GEORGE AND MARTHA
WASHINGTON

GEORGE AND MARTHA WASHINGTON

A Revolutionary Marriage

FLORA FRASER

BLOOMSBURY

LONDON · OXFORD · NEW YORK · NEW DELHI · SYDNEY

Bloomsbury Publishing
An imprint of Bloomsbury Publishing Plc

50 Bedford Square
London
WC1B 3DP
UK

1385 Broadway
New York
NY 10018
USA

www.bloomsbury.com

BLOOMSBURY and the Diana logo are trademarks of Bloomsbury Publishing Plc

First published in Great Britain 2015

© Flora Fraser, 2015
Maps by David Lindroth

Flora Fraser has asserted her right under the Copyright, Designs and
Patents Act, 1988, to be identified as the Author of this work.

British Library Cataloguing-in-Publication Data
A catalogue record for this book is available from the British Library.

ISBN: HB: 978-1-4088-0909-9
ePub: 978-1-4088-3596-8

2 4 6 8 10 9 7 5 3 1

Typeset by Newgen Knowledge Works (P) Ltd., Chennai, India
Printed and bound in Great Britain by CPI Group (UK) Ltd, Croydon CR0 4YY

To find out more about our authors and books visit www.bloomsbury.com.
Here you will find extracts, author interviews, details of forthcoming
events and the option to sign up for our newsletters.

For
Paul and Daisy, beloved New Americans

CONTENTS

BOOK THREE: AFTER THE WAR, 1784–1802

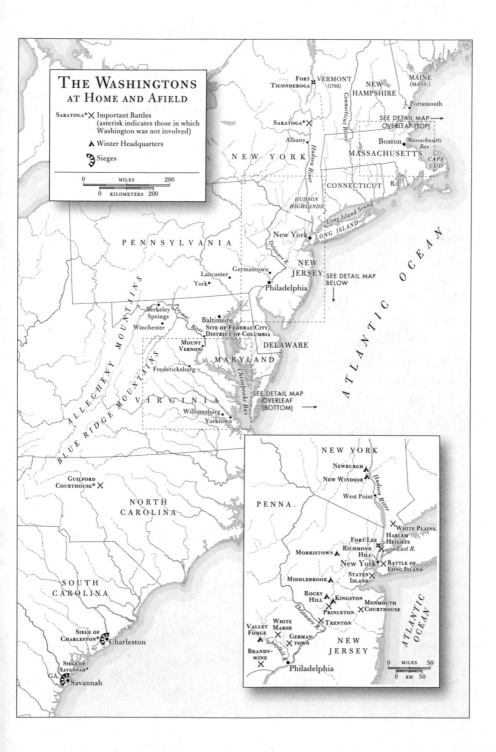

THE WASHINGTONS
AT HOME AND AFIELD

SARATOGA*✕ Important Battles
(asterisk indicates those in which
Washington was not involved)

▲ Winter Headquarters

⌇ Sieges

| 0 | MILES | 200 |
| 0 | KILOMETERS | 200 |

MAINE
(MASS.)

• Portsmouth

SEE DETAIL MAP
OVERLEAF (TOP)

FORT ✕ VERMONT
TICONDEROGA (1792)

NEW
HAMPSHIRE

SARATOGA*✕

Albany •

NEW YORK

Connecticut River

MASSACHUSETTS

Boston • Massachusetts
Bay

CAPE
COD

CONNECTICUT R.

HUDSON
HIGHLANDS

Hudson River

Long Island Sound

New York • LONG ISLAND

PENNSYLVANIA

NEW
JERSEY

Delaware R.

SEE DETAIL MAP
BELOW
↓

Lancaster • Germantown •
York •
Philadelphia •

ATLANTIC OCEAN

Berkeley •
Springs
Winchester •

Potomac River

Baltimore •
SITE OF FEDERAL CITY/
DISTRICT OF COLUMBIA

DELAWARE

MOUNT
VERNON •

MARYLAND

Fredericksburg •

Chesapeake Bay

SEE DETAIL MAP
OVERLEAF
(BOTTOM) →

VIRGINIA

Williamsburg •
Yorktown •

ALLEGHENY MOUNTAINS

BLUE RIDGE MOUNTAINS

GUILFORD
COURTHOUSE* ✕

NORTH
CAROLINA

SOUTH
CAROLINA

SIEGE OF
CHARLESTON* ⌇ Charleston

SIEGE OF
SAVANNAH*
GA. ⌇ Savannah

Detail map

NEW YORK

NEWBURGH ▲
NEW WINDSOR ▲

Hudson River

West Point •

PENNA.

WHITE PLAINS ✕

HARLEM
HEIGHTS ✕
FORT LEE
RICHMOND East R.
HILL

MORRISTOWN ▲

New York • ✕ BATTLE OF
LONG ISLAND
STATEN
ISLAND

MIDDLEBROOK ▲

ROCKY ▲
HILL ▲ KINGSTON
PRINCETON ✕ MONMOUTH
✕ COURTHOUSE

Delaware R.

TRENTON ✕

VALLEY WHITE
FORGE ✕ MARSH
✕ GERMAN-
✕ TOWN

NEW
JERSEY

BRANDY-
WINE ✕

Schuylkill R.

Philadelphia •

ATLANTIC
OCEAN

| 0 | MILES | 50 |
| 0 | KM | 50 |

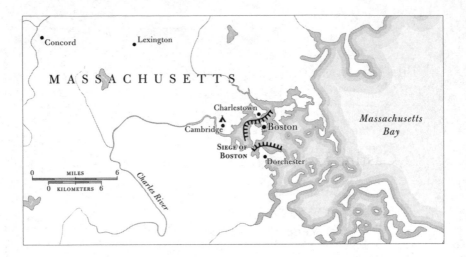

Prologue

Casting Lots for his Garments, July 1802

*There was something in the whole
scene . . . that shocked me*

An extraordinary meeting of Martha Washington's heirs and legatees took place on Thursday 22 July 1802 'up stairs' at Mount Vernon, the plantation home on the Potomac in Virginia where she had died two months earlier. Those gathered were mostly related either by blood or by marriage to Martha, George Washington's widow. The 'Private sales' that now took place were of personal effects that had belonged to the commander and President himself. Among these items, which had passed to Martha on George's death in 1799, were a gold watch, chain and seal, a box of shaving soap, Masonic aprons, sunglasses, a ruler, a 'sandwich box' and a hat.[1]

William Thornton, architect of the new 'Federal City' near by that Congress had named after the nation's first President, was deeply offended. He wrote to Thomas Jefferson that the legatees had '*cast lots for his* [Washington's] *garments!* There was something in the whole scene, and in the general proceedings, that shocked me. But it was a scene which, although devoid of feeling, *was not without interest.*' Public sales of items judged less personal had already occurred over the two previous days, in accordance with

the will Martha had made in September 1800. They were held in
order to provide for the education of two of her nephews and a
great-nephew. They offered, besides, opportunities for an idola-
trous public as well as family and friends to obtain certain
paraphernalia of the marriage that is the subject of this book.
Jefferson, President since 1801, wanted the large 'terrestrial globe'
that stood in his predecessor's library.[2] Martha's grandson,
Washington Custis – George Washington Parke Custis, in full –
bought, among many other items, a 'markee', one of the campaign
tents that had served General Washington and the Revolutionary
army a quarter of a century earlier.[3] Custis also purchased a trunk.
His sister, Eliza Parke Custis Law, was later to claim that in it their
grandmother had stowed her possessions when she joined her
husband every winter of the war.[4] George and Martha had already
willed to friends and relatives other memorabilia, pictures, prints
and household items. These poignant sales, public and private,
effaced further vestiges at Mount Vernon of a marriage that had
endured and only strengthened over forty years.

   These sales also served to feed the cult of Washington the hero, the
stern and judicious Father of the Nation. The cult reached its apogee
with the dedication in the United States capital in 1885 of the
Washington Monument, then the tallest building in the world. For
the cult, Martha Washington was an irrelevance, even an inconvenience. No wife or Mother of the Nation was wanted in the virile
American nineteenth century. No woman's portrait appeared on any
US postage stamp during that century. (Martha's head eventually
graced the dark lilac eight-cent stamp in 1902.) Admittedly, Martha
was portrayed on the silver dollar certificate of 1886, becoming the
only woman ever to have appeared on US paper currency.* Ten years
later, though, when the beautiful Educational Series of 1896 was
launched, Washington's portrait joined Martha's on the certificate.
This pairing was a rare concession to the reality of the life of the
Father of the Country. The numinous wording of the funeral address
that Henry 'Light Horse Harry' Lee gave in 1799 lingered, and

---

* At the time of writing, she still holds that distinction.

Washington was celebrated as 'First in war, first in peace and first in the hearts of his countrymen'. Men – and women – forgot that Lee, who knew both Washingtons well, had also declared the founding father 'to the dear object of his affections' – Martha – 'exemplarily tender'.[5] As the man faded from memory and the monument came into being, Washington was seen as a man of destiny, and men of destiny customarily bestride the world alone.

No one during the Washingtons' lifetime would have thought of ignoring Martha. Officers welcomed her arrival in camp during the bleak winter months at Valley Forge and Morristown. They knew that her husband's temper, which was uncertain, would mellow with her arrival and his morale improve. Among Washington's greatest achievements as Commander-in-Chief was keeping together for eight years an army of officers and other ranks who were, though paid, volunteers and, more often than not, on very short enlistments. He owed much to affable Martha, an assiduous hostess at headquarters to Congressional committees, state representatives and foreign envoys.

Later, forging with her husband a Presidential style in New York and Philadelphia, Martha Washington was strong, capable and tough. Where her husband was concerned, she remained as romantic as a young bride all their married life. Her instinctive preference was for the man of action, not the head of state. Following George's death in 1799, she commissioned a memorial miniature showing him as a younger man in military uniform. Her own age and grief are not disguised in a companion miniature. Following Martha's own death and interment beside George in the vault at Mount Vernon, the miniatures were separated. In 2008 they were reunited at the Yale University Art Gallery, luminous and palpable souvenirs of a remarkable union.[6]

This book is necessarily an oblique look at the Washingtons' marriage. Though they wrote constantly to each other when apart, very little of this correspondence survives. Martha burnt all that she had to hand after George's death, forestalling requests from his many contemporary biographers for a viewing. Accordingly, it is for the most part through the medium of their correspondence with others, and through contemporaries' descriptions of their relationship, that I present their life together.

There are two twentieth-century Washington experts to whom I owe much. John C. Fitzpatrick edited, in thirty-seven volumes, *The Writings of Washington from the Original Manuscript Sources* (1931–44). Douglas Southall Freeman wrote, in the 1940s and 1950s, a detailed multi-volume biography, *George Washington*, based on Fitzpatrick's *Writings*. The importance of the wealth that Martha brought George, her first husband having died intestate, pervades both works. The couple's life together and apart is to be found nowadays on the page and in the ether in the form of *The Papers of George Washington*, the brainchild, in 1968, of the Mount Vernon Ladies' Association and of the University of Virginia. Invaluable, authoritative, both print and digital editions – as yet incomplete – have been the richest of seams to mine.

I should mention, in connection with eighteenth-century letters, journals and dispatches, that the originals are strewn with strange spellings and stray capitalizations, like so much salt and pepper. I have preserved, in my text, some of them to give a flavour of the whole. The authoritative texts are located at the sources indicated in the Notes.

John Adams posed a question, in 1816, that many have asked since: 'Would Washington have ever been commander of the revolutionary army or president of the United States, if he had not married the rich widow of Mr Custis?'[7] I would answer that Washington's marriage was, in more than one sense, the making of him. Martha imbued George not only with wealth but also with a confidence he had earlier lacked. Together this couple, loyal British subjects when they married in 1759, became disaffected with rule from London, with remarkable consequences for their union as much as for the future of the American colonies.

Martha gave Washington a role as a paterfamilias, though he fathered no children. He was an attentive guardian, at Mount Vernon, to her children by her first husband and, later, in Virginia and in Presidential residences to two of her four Parke Custis grandchildren. All four of her grandchildren regarded Mount Vernon as their personal fiefdom and were accordingly resentful when Judge Bushrod Washington, the President's nephew and principal heir, inherited the plantation, following Martha's death. They bid at the various sales in 1802 for the most mundane objects. One granddaughter, Martha Parke Custis Peter, acquired, thanks to her husband Thomas Peter, 'four cracked bowls' and a broken thermometer, as well as costly looking glasses.[8] The Peters had a home, Tudor Place, built in Washington, DC, in which their heirs lived till 1983. On public view there now are one of Washington's wartime camp stools and pieces from the Sèvres china service used during the Presidency.

Martha's only grandson, Washington Custis, was prone even in old age to refer to himself as the 'child of Mount Vernon'. He was imaginative with his acquisitions. At Arlington House, the home he had built across the Potomac from the Federal City of Washington, he staged an agricultural fair near the river bank every spring on his birthday. Guests were invited to watch imported merino sheep being sheared and to toast 'the best specimens of sheep and wool'. The 'markee' which had sheltered George Washington in the Revolutionary War was a central attraction.[9]

Bushrod Washington, a Supreme Court associate justice till his death in 1829, lived little at Mount Vernon. The house was depleted. The estate was difficult to manage. His uncle's slaves had been manumitted before Martha's death, and her dower slaves had passed into the keeping of her grandchildren thereafter. Andrew Jackson, fresh from victory over the British at the battle of New Orleans, was shocked in 1815 to find the Washingtons' tomb overgrown with cedars.[10] The estate lacked both attention and funds and, after Bushrod's death in 1829, continued to deteriorate under the care of two further relatives. The cult of Washington only amplified as time and disuse erased all traces of his domestic life with Martha at Mount Vernon.

Washington Custis displayed at Arlington House, among other relics, the General's uniform, his battle sword with its hanger and his camp chest. Custis was custodian, as he saw it, of the Washington legend. It was a legend in which Martha did not feature. Nevertheless, the house was hung with portraits that had come to Custis by descent from his grandmother, including those painted at Mount Vernon and elsewhere during the Washingtons' marriage. Custis's daughter and heir, Mary – Martha's great-granddaughter – married, in 1831, fellow Virginian Robert E. Lee, son of 'Light Horse Harry'. They brought up their many children at Arlington House, and the young Lees received first-hand knowledge of the relics and portraits from their Custis grandfather, who died only in 1857.

At the outbreak of the Civil War, Lee became General Robert E. Lee of the Confederate army, and his wife, Mary Custis Lee, fled south as Union troops approached Washington, DC. Some of the souvenirs from Washington's military career that Washington Custis had accrued at Arlington were left behind when Mrs Lee headed south. They passed into government hands, and the grounds of Arlington were destined to become the nation's pre-eminent military cemetery. Mrs Lee, before she fled, had spirited south family portraits, papers and silver. They were buried outside Lexington, Virginia, when Union troops neared that town, and dug up after the conflict ended. The papers, Mrs Lee recorded, were found to be 'destroyed by mould and damp and were *perfectly illegible*.'[11] After the war General Robert E. Lee became President of Washington College in Lexington, renamed Washington and Lee University after his death in 1870. Here, in the Lee Chapel and Museum, the portraits of George and Martha, and of her children, that were ferried south from Arlington, are still located. The majority of the papers, restored, are now in the Virginia Historical Society in Richmond. They include incomplete Guardian Accounts for Martha Parke Custis's children in tattered quarto books.[12] Martha's hand in the upbringing of these children and Washington's concern for their wellbeing are everywhere to be seen in these records, once kept so painstakingly, so far from Richmond. At Mount Vernon Washington kept 'exact copies of the [Guardian] Accts settled with the General Court annually' in a 'Marble colour'd folio Book' ledger.[13] In the 1980s, dilapidated, disbound pages of accounts in Washington's handwriting at Washington and Lee University Library, Lexington, were identified as the complete contents of this folio book, restored and reordered.[14]

The long journey towards a revival of interest in Martha Washington may be said to have begun in advance of the Civil War. Mrs Robert Cunningham, a Southern lady who had been brought up near Mount Vernon, passed near the house and grounds on a nostalgic river cruise in 1853 and wrote to her invalid daughter in Philadelphia: 'I was painfully distressed at the ruin and desolation of the home of Washington, and the thought passed through my mind: Why was it that the women of his country did not try to keep it in repair, if the men could not do it?'[15] The rest is, as they say, history. Her daughter, Miss Ann Pamela Cunningham, successfully made it her business to solicit funds from ladies of 'the Union', and on 6 April 1858 John Augustine Washington III, the then owner, sold the estate to the Mount Vernon Ladies' Association of the Union for $200,000.

At the house a few items remained. All were of historical value, but none was associated with Martha Washington. After the Civil War, Miss Cunningham began to fill the house with other objects that had once had a place there. Many of those that first came back were intimately associated with Martha, including her granddaughter Nelly's harpsichord and the Washingtons' bed. There was a limit to the Ladies' Association's interest in her. It was only of the President that Miss Cunningham spoke to her Board when she retired in 1874 as Regent of the association she had founded: 'Ladies, the Home of Washington is in your charge. *See to it that you keep it the Home of Washington!* Let no irreverent hand change it: no vandal hands *desecrate* it with the fingers of – *progress*! Those who go to the Home in which he *lived* and *died, wish to see in what he lived and died*!'[16]

Since then there has been a sea change at Mount Vernon. In fact, something of a revolution has taken place, though not one in which 'vandal hands' have been involved. Today the governing body encourages its many visitors to view the estate as the home of all who lived there, including the slaves who worked in the house and in the fields. The Donald W. Reynolds Museum and Education Center at Mount Vernon and mountvernon.org, the associated website, further this work. The mansion itself is imbued with the presence of Martha Washington, thanks to research into different aspects of her life. Joseph E. Fields published in 1994 *"Worthy Partner": The Papers of*

Martha Washington. Ellen McCallister Clark's admirable *Martha Washington: A Brief Biography* marked the bicentenary of her death in 2002. The marthawashington.us website at the Roy Rosenzweig Center for History and New Media, George Mason University, and the National First Ladies' Library, Canton, Ohio, continue this work of reassessment. Mary V. Thompson, Research Historian at Mount Vernon, is the author of *'In the Hands of a Good Providence': Religion in the Life of George Washington* (2008). She has shared unstintingly with others her growing knowledge of George and Martha's lives together since she was first, in 1980, a Museum Attendant and Historic Interpreter at the estate.

Can we know the Washingtons? If any image of Martha is known today, it is the grandmotherly 'Atheneum' portrait of her painted by Gilbert Stuart in 1796. An enormous cap dominates. The image of Washington that is perhaps best known today is the one on the dollar bill, derived from a companion portrait by Stuart. The couple were then well into their sixties and had been married nearly forty years. A year later George was to dash a lady's suggestion that a bundle of letters from his wife to him constituted 'love letters'.[17] But husband and wife were more ardent earlier. In the first years of the war, an officer noted, 'Mrs Washington is excessive fond of the General and he of her. They are very happy in each other.'[18]

What is above all necessary for the reader today to bear in mind is that when Martha and George married, they were both in their mid-twenties. Martha was the elder by only eight months, and a very attractive and wealthy young widow. Since she was a girl, she had been living in the same Virginian parish, first at home, then as the wife of a much older husband. Following that first husband's death Martha is pursued by George, a colonel in the colonial service. He sweeps her north and away from her family and friends. If this book leaves the reader with any image, I hope it will be of a couple who were of an age, and who were both friends and lovers.

There have been many visitors to Mount Vernon since the Ladies' Association opened its doors to the public. Perhaps the most incongruous duo who ever stood before the Washington vault were Eleanor Roosevelt and Madame Chiang Kai-shek. Resplendent in furs, FDR at their side, these wartime allies were photographed on 22 February 1943, the anniversary of the first President's birth, about to lay a handsome wreath on his tomb.[19] History does not relate whether Martha's tomb was similarly honoured. But in a radio broadcast on that same anniversary in 1935, Mrs Roosevelt, who blazed her own trail at the White House, had spoken admiringly of Mrs Washington: 'She was a pioneer and maker of precedents, and we can be grateful that she took an interest in public affairs and did her duty in the way that she considered compatible with the standards and customs of the day.'[20]

Queen Elizabeth II, when on a visit, as Princess Elizabeth, to Mount Vernon in November 1951 while her father was still king, is held to have remarked, 'It's a cosy little place.'[21] Indeed, in England the home commonly termed 'the mansion' would rank as a small manor house, albeit one with a spectacular view. More importantly, 'cosy' is not an epithet that anyone would have used on viewing the house while Washington lived there alone in the late 1750s. Before the expectation of marriage to Martha dawned, in Virginia George was a lonely and even cantankerous young bachelor, with what he viewed as dismal prospects. It is with this lonely bachelorhood that *George and Martha Washington* now begins.

BOOK ONE

The Colonel and his Lady,
1758–1775

Colonial Colonel

. . . no prospect of preferment . . .

George Washington, anxious by nature, was fractious in the spring of 1758 at Mount Vernon, his plantation home on the Potomac River in northern Virginia. Six years earlier, the young man had seen his older half-brother Lawrence waste away from 'decay', as tuberculosis was then termed, and die at Mount Vernon while still in his early thirties. Now George himself had, as he wrote on 4 March 1758 to Colonel John Stanwix, a British officer serving in America and formerly his commander, 'some reason to apprehend an approaching decay'. While serving with his regiment in north-western Virginia the previous year, he had suffered for months from a 'bloody flux', or dysentery. In November he had retreated to Mount Vernon, a home that he rented from his brother's widow. Here he dieted on medicinal jellies and brooded on his misfortunes. He wrote to Stanwix in March that his constitution was greatly injured: 'nothing can retrieve it but the greatest care, and most circumspect conduct'.

To compound his dejection, as he informed Stanwix, Washington saw 'no prospect of preferment' – or promotion – 'in a military life'.[1] He had served in the Virginia Regiment since it was raised in 1754, and was now its colonel. But he had failed, like so many 'provincial' or colonial officers, to win a commission in the regular British army. First settled by the Virginia Company in 1607, Virginia had come under the direct rule of James I of England in 1625. Within

America the colony was often named the 'Old Dominion'. It was the fifth dominion that the Crown claimed, Scotland, Ireland and France, besides England, being the others. After the 1707 Act of Union united the English and Scottish thrones as the kingdom of Great Britain, Virginia's seal featured the words, 'En Dat Virginia Quartam' – Virginia Makes a Fourth. (Ireland was to remain a separate kingdom until 1801, at which time the claim to France was finally dropped.) Twelve other colonies on the American eastern seaboard were established, the last being Georgia in 1733. New Hampshire, Massachusetts, Connecticut and Rhode Island were known as the New England colonies. New York, with Pennsylvania and Delaware, constituted the Middle Colonies. Virginia and Maryland were known together as the Chesapeake Colonies or, with North and South Carolina and Georgia, as the Southern Colonies. Britain had other colonies, too, on the Atlantic coast of America, both north and south of the Thirteen Colonies, as the above named were known. Newfoundland and Nova Scotia were among those to the north; the Floridas, with other colonies in the British West Indies, lay to the south. Meanwhile Canada and Louisiana were part of New France.

In principle, there was nothing to prevent colonial subjects serving in the British army. In practice, the War Office in London advanced the claims of young Englishmen with 'interest' – an influential patron – in the metropolis. As a result of his ill health and poor military prospects, as Washington now wrote to inform Stanwix, he meant to quit his command and retire from all public business.[2] It was a dismal outlook for one who had turned twenty-six on 22 February of this year and who had exulted, till his recent illness, in physical strength and stamina. George had been born at Pope's Creek, Westmoreland County, Virginia, on land near that originally settled by a Washington ancestor in 1657. His birthdate was 11 February 1732, according to the Julian calendar that Britain and its colonies then followed. After the Gregorian calendar was adopted in 1752, entailing a loss of eleven days in that year, Washington gave the date of his birth as the 11th, Old Style. But he kept its anniversary on the 22nd, New Style.

Washington's physical strength was to become legendary later in his life. At Home House, the small plantation outside Fredericksburg, Virginia, to which his parents moved when he was young, he could pitch a stone across the wide Rappahannock River, according to 'Parson' Weems. Mason Locke Weems is also author of the story that when aged six, George swung at his father's cherry tree with a hatchet and could not tell a lie.[3] Though Weems published his narrative in 1800, the year after Washington's death, the infant Hercules of myth was father of the flesh-and-blood man. George Mercer, the Colonel's aide-de-camp in the Virginia Regiment, reportedly wrote in a letter of 1760 that Washington was 'straight as an Indian, measuring 6 feet 2 inches in his stockings'. His frame, according to this letter, was 'padded with well developed muscles, indicating great strength'.[4] This impression of 'great strength' Washington conveyed for most of his life.

When Washington wrote to Stanwix, in the spring of 1758, both health and strength were in abeyance. Upon his arrival at Mount Vernon the previous November, he had outlined to a neighbour, Mrs George William Fairfax of Belvoir, the regimen that a local reverend, who doubled as physician, had prescribed for him: 'He forbids the use of meats, and substitutes jellies and such kind of food . . . I have no person that has been used to making these kind of things, and no directions.' George's younger brother John Augustine, with his wife Hannah, looked after Mount Vernon and kept house while its tenant served with his regiment. Now, in his sister-in-law's absence, George applied to Sally Fairfax: 'I find myself under a necessity of applying to you for your receipt [recipe] book for a little while, and indeed for such materials to make jellies as you think I may – not just at this time – have. For I can't get hartshorn shavings [gelatin] anywhere.' Of hyson, or green, tea, he wrote: 'I am quite out, and cannot get a supply anywhere in these parts.' He begged also a bottle or two of 'mountain or canary [sweet] wine'. The Reverend Charles Green had ordered him to take a glass or two each day, mixed with 'water of gum arabic'.[5]

The bachelor Colonel had been confident that Sally Fairfax, whose husband was away on business in England, would provide. Not only did the Mount Vernon lands border those of Belvoir, where her father-in-law, Colonel William, had built a handsome brick mansion in the 1730s, but Lawrence Washington had married the master of Belvoir's daughter Ann in 1743, when she was fourteen. Furthermore, in that same year Lawrence and George's father, Augustine Washington, had died unexpectedly at home in Fredericksburg. Over the succeeding years George – aged eleven when his father died – completed a sketchy education in Fredericksburg and spent time increasingly at Mount Vernon. At Belvoir Colonel William took an interest in the boy and George Washington responded with enthusiasm.

Fairfax was a man of influence as well as one with close connections to the English nobility, being cousin and land agent to Thomas, 6th Lord Fairfax of Cameron. He also served on the Governor's Council in Williamsburg and was at one time its President. As senior colonial official in the county, besides, he commanded, with the rank of colonel, the local militia. This was the home guard composed of able-bodied men in the neighbourhood, who were formally under the command of the resident Royal Governor, or deputizing Lieutenant Governor of Virginia. As in other colonies, they turned out, bearing arms, a few times a year for training by an adjutant. About a quarter of them trained more regularly, and were known as minutemen, from the requirement that they respond at a minute's notice to news of public danger or affray.

George Washington benefited greatly from Colonel William's professional relationship with Lord Fairfax. This peer had inherited a vast tract of Virginia, five million acres in all, land that had originally been granted in 1649 by King Charles II, living in exile in France during the English Civil War, to several supporters. On his restoration as king in 1660, the grant assumed substance. By 1719, the land was vested in Lord Fairfax alone and known as the Fairfax Proprietary. Eccentric but tenacious, he triumphed, in 1745, in a boundary dispute with the Virginia government in the Privy Council in London. His lands included the entire Northern Neck, as the peninsula between the Potomac and Rappahannock Rivers that jutted out into Chesapeake Bay was known. The extent of his land to the north-west satisfactorily settled, he made his home in the seclusion of the

Shenandoah Valley, and left it to his cousin William to administer the Proprietary.

It is easy to see why life at Mount Vernon and at Belvoir attracted the young George Washington. His father had been a restless spirit who invested in land and iron mines with no great success. What little income Home House – the family farm in Fredericksburg and his inheritance from his father – yielded was swallowed up by the demands of George's mother and younger brothers and sister who continued to live there. He was in need of a profession and an income. But his mother, Mary Ball Washington, in 1746 stood out against a plan endorsed by Colonel William that George should join the British navy. A friend wrote to Lawrence, who had himself served as a captain of marines in the Spanish Caribbean five years earlier: 'She offers several trifling objections such as fond and unthinking mothers habitually suggest; I find that one word against his going has more weight than ten for it.'[6]

Mrs Washington's will prevailed, her half-brother, the merchant Joseph Ball, adding, from London, his disapproval of the scheme: 'as for any considerable preferment [promotion] in the Navy, it is not to be expected, [as] there are always too many grasping for it here [in England], who have interest [connections], and he has none'.[7] Colonel William stepped into the breach and became young George's patron. He dispatched him in 1748, when the boy was just seventeen, to survey Fairfax Proprietary lands on the south branch of the Potomac River, west across the Blue Mountain range. While the boundary of the Northern Neck had been in doubt, there had been extensive occupation of the area. Now Lord Fairfax's tenants were eager to obtain valid grants from the 'Proprietor', as the peer was known. A profitable position for Washington followed a year later when he was appointed county surveyor for Culpeper County, a newly established district in south-western Virginia. Over the next few years, he conducted 199 surveys in that county and in other parts of western Virginia.

The environs of Mount Vernon and Belvoir were undergoing substantial change. In 1749 Colonel William Fairfax acted in concert with the 'Proprietor', and with George Mason of neighbouring

Gunston Hall and others to found a new harbour town on the Potomac. Alexandria, as the Fairfax County town was named, swiftly became a thriving port and a centre for neighbourhood business and gaieties, including horse races and assemblies. More sombrely, the market square saw the sales of African-Americans, who worked in these founders' households and fields. Alexandria was to become a town of some importance to George Washington.

In 1752 Lawrence died, and his only child, a daughter, survived her father by only two years. George would inherit Mount Vernon one day, if he outlived Lawrence's widow Ann, who remarried and moved away. For the moment he rented the plantation from her. But five adventurous years – mostly on the frontier with New France – elapsed before ill health led Washington to seek a permanent residence at the plantation. His younger brother John Augustine, released, moved away with his wife to Wesmoreland Country.

In December 1753 Robert Dinwiddie, Lieutenant Governor of Virginia – deputing for the Royal Governor, the Earl of Albemarle – dispatched Washington, then a major in the county militia, on a mission to tell the French commander, Jacques Legardeur de Saint Pierre, to leave the forks of the Ohio. The Frenchman refused.

The following spring the Virginia Regiment was raised, specifically to defend the colony's interests at the forks of the Ohio against French Canadian incursions from the north. Washington, now a lieutenant colonel of the regiment, was dispatched again by Dinwiddie with more aggressive orders, and was joined by Mingo allies, members of the Iroquois Confederacy. Both the British and the French governments wooed the Six Nations, important Native American tribes – among them the Mohawks, the Oneidas and the Senecas – who inhabited the region. They were known collectively as the Iroquois. While each tribe was autonomous, they had long before formed a defensive confederacy, with an elected Grand Council of fifty sachems, or elders. The Virginians and their Native American allies ambushed a French patrol, shots were fired, and the enemy commander, Joseph Coulon, Sieur de Jumonville, was brutally killed by the Mingo. Hostilities had begun between European powers in North America that were to become known as the French and Indian War and endure till 1760. Spreading to a wider world, the conflict would – as the Seven Years War – end only in 1763. Knowing little of such mighty consequences or that, in a few months, he would surrender a stockade, Fort Necessity, to the French, Washington wrote to his brother, John Augustine, a few days after the Jumonville affair, 'I fortunately escaped without a wound, tho' the right Wing where I stood was exposed to & received all the Enemy's fire and was the part where the man was killed & the rest wounded. I can with truth assure you, I heard Bulletts whistle and, believe me, there was something charming in the sound.'[8]

During a campaign the following year that became notorious, ending in defeat and death for the British commander, Edward Braddock, Washington acted a hero's part, and in 1756 was commissioned colonel of the Virginia Regiment serving in frontier garrisons. He hoped that Lord Loudoun, currently Royal Governor of the colony as well as Commander-in-Chief of the British forces in America, would take the Virginia Regiment into the army establishment. But Loudoun, following the example of previous noble incumbents, never visited Virginia, instead relying on lieutenant governors – usually British commoners – to act in his place. Washington's hopes for a regular British army commission faded. Living in retirement at Mount Vernon, as he now resolved to do, he would cease to jockey for position in the world and depend on neighbours such as George Mason of Gunston Hall and the Fairfaxes of Belvoir to enliven his existence.

The Fairfaxes were a sophisticated tribe, an English family who regarded London, rather than Williamsburg, as the centre of their world. George Washington, who once copied out an entire etiquette book, *Rules of Civility*, looked to them as models of how to behave.[9] But to English eyes the Fairfax establishment would have seemed more than a little wild and colonial. William, when Governor of the Bahamas in the 1720s, had taken as his first wife Sarah Walker, a woman whose mother was a 'free black' – the term in general use to denote an African in the Americas not a slave. Any child of a free black mother was born free, while any child born of a slave mother was born into slavery.

Colonel William's second wife had no African blood. She had this fault in the eyes of the local parson's wife: though Deborah had a large house, four stepchildren and two children at Belvoir to care for, Mrs Green asserted, she 'lay long abed'.[10] Mrs Fairfax took umbrage at this remark, and an estrangement between the two households developed. It would seem, though, the young women of the Fairfax family circle enjoyed remarkable licence at Belvoir, before and after Deborah's death in 1748.

William was not afraid, despite his elder children's African blood, to solicit favours from Fairfax relations. When planning to send his eldest son to school in England, he wrote, 'he has the marks in his visage that will always testify to his [Fairfax] parentage'.[11] George William was, despite this avowal, to find his African blood trouble-some following his father's death in 1757. While Washington was on sick leave at Mount Vernon that year, his neighbour was in England, trying to secure the post of Collector of Customs for the Northern Neck that his father had held. George William was also eager to convince an uncle in England, Henry Fairfax of Towlston, with a fortune to leave, that he was, in his wife Sally Cary Fairfax's words, 'not a negro's son'. They feared that Henry might leave his wealth elsewhere.[12]

In Virginia, a free black grandmother was less of a hindrance. Lawrence Washington and John Carlyle, grain merchant in Alexandria, had not hesitated to marry George William's sisters, Ann and Sarah. George William had had no difficulty, in 1748, in marry-ing Sally Cary, the eligible daughter of Willson Cary of Hampton. Sally's sisters Ann and Mary Cary, before and after they married, were frequent visitors to the estate on the Potomac. George Washington was young and impressionable. While at Belvoir in about 1750, though pining for 'Sally', an unidentifiable 'lowland beauty' in Fredericksburg, he wrote: 'I might, was my heart disen-gaged, pass my time very pleasantly as there's a very agreeable Young Lady Lives in the same house (Colonel George [William] Fairfax's Wife's sister) . . .'[13] Mary Cary was probably this companion. Much later, in a letter to George William, he declared that he counted his days at Belvoir 'the happiest moments of my life'.[14] Surveys and – later – campaigns with the Virginia Regiment notwithstanding, he engaged vigorously in courtly correspondence with the ladies of the Fairfax circle. They, on the other hand, seem to have enjoyed driving the young man to distraction, as first one and then another toyed with his affections.

Sally's sister Ann became in 1751 the wife of Williamsburg lawyer, Robert Carter Nicholas. In 1754 Mary Cary married too, elsewhere in Virginia. Washington's attention shifted to another of the circle – George William's sister, Mrs Carlyle. But she wrote to him while he was on the frontier in 1754. He must not expect any further correspondence, she warned, 'to be carried on (on my side) with the spirit it ought, to enliven you, which would be my desire if I could'. In a tantalizing sentence she hints at a previous flirtation: 'Those pleasing reflections on the hours past ought to be banished out of your thoughts; you have now a nobler prospect, that of preserving your country from the insults of an enemy . . .'[15]

By the following year George William's wife, Sally Cary Fairfax herself, is the target of an impassioned and querulous letter that the young man drafted. She had requested, when they had met recently, that he should inform others, in place of her, that he had reached camp safely. His drafted reply is full of crossing-outs and substitutions: 'This I took as a gentle rebuke and polite manner of forbidding my corresponding with you; and conceive this opinion is not ill founded when I reflect that I have hitherto found it impracticable to engage one moment of your attention.'[16] Washington softened the tone of the letter he eventually sent, but had to wait till his return to Mount Vernon from garrison duties for a reply. It was a note written jointly with two other ladies: 'if you will not come to us, tomorrow morning very early we shall be at Mount Vernon'.[17] Although the ladies of the Fairfax circle enjoyed the attentions of this handsome young neighbour, sometimes he pressed too hard.

Washington's affairs of the heart, by the time he reached the age of twenty-six in February 1758 – whether with 'Sally' of Fredericksburg, with the Misses Cary, with Sarah Fairfax Carlyle of Alexandria, or with Sally Cary Fairfax at Belvoir – may be characterized as tentative and awkward. The objects of his attentions were generally unavailable. Sexual desire he probably satisfied, following other Virginian planters, with servants or slaves on the plantation at Mount Vernon or with tavern 'wenches', serving maids in Alexandria. Additionally, when stationed on the frontier, he may have engaged with women outside the fort. But did he take advantage of George William's absence in England to pursue Sally Cary Fairfax more closely? Letters that Washington wrote to Sally in September 1758 hint at recent passionate passages. Notwithstanding, when Washington wrote to her in March 1758, on the same day that he had poured out his troubles to Stanwix, business was to the fore: 'If you, or any of the young ladies have letters to send, or other commands that I can execute, I should be glad to be honoured with them, and you may depend upon my punctuality – please to accept my compliments yourself, and offer them to the young ladies, and believe that I am with great truth and sincerity, dear madam, your most obedient and obliged George Washington.'[18]

Next day Washington was off, on the move after months of leave. Williamsburg, the colonial capital, which lay a hundred miles south of Mount Vernon, was his destination. The careful log of expenditure that Washington kept, and which survives, allows us to follow the progress of an expedition that was to have several important outcomes. The most important, where this narrative is concerned, involved the payment of gratuities in March and June to servants of Mrs Martha Dandridge Custis, a wealthy young widow with two small children.[19] Following the death the previous year of her husband, Daniel Parke Custis, she had chosen to manage on her own behalf and for her children an extensive plantation known as the White House situated on the banks of the Pamunkey, thirty miles west of Williamsburg. There were substantial holdings also in other parts of the colony. She had been grappling successfully, as well, with a lawsuit of long standing that threatened the estate. Martha Custis was, in short, a woman of considerable mettle, and one who was to become within the year Martha Washington.

Dandridge's Daughter

I shall yearly ship a considerable part
of the tobacco I make to you . . .

Petite, at five feet, with brown hair and hazel eyes, Martha Dandridge Custis was aged twenty-six in March 1758 – she would turn twenty-seven on 13 June [2 June, old style] – and was described about this time as an 'agreeable widow'.[1] The lawyers and tobacco agents who had had to reckon with her brisk correspondence since her husband Daniel Parke Custis's death might have tempered this praise. Agreeable for certain, in Washington's eyes, were a town house in Williamsburg, the White House on the Pamunkey River, and the Parke Custis acreage that Martha and her children had inherited on Daniel's death. The whole comprised one of the larger fortunes in Virginia. There was one fly in the ointment – the so-called Dunbar suit. This lawsuit of forty years' standing, in which plaintiffs in Antigua threatened the Parke Custis estate, had come to trial in the General Court in Williamsburg in April 1754 and been dismissed. It had then gone to the London Privy Council, which heard appeals from the colonies. In the summer of his death, Daniel had been waiting to hear the outcome of the plaintiffs' appeal. In December 1757, Martha had learned that the dismissal had been overturned on appeal. The plaintiffs could seek a retrial in Virginia.

This lawsuit had its origins in ambiguous wording regarding the payment of debts in the will of Daniel Parke. This Virginian – Daniel Parke Custis's maternal grandfather – had been rewarded for services to the Crown at the battle of Blenheim in 1704. Made Governor of the Leeward Islands in the West Indies, he had proved corrupt and debauched in the post. Islanders in revolt against his arrogant rule had murdered him in Antigua in 1710. In his will of the previous year, he had left to his daughter Frances Parke Custis, wife of John Custis IV of Arlington, Virginia, and to her heirs, his considerable wealth and acreage in England and Virginia. The condition was that they bear the name of Parke, in which he took pride. Frances Custis's young children Daniel – Martha's future husband – and his sister adopted the name. Parke bequeathed a thousand pounds to his other daughter, Lucy Parke Byrd, wife of William Byrd II, again on the condition that her children – two daughters – adopt his name. But the Governor's will contained a surprise. Should Lucy Chester, an infant in Antigua, take the name of Parke, he willed her property in the Leeward Islands valued at £30,000. The child was popularly assumed to be her benefactor's daughter, and her mother, Katherine Chester, his mistress. In Virginia the Custises were scandalized, but were advised that a challenge to the will would be fruitless.

Time passed. Frances Parke Custis and her sister, Lucy Parke Byrd, died young, as did wealthy Miss Chester in Antigua, soon after she had married a fellow islander, Thomas Dunbar. He accommodatingly altered his name to Dunbar Parke. But the Governor's will took on new life, though the orginal legatees were dead, in the early 1720s. Dunbar Parke claimed, as plaintiff, that Daniel Parke had wished to leave his insular property free of all encumbrance. It was therefore, he argued, for the Virginia heirs to meet some £6,000 of debts in Antigua that he had settled. John Custis IV hotly contested the claim. The wording of the will being ambiguous, for over twenty years both Antiguan plaintiffs and Virginian defendants enriched lawyers who disputed the point. Though Dunbar Parke himself died in 1734, his brother Charles adopted the name of Parke, and he and his children pursued the claim and brought it before the General Court in 1754.

When Daniel Parke Custis chose her as a bride in 1749, Martha – then Miss Dandridge of Chestnut Grove, New Kent County and aged about eighteen – knew little of Chancery suits. Described then as 'beautiful and sweet tempered', she had had much to endure.[2] Daniel's father, John Custis IV, while a shrewd man of business and a botanist with a celebrated garden at his town house in Williamsburg, was also eccentric and quarrelsome. Having first seemed to favour the match, he then objected to Martha as a wife for his son. But Martha showed herself a confident young woman and one capable of dealing with an irresolute suitor and a volatile head of the family.

Daniel, aged thirty-eight in 1749, was more than twenty years older than Martha, and a bachelor who lived quietly at the White House on the Pamunkey River, tending his tobacco crop. Though handsome in a swarthy way and undeniably rich, he had at least once failed to succeed in a marital venture when his father could not agree terms with the bride's family. Unlike his father, who was a member of the Governor's Council in the capital, Daniel took no part in public life beyond serving as an officer of the local militia and acting as vestryman at his parish church, St Peter's, New Kent. Martha's father, John Dandridge, who was clerk of New Kent Courthouse, was also a member of this vestry. Like many others, he incurred John Custis's wrath, according to friends of the old man. His crime was to have fathered a daughter so 'much inferior . . . in point of fortune' to Daniel. Chestnut Grove, the modest Dandridge home where Martha grew up a few miles downriver from her suitor's home, stood in only 500 acres, and its workforce of slaves numbered fewer than ten.

Not content with rejecting Martha on the ground of fortune, John Custis IV, it seems, also objected to her as a bride because of an animus he bore against the entire Dandridge clan. Martha's wealthy and well-connected uncle William, though by then dead, had been an adversary of Custis's on the Governor's Council for many years. Custis expressed his displeasure by presenting Williamsburg friends Matthew Moody and his wife with gifts of furniture and horses and family plate. To remonstrances, he allegedly replied that he preferred the Moodys to have them 'rather . . . than any Dandridge's daughter or any Dandridge that ever wore a head . . . he had not been at work all his life time for Dandridge's daughter . . .'[3]

Daniel Parke Custis feared that his father would go further. John Custis extravagantly favoured 'Black Jack', a former slave whom he had freed in 1748 and on whom he had settled 250 acres. 'Black Jack' was certainly the son of Custis's slave, Alice, and very probably his own illegitimate son. Daniel feared that his capricious father would disinherit him in favour of the boy, and hesitated to marry without his father's consent. But seventeen-year-old Martha carried the day. The eldest of a large family, she knew what it was to deal with tantrums, and turned away Custis's wrath with a 'prudent speech', according to Daniel's friend and attorney James Power. Whereupon the contrary old man declared that he would rather his son married her 'than any lady in Virginia'.[4] Following this statement, and before he could recant, Custis fell ill, died, and was buried in the autumn of 1749, leaving most of his worldly goods, including the mansion in town, to the son he had tormented. The will made provision for 'Black Jack', directing that he be accommodated with a house furnished with Russian leather chairs, black walnut tables and feather beds. But the young man was not destined to enjoy such comfort for long. Within two years he had died of a fever. Meanwhile Daniel and Martha had married in May 1750 and set up home together at the White House.[5]

Daniel Parke Custis had already proved a good manager of the acres lying in and about New Kent County. 'If everyone would take the same pains with their tobacco and fling away as much [substandard leaf] as I do,' he wrote to London merchant Robert Cary in 1755, 'there would not be such complaints of the inspectors [in England] as there are.'[6] He administered competently the enlarged estate that he inherited on his father's death, and lived quietly with Martha at the White House. In six years they produced four children.

The standard of living Martha now enjoyed was far higher than that at her childhood home. Both plantations were situated on ground close to the slow-moving Pamunkey River and shrouded from the summer heat by oaks, hickories and maples. Low-lying agricultural fields and freshwater marshes formed part of a distinctive riparian terrain where bald eagles and great blue herons nested and fished. The shallow, winding river was the life-blood of the locale, and, at different points where the course narrowed, ferry crossings connected neighbouring families. Many of those families were also connected by blood. It was a pleasant neighbourhood, and one with which Martha was intimately familiar from birth.

Before her marriage Martha had, it seems, spent some years 'up the country' – possibly in the wealthier atmosphere of Elsing Green, her uncle William's brick mansion, on the northern banks of the river.[7] Elsing Green contained, among other treasures, one of the few picture galleries in Virginia – a nod, perhaps, to the Dandridge family's artistic heritage: Martha's paternal grandfather had been a master painter-stainer in London. Another London relative, recently dead, had been her uncle, Bartholomew Dandridge; a pupil of Sir Godfrey Kneller, he was a celebrated portrait painter, whose image of Frederick, Prince of Wales was widely reproduced. In future years Martha was to play an important part in disseminating images of her second husband. Even during her first marriage, John Wollaston, an English painter popular in Virginia, obtained the commission, in 1757, to paint portraits of her and of Daniel. He also painted a double portrait of their children then living. A scarlet cardinal bird – emblem of Virginia – perches somewhat improbably on three-year-old Jacky's fist. Jacky is breeched and in coat and waistcoat, while his sister, Patsy, only a year old, is propped up, doll-like, in a satin dress.[8] Another portrait, *The Custis Children*, attributed to Matthew Pratt, probably dates from the time of her second marriage.[9]

Not only did Martha have an artistic eye. She also had, like many Virginians, a connoisseur's approach to material goods. Luxurious apparel and furnishings, china and silver – all imported from England – were badges of rank in this society. At least once a year she ordered from London suppliers fashionable and costly clothes for herself and her children and household articles of quality, as Daniel Parke Custis's invoice book, noting each year's commissions, attests. Robert Cary and Co. in London was, historically, the London merchant house which had dealt with the majority of the Parke Custis tobacco. The trade that they entered into with Daniel was mirrored in the transactions between dozens of other houses or firms in British ports and other Virginian families. Each year Daniel shipped to London, together with the hogsheads (barrels containing a thousand pounds of tobacco) from the numerous plantations, an invoice listing the innumerable items required at the White House and elsewhere over the course of the following year. Upon reception of the shipload, Cary and Co. sold the tobacco, for prices that varied dramatically. At the same time they applied to ironmongers, mantua-makers, cobblers and coachmakers – to name a few of the relevant suppliers – for the items requested on Daniel's invoice. The credits from the tobacco sales and debits from the inventory purchases were entered. Six months later, a ship bringing such goods as had been obtained would appear in the York River, with a load to be trans-ferred to the Pamunkey tributary and ultimately to the Parke Custis estate.*

Invoices for the years following their marriage show the reliance Daniel and Martha placed on their London suppliers. A smart 'two wheeled chair' or carriage, painted a 'pleasant stone colour' and adorned with 'gold shields, arms and crest', was acquired in 1750. The following year's invoice listed a 'blue and white' tea and coffee service, and a silver sugar dish 'with a cover to fit very close'. On this dish, and on a milk pot, on a stand and on twelve salvers, all to be of silver, Daniel instructed that his arms be engraved. On a practical note he added: '2 brushes to clean silver with'. The agent was to procure, in 1752, among many other items, 'two pairs of very neat silver shoe buckles for Mrs Custis's own wear' and 'one piece of fine flowered calico for Mrs Custis'. At the same time an order was placed for 'a fashionable cap and feather for my son, about two years well grown'.[10] Planters had to think far ahead in making out their invoices.

---

* Sterling was always in short supply in Virginia. From 1755 some paper currency – technically, bills of credit – was printed in the colony as part of the war effort and, denoted in pounds, shillings and pence, was known as 'current money'. (Because other colonies issued their own paper currency, that printed in Williamsburg was also distinguished as 'Virginia currency' or 'Virginia money'.) The worth of colonial currencies against each other and against sterling fluctuated. At this time Virginia money was worth about seventeen shillings in the pound sterling. Spanish coins – gold ones known as pistoles, worth nearly a pound sterling, and silver pesos or dollars, worth about five shillings – also circulated in the colonies, as did smaller denominations of Spanish and Portuguese coin or 'specie'. The system of credit with London agents on which Virginia planters relied had the advantage that no exchange rate was involved.

Martha had given birth on 19 November 1751 to a son and heir, to be known for his short life as Daniel Parke Custis II. But by the time this consignment from London had made its way across the Atlantic and to the Pamunkey, it would be the autumn of 1752 and the child a year old.

Time passed and the invoice sent to merchant Thomas Godwin the following year includes: '5 pairs of pumps [shoes] for my son, about 2½ years old, of different sizes'. By then, Frances Parke Custis, a sister for young Daniel II, born on 12 April 1753, had joined the family. Orders, looking ahead, are placed with Cary and Co. for '2 caps, for a girl about one year' and for three pairs of pumps 'for a girl about one year old of different sizes'. Like the earlier order for the tea and coffee service, a commission for twelve silver beakers – 'each of them to hold one pint with my arms engraved on them' – suggests that, even in the quiet surroundings of the White House plantation, the Parke Custises as a couple upheld the Virginian tradition of sociability and hospitality. Was this Martha's influence? How did she deal with a husband so much her elder, so long a reclusive bachelor? She appears to have charmed him into spending a fortune. In 1754, for instance, Daniel ordered Robert Cary to obtain '18 yards of the best pink tabby [watered silk] with a fashionable white satin stripe with binding for the same, and no lining'.[11] In addition, that year a London merchant, owner of an establishment called The Lock of Hair in Fleet Street, was commissioned to make for Martha an 'extraordinary white cut peruke and dress and a set of curls of best natural curled hair and newest fashion'.[12]

Although Daniel made so many purchases, both necessary and lavish, for his family and home, in other matters he was cautious, especially once the Dunbar suit was on appeal in London. Just as it was the duty of every Virginian to offer hospitality to anyone who came calling, so it was considered the duty of a gentleman in Virginia to grant loans to family, friends and neighbours. Daniel became creditor to some, but declared, in November 1754, that he 'never would meddle with one farthing' he had in England until the lawsuit was over. If it should go against him, he affirmed, 'all that I have in the world would scarcely do . . . [to meet the Antigua plaintiffs' demands].'[13] Once Martha had control of the estate, she showed herself a true Virginian and ended this rule of prudence that friends and neighbours no doubt viewed as parsimony.

While Martha was in her early twenties and Daniel in his early forties, a sombre item appears in the invoice for 1754: 'tomb for my son'. The Parke Custises' son and heir Daniel II died in February that year, aged two or three, and was buried in the old Parke grave-yard at Queen's Creek near Williamsburg. His parents went into mourning for fifteen months, as was prescribed for the death of a child or parent. For an initial six months deep mourning was observed, and Martha wore unrelieved black. In her jewellery, she abjured coloured stones. For a further six months, known as half mourning, touches of white might alleviate the dark palette. During second mourning, the last part of the prescribed period, lavender, mauve, grey and other muted shades were permitted. Daniel II's sister, Frances or 'Fanny', lived to wear '3 pr of mittens to fit a girl of 2 years old' as well as the 'fine thread', 'worsted' and 'scarlet' stockings that figure on the invoice sent to Robert Cary and Co. in 1754.[14] She lived also to become elder sister to John Parke Custis, to whom Martha gave birth on 27 November of that year, and to Martha, born some-time in 1756.[15] Daniel ordered 'two pairs of red satin shoes for Fanny, 2 years old' in 1755, as well as '2 fashionable necklaces' and 'one fashionable hat for my daughter, 3 years old'.[16] But further additions to Fanny's wardrobe stopped abruptly. In April 1757 the child died, eleven days short of her fourth birthday and, like her brother before her, joined Parke forebears in the Queen's Creek cemetery. Thus in the space of three years Martha gave birth to her two younger chil-dren, and lost her two older ones. In addition, her father, John Dandridge, had died unexpectedly while in Fredericksburg in August 1756, and she was still in half-mourning for him. Her daughter's death caused her to resume deep mourning.

Wollaston's stiff, doe-eyed portraits of 1757 show the reduced family – Daniel and Martha and their surviving children, John or 'Jacky' and Martha or 'Patsy' Parke Custis.[17] At this date Martha was still only twenty-five, Jacky and Patsy two and a half and about one. Deaths in childhood in this period were common, and there was no reason why more children should not follow. But only three months after the death of his elder daughter, Daniel himself was abruptly taken ill in July. Despite the attentions of a Williamsburg doctor, he died the following day.[18] The flurry of grief, mourning and burial arrangements included Martha's sending to Cary and Co. for the shipping of 'One handsome tombstone of the best durable marble to cost about £100'.[19] Her husband and two elder children now all lay in the Queen's Creek plot. Martha, still in black for Fanny, must wear mourning for two more years, the period prescribed following the death of a husband. A year of deep mourning was succeeded by six months of half mourning and six of second mourning. An exception was made only if, after the initial year, she acquired a serious suitor. She might then resume everyday attire.

This catalogue of deaths when she was in her early twenties must go some way towards explaining an anomaly in Martha's character. All her future life she was to be, for one so capable and strong-minded, exceptionally nervous and fearful about the health of her children and, later, of her grandchildren. To the immediate challenges of widowhood and of mothering her fatherless children, she rose confidently. With the children, she had ample help in the shape of the White House house slaves and servants. Lawyers, including her brother Bartholomew Dandridge and Robert Carter Nicholas supported her in the decision she took to administer the large Parke Custis estate herself. She did it for the most part with aplomb, although her late husband would have deplored her improvidence in making loans to family and friends. A steward, Joseph Valentine, supervised the work of the plantation overseers and the field slaves, and answered to her. Martha herself undertook the necessary correspondence with shipping agents in London concerning the dispatch and insurance of the hogsheads crammed with tobacco leaf, which she sent from the estate for sale across the Atlantic.

'I shall yearly ship a considerable part of the tobacco I make to you,' she wrote in August 1757 to Robert Cary and Co., 'which I shall take care to have made as good as possible and hope you will do your endeavour to get me a good price . . .' She sent that year thirty-six hogsheads in all – that is, some 36,000 pounds of tobacco. 'I shall want some goods this year for my family,' she added, 'which I have inclosed an invoice of and hope you will take care they are well bought and sent me by your first ship to this river [the James River].'[20]

As Daniel had died before composing the year's invoice, she filled it out herself. For once, there are no items of adornment for Martha. For her mother, Frances Jones Dandridge, who was now observing second mourning for her husband, Martha's father, there was only a pair of 'very well made silk pumps'. Martha's daughter Patsy, going on a year and a half, was to receive only such 'pumps' or shoes as are most proper for 'such a child'. For Jacky, now the sole male Parke Custis and a child in whom his mother vested much, Martha commissioned, besides two pairs of calf leather pumps, '1 pair calves' leather shoes, red heels, well sewed'.[21]

Martha was not long widowed when she heard with concern that the Privy Council in London had overturned the dismissal in Virginia of the Dunbar suit. The Antigua plaintiffs were therefore free to seek a retrial in the General Court in Williamsburg. In December 1757 she wrote to John Hanbury and Co., rival agents to Cary and Co. in London, who received some Parke Custis tobacco, expressing her surprise at this outcome. She had been advised in Virginia, she informed the firm, that 'Mr Custis [her late husband] was very unfortunate in losing so good a cause.' In lieu of further animadversions on the London lawyers' capabilities, she asked for a 'particular' – or detailed – account of 'the charges of the lawsuit'. Refusing all accommodation with the plaintiffs, though the case would very likely proceed to retrial in Williamsburg, she wrote, 'no doubt the matter will turn out in my favour'.[22] Martha's attorney was to prevail, late in 1758, on John Robinson, Speaker of the House of Burgesses, to act as guardian – in legal matters – to her children. In his father's place, four-year-old Jacky was now 'chief defendant' in this and any other lawsuit that might be brought against the estate. Martha and her daughter were also liable.[23]

Martha Dandridge Custis, while fully and competently engaged in this Atlantic trade and while conducting herself ably in a complicated Chancery suit, had nevertheless inhabited a narrow milieu all her twenty-six years, venturing no further than to other houses on the Pamunkey or before marriage to Williamsburg. In the colonial capital she found many friends. Her mother, Frances Jones Dandridge, was related to half the lawyers and clerics in the capital as well as to numerous burgesses. But Martha had not even found her husband in the capital: she had married a Pamunkey neighbour, and upon marriage had settled in the self-same parish in New Kent County where she had grown up. Her encounter with George Washington in March 1758 would introduce her not only to life in northern Virginia but, by degrees, to a wider world than the younger Martha could ever have dreamed of.

3

North and South

. . . the animating prospect of possessing Mrs Custis.

Upon his arrival in Williamsburg in mid-March 1758, Washington was assured by Dr John Amson, at a cost of £3 2s 6d, that his life was not in danger and that there was nothing to prevent him rejoining his regiment.[1] Nevertheless he persisted in resigning his commission. General John Forbes was the British commander of an expeditionary force charged with seizing Fort Duquesne, the fortress that commanded the forks of the Ohio River, from a French garrison. He was sorry to hear of George's decision, writing in March to the President of the Governor's Council in Williamsburg: 'he has the character of a good and knowing officer in the back countries'.

The young Colonel had chosen a critical moment to resign. The Virginia House of Burgesses was on the point of raising a second Virginia Regiment to supplement the first, in which he had served. Both were to join Forbes's British regulars in the assault on the French. Forbes urged intervention on President John Blair: 'If he [Washington] . . . would serve this campaign, I should be glad that you ordered his regiment to repair to Winchester directly.'[2] Honeyed words from Blair – Acting Governor of Virginia in a lull between lieutenant governors – resulted in a compromise. Washington would indeed serve in the campaign but, it was understood, would resign at its end. Writing to Forbes the following month, Washington hoped that the General's good opinion of him would continue: 'it is the greatest reward I expect for my services in the ensuing campaign'.[3] With retirement to Mount Vernon to follow, promotion was no longer at issue. But he intended to have a companion in that retirement.

By early April Washington was with his regiment at Winchester, in north-western Virginia. Until late in the year they were to be employed in manoeuvres in the Ohio country directed by Forbes with the aim of clearing a path to Canada. But while he was still in Williamsburg in March, he noted in his ledger two entries which introduce 'Mrs Custis'. On the 16th we have: 'By Mrs Custis's servants 30 shillings'. And an entry for the 25th of the month shows 'Mrs Custis's servants' being paid a further thirty shillings.[4]

There are pretty stories about the Washingtons' initial meeting, including a chance encounter at this time at the home of one of Martha's neighbours on the Pamunkey River.[5] Most probably, Williamsburg being a small place with a total population of under 4,000 and a 'society' far smaller, they had met previously. Robert Stewart, a fellow officer in the Virginia Regiment, implied as much when he wrote from the Winchester garrison, shortly after his fellow officer's marriage, congratulating Washington on his 'happy union with the Lady that all agree has long been the just object of your affections'.[6] When Washington first tipped Martha Dandridge Custis's servants, her brother-in-law Colonel Burwell Bassett was probably present, as his servants received '4 shillings, fourpence ha'penny'.[7] Bassett and his wife – Martha's younger sister, Anna Maria or 'Nancy' – lived at Eltham, a Pamunkey plantation. Where the two visits indicated by the payments took place, whether town or country, we cannot know. Like the Bassetts, Martha went periodically on business and for pleasure into Williamsburg. The question of who suggested that Washington pursue the 'widow Custis' is of more interest. It was not all because of her fine hazel eyes that he came calling.

Among those who had advised young Mrs Custis upon her husband Daniel's unexpected death at the age of forty-six the previous year was the lawyer Robert Carter Nicholas. With his wife Ann, he often visited her sister, Sally Fairfax, at Belvoir.[8] In January 1758

Washington had also consulted the lawyer professionally.[9] Possibly Nicholas, who knew as well as anyone of Washington's military disappointments, of his loneliness, and of the young widow's circumstances, advised the young planter to woo Martha.

She was, by any standards, a wealthy widow. Daniel Parke Custis had died intestate. In accordance with English common law which obtained in the colony, therefore, all his personal property, minus his lands and slaves, was divided equally between his widow and children. This comprised, in England, £10,000 sterling in cash, stocks and bonds and, in Virginia, personal property – including slaves – valued at £30,000 current money. Two-thirds of his Virginian lands, amounting to 17,779 acres, were vested immediately in his son and heir, as were two-thirds of his slaves – 285 in number. Eight thousand acres, the Custis mansion in Williamsburg and 126 slaves were settled on Martha for life. Should she take a new husband, this dower share, as well as her share of her late husband's personal property, would come under his control. Supposing this second husband predeceased her, both shares reverted to her. At her own death, land and slaves would revert to the Parke Custis estate. She might bequeath her share of personal property where she liked, including to her second husband, if he survived her. But that was to look ahead.

On the debit side for a young man contemplating matrimony with Mrs Custis, there was the Dunbar suit. It might be decided against the Parke Custis estate, when and if it came back to the General Court in Williamsburg for retrial. But it might never come into the courts. If it did, it might continue to seesaw between those of Virginia and London. Moreover, Virginians in colonial times were gamblers. John Mercer of Marlboro on the Potomac had long been the Parke Custis lawyer in Virginia regarding the Dunbar suit. He was aware that the Parke heirs in Antigua, though successful in London, were not yet in a position to seek a retrial in Williamsburg. Such information was easily forthcoming from him, from his nephew, George Mason, Washington's neighbour, or from Mercer's own son in the second Virginia Regiment – another George.

Other suitors for Martha's hand were circling, as an April 1758 letter to William Byrd III, a connection of her children, makes clear:

'C.C. is very gay and says he has attacked the widow Custis'.[10] 'C.C.' was probably Charles Carter of Cleve, who was already, aged fifty, twice widowed. He did not succeed with Martha Dandridge Custis. As is apparent from further entries in Washington's cash book, the Colonel now pursued Martha with all the tenacity and deadly purpose he had previously shown in pursuing the French and their Native American allies. But the outcomes of the engagements were very different. Where Washington and the forces with which he fought failed to make headway against enemy positions, with Martha he swept to victory.

On Washington's part this was no relationship with love or lust at its root, such as he had initiated with the Fairfax ladies. Martha was, to employ Stewart's words, a 'just object' of the bachelor's affections. He could tend his estate at Mount Vernon with the aid of the income from Martha's dower lands in southern Virginia. With a wife also came the prospect of heirs. Moreover, in the social hierarchy of the colony, he belonged to the second tier of planters. As guardian and stepfather to the rich and well-bred Parke Custis children, he would derive worldly benefit. Washington was to describe Martha, soon after their marriage, as an 'agreeable partner'.[11] Five months later, in a letter to the same correspondent, she had become 'an agreeable Consort for Life'.[12] With time, as this book will show, Washington would come to look on his wife as infinitely more than 'agreeable'. But thirty-five years after his marriage he warned a young woman eager to wed:

> . . . love is too dainty a food to live upon *alone*, and ought not to be considered farther, than as a necessary ingredient for that matrimonial happiness which results from a combination of causes; none of which are of greater importance, than that the object on whom it is placed, should possess good sense – [a] good disposition – and the means of supporting you in the way you have been brought up . . .[13]

The woman he courted in 1758 possessed all three of the qualities he praised – sense, disposition and means.

What made Martha Dandridge Custis fix on Washington as a husband? Did he seem to her, to use his own tepid terminology, merely an 'agreeable partner'? Or did Washington's attentions awaken in Martha feelings of passion and of romantic love? In contrast to several other Virginia planters free to marry at this date, he was not an especially appealing prospect, though respected, as we have seen, as a 'useful' soldier. His account of the 1753 mission to Legardeur de Saint Pierre was, at the behest of the colony's Acting Governor, published in Williamsburg the following year. Its sonorous title in full was 'The Journal of Major George Washington, Sent by the Hon. Robert Dinwiddie, Esq.; His Majesty's Lieutenant-Governor, and Commander in Chief in Virginia, to the Commandant of the French Forces on Ohio'. He had come out well from Braddock's fatal march on Fort Duquesne later in 1754. He had made continual small but shrewd land purchases in the frontier lands. But his brother's widow, Ann Fairfax Washington, who had remarried and moved away, would own Mount Vernon until her death. Washington, who farmed the plantation, kept what income he could make from the tobacco he grew – in 1757, £4,000 odd.

In short, the disparity in wealth between George Washington and Martha Dandridge Custis at the time of their meetings in March 1758 was striking. According to Washington's own later testimony, Martha's uncle Francis Dandridge, a wealthy merchant in London, censured the match.[14] But sociable, confident Martha knew her own mind, whether she was out to marry wealthy Daniel Parke Custis or plan a new life with a second husband. She withstood this disapproval and occupied herself with her tobacco trade, sending seventeen hogsheads of tobacco to Hanbury and Co. in London in June 1758: 'as tob[acc]o is now very scarce, and it is certain very little will be made [out of] the ensuing [forthcoming] crop, I hope I shall get an uncommon price for this tobacco. Inclosed is a bill of lading for it. I wrote to you for insurance, which I don't doubt but you have made.'[15] Martha may have had help in framing the letter, but her business sense was admirable.

Martha was indeed now an experienced businesswoman, having managed the estate for a year. She was confident in her commissions, whether asking Cary and Co. to procure items for herself, for her children or for the plantation. When necessary, she was critical of what arrived, declaring a dress she had sent to be dyed as 'very badly done'. In an order that included 'a handsome bureau dressing table and glass, mahogany', needles and pins, '4 handsome chafing dishes, raisins and currants', there was also 'for the negroes . . . 6 dozen broad [field] hoes'.[16] There was little, in short, that Martha, like other Virginian planters, did not procure from England in exchange for the hogsheads of tobacco they sent for sale there. The problem with this system of barter for the colonists was that their demands very often outstripped the value of the tobacco dispatched.

Washington's pursuit of Martha continued through the summer of 1758, as the following entry in his account book shows: 'June 5 – By Mrs Custis's servants 14/6'.[17] Washington had returned on a brief visit to Williamsburg to requisition supplies urgently needed for Fort Loudoun, the frontier garrison at Winchester in western Virginia where he was stationed with his regiment. But his visit to Martha seems to have been at the expense of normal civility. He did not stay to greet Francis Fauquier, the new Lieutenant Governor who arrived in the colony that same day. Dissembling slightly, he wrote to Fauquier in apology on 17 June: 'the business that carried me there was of too urgent a nature to admit of delay when I had once got it accomplished'.[18]

Had he also by now persuaded Martha to endow him with her hand and worldly goods? It is unclear at what point during the year, and whether by correspondence or in person, Washington and Martha agreed to marry. As has already been noted, only a few items of the couple's correspondence with each other survives, and none from this period.

Martha's extant correspondence for 1758 consists of business letters, several of them about the Dunbar suit. One item in her 1758 invoice to Robert Cary and Co., which includes a request for '2 Dresden [lace] worked handkerchiefs [neckerchiefs]', is interesting. She required 'One Genteel suite of clothes for myself to be grave but not Extravagant nor to be mourning'. As we have seen, after a year, should a suitable marital prospect emerge, she was free to discard further mourning. She sent a 'night gown' – informal dress – to be dyed a 'fashionable colour fit for me to wear'. She expected it to be 'dyed better' than the one she had sent the year before. It would, besides, furnish a measure for gowns of 'the best Indian [chintz]' – one dark, one on a 'white calico ground, to be made of very fine Calico' – which she now commissioned.[19]

Nowhere else is marriage hinted at. We must guess at her feelings as she contemplated exchanging, with her children, a familiar landscape and family and friends she had known all her life for a life in remote northern Virginia. And if life on the majestic Potomac would be an unknown to conjure with, how much more so would be George Washington as a husband?

In contrast to Daniel Parke Custis, George was Martha's contemporary. He was, also unlike reclusive Daniel, ambitious, for all his talk of retirement, and of an adventurous spirit. Daniel had had dark good looks. Washington, pale-skinned and with chestnut hair, had fine, classic features. He was, besides, a man of unusual height and with a powerful physique. And, last but not least, when Washington came calling, he was a serving officer in uniform. An entire chapter could be dedicated to the susceptibility of Eve, since time began, to Adam in military attire. Looking ahead to descriptions of George and Martha's relationship in the course of what would prove a forty-year marriage, to employ vocabulary of the battlefield, we may posit that capable, sensible Martha was smitten by Washington. She remained felled by love all her life. But she also had a strong urge to care for and mother others. This impulse possibly originated in her position in the family where she was eldest of eight. She may also have responded to a fragility in her apparently stalwart suitor. Others, among them William Fairfax, had exerted themselves on behalf of Washington when he was younger. Initially, Martha may well have relished the prospect of cherishing her husband as much as the prospect of being cherished.

George, for all his physical grace, was nervous at home and stiff and uncertain in company, except with intimates or fellow officers. Martha instilled in him a self-confidence which had hitherto been lacking. Under her tutelage he was to embrace possibilities of friendship and family life. As he grew in self-confidence at Mount Vernon, so he would be called on repeatedly to act as arbiter in vexed parochial and familial disputes. In due course, that local experience, born of partnership with Martha, would be of use in a great national struggle.

All this year, whether stationed with his regiment in Winchester or campaigning with Forbes against the French at Fort Duquesne, Washington was making strategic and practical decisions with a view to settling at home. He had joiners add an extra storey to the house, which had previously featured only a ground floor with two bedchambers, a parlour and a dining room. He stood for the first time for the House of Burgesses in July, and was duly elected to represent Frederick County, the district in which Winchester lay. But he makes mention of Martha only once, in a letter to Sally Fairfax of 12 September 1758. She had apparently responded to criticisms he had made of his superior officers in their conduct of the Ohio campaign. He protested: 'If you allow that any honour can be derived from my opposition to our present system of management, you destroy the merit of it entirely in me by attributing my anxiety to the animating prospect of possessing Mrs Custis.'

Thereupon Washington, though on the brink of marriage to Martha Dandridge Custis, writes to Sally Fairfax: ''Tis true, I profess myself a votary to love – I acknowledge that a lady is in the case – and further, I confess, that this lady is known to you.' The awkward code and flowery sentiments do not obscure the fact that 'this lady', far from being Martha, was none other than Sally herself. 'I feel the force of her amiable beauties in the recollection of a thousand tender passages', he continued, 'that I could wish to obliterate, till I am bid to revive them – but experience alas! sadly reminds me how impossible this is . . .' He concludes: 'there is a destiny, which has the sovereign control of our actions – not to be resisted by the strongest efforts of human nature'.[20] The reader is at a loss to know if the 'thousand tender passages' to which the bachelor Colonel refers indicate unrequited passion, stolen kisses or a full-blown affair. But he plainly sees his forthcoming marriage to Martha as a sacred undertaking – directed by 'a destiny'.

In later life at times of crisis Washington would invoke the name of 'destiny' and also that of 'Providence', entities that he believed guided him at crucial moments. In England at this time many valued reason and science above the traditional teachings of the Church, and preferred to account for the workings of the world without recourse to prayer. In eighteenth-century Virginia belief and politics were pragmatic. Washington joined the Freemasons' Lodge in Fredericksburg, and later that of Alexandria. Like his neighbours, he was church-going and served, with them, as a vestryman in the local parish. In this post they were responsible for appointing the minister, keeping up the fabric of the church, and administering justice and relief for the poor. In short, the 'destiny' Washington invoked when about to embark on marriage was roughly equivalent to an Almighty who looked favourably on him.

Washington wrote one more letter to Sally, on 25 September. He ended it: 'you ask if I am not tired at the length of your letter? No, Madam, I am not, nor never can be while the lines are an inch asunder to bring you in haste to the end of the paper . . . believe that I am most unalterably your most obedient and obliged George Washington.'[21] 'Unalterably' he might be Sally Fairfax's, but this did not prevent George from proceeding with resolute steps towards his 'sovereign destiny' – marriage with Mrs Custis.

Mount Vernon, Fairfax County

*Mr Bassett will inform you of the mirth and
gaiety that he has seen.*

Washington ended his career in the colonial service on a high note. He had helped, with the Forbes Expedition in November 1758, to end the long French hegemony at the forks of the Ohio. It would be long before, in a very different conflict but again on American soil, he would again commit to war. Dr James Craik, the regimental surgeon, wrote on 20 December from Fort Loudoun, Winchester: 'We are very anxious here to know the fate of the troops, and who will be commander when the regiment meets with that irreparable loss, losing you.'[1] Washington took a parting shot at higher authorities, bidding farewell to his fellow officers: 'had everything contributed as fully as your obliging endeavours did to render me satisfied, I never should have . . . had cause to know the pangs I have felt at parting with a regiment, that has shared my toils, and experienced every hardship and danger, which I have endured'.[2]

By the time he wrote this letter, dated 'New Kent County, 10th January, 1759', Washington was a married man of four days' standing. Twelfth Night – 6 January – had seen the couple wed and the 'widow Custis' take the name of Martha Washington. Martha's granddaughters handed down to their descendants remnants of yellow brocade and lace and a dainty pair of sequinned shoes they supposed her to have worn on the occasion.[3] Probably the Reverend

David Mossom, longstanding minister at St Peter's Church, New Kent, officiated, and we may assume members of Martha's family were witnesses. Where the couple exchanged vows is in doubt. Later recollections of local inhabitants and Dandridge kin claim the White House as the locale, and make mention of a wedding feast and festivities lasting several days.[4] Possibly, despite the inclement season, the Washingtons married in Mossom's handsome brick church in the New Kent woods, and banqueted later at Martha's home.[5] The bridal couple's feelings on the day about each other are also a matter of supposition. Much later, Washington was to write, 'I have always considered marriage as the most interesting event of one's life – The foundation of happiness or misery.'[6] He and Martha had now laid a foundation that would withstand in time the seismic shocks of war and revolution.

Though it does not survive, the Washingtons' marriage certificate was at least 'properly . . . authenticated' when George sent it off to Robert Cary and Co. in early summer. From now on, he informed Cary, the firm was to address to him all letters 'which relate to the affairs of the late Daniel Parke Custis, Esquire'.[7] Martha's days of superintending the family estates, corresponding with the London agents and consulting with Williamsburg lawyers were over. Moreover from now on Washington, assuming the role of guardian as well as that of stepfather to her children, kept meticulous accounts on their behalf.

Washington took his place for the first time in the House of Burgesses in Williamsburg and was appointed to an important standing committee. In addition, Speaker Robinson returned him the thanks of the House on 26 February 1759 for five years of 'faithful services to his Majesty and this colony'. The assembly was grateful also for 'his brave and steady behaviour' from the 'first encroachments and hostilities of the French and their Indians to his resignation after the happy reduction of Fort Duquesne'.[8] At the beginning of April the new Burgess obtained permission to be absent for the remainder of the House sessions. An urgent note that Washington wrote to John Alton on 5 April gives us the reason why: 'I have sent Miles on today to let you know that I expect to be up tomorrow, and to get the key from Colonel Fairfax's which I desire you will take care of . . .' Alton had formerly been his master's 'body servant', or valet, and was now steward at Mount Vernon. 'Enquire about in the neighbourhood, and get some eggs and chickens, and prepare in the best manner you can for our coming. You need not however take out any more of the furniture than the beds, tables and chairs, in order that they may be well rubbed and cleaned.'[9] The Washingtons, with the Parke Custis children, were on their way home.

Coming, in the spring of 1759, from New Kent County, where woods and fields and near neighbours had bounded her parish world, Martha was unfamiliar with the more dramatic scenery that northern Virginia offered. For the sluggish Pamunkey, whose many ferries facilitated neighbourly visits, she had exchanged the majestic Potomac, three-quarters of a mile wide below the promontory on which Mount Vernon stood. Ferries were few and the wind often high, discouraging passenger traffic. However, a steady stream of visitors came by road, and Martha's new home was a small but pleasing house, two storeys high and recently faced with cream rusticated wood in imitation of stone. In its windows blinked 'two hundred and fifty squares best Crown glass' with which Washington had replaced earlier and inferior windowpanes.[10]

The carriage entrance at the front of the house faced a bowling green, beyond which lay the road to Alexandria. The garden at the back gave onto lawns above the river. Within, a central hall on the ground floor gave onto a bedroom, parlour, study and dining room. Above were further bedrooms, reached by a substantial staircase situated close to the front door. Washington had always been eager that the house should be stylishly equipped. From the 'cold and barren frontiers' of Virginia, on garrison duty in 1757, he had commissioned Richard Washington, in London, to 'procure [wall] paper for 5 Rooms', to differ in their colours. Wanted also was 'paper of a very good kind and colour for a Dining Room', and two square mahogany tables, 'to join occasionally'. All was to be 'fashionable – neat – and good'.[11] The agent had obliged, and dispatched eight dozen yards of blue, green, yellow, Chinese and Indian floral wallpaper and twelve of crimson, with matching borders. In addition, '12 Mah[ogan]ay best gothick Chairs, wt. Pincushion Seats, stufft in the best manner & coverd with horse hair' crossed the Atlantic, and a 'neat landscape – after Claude Lorrain' now surmounted a 'fine, new, veined marble chimney piece slab, and covings'.[12] For the master bedroom the Washingtons this year ordered a handsome four-poster bed with blue and white hangings.[13]

No amount of imported finery could disguise the fact that the rooms at Mount Vernon were of small proportions. The hall was, in consequence, a room that was regularly used to accommodate larger or more important parties. In the spring of 1760, for instance, Washington extended an invitation to dine to Lord Fairfax, who was staying at Belvoir. The peer was generally to be found living in eccentric isolation at Greenway Court, a log lodge that he had built near Winchester. On this occasion he was graciously pleased to accept the invitation. Among the company who came with him was Bryan Fairfax, George William's younger half-brother, who had recently ended up in jail in Annapolis after a long debauch. Apparently chastened by the experience, he had married Sally Fairfax's younger sister, Elizabeth, and was now settled at a house in the neighbourhood. He was now his elder half-brother's heir, and indeed stood third in line to inherit the barony of Fairfax from his noble cousin. Washington had, the previous autumn, obtained a commission for William Fairfax, George William's younger full brother, in a British expedition headed north with the aim of seizing Quebec from the French. In the successful British assault that followed in September 1759, both the victorious general, James Wolfe, and his French opponent, fell. So too did Billy Fairfax. The French were to retreat to Montreal this year, and, in the autumn, surrender there. The theatre of war would shift to Europe and elsewhere.

The Fairfax presence on the Potomac was further reduced when the master and mistress of Belvoir left in the spring of 1760 for England. George William had still to settle a part of his father's estate. While he was away, Washington supervised his friend's Virginia estate, and received in return intelligence from the metropolis. Fairfax wrote, in 1761, of rumours that George III, who had succeeded his grandfather the previous September, was to marry a Brunswick princess and that an 'immediate peace' was to ensue.[14] The young king took instead as his bride Charlotte of Mecklenburg-Strelitz, and the Peace of Paris was not signed until 1763. Washington devoutly hoped that it would be 'of long continuance and introductory of mutual advantages to the merchant & planter . . .'[15] Like other Virginia planters, he had suffered from seizures by enemy French and Spanish vessels of ships bound for England with tobacco and with goods westward. There was no thought in his or Martha's minds, busy as they were with the plantation and the children, that the British response to the peace would ultimately bring war in its wake. Washington was intent on procuring the land bounty – 200,000 acres at the forks of the Ohio and elsewhere – promised him and those others who had joined the Virginia Regiment on its formation in 1754, once the war was at an end. These western lands, whenever they should be forthcoming, would substantially increase his acre-age, and offered virgin ground for planting tobacco, if the Mount Vernon yield slowed. It was a crop that ultimately exhausted the soil, if intensively farmed. Virginian landowners, dependent on the plant as a cash crop, did not practise rotation.

If the cultivation of tobacco at Mount Vernon brought anxiety, the situation of the house provided solace. One had only to open the door at the back of the hall to step on to lawns with sweeping views of Maryland across the river. Mount Vernon was now no longer the bachelor house devoid of comforts from which Washington had written to Sally Fairfax, begging for jellies to mend his health. Washington, inclined to be querulous, was a very contented married man.

This is apparent in a letter that he wrote, only nine months after his marriage, to Richard Washington in England. He referred to 'The longing desire, which for many years I have had, of visiting the great metropolis of that kingdom [London]'. That desire, he now accepted, was unlikely soon to be satisfied: '. . . I am now tied by the leg and must set inclination aside.' He was not complaining. 'I am now, I believe, fixed at this Seat with an agreeable Consort for Life, and hope to find more happiness in retirement than I ever experienced amidst a wide and bustling World . . .'[16]

The following year, 1760, Martha gave her brother-in-law, Burwell Bassett, who had been visiting, a letter to take home to his wife, Nancy: 'Mr Bassett will inform you of the mirth and gaiety that he has seen.'[17] The Washingtons' relationship had to withstand one specific strain, as the years of their marriage multiplied. Martha had given her first husband four children. She and George were, and remained, childless. No reference to any 'accident', or miscarriage, no repining concerning the want of an heir, survives. Was Washington infertile? There is no one convincing explanation of the matter. We may assume that it represented a nagging anxiety at least, with hope and disappointment thrown in.

Mount Vernon was now astir after years of comparative neglect while Washington had been at the frontier. He later told his former fellow officer, Robert Stewart, that he 'had provisions of all kinds to buy for the first two or three years; and my plantation to stock . . .'[18] With a compound of capital investment and innovative methods of agriculture, he was convinced that he could stimulate both quality and price of the tobacco he grew at Mount Vernon. Among other books he sent for from Cary was one with the seductive subtitle: *A Plain, Easy, and Demonstrative Method of speedily growing Rich, by a Country Gentleman*. He informed the London agent that he would now add to the Parke Custis freight he dispatched from the York and Pamunkey his own Potomac tobacco.[19] George Washington had once been grateful to Colonel William Fairfax for the introduction to his namesake, the London agent Richard Washington. The illustrious London firms he now did business with – Cary and Co., Capel and Osgood Hanbury, and James Gildart – were more enterprising in procuring the 'neat and fashionable' goods that the Washingtons were eager to acquire.

Martha presided over a household that included thirteen house slaves, many of them Parke Custis dower slaves who had accompanied her north. On Doll, a cook-housekeeper, she relied. Lame Alice was a 'sempstress' or seamstress, charged annually, with others, with making clothes and stockings from cheap imported cloth for each of the field slaves. In the nursery quarters a boy named Julius wore the Parke Custis livery to proclaim his position as Jacky's attendant.

Molly, another sempstress, and Rose looked after his younger sister, Patsy. In the autumn of 1761 the children began lessons with a tutor, Walter Magowan, who took up residence at Mount Vernon. In the Guardian Accounts he kept for Jacky and Patsy, Washington charged half Walter Magowan's salary to each of the children.[20] The children, Martha wrote proudly the following year, 'learn their books very fast'.[21]

Never far away lurked the medical men. Martha suffered from measles and then from whooping cough in the years following her marriage. Washington himself was plagued by episodes of the 'ague' or malaria. Only Jacky was in general in robust health. Patsy had worrying 'fits' a year after her move north, in 1761, when she was only five or six. Martha wrote to Margaret Green, the local minister's wife: 'I have the pleasure to tell you my dear little girl is much better. She has lost her fits and fevers both, and seems to be getting well very fast. We carried her out yesterday in the chariot and the change of air refreshed her very much.'[22] But these 'fits and fevers' would recur, and increase in frequency and in severity, as Patsy grew older.

The Reverend Green, when not officiating in church, acted as physician to the family. For a time Dr Laurie of Alexandria tended, for a lesser fee, to the field slaves. They led a crowded existence in log cabins grouped together in the different quarters of the plantation. Diseases, malaria and smallpox included, spread easily. On occasion Laurie also doctored the family, not always satisfactorily. He appeared at the house one evening in April 1760: 'I may add, drunk,' Washington noted.[23] The doctor 'blooded' Martha in the morning, but what Washington termed 'his incapacity to attend the calls of his profession' increased.[24] Well before the medic's early demise, the Washingtons turned to Dr William Rumney, a new doctor who had set up his stall in Alexandria. He treated sick slaves and, in addition, ministered to Patsy, as her fits and fevers worsened.

Martha did not lose touch with her family in New Kent County. She visited her mother periodically at Chestnut Grove. She saw her brother, the lawyer Bartholomew Dandridge, when she was in Williamsburg with Washington, and was intimate with her sister Nancy Bassett. They corresponded freely about their home lives and about Dandridge family concerns. 'I am very sorry to hear my mamma is still complaining and her staying at home so much as she does, I believe, is a great hurt to her,' Martha wrote in 1762. 'I hope she is happier at home than she seemed when I was down.' Referring to their younger sister who, aged thirteen, was still living with their mother, she added: 'I should be glad [if] you would take care of Betsy and keep her in proper order. She has her own way so much at home, I am afraid she will be quite spoiled.'[25]

Washington kept a kind of farmer's journal. Here he entered weather conditions and dates on which plantings, fellings and harvests had taken place. He jotted down prices paid, recorded visitors to Mount Vernon, and noted visits and journeys he and Martha and the children made. Entries for January 1760 offer a snapshot of the Washingtons' early married life. When the diary opens, Martha is suffering from the measles, and Nancy Bassett is visiting. An entry for the 2nd begins: 'Mrs Barnes . . . ' – a relation on his mother's side living in the area – '. . . returned home in my chariot, the weather being too bad to travel in an open carriage – which, together with Mrs Washington's indisposition, confined me to the house, and gave me an opportunity of posting my books [transferring accounts to ledgers] and putting them in good order.' Three days later the Reverend Green came to prescribe for Martha, and Sally Fairfax came visiting that same morning. 'Just as we were going to dinner Captain Walter Stuart' – a former colleague of Washington's in the Virginia Regiment – 'appeared with Dr Laurie.' Some of the slaves had come down with the measles. 'The evening being very cold, and the wind high, Mrs Fairfax went home in the chariot . . .'

As the chariot did not return in time next day, the Washingtons were prevented from going to Pohick Church, an old wooden building soon to be replaced by a brick structure, about seven miles from Mount Vernon. Next day Mrs Bassett accompanied her brother-in-law into Alexandria. They visited, among others, a merchant, Mr Kirkpatrick. Here Washington ordered a keg of butter weighing seventy-one pounds, destined to be stored underground. Washington also asked Dr Craik, the Virginia Regiment surgeon, now living in retirement, to find him a gardener. Following a visit by the

Washingtons and Nancy to the Fairfaxes at Belvoir, on the 12th George escorted his sister-in-law part of the way home to Eltham.[26]

There was entertainment to be had in Alexandria in February, though the month also brought snow, ice and rain. To promote the harbour town, the leading men of the town and of the neighbourhood, including Washington, regularly acted as managers of balls and assemblies. From the beginning of their marriage both Washingtons were regular in their attendance at these occasions, including, in January 1769, 'the Monthly Ball' – probably a subscription affair.[27] These provincial gatherings were not always of the standard that obtained in Williamsburg, let alone the far-distant metropolis that was London. Following the ball in February 1760 Washington had no complaint of the 'music and dancing . . . the chief entertainment' provided. He and Martha stayed the night at the Carlyles' imposing mansion in town, and may not have reached it till late into the night. Inhabitants of other colonies, as well as visitors from Europe, were astonished at how hard and how long Virginians would dance. But he was offended by the supper the ball managers offered: only 'great plenty of bread and butter', some biscuits with tea, and coffee, 'which the drinkers could not distinguish from hot water sweetened'.[28]

Later this summer Martha congratulated Nancy on the birth of a second daughter: 'I wish I could say boy, as I know how much one of that sex was desired by you all.' She added, as an experienced mother: 'I also hope you are out of all fear of sore breasts before this time.'[29] Visits to Mount Vernon that Nancy planned did not always take place. She was rapidly becoming the mother of a large family. If her younger sister's fecundity caused Martha to mourn the continuing want of an heir at Mount Vernon, she made no mention of it. After Nancy cried off a visit, owing to family illness at Eltham, in the spring of 1762, Martha wrote: 'It was a very great disappointment to me your not coming as we had so long expected you . . . I have had a very dark time since I came home. I believe it was owing to the severe weather we have had. I think I never knew such a winter as it has been . . .'[30] From Martha, so positive and cheerful in general, this is a remarkable admission. The weather did not usually so affect her. Possibly Nancy knew of another cause for Martha's 'dark time'.

Thoughts of a miscarriage or hopes of pregnancy dashed arise. But this year Martha seems to have been in a nervous state generally, and the Washingtons' marriage suffered accordingly.

She told Nancy in August 1762 of a fortnight's visit she had paid with her husband to his brother, John Augustine Washington, in Westmoreland County. She had taken Patsy with her, but left Jacky at Mount Vernon: 'for a trial, to see how well I could stay without him'. It was a disaster. 'If I at any time heard the dogs bark or a noise out, I thought there was a person sent for me. I often fancied he was sick or some accident had happened to him.' The upshot was, she no longer felt able to accompany Washington when he went down to the House sessions in Williamsburg. She wrote to Nancy: 'nothing but my children's interest should prevent me the satisfaction of seeing you and my good friends'. There is more than a hint that she pined for the gaiety of the colonial capital. 'If I could leave my children in as good care as you can, I would never let Mr Washington come down without me,' she affirmed.[31] But she was adamant. Martha committed herself to the care of Jacky and Patsy at Mount Vernon. Washington came and went to the Parke Custis estates 'below', and to Williamsburg, on increasingly vexatious business.

'I do not like to recriminate on a subject,' he wrote ominously to Cary and Co., going on to do exactly that, on 26 April 1763. Another agent, he was informed, had sold George William Fairfax's tobacco for twelve shillings a hundredweight. It was, Washington wrote, 'of the same kind exactly' as some he had shipped to Cary, and for which he had received a much lesser sum. He could 'conceive no reason therefore' why his neighbour's tobacco should so far outsell his.[32] The truth was, the soil varied dramatically between even neighbouring plantations, owing to a number of factors. But he might well complain of the prices the London agents paid for his crops. Not only were all his – expensive – efforts to improve his farmland failing. Other sums, gone to rescue Mount Vernon from neglect, had, as he told his friend Robert Stewart, 'swallowed up, before I well knew where I was, all the money I got by marriage – nay more, brought me in debt . . .' He had just received a statement of his account with Cary and Co., showing that he was in their debt. It was, he wrote to Stewart, 'transmitted to me with the additional aggravation of a hint at the largeness of it'.[33]

Washington had prided himself on being a good manager. He was disconcerted to find he was in the company of those Virginians who ignored their balance sheets with the agents in London and spent profligately. He had been too complacent. With Martha, he had ordered luxuries as well as staples too freely. The first period of contentment in the Washingtons' marriage was at an end. Now husband and wife had to pull together if they were to escape the spectre of debt that hung over every colonial planter's head. In mitigation, he wrote to Stewart, he owed to no one in Virginia, unlike many others whose estates the public gazettes ultimately offered for sale. The land bounty he was owed, when paid, would bring more acreage in the west. George was resourceful and determined, and Martha was to prove as tenacious in her pursuit of economy as she had been eager for opulence.

Family Affairs

. . . a promising boy . . . and will possess a very large fortune.

The Washingtons had to contend with the unfavourable character of the tobacco trade. Furthermore, the Peace of Paris, signed on 10 February 1763 by Britain, France and Spain, brought in its wake Native American incursions in the back country. These threatened the stability of George's investments westward. Although he had not as yet received his portion of the land bounty due members of the Virginia Regiment who had signed up in 1754, since first serving on the frontier and even before that he had been accruing parcels of land there. With the Peace, ownership of all lands in North America east of the Mississippi formerly French had passed to Britain. Native Americans long settled in those regions regarded their new overlords with mistrust. Sir Jeffery Amherst, British Commander-in-Chief in North America since September 1758 and Governor of Virginia since September 1759, refused to pay village chiefs the customary tribute. Moreover, British colonists from Virginia and elsewhere settled in the west without regard for Native American claims on the land. Urged on by a charismatic chief, Pontiac, the different Indian nations combined to attack British garrisons and settlements. Disturbed, George conducted a tour of inspection of his western lands, which were mostly rented out to tenant farmers. He wrote, on his return home, in July 1763: 'it is melancholy to behold the terror that has seized them [the frontier Virginians], and the fatal consequences that must follow, in the loss of their harvest and crops; the whole back country being in forts or flying . . .'[1]

Political affairs in London and in Williamsburg were no less alarming. That May the House of Burgesses had been unexpectedly ordered to assemble. The value of current money, as opposed to sterling, which the colony had issued over six years of war with the French and Indians, had fallen steeply. It was now about a third of sterling's value. Other colonial currencies had similarly depreciated. When the House assembled, Governor Francis Fauquier informed the representatives that the Board of Trade required them to supply to British merchants greater 'security in recovering sterling debts due from this colony to them'.[2] In consequence, a Currency Act forbidding further issue of current money was making its way through Parliament in London. This announcement effectively blocked the colony from raising and funding regiments to combat the turmoil on the frontier. Instead, militia were drafted in to aid the British regiments, which were part of a force policing the colonies following the Peace at an annual cost of £225,000.

The turbulence in western Virginia lessened after a Royal Proclamation designed to appease the Native Americans was issued in October. This forbade colonists to settle west of a 'Proclamation Line', or boundary line, running from Georgia in the south as far as New England and the length of the Appalachian mountains. The lands west of this Line were reserved for Native American occupation. Colonists with farms beyond the Line and others who viewed the west as ripe for development were not the only losers. In the 'Indian Reserve', too, lay the acres that had been promised in 1754 to Washington and others. In addition, the Proclamation instructed colonial governors to make land grants to all veterans of the war, ranging from 50 to 5,000 acres depending on rank. The latter area was due Washington, as a colonel of his regiment. This land also, lying west of the Line, the Virginian Governor was powerless to grant. Washington regarded the concession to the Native Americans as what he later termed a 'temporary expedient' and did not give up hope of claiming, at a later date, the land due him.[3] He interested himself in a project to drain the Great Dismal Swamp that lay south

of Williamsburg, convinced that there was 'excessive rich' land under
the mass of reed and fallen tree branches that clogged the desolate
expanses.[4] His crops at Mount Vernon were a more pressing concern.
In July he wrote to his brother-in-law Bassett of 'rust' that blighted
the wheat, and of 'continual and excessive rains' that had caused
weeds and grass to grow in abundance and smother his maize and
tobacco.[5] In short, though the French and Indian War was at an end,
the Virginian planter's lot in the mid-1760s was not an easy one.

Martha's children were growing up fast, as the Guardian Accounts
that Washington kept so scrupulously and invoices sent to Cary and
Co. on their behalf attest.[6] While the Washingtons strained to keep
their own expenditure in check, they took pains to accord both children accoutrements that advertised their standing, including liveries
for their attendants, crested silverware, and refined or 'handsome'
dress. Jacky, Washington was to inform a schoolmaster into whose
care his stepson passed, was 'a promising boy – the last of his
family – and will possess a very large fortune'.[7] Tobacco from the
Parke Custis lands on the Pamunkey and York rivers continued to
yield well and command substantial prices in London. Patsy, though
she owned no land or slaves, had received a third of her father's
personal estate in cash, stocks and bonds. Belonging, like her
brother, to the first tier of Virginia planter families, she could expect
to marry another of that charmed and wealthy circle.

When Patsy was seven or eight, in 1764, Martha asked Robert
Cary and Co. to pass a note to Mrs Shelbury, a milliner in London's
Dean Street in Soho, who had previously supplied her with ruffles. 'I
have directed all the goods for Miss Custis's use to be got from you,'
Martha wrote, and instructed the milliner to send 'Such things as
Misses of her age usually wear here . . . if you can get those which
may be more genteel and proper for her, I shall have no objections to
[it] . . .' Reverting to prudence, she made the proviso that if
Mrs Shelbury selected items of superior quality, she should do it
'with frugality'. Patsy being so young, 'a superfluity, or expense in
dress would be altogether unnecessary . . .' Martha ordered for herself
stays that she specified, with the Virginian summer heat in mind,

must be 'good, easy made and very thin'. She had one last instruction to give: 'Mr Washington wrote to Mr Cary in February last to purchase of you a French [pearl] necklace & earrings for me. I would rather choose a blue Turkey stone [turquoise] necklace and earrings sent in their place, if the price does not exceed two guineas.'[8] It was a woman's prerogative to change her mind, even when the woman was of as firm a character as Martha.

Prowess in the ballroom was deemed in the colony the mark of a gentleman or of a lady. Washington himself was for most of his life admired for his elegance and stamina on the dance floor, although Martha, with time, ceded her place to younger women. Jacky and Patsy, rising ten and eight, were inscribed annually as scholars of 'Mr MacKay', dancing master.[9] Later they shared with other children of the neighbourhood in classes that a Mr Christian gave in one or other of their homes.[10] Further tuition in the 'polite arts' for the children was supplied by John Stedlar, an itinerant music master, originally from Germany, who had served in the recent war. The spinet, or small harpsichord, that occupied pride of place in the Mount Vernon parlour was Patsy's province. A fine instrument, it had been procured by Robert Cary in 1761 from 'Mr Plinius, harpsichord maker in South Audley Street'. Washington had instructed the agent to ask for it 'as for himself or a friend'. If it was known to be for export, the cabinetmaker would, George feared, supply something inferior and at an inflated price.[11] Though Washington himself played no instrument, before her marriage to Washington Martha had sent for a copy of the 'Bullfinch . . . a choice collection of . . . English songs set to music', and there is an indication that she joined the lessons Stedlar gave.[12] She later made a granddaughter at Mount Vernon do long hours of keyboard practice, and Patsy's hours at the spinet were very likely arduous. In addition, Stedlar taught Jacky the 'fiddle', or violin, and requests for new 'fiddle strings' over the years indicate that he persevered with the instrument.

In the Guardian Accounts valuable horses, handsome saddlery and stabling bills feature over the years, as Jacky and Patsy became confident riders and ventured further afield. Horsemanship was another central plank in the composition of Virginians – be they gentleman or lady. That Jacky should have a good seat in the saddle was essential. When he was older, there would be careful choices for him to make – of riding horses, hunters and carriage horses for his personal use and stallions and mares for breeding. Patsy would in due course, like her mother, keep at least one riding horse.

Walter Magowan continued resident at Mount Vernon and gave the children their formal lessons. Neither Martha nor George had inhibitions about speaking their mind when others failed to meet their rigorous standards. It is unlikely that they were anything but strict where Jacky's and Patsy's manners and deportment were concerned. Washington was also eager that Jacky should acquire an education that would distinguish the boy from so many of his peers who frittered away their lives – and patrimony – gambling, at the races, foxhunting, and neglecting their estates. Washington himself, like all his contemporaries, spent his share of time and money at the gaming tables and in taverns and sponsored race meetings in Alexandria and elsewhere. But he was ever moderate in these avocations. Keenly aware of the inadequacies of his own education, he now had the satisfaction of ordering, for Jacky and Magowan to look over together, Cicero's *De Familiaris* and Erasmus' *On Follies*. When aged thirteen, the boy began work on 'the Greek testament'.[13] Attendance at a 'sleight of hand' performance the previous year in Alexandria, where Jacky incurred a charge of sevenpence, is a rare frivolity in the records Washington kept.[14]

The children were not without friends, either within the neighbourhood or further afield. Washington was to write to a rich merchant uncle of Martha's in London in 1765 that they rarely saw his wife's relations 'below' more than once a year – 'not always that'.[15] In the case of the Bassetts that was not strictly true. Not only did the Bassetts visit Mount Vernon, but now that Jacky and Patsy were older, Martha stayed with them in the autumn at Eltham, while Washington conducted business in Williamsburg. The elder Bassett children were of an age with Jacky and Patsy; the youngest child, Frances, or 'Fanny', was born in 1767. Martha's mother, Frances Dandridge, stayed firmly on the Pamunkey, maintaining a home at

Chestnut Grove for her youngest daughter, Betsy, who was in 1764 fifteen and unmarried. The elder of Martha's brothers, William, lived there too and farmed the small plantation for his mother. Between Martha and her mother appears to have prevailed that mixture of affection and irritation that can characterize relations between a mother and eldest daughter of strong wills. They may have both been grateful that Martha's marriage had put several days' travelling distance between them. Bartholomew, her younger brother, who had three daughters, lived, when in New Kent, at Pamocra, a 'dower' Burbidge plantation come to him by marriage, and acted for Dandridge family members in Williamsburg when a lawyer was needed.

As for the children's paternal relations, there were no other Custises, and in practice Jacky and Patsy saw little of their Byrd connections. There was a brood of ten Carters at Cleve, an imposing mansion in Gloucester County, descendants of Daniel Parke's daughter, Lucy Parke Byrd. But Cleve, on the Eastern Shore of Virginia, lay remote from Mount Vernon. Martha and George and the children, on the other hand, routinely saw much of Washington's own brothers' and sister's families in northern Virginia. Washington was devoted to his only sister, Betty, sixteen months his junior, who resembled him in her features and even in her stature, it is said. She was the second wife of Fielding Lewis, an enterprising Fredericksburg merchant. Their palatial home, Millbrook, was a lively and luxurious resting-place where the Washingtons and the children were accustomed to stay when journeying to Williamsburg. The elder Lewis cousins were of an age with Jacky and Patsy. George and Betty's mother, Mary Ball Washington, remained at Home House just outside the town. This residence offered sparse comfort, but Mary Washington, as set in her ways as Frances Dandridge, could not be persuaded to move into town.

Both George Washington's elder half-brothers were now dead. He had three full brothers, all younger than him, all married and with children. Samuel, next in age to him, lived at Chotank in Stafford County, twenty miles east of Fredericksburg. At Chotank also lived a cousin, Lund Washington. In response to the demands of estate business George offered him, in 1764, the position of land agent. Eager to accrue funds to one day purchase a farm of his own, Lund accepted the job and took up residence with George and Martha. Next in order of the brothers came John Augustine. He and his wife Hannah Bushrod Washington lived at Bushfield Hall, on a tributary of the Potomac in Westmoreland County. Their circle included the Carters at Nomini Hall and the Lees at Stratford Hall, who provided Tidewater hospitality of a magnificence unknown in Alexandria and Fairfax County, when George and Martha visited. Washington was grateful for John Augustine's help in managing Mount Vernon while he himself was on the frontier. He meant to will the estate to this brother or his heirs, should Martha fail to produce a son. But the couple at Mount Vernon still lived in hope. Washington, cautious, said nothing of his intentions. Charles, youngest of all the brothers, was a magistrate in Fredericksburg. Later he was to move west and found Charles Town in Frederick County.

The comings and goings of these Northern Neck relations, be it for a christening – but never at Mount Vernon – or a ball, for Christmas or Easter or for no special reason, were a source of enjoyment for George and Martha, as well as an obligation. All were made welcome by Martha. Sociable, practical and familial, she was a consummate hostess. Return visits were obligatory, and the stays in each place prolonged.

At home Washington had turned aside from growing tobacco to sowing wheat and had it in mind to grow hemp and flax, for which the British government had declared a bounty. He continued his attempts to improve all aspects of the estate. When he grafted, in March 1763, a 'fine early May cherry', and, the following March, 'the black pear of Worcester . . . a large coarse pear for baking', he acknowledged in both cases his benefactor, Colonel George Mason.[16] In return, Washington was to keep Mason abreast of some extraordinary transactions that occurred in the House of Burgesses, beginning in December 1764. A Committee of the whole House sent an Address, Memorial, and Remonstrance to King George III, the House of Lords and the Commons respectively. They protested, though they protested humbly, against the news that a Stamp Act was to be passed in England in order to raise revenue for the defence of the American colonies. Legal papers, newspapers, magazines and even playing cards were all to be printed on paper embossed or stamped in Britain. This paper was to be brought to the colonies and paid for in British pounds. Since Virginia's foundation, it had been in the remit only of the colony's legislature, the burgesses submitted, to raise internal, or direct, taxes.

The Act was passed, despite all protests, in March 1765. 'We might as well have hindered the sun's setting,' Benjamin Franklin, agent for Pennsylvania, in London, was to write four months later to Charles Thomson in Philadelphia. He counselled 'Frugality and industry'.[17] Mason, like Washington, had a seat in the House, but, long paralysed by gout, went to Williamsburg rarely. He had anyway the habits more of a philosopher than of a politician, and liked to read, sitting at a table in the Gunston Hall parlour, while his ten children streamed about him. Yet Mason made his mark as much as anyone in the colonial resistance that followed the passage of the Act and, following its repeal in 1766, of other revenue Acts that came after. He had had the run of his uncle John Mercer's law library in youth, though he had never practised. His chosen weapon was natural law, and his chosen conduit George Washington, a Potomac neighbour whose own scanty knowledge of law came principally from boundary disputes.

Washington was, for all his lack of education, a diligent student and an able collaborator with Mason. It would appear from an emollient letter that he wrote in September 1765 to Martha's uncle, London merchant Francis Dandridge, that Washington regarded the Stamp Act as an 'unconstitutional method of taxation'. He did not ally himself with that 'Speculative part of the colonists' who regarded it as a 'direful attack upon their liberties'.[18] Samuel and Charles Washington were to become members of a brash Westmoreland Association that threatened violence against government officials. George sought Mason's advice, and returned to Williamsburg time and time again with his instructions in mind if not on paper. Martha was not only to play hostess to the pair as they consulted anxiously at Mount Vernon, she was to cheer their partnership all the way. The course they steered was to lead to an increase in intimacy with those who supported their initiative. But it led also to division between the Washingtons and those like the Bryan Fairfaxes, who hesitated to criticize the London government. Of division between husband and wife, there would be none.

6

Acts and Associations

*. . . many Luxuries which we lavish our
substance to Great Britain for . . .*

From London in August 1765 Virginia Regiment veteran Robert
Stewart had written to Washington. He entrusted his letter to George
Mercer, formerly Washington's aide-de-camp at Fort Loudoun and
then in England. Mercer, wrote Stewart, 'returns to collect a Tax
upon his native Land'. Earlier in the summer, thanks to the influence
of his father John Mercer at home, George had been appointed Stamp
Distributor for Virginia. With the cargo of taxed paper that he now
brought across the sea came Stewart's more welcome letter to
Washington. The veteran recalled 'the many very pleasant days I
have so agreeably passed in your most desirable Company' and sent
his 'dutiful and affectionate respects' to 'Your Lady'.[1]

Many very pleasant and sociable days continued to occur at
Mount Vernon. Washington was more than usually occupied on his
farms. He was sowing and reaping hemp and flax for the first time
with mixed results. The children's social circle was widening as they
got older. Patsy was friends with a group of girls from Alexandria –
the daughters of merchants John Carlyle, William Ramsay and John
Dalton – who accompanied their elders when they visited Martha.
Visits to 'the play' in town amused the whole Washington family.
Churchgoing also, with the opportunities for display, was not
entirely without its rewards. It was impossible, however, to ignore

the coming enactment of the Stamp Act on 1 November. On this date George Mercer would attempt to sell his sheaves of stamped paper in Williamsburg. Virginians, pre-eminent among Americans in their resistance to the Act, intended to refuse to purchase it. Washington discussed the implications in the letter he addressed in September to Francis Dandridge, Martha's surviving paternal uncle, in London.

This elderly, rich – and dying – relation had apparently broken off a correspondence with his niece when she married her second husband. 'I should hardly have taken the liberty, Sir, of Introducing myself to your acquaintance in this manner, and at this time', wrote Washington, 'lest you should think my motives for doing it arose from sordid views . . .' A letter he had received this summer from Cary and Co. had given him 'Reason to believe that such an advance on my side would not be altogether disagreeable on yours.'[2] The legacy-hunter was disappointed. When Dandridge died later that year, he left £600 to his sister-in-law, Martha's mother, and nothing to Martha. Like tobacco, flax and hemp, bequests required intensive cultivation.

In Stewart's August letter to Washington, he had referred to copies circulating in London of 'some very warm and bold Resolves', passed by the Virginia legislature.[3] These were the so-called Virginia Resolves, or Resolutions, that young Patrick Henry, lawyer turned Burgess, had unexpectedly submitted late in May of this year. They were carried in the House, admittedly by a narrow margin and at a time when most planters, Washington included, had left for home. Four of the Resolves Henry proposed made innocuous reference to the original settlers of Virginia, and to the charters granted them by James I. These entitled colonists to all 'liberties, privileges and immunities' enjoyed by British subjects 'abiding and born in the realm of England'. The audacious fifth Resolve, referring to the Virginia legislature's right to tax the colony, asserted: 'every Attempt to vest such Power in any person or persons whatsoever other than the General Assembly aforesaid has a manifest Tendency to destroy British as well as American Freedom'.[4] The reference to the Stamp Act passed in London and taxing Virginians was clear.

Thomas Jefferson, then a young clerk, observed from the lobby the violent debate that followed. He was to write of Henry: 'He appeared to me to speak as Homer wrote.'[5] The Speaker of the House, John Robinson, challenged Henry with the cry of 'Treason'. The Burgess, in mid-flow, concluded a sentence that had begun 'Caesar had his Brutus, Charles the First his Cromwell,' with the more peaceable phrase: 'and George the Third may profit by their example.' But he added, gazing defiantly at Robinson: 'If this be treason, make the most of it.'[6]

Following the passage – by one vote – of this last Resolve, it was revoked the following day. Governor Fauquier made haste, on 1 June, having once given his assent to bills presented, to dissolve the House. After a new House of Burgesses was elected in July, he issued proclamation after proclamation to prorogue it. As a result, no representatives could attend the Stamp Act Congress that New York hosted this autumn. But the damage was done. Over the course of the summer all five Resolves circulated throughout the colonies. General Gage, Commander-in-Chief in North America, wrote home to Secretary of State Henry Conway that they 'gave the signal for a general outcry over the continent'.[7]

In Virginia itself opposition to the Act was intense. In September, while George Mercer was still crossing the Atlantic, Richard Henry Lee, John Augustine Washington's wealthy neighbour, orchestrated a procession which marched on the Westmoreland County courthouse. It was made up largely of Lee's slaves with some additional white 'tag rag and bobtail', John Mercer was later to write indignantly. They carried effigies of George Grenville, the Minister who had originally introduced the Stamp Act, and of George Mercer himself. The slaves, acting as 'sheriffs, constables, Bailiffs and hangman', hanged the dummies at the public gallows and then burnt them.[8] Lee afterwards published the supposed 'dying words' of Mercer, all confession and contrition.[9]

George Mercer had been previously esteemed in the colony for his services as an officer. But the public mood was ugly when he disembarked at Williamsburg on 30 October, leaving his odious cargo of stamps on board. A great many 'gentlemen of property . . . some of them at the head of the respective Counties' and 'merchants of the country, whether English, Scotch or Virginian', were in town when Mercer arrived, as Governor Fauquier subsequently reported to the London Board of Trade. They waylaid Mercer and demanded that the Distributor resign his office.[10] He volunteered to give an answer two days later and proceeded to meet the Governor, who was, with the Speaker and Council, at Mrs Campbell's coffeehouse in the Exchange. But the planters and merchants were not satisfied.

They passed messages, requiring an earlier answer. The Distributor stood firm. Frustration mounted. As dusk was gathering, a cry went up, 'Let us rush in', and some of the malcontents stormed the coffeehouse. Though they were repulsed, Mercer agreed to give his answer instead the following afternoon. Through the 'thickest of the people' he then proceeded, walking side by side with Fauquier, so that he would not be 'insulted', to the Governor's Palace. There he spent the night.[11]

Humiliation followed for the government. Mercer appeased his detractors with his decision, the following afternoon, to resign. The day after, he appeared in the General Court to say that he had no stamped paper to distribute. It was the signal for the stagnation of business in the colony. Without the stamps, the General Court could not function, and it adjourned. Without the stamps, the shiploads of tobacco that sailed every spring for England could not be certified. Planters and merchants were jubilant, despite the economic hardship entailed. The following February Richard Henry Lee instigated what became known as the Westmoreland Association. He had the support of two of Washington's brothers, Samuel and Charles. More than a hundred members of other leading families of the area also became 'Associators'. They swore to 'exert every faculty to prevent the Execution of the said Stamp Act in any Instance whatsoever'. In particular, they threatened 'every abandoned Wretch . . . so lost to Virtue and public Good' as to use stamped paper.[12] One Archibald Ritchie had rashly announced at Richmond his intention to clear with the reviled paper from some unknown source a cargo bound for the West Indies. He had since privately recanted. But Lee would not be baulked of his theatre. A 'Committee of Safety', on 28 February

1766, forced Ritchie out of his Hobbs Hole house to swear fealty in public to the Association. The Associators and a crowd of onlookers – three or four hundred men, some armed, according to newspaper reports – witnessed the merchant express his remorse for having formed 'so execrable a design'.[13]

As unrest in the colony grew, Fauquier continued to prorogue the House of Burgesses, which was to meet for the first time in November 1766. Washington left Mount Vernon only on estate business. His response to the vicissitudes of the Stamp Act was not to rail against government or resort to violence like his brothers. In September 1765 he, echoing Benjamin Franklin, had written regarding the revenue Act shortly to be imposed on the colonies: 'the Eyes of our People – already beginning to open – will perceive, that many Luxuries which we lavish our substance to Great Britain for, can well be dispensed with whilst the necessaries of Life are (mostly) to be had within ourselves – This consequently will introduce frugality, and be a necessary stimulation to Industry.'

This was a radical proposition for a Virginian to make. Washington and Martha positively delighted in luxury, and had taken pains in earlier years to obtain the very latest and best from England. But they had already retrenched, on finding themselves in Cary's debt. Artisans in America were becoming more sophisticated in their manufacture. In return for furniture, millinery, saddlery from New York or Philadelphia, as well as the 'necessaries of life' – cloth, food, medicines – Washington had wheat to sell in the domestic market. As swiftly as agitation in Virginia had brewed, it subsided. News came of the repeal of the Stamp Act in London in the spring of 1766. Washington had guessed correctly in September: 'if a stop be put to our Judicial proceedings I fancy the Merchants of Great Britain trading to the Colonies will not be among the last to wish for a Repeal of it'.[14]

Washington accepted Cary and Co.'s assurances that they had done their utmost to promote annulment of the Act, responding drily that he was a friend to any who had done so. He added, regarding a recent order: 'the Wheat Riddles [sieves] are so entirely useless that I shall be under a necessity of sending them back, or keeping

them by me as useless lumber'.[15] Sometimes the deficiencies of the
consignment trade were glaring, and the stranglehold in which the
British agents had the Virginians hard to bear. Three years hence
Washington was to write to Mason: 'that the Colonies are consider-
ably indebted to Great Britain, is a truth universally acknowledged'.
He added, 'That many families are reduced, almost, if not quite, to
penury & want, from the low ebb of their fortunes, and Estates daily
selling for the discharge of Debts, the public papers [newspapers]
furnish but too many melancholy proofs of.'[16] Washington,
determined never to see Mount Vernon or the Parke Custis lands
advertised for sale in the *Virginia* or *Maryland Gazette*, continually
took measures to reduce his own indebtedness to Cary by whatever
means he could discover. In 1767, for the first time, 1,500 ells of
cloth and linen were woven at the plantation, rather than imported,
and Washington, in his accounts, estimated that this was at a considerable saving.

A Declaratory Act was passed at the same time that the Stamp Act
was repealed. It affirmed the Crown's right to tax any part of its
empire whenever it suited, but no one in Virginia was inclined to
dwell upon this. At last in November 1766 Fauquier summoned the
House of Burgesses to meet. As though he had never incited violence
and unrest, Richard Henry Lee served on a committee which
acknowledged the 'tender Regard shown to the colonists' Rights and
Liberties' by the King.[17] Unfortunately this 'tender regard' was not
to last for long. Just a year after repeal of the Stamp Act, Chancellor
of the Exchequer Townshend promoted Acts imposing a tax on tea,
paint and other items that were customarily exported from England
to the colonies. The new minister was reviled in Virginia. But neither
an official protest in the House of Burgesses nor less orderly agitation elsewhere had any effect. The government in London had
ordained that the colonies should pay towards their own military
defence.

As the politics of colony and Crown grew more embattled,
Washington was often away, in Williamsburg and inspecting the Parke
Custis estates, or pursuing land claims in the west or south. Martha
kept up a constant correspondence with her husband when he was

absent. Lund Washington wrote to his cousin from Mount Vernon, giving details of the lambing and of a runaway slave, on 30 March 1767. Martha added this misspelled but confident postscript, making it clear that the couple's relationship was both intimate and easy:

> My Dearest
>
> It was with very great pleasure I see in your letter th[at] you got safely down we are all very well at this time but it still [is] rainney and wett I am sorry you will not be at home soon as I expe[ct]ed you I had reather my sister woud not come up so soon, as May woud be much plasenter time than april we wrote to you las[t] post as I have nothing new to tell you I must conclude my self your most Affcetionate [*sic*]
>
> Martha Washington[18]

This is one of only two missives extant from Martha Washington to her husband. The other is a postscript to a letter from Jacky to his stepfather. It may serve as representative of many hundreds of letters that we know, from references in other letters, that she wrote him.

Cheerful, practical and loving, she wrote as, increasingly, she looked. Although only thirty-six in June while George was thirty-five, Martha was filling out with the years. The stays and dresses that came from London were of a larger measure than before. Washington himself had not renounced his soldier's figure, and the London tailors received no fresh instruction for his suits. But Martha and George had always been of comically different build – she so small, he so tall. That her girth was increasing does not seem to have disturbed him. Though a reserved man, he spoke openly of the happiness it was to be married to his wife and marked, even at a time of privation, their wedding anniversary.

This summer of 1767 Martha and George made a journey to Warm Springs, a mountain spa in western Virginia long known for its medicinal purposes. Mineral springs flowed at a temperature of 72 degrees down from Warm Springs ridge. Washington had previously accompanied his ailing brother Lawrence here. The focus of this visit, which lasted a month, appears to have been Martha's health.

There was a widely held belief at this time that 'taking the waters' could induce fertility in women. The George William Fairfaxes, also childless, went with them. The journey was formidable, the spa was rough and ready, they had to bring with them all their supplies. Were Washington and Fairfax hopeful that their wives might become pregnant? If so, both were disappointed.

In Williamsburg in early November 1768, Washington joined his fellow planters and the merchants of the town in welcoming Lord Botetourt, the new Royal Governor of Virginia, who had arrived days before. Botetourt, recently elevated to the peerage and also appointed a Lord of the Bedchamber, came with instructions from the King in Council to converse with 'the principal persons of influence . . .' He was to 'endeavour to lead them . . . to disclaim the erroneous and dangerous principles which they appear to have adopted'. In addition, for fear that any 'sudden commotion of the populace' might require troops to be ferried in from Boston, the ship on which he had come, HMS *Rippon*, remained in the harbour.[19]

Though there was great commotion in Williamsburg upon the Royal Governor's arrival, it was laudatory and even adulatory. The usual complaints about the Townshend Acts were barely audible. It had been eighty years since a Royal Governor had chosen to live in the colony. Three successive peers had deputed their duties to Lieutenant Governors, of whom the last was Francis Fauquier, recently deceased. Washington dined out in company with the new Governor and, with others, attended receptions at the palace replete with pomp and ceremony. Botetourt, writing home to Lord Hillsborough, Secretary of State for the Colonies, declared that he liked the style of the Virginians 'exceedingly'.[20] Conversations and correspondence between Washington and George Mason on the Potomac the following spring bore radical fruit, which caused him to change his opinion.

Washington wrote to his neighbour on 5 April 1769: 'At a time when our lordly Masters in Great Britain [the British government] will be satisfied with nothing less than the deprivation of American freedom, it seems highly necessary that something shou'd be done to avert the stroke and maintain the liberty which we have derived from our Ancestors . . . no man shou'd scruple, or hesitate a moment to use a–ms [arms] in defence of so valuable a blessing, on which all the good and evil of life depends.' More cautiously he continued: 'Yet A–ms [Arms], I wou'd beg leave to add, should be the last resource; the dernier resort.' Addresses to the throne and remonstrances to Parliament had proved futile. He concluded: 'starving their Trade & manufactures, remains to be tryed'.

Washington and Mason studied together a non-importation association that Philadelphia merchants had drawn up for Pennsylvania. The Philadelphia association, modelled on others in Boston and in New York, aimed to force the repeal of the Townshend Acts by proscribing luxury goods from Britain. In Philadelphia, merchants alone had become signatories to the association. Maryland merchants pointed out that, in the southern 'tobacco colonies', individual planters, quite as much as merchants, were responsible for imports. They must therefore also sign any agreement. Washington wrote to Mason that he believed that such an association would furnish Virginian planters 'with a pretext to live within bounds' and curb their habit of living to the hilt 'till ruin stares them in the face'.[21]

Mason, though suffering from a cold and erysipelas at Gunston Hall, responded the same day and set to work to draft an Association for Virginia. 'Our all is at stake', he wrote, 'and the little conveniences and comforts of life, when set in competition with our liberty, ought to be rejected not with reluctance but with pleasure . . .' He was keen to 'retrench all manner of superfluities, finery of all denominations', and was of Washington's opinion: 'it is amazing how much this (if adopted in all the colonies) would lessen the American imports . . .'[22] The Association agreement that he now drafted at Gunston Hall banned the import of, among other British goods, 'watches, clocks, tables, chairs, looking glasses, carriages, joiners' and cabinet work of all sorts.' Also proscribed were 'upholstery of all sorts, trinkets and jewellery, plate, and gold[smiths'] and silversmiths' work of all sorts'. In line with Mason's previous remarks about 'finery', the draft agreement forbade the import of 'ribbon and millinery of all sorts, lace of all sorts, India goods of all sorts (except spices), silks of all sorts (except sewing silk), cambrics, lawn, muslin, gauze'. Dearer cottons and linens were proscribed, as well as dearer 'woollens, worsted, and mixed stuffs', and dearer broadcloth and narrow cloth. Even 'hats, stockings, shoes and boots' featured, as well as saddles and 'all manufacture of leather and skins of all kinds'.[23] Should the Association be embraced, Martha and Patsy must find substitutes at home for their lace and gloves and satin slippers. Jacky's guns and Washington's 'superfine' coats must come from Philadelphia or New York.

Late in April, though he seldom stirred from home, Mason stayed three days at Mount Vernon to work on the draft agreement with Washington. By the 28th Mason, back home and passing the document in review, sent over some last amendments. Two days later Washington left for Williamsburg, carrying with him the draft Association. He also had commissions from Mason for 'a pair of toupee [curling] tongs' and, for the Misses Mason, 'two pairs of gold snaps . . . small rings with a joint in them, to wear in the ears, instead of earrings'.[24] Upon his arrival in town in early May, he lodged as usual at Mrs Campbell's, attended the House, dined in company and played cards.

In mid-May proceedings in the House took an unconventional form. Resentment flared, following a British move to have colonists who were accused of agitation amounting to treason removed to England for trial. Washington was among burgesses who adopted a series of resolutions reasserting their sole right to lay taxes on their fellow colonists, and asserting their sole right to try their fellow colonists. The burgesses denounced the British government's move, while beseeching the King's intercession as 'father of all his people' on their behalf. These bold resolutions not unnaturally attracted the attention of Governor Botetourt. He called the burgesses to the Council Chamber. There, he informed them, 'I have heard of your resolves, and augur ill of their effect.' He dissolved the House immediately.[25]

Uproar ensued outside, and a good part of the burgesses walked down the street and gathered in the Apollo Room at the Raleigh Tavern. They formed themselves into a makeshift assembly, with Speaker Peyton Randolph elected as moderator. Here, in the Apollo

Room on 17 May 1769, in an animated atmosphere which still lacked firm purpose, Washington came to the fore. Appointed to a Committee that sat the next day till ten at night, he submitted the draft Association which he and Mason had constructed the previous month. It was approved by the Committee. Next day eighty-eight burgesses, including Washington, Patrick Henry, Robert Carter Nicholas, Richard Henry Lee and Thomas Jefferson – newly elected to the House for Albemarle County – were signatories. They must now personally exhort their fellow citizens at home to sign copies of the Association that would now circulate, a formidable task. The non-importation agreement was to come into force on 1 September, with all the signatories pledging to 'promote and encourage Industry and Frugality, and discourage all Manner of Luxury and Extravagance'.[26]

Washington and his colleagues, satisfied, toasted the King, Queen and Lord Botetourt to complete their proceedings. In these acts of fealty they saw nothing odd. They also attended the 'splendid ball and entertainment at the Palace', marking the birthday of Queen Charlotte, the Queen Consort, the following day.[27] Radical Washington and his fellow planters might be in their economic plans. Like most colonists at this time, they held the British government responsible for the ills visited on them and not the King or his representative in Virginia. The next day Washington left Williamsburg for home, bearing with him, as well as news of political success, the 'gold snaps' he had procured for the Mason girls.

At home Washington found a large party assembled. The races, an Alexandria barbecue and attendance at Pohick Church were subsequent diversions. George and Martha stood sponsors, or godparents, to Ferdinando Fairfax, a third son for Bryan Fairfax. Washington's mind, however, was much occupied with the implementation of the agreement he had promoted and signed. He told his brother-in-law Burwell Bassett in June: 'The Association in this and the two neighbouring counties of Prince William and Loudoun is complete, or near it. How it goes on in other places I know not, but hope to hear of the universality of it.'[28] He sent a very modest invoice this year to Cary and Co. in July, writing that he had 'very heartily' entered into the Association, and was 'fully determined to adhere religiously to it'.[29] The question was, would others?

The Association frowned on 'all Manner of Luxury and Extravagance', but signs of the 'universal retrenchment', for which Washington, Mason and others had hoped, proved sparse. Within two years all sanctions on British imports in Virginia were virtually at an end. The Association had failed to live up to its promise as a club with which to beat the British government. Many of the merchants of the colony acted, in the words of Burgess Francis Lightfoot Lee of Stratford Hall, as 'traitors' and ignored the agreement that they had signed. The 'country gentlemen' or backwoodsmen planters, who played no part in colony politics, had been 'indolent'. They either omitted to sign the agreement or else, having signed, ordered from Britain and purchased from Virginia merchants goods proscribed by the Association.[30]

Washington, with Mason, was instrumental in June 1770 in securing a new Association. It was, the former wrote to George William Fairfax in England, 'formed much upon the old Plan, but more relaxed'.[31] Upward of three hundred merchants, including John Carlyle and Robert Adam of Alexandria, were signatories, as were a further thirty-odd planters including Washington. This agreement called for county committees to police imports, and for a boycott of those merchants who imported goods on the proscribed list. Washington and Mason, as members of the Fairfax County Committee, interrogated two local merchants in July 1771 about cargoes including 'silver handled knives and forks' and 'nine men's fine hats', both proscribed items.[32] By and large the committees failed to control the volume of goods imported against the spirit and letter of the Association.

The British government lifted in March 1771 the tax on all but tea and a few other exports, though the American Board of Customs remained in place in Boston. For this surprising turn of events, civil disobedience in Boston and the establishment there of two regiments of foot were responsible. Disaffection culminated in a bloody clash of townsmen and soldiers in March 1770. Five townsmen lost their lives in what became known as the Boston Massacre. The British government, yielding to the temper of the times, scaled down the odious Revenue Act. In other colonies, Associations had, in response, disbanded. Washington and Mason would both have liked to continue the Virginia boycott, encouraging planters and merchants to favour domestic manufacture and eschew luxury goods. They were not proof against the commercial instincts of merchants, on the one hand, and against the habits of planters, on the other. They reluctantly recommended to Peyton Randolph, Chair of the Association, an end to the sanctions on all goods except tea 'and such other articles as are, or may be, taxed for the purpose of raising revenue in America (which, we trust, will never be departed from until our grievances are redressed)'.[33]

At a general meeting of this later Association in Williamsburg in July 1771, it was duly agreed that sanctions on – taxed – tea, paper, glass and painters' colours of foreign manufacture alone should remain. The Washingtons, nothing if not pragmatic, sent invoices immediately to Robert Cary, on their own behalf and that of Jacky and Patsy. Orders for crested rings, morocco prayer books, satin slippers and pickled walnuts jostled for space. The few years of sack-cloth and retrenchment were over. Once more, whether their estates could bear the expense or not, every Virginian would be at pains to appear as 'neat' and 'fashionable' as they imagined the inhabitants of the 'metropolis', London, to be.[34]

Fevers and Physicians

Miss Custis's Complaint . . . rather increases than abates.

At Mount Vernon the welfare of Patsy Parke Custis was a matter of concern to George and Martha. She began to suffer frightening 'fevers and fits' in 1768 when she was about twelve. These episodes, which would increase in frequency and in strength as the months and years went by, appeared, to her mother's and Washington's infinite distress, impervious to medical aid. Mount Vernon, till now a haven of calm when financial worries did not impinge, was set to become the scene of frustration and sorrow.

There had been no suggestion earlier that Patsy was in poor health. When the Washingtons were at Warm Springs in the summer of 1767, Lund had written to inform them of life at home: 'The Children are very well & were Yesterday at Alexandria Church with Miss Guess [Gist, a local spinster] who called & carry'd them up in the Chariot. Let Colonel Fairfax know his family are well & he has a plenty of Rain – this day with us is very rainy.'[1] For some time Patsy learnt her lessons alongside her brother, and she received her own copy of *Ruddiman's Rudiments* (of the Latin tongue). Subsequent Latin and Greek grammars and texts were charged to Jacky alone, and her formal education seems to have ceased entirely when the children's tutor, Magowan, left before Christmas 1767. The following June her brother, aged thirteen, was enrolled as a pupil at the school that clergyman Jonathan Boucher had established in his parish about six miles from Fredericksburg. Patsy devoted hours to music lessons with Mr Stedlar. Washington ordered on her behalf from London song books and music-composition books as well as books of prayer, and she continued to take part in dancing classes.

Anxiety about Patsy's health first surfaced in February 1768. Washington returned on the 24th from a day that he had spent duck shooting – 'killed 2 Mallards & 5 bald faces', he noted in his diary – to find William Rumney at dinner. Many of the Alexandria medic's visits to Mount Vernon were purely social, and he often joined Washington and others out foxhunting or shooting. On this occasion Dr Rumney in his official capacity prescribed twelve powders for Patsy, as well as 'a vial of nervous drops' and valerian, a substance then in common use as an antispasmodic. Next morning, Rumney departed, and Washington went out with his gun again: 'Killd 2 ducks – viz. a sprig tail and Teal'. Two days later Mr Stedlar came as usual so as to give Patsy and her brother their music lesson.[2]

Three months later Jacky was preparing to become Mr Boucher's pupil. Washington noted, following a visit to Belvoir, on 14 June: 'Sent for Doctr. Rumney to Patsey Custis, who was seized with fits.' Once more the physician prescribed valerian and 'nervous drops'. Now he also bled his patient. In July he experimented with capsules of musk, another anticonvulsant.[3] We catch sight of the convulsions that incapacitated Patsy periodically in her stepfather's almanac and diary notations, and in other doctors' bills and cash accounts. They were almost certainly epileptic seizures. Epilepsy is currently defined as short episodes of symptoms caused by a burst of abnormal electrical activity in the brain. Washington recorded Patsy's fits in the margins of his almanac for some months in 1770 and passed judgement on their severity. In July, beside three dates, he noted: '½ fit'. These may have been some form of partial – or petit mal – seizure, characterized by loss of awareness, and lasting between ten or fifteen seconds and two minutes. Only a part of the brain is involved and these 'fits' do not tax the sufferer unduly. From the outset – in 1768 Washington used in the phrase 'seized with fits' – Patsy very likely also suffered grand mal episodes, which may last up to five or ten minutes. The electrical storm pervades the whole brain.

Grand mal episodes, being violent in nature and causing nervous and physical exhaustion, are frightening to behold and potentially dangerous to the sufferer. Washington noted in his 1770 almanac beside twenty-six different summer dates variously 'Fit', '2 fits', '3 fits' and 'Ditto'. On 31 July he wrote: '1 very bad ditto'.[4] Typically in a grand mal seizure the sufferer goes rigid and, if standing, falls to the ground. Next, her arms and legs begin to jerk. Her eyes may close or roll back in their sockets, she may bite her tongue or cheek, and incontinence may occur. Patsy would afterwards very likely have proceeded to sleep deeply before waking confused and with no memory of the episode. From the first, the Washingtons appear to have taken practical steps regarding the danger that these 'fits' posed to Patsy. George made this entry in his cash accounts for December 1768: 'Mary Wilson came to live here as a House keeper a[t] 15/. [fifteen shillings] Pr. Month.'[5] Previously Martha had superintended all. This appointment points to the mother's need to supervise her daughter's health closely and depute duties where she could.

Between episodes Patsy was resilient, as an entry in Washington's diary during the harvest season of 1768 shows: 'Rid [Rode] to Ditto [the wheat field in Dogue Run, a part of the plantation two miles from the main house] in the forenoon with my Wife & Patsy Custis.'[6] A commission from London that summer for a 'very handsome and fashionable' saddle 'with bridle and everything complete' for Patsy's use, and other riding equipment charged to her account over the next years, confirms that she continued to ride out.[7] Patsy accompanied her mother and stepfather in August when they went on a fortnight's visit to the Samuel Washingtons at Chotank. Jacky joined them from school, and the family party continued to the John Augustine Washingtons in Westmoreland County. Patsy was apparently well, although Jacky fell ill with an 'intermitting fever, attended with bilious vomitings'. Washington wrote to the Reverend Boucher on 4 September, to apologize for the boy's late return to school: Martha had insisted on taking Jacky take home with them to convalesce.[8] The clergyman, in reply, ascribed Jacky's gastric disorder to glut-tony: 'he is fond of fruit, and what is worse for him, he is fond of cucumbers'.[9]

Washington noted on 20 September: 'Mrs Washington & the two Children went up to Alexandria to see [George Farquhar's] *The Inconstant, or Way to Win Him* acted.'[10] Jacky only started back to school on 20 October, having missed a good two months of lessons. Martha, placing much less emphasis than her husband on Jacky's education, reserved her own enthusiasm for making much of her son at home and finding reasons to prolong his stays there.

Returning home from Williamsburg in early November 1768, George brought north his sister-in-law, Betsy Dandridge. Martha had feared their mother spoilt Betsy when she was younger. Now in her late teens, the girl, who had no dowry, was as yet unmarried, and she remained some months at Mount Vernon. No husband emerged from the ranks of young men of the neighbourhood she encountered on visits and at public balls in Alexandria. She settled, in 1773, for a cousin at home, John Aylett. The future for Betsy's wealthy niece, though she was cosseted and cherished, was in doubt. Rumney again bled Patsy in November 1768. When she was rising thirteen, he treated her once more with a 'vial of drops' and more musk capsules at Epiphany 1769 – the Washingtons' tenth wedding anniversary.[11] Jacky, claiming to be affected by his sister's 'disorder', stayed on at home after Christmas till near the end of January 1769. Washington apologized to Boucher: 'After so long a vacation, we hope Jacky will apply close to his Studies, and retrieve the hours he has lost from his Book since your opening School – he promises to do so, & I hope he will.'[12]

Attempts to find a cure for Patsy dominated the new year. Hugh Mercer, a Scot and celebrated apothecary in Fredericksburg who had served earlier as a surgeon in the British army in America, consulted at Mount Vernon with Rumney on 31 January 1769. He advocated 'mercurial pills, purging pills, and ingredients for a decoction'.[13] Neither these nor any other treatments were effective. Washington made this entry in his diary in February: 'Joshua Evans who came here last Night put an Iron [finger] Ring upon Patcy (for Fits) and went away after Breakfast.'[14] Evans – probably a blacksmith of that name from Loudoun County – charged a guinea for this cramp ring, a device medieval in origin. The doctors' bills were far higher, the benefits of their treatments as nebulous. Rumney's account for the year ran to £19 6s 6d, and Mercer, for his consultation, was paid £6.[15] But there was 'no alteration for better or worse in Patsy', as Washington informed Burwell Bassett that June.[16]

In a renewed attempt to find a cure, George and Martha took Patsy to Warm Springs in August 1769. (Ever the careful accountant, Washington ascribed all the costs of the summer journey to his ward's account, as the enterprise was for her benefit.) The journey would appear to have been to no avail. In the autumn, Patsy accompanied Washington and her mother south. Dr John Sequeyra, graduate of Leyden University and member of a distinguished family of London physicians, had set up his stall in Williamsburg years earlier. He reviewed her case, saw her at Eltham on three occasions and in town on five, and submitted a bill for £10 15s. Pasteur, the apothecary in Duke of Gloucester Street, supplied a course of medicine. A brief respite from medical appointments was afforded Patsy on 2 November when, in company with her mother and stepfather and the Bassetts, she ate oysters at Mrs Campbell's hostelry in town.[17]

The following July, when Patsy was about fourteen, Washington was to write to Thomas Johnson, a Maryland lawyer, whose brother was a doctor: '. . . Mrs Washington wou'd think herself much favour'd in receiving those Simples' – concoctions – '& direction's for the use of them, which your Brother Administers for Fitts – Miss Custis's Complaint has been of two years standing, & rather Increases than abates.'[18] Cargoes of John Johnson's herbal preparations were subsequently ferried to Mount Vernon, and for some time Johnson himself was a regular visitor to the house. Recommending that Patsy keep her body 'cool and open', he further urged on her 'light cooling food' – frumenty, a kind of porridge, made either of barley or of wheat.[19] The implication is that some at least of Patsy's seizures occurred when her temperature was high. In June 1771 Washington agreed that Boucher should send more 'physic' from Dr Johnson, 'as he has been so obliging to provide it . . . tho', if [it be] some of the last, nothing is to be expected from it; that was used without having in the smallest degree, the desired effect . . .'[20]

As Patsy turned fifteen and then sixteen in 1771 and 1772, invoices sent to Robert Cary and Co. for luxury items – necklaces, suits of Brussels lace, songbooks, riding hats – continue to reflect her status as a wealthy young woman. But she was no better, as entries in Washington's Guardian Accounts indicate: '4 bottles of Fit drops of Mr John Carter' and '2 bottles of Norris's drops.'[21] Dr Norris advertised the drops purchased on her account as a cure for fever. Dr Hammond promoted bottles of 'essence of antimony', one of which features in the Guardian Accounts, as a cure for spasmodic and other 'nervous weaknesses'. Washington wrote to Boucher in February 1771: 'Mrs Washington requests the favour of you to get her 2 Oz. of the Spirit of Ether' – another antispasmodic – 'if such a thing is to be had in Annapolis, for Miss Custis.'[22] Nearer to home Dr Rumney continued to administer medicine at Mount Vernon. In addition, the Guardian Accounts for Patsy show a large sum, £5 10s 6d, Maryland currency paid in 1773 to Dr James Craik of Alexandria. The acquisition of a parrot at £1 16 shillings, Virginia currency, in April of that year may have done more to lift the afflicted girl's spirits than all the medics who attended her with their nostrums to no discernible effect.

Patsy's illness was taking its toll, and a miniature painted of her in 1772 shows a girl shockingly wan and pinched. One can hardly connect her to the healthy child of the earlier portraits. Charles Willson Peale, the young artist from Philadelphia who took her likeness, much later recalled, 'we danced to give Miss Custis exercise, who did not enjoy a good state of health. She was subject to fits . . .'[23] Jacky, painted by Peale at the same time, on the other hand, brims with vitality, and is plainly an elder version of the younger child.

Wan of face Patsy might be, but her person did not lack for adornment. A request for the *Lady's Magazine* indicates that she enjoyed, with her mother, a healthy interest in dress. Other requests – for a velvet collar, a fan, a firestone necklace and earrings, jewelled hairpins and shoe buckles – reflect that fondness. Silk shoes, one pair striped with gold, one with silver, swelled the order.[24] Patsy continued, when well, to lead an active life. She paid visits and went to church with her family like any of her peers. Neighbour John Posey's daughter Milly – formally Amelia – was much at Mount Vernon and shared, in 1770, Patsy's dancing lessons with Mr Christian. Milly also accompanied her friend two years later to a ball in Alexandria.[25] And Patsy travelled with the Washingtons as far afield as Williamsburg in the autumn of 1772. One may assume that they were unwilling to leave her to 'fit' in the company of housekeepers and house slaves.

Martha had been morbidly anxious, since her children's extreme youth, about their health, and Patsy's fits were hard to bear. Moreover, abnormal and sudden falls, jerking limbs and frothing at the mouth were hardly genteel behaviour in anyone, let alone in a young heiress who might normally expect to attract suitors of her own high rank. Yet Martha and George, far from being ashamed of Patsy and her condition, canvassed opinion widely for a cure, and took no pains to hide Patsy's fits from anyone, or indeed hide Patsy herself away. When Associations did not preclude such purchases, the invoices sent to London on Patsy's behalf – for necklaces, for silks and for satin dancing slippers – were as exacting as for any other 'young miss' of her age, and gave no hint of debility.[26]

That Patsy attended formal occasions, dressed according to her station, is evident from a letter of complaint that Martha addressed in July 1772 to a London milliner, Mrs Thorpe. Martha had ordered a 'handsome suit of Brussels lace' – comprising cap, tippet, ruffles and tucker for formal occasions – 'to cost £20' for her daughter. Upon the consignment's arrival at Mount Vernon, it was found that cap and tippet were missing. Moreover, the lace that did arrive, Mrs Washington complained, was set on 'plain joining net, such as can be bought in the milliners' shops here at 3/6 per yard'. Martha had shown the offending items to 'several ladies who are accustomed to such kind of importations'. All agreed that they were 'most extravagantly high charged'. Miss Custis could ill afford to do without even the incomplete suit of lace that had been sent, wrote her mother, else these 'hard bargains' would have been returned. Martha now sent for another 'suit of fashionable lace', at a price 'not to exceed £40', with strict instructions that it was to include a cap with lappets, ruffles and tippet or handkerchief.[27]

Patsy, in her costly ruffles and tucker or wearing a cap 'of Minto lace' that her mother ordered her, was no invalid living in the shadows of society. Virginia society was forgiving, Governor Lord Dunmore being among those who commiserated upon Patsy's debility. But how did she combine an active social life with an illness whose alarming and uninhibited symptoms were so unmaidenly? Artist Peale in 1772 noted that Mrs Washington 'never suffered her to be a minute out of her sight'.[28] One may imagine that, at the first sign of a fit developing, Patsy was whisked into some private setting. Courtship and marriage and progeny did not lie in the future for her. Unspoken though implicit in all arrangements was the understanding that in lieu of a husband, her mother and stepfather would cherish Patsy at home, their daily anxiety about her fits undiminished, as she and they aged. The Washingtons, celebrating thirteen years of marriage in January 1772, had need to draw on all the reserves of mutual affection and understanding that had accumulated in those years.

The Schooling of Jacky Custis

His Mind . . . more ever turnd to Dogs Horses & Guns. . . .

In July 1771 Washington had ordered for Martha from London 'a handsome white satin cloak', ten yards of pea green lutestring – a glossy silk – and a dozen silk pocket handkerchiefs. He also asked Robert Cary to procure '2 handsome Gauze Caps for a middle aged Woman'. In years to come, an older and more redoubtable Martha, chins and all, grey hair tucked into a succession of large caps, stiff and frilled, would become an image familiar to many. She would rarely be seen – or painted or otherwise described – without this armour. But at this time, when she was aged forty, she was still a stylish woman. Her hair was thick and chestnut brown, and these 'Gauze Caps' would very likely have been ornamental rather than enveloping.[1] The following year's invoice, for instance, includes an order for '2 handsome caps of mignonette lace, one to wear in [formal] dress, the other with a nightgown [casual dress]'.[2]

Martha wears no cap in a miniature by Peale, for which she sat in this latter year, 1772, and which Washington charged to Jacky's account.[3] Instead, a silk scarf with a thin gold stripe, pinned in her hair with pearls, twines round the back of her head to fall over one shoulder. Round her neck are more pearls, and, at the neckline of her dress, a thin lace fichu is collar to a heavier lace border. She looks elegant and, with clear, wide eyes and long, curved smile, content. Jacky's inattention to his studies, however, as much as Patsy's declining health, was cause for concern.

In the summer of 1770 Martha's son had followed Jonathan Boucher, when the clergyman obtained a living in Annapolis, Maryland, and set up a new school in that lively commercial town. It soon attracted, besides Jacky, a number of scholars. Boucher suggested that he should in the course of time lead young Parke Custis on a Grand Tour of Europe: 'it is to be hoped . . . that it will stimulate Him to pursue his Studies with greater Earnestness, when He recollects how often He must be put to the Blush, if He appears illiterate amongst Men of Letters, into whose Company, in Travelling, He will often fall'.[4] George and Martha gave serious consideration to this proposal. Before thinking himself 'at liberty to encourage this plan', Washington was to recall a year later, he judged it 'highly reasonable and necessary . . . that the mother should be consulted'. Accordingly he laid Boucher's letter and suggestions before Martha, and 'desired that she would ponder well'. Her considered answer, he reported, was: 'if it appeared to be his [Jacky's] inclination to undertake this tour, and if it should be adjudged for his benefit, she would not oppose it, whatever pangs it might give her to part with him'.[5]

In the late winter of 1771 it seemed that this scheme to expand Jacky's horizons was about to take final shape. Lord Fairfax's younger brother and heir, Colonel Robert Fairfax, on a prolonged visit to his American relations in Virginia, expressed his approval of the plan. On the point of returning to England, the Englishman expressed a wish for a meeting with Jacky and his would-be cicerone, Boucher. 'The warmth with which he has made a tender of his Services', Washington continued, '& the pressing Invitation to make use of Leeds Castle' – a Fairfax stronghold in England, formerly a royal residence – 'as a home in vacation time [during Jacky's projected residence at an English university], are too obliging to be neglected.'[6]

Discussions about Jacky being inoculated against smallpox before the projected journey then occupied the family. Washington himself had contracted the disease while in the West Indies with his brother Lawrence in 1754. In consequence, he rode immune over his plantations and could venture into the dwellings of sick slaves when outbreaks of smallpox occurred. Martha and her children had not been inoculated, and were always in danger of infection. Regardless of whether Jacky was to tour Europe, inoculation was proving efficacious in a colony where outbreaks of the disease could sweep an area, spread fast in crowded slave quarters, and readily infect planter households. Numerous enterprising doctors now offered the procedure in clinics and hospitals, some of them more salubrious than others. It involved the patient being – lightly – infected with the pox. Occasionally a great many pustules formed, and unlucky patients were scarred. Very occasionally a virulent case of smallpox resulted, and proved fatal. But under the care of an experienced doctor such tragedies were rare.

Unfortunately, at Mount Vernon in the spring of 1771 Martha's old fears about her children's wellbeing resurfaced. Washington was to tell Boucher that Martha had 'often wished, that Jack would take & go through the disorder [smallpox inoculation] without her knowing of it; that she might escape those Tortures which Suspense would throw her into, little as the cause might be for it'.[7] Now she and Jacky imbued each other with anxiety about the procedure. He left home for school in early April with, George and Martha believed, no intention of proceeding to Baltimore, where a suitable clinic had been identified. But Jacky went directly from Annapolis to Dr Stevenson's and put himself willingly under the doctor's care. Wrote Boucher of his mercurial charge: 'He was very eager for it, & in high Spirits.'[8]

At this point a curious correspondence ensued, shedding some light on relations between the master and mistress of Mount Vernon. Washington, responding to Boucher, begged the clergyman not to write to him direct again, but 'under cover to Lund Washington, & in a hand not your own'. Martha believed Jacky had resolved to postpone the procedure, Washington wrote. Nonetheless, he continued, 'her anxiety & uneasiness is so great, that I am sure she could not rest satisfied without knowing the Contents of any Letter to this Family of your Writing'. Were she to know that Jacky was 'under Inoculation, it would', Washington wrote, 'put an infallible stop' to her journey to Williamsburg '& possibly delay mine; which would prove very injurious'.[9] Washington was bound to submit his Guardian

Accounts to the General Court, which sat during the months of April and October only.

Information came from Boucher, dated 19 April, that Jacky was now out of all danger: 'in Dr Stephenson's own Phrase, He cannot now die if He would'. Martha was told of this, and was apparently satisfied. She and Patsy accompanied Washington when he journeyed south, on the 27th, to Williamsburg. A conscientious reporter, Boucher had added in his letter of the 19th: '. . . Jack's [blisters], as I remember, are one on his Neck, another by his Ear, one on his Breast, two on one Arm & one on Another, & two on one Leg; not one on his Face.'[10] Indeed, gregarious Jacky felt so well after his adventure that, rather than hasten to show an unmarked face to his mother or return to his studies, he stayed on in Baltimore to attend the wedding of 'a Mr Gough, a gentleman of rank and fortune'. So Boucher, 'exceedingly displeased' but impotent in Annapolis, informed the Washingtons on 3 May.[11] But if those around him – though never Martha – cursed Jacky for his thoughtlessness, or despaired of him and his sybaritic ways, he was always quick to show penitence, promise reform and win forgiveness. Book learning he might not have; charm he had in abundance.

Though Jacky was now immune to smallpox, the plans for his Grand Tour slowly crumbled. First, Boucher secured the promise from Governor Eden of Maryland of a good parish in Prince George County, midway between Annapolis and the eastern shore of the Potomac. The duties of that parish, which he was to take up in December 1771, required his remaining in the colony. Jacky's mother and stepfather had no interest in Jacky travelling abroad without the clergyman, as Washington made clear on 5 June: 'to Embark on a Tour of the kind you proposed without a Conductor; as pleasure and dissipation without a kirb, would leave little room for study, & more than probably end in his Ruin'.[12]

Washington expressed a wish at numerous times in his life to visit England and also France. He had initially embraced the scheme for Jacky's improvement abroad. Boucher had spared no ink to describe an ugly alternative, should Jacky remain at home: 'Sunk in unmanly Sloth'. His estates would soon be left to the Management of 'some worthless overseer', and Jacky himself, entangled in some matrimonial adventure, in which passion would dominate over reason.[13] Now both Washington and Martha had serious doubts about the benefits of a Grand Tour. When Boucher won from the Governor permission to travel for a year, Washington cavilled at the exorbitant expense of the expedition proposed. In Williamsburg the Dunbar suit was in danger of at last coming to trial in the General Court. George Wythe, representing the Antigua plaintiffs – now Thomas Dunbar's grandsons, John and Joseph Dunbar – had filed an attachment. Washington retained Edmund Pendleton, as well as John Randolph and James Mercer, at no small cost to the Parke Custis estate. Five years earlier these same plaintiffs had suggested settling out of court. That had come to nothing but had engendered a flurry of correspondence and invoices. Preparations now for trial were similarly urgent, but there was as yet no date. Though Washington could not know it, the Antigua plaintiffs were never to have that hearing in the General Court, the fear of which featured so large in all his calculations during his wards' minorities.

Washington's vicarious pride in the Parke Custis wealth and acreage, of whose splendours he had boasted when first enrolling Jacky among Boucher's scholars three years earlier, was now much muted. He wrote to Boucher on 9 July 1771: 'his [Jacky's] estate is of a kind that rather comes under the denomination of a large than a profitable one. He has a good deal of land and a great many slaves, it is true, but the former is more to be esteemed for the situation than the produce, being of an indifferent quality and much worn, so that large crops cannot be made from them.'

This gloomy assessment of Jacky's landholdings on the York and Pamunkey, where previously their yield had far outstripped that of the Washington holdings on the Potomac, calls for some explanation. The slow degeneration of a tobacco plantation where the crop was farmed without rotation, as was the practice among Virginians, hungry for barter with London merchants, was inevitable. Washington could counter the slide in fortunes of his own Parke Custis dower lands by expanding west and investing in schemes to acquire land elsewhere. At Mount Vernon he had turned to planting wheat and other crops in place of tobacco. As Jacky's guardian answerable to the General Court he was unwilling to involve his stepson in such gambles, and the boy – land rich, cash poor – must stand or fall by his ancestral acres and by hallowed Virginian agricultural practices. In the circumstances, and given, in addition, that the tobacco yield on all plantations varied wildly from one year to another, a Grand Tour of the kind Boucher proposed would be a drain on Jacky's income difficult to justify.

Washington made mention now of Jacky's education, which he judged 'by no means ripe enough for a tour of travelling'. In particular, the boy was wholly ignorant of French – a language 'absolutely necessary to him as a traveller'. Notable too was the boy's apparent indifference to the project: 'if his mother does not speak her sentiments, rather than his, he is abundantly lukewarm in the scheme'. Above all, wrote Washington, 'there is a possibility, if not a probability, that the whole design may be totally defeated'. In short, Martha no longer supported the project. Her earlier declaration that she would not oppose the journey if it were to be of benefit to her son she still adhered to: 'but in so faint a manner', wrote Washington, 'that I think, what with her fears and his indifference . . . it will soon be declared he has no inclination to go . . .' That there had not been the usual openness between the Washingtons in recent months regarding the project emerges from Washington's subsequent tentative phrasing: 'I do not say that this will be the case; I cannot speak positively.' But he continued: 'Several causes, I believe, have concurred to make her view his departure, as the time approaches, with more reluctance than she expected.'[14]

Washington had referred in an earlier letter to the 'doubts of her friends', their number probably including her brother-in-law Bassett and brother Bartholomew Dandridge. All had counselled against the venture: 'some on acct of the expense; others, as being almost the last of a Family, think he should run no risks that are to be avoided'.[15] In this letter of July he made plain the principal cause of Martha's reluctance to part with Jacky: 'The unhappy situation of her daughter has in some degree fixed her eyes upon him as her only hope.'[16] In the face of this quiet but painful objection, the subject of a Grand Tour for Jacky was dropped, and never raised again. No one knew how long his sister's life would be prolonged.

Peale's haunting image of Pasty and his miniatures of Martha and of Jacky, which provide so lucid a picture of their appearances, were painted over the course of a week and as something of an afterthought. He came to Mount Vernon in May 1772 with a letter of introduction from Boucher and in the hope that the master of the house, of whom no portrait then existed, would sit to him. 'Inclination having yielded to importunity', as Washington informed Boucher, the sittings took place and a three-quarter-length portrait was the result.[17] Washington – clothed, despite his growing concerns about British government measures, in the blue coat and red waistcoat and breeches which he had worn to serve his King against the French and their Indian allies – looks resolute and stern.[18] The truth was, as the reluctant hero wrote wryly, he was posing 'in so grave – so sullen a Mood – and now and then under the influence of Morpheus [Sleep], when some critical strokes are making, that I fancy the skill of this Gentleman's Pencil, will be put to it, in describing to the World what manner of Man I am'.[19] As soon as he could, Washington escaped west on business, leaving Peale to finish painting the 'drapery', or details of his uniform, and his more artistically minded wife and children to entertain the artist further and sit for their own souvenirs of the visit.[20] Daniel Parke Custis's portrait, a pair to the Wollaston portrait of Martha till now, could at last be relegated to a less prominent place in the house. Jacky, meanwhile, had his memento of his mother to remind him of home when at his studies elsewhere.

When Jacky was in Annapolis, Washington had been fearful for his stepson's morals. In December 1770 he had written: 'Jacky Custis now returns to Annapolis – His Mind a good deal relaxed from Study, & more than ever turnd to Dogs Horses & Guns; indeed upon Dress & equipage, which till of late, he has discoverd little Inclination of giving into.' Jacky was not to sleep elsewhere than under Boucher's roof, he instructed, unless the clergyman could vouch for the character of the hosts. Nor must Boucher 'allow him to be rambling about at Nights in Company with those, who do not care how debauchd and vicious his Conduct may be'.[21] Boucher, engaging, candid and willing as ever to concede fault, in his reply promised close supervision. But he characterized his pupil as 'exceedingly indolent . . . surprisingly voluptuous . . . one would suppose nature had intended him for some Asiatic prince'. In some horror the Washingtons will have read the clergyman's confession that another pupil, Mr Galloway – 'wild, volatile, idle and good natured' – had led Jacky astray. Further, Mr Galloway had a sister, 'young and pretty', who had caught the boy's eye when she was in town – 'about the time of the players [company of actors] being here'. Mused Boucher: 'Jack has a Propensity to the Sex, which I am at a Loss how to judge of, much more how to describe.'[22]

In a letter of the following February Washington returned to the theme, writing that he wished to 'prevent as much as possible his connecting with Store boys [shop assistants], & that kind of low, loose Company'.[23] Again and again he stressed the importance of a good education, and his dissatisfaction with his stepson's progress: '. . . I cannot discover that he is much [further] in Latten', he protested in June, 'than when he left Mr Magowan, know[s little] Arithmetic and is quite ignorant of the Greek Language, which he had begun under the Tuition of that Gentleman . . .'[24]

In vain did Washington urge French, geometry and philosophy as fit subjects for Jacky to study. He begged Dr John Witherspoon, the President of Princeton College, for advice. Boucher, in November 1771, was complacent. Had Dr Witherspoon examined his student, he allowed, the college President would not have found Jacky 'possessed of much of that dry, useless, & disgusting School-boy kind of Learning fit only for a Pedant'. But he considered his pupil 'not illy accomplished, considering his manners, Temper, & Years, in that liberal, manly & necessary Knowledge befitting a Gentleman'. He added blithely: 'I ever did hold in abhorrence that servile System of teaching Boys Words rather than Things; & of getting a parcel of Lumber by Rote.'[25]

The Washingtons did not remove Jacky from the lax grasp of this insouciant master. In December 1771 the young man followed Boucher to the parish of St Barnabas in Maryland, which had been promised the clergyman, some twenty miles from Mount Vernon across the Potomac. Jacky soon became friends with Charles Calvert, another pupil, whose home, Mount Airy, a plantation of 4,000 acres, lay nearby. The rambling Calvert household – Charles was one of ten children, a number that would ultimately rise to thirteen – was easygoing and hospitable, and Jacky found his fellow pupil's eldest sisters, the Misses Elizabeth and Eleanor Calvert, delightful. Charles's father, Benedict Calvert, though illegitimate, could boast the 5th Lord Baltimore as his sire. Sir Robert Eden, Governor of Maryland, and his wife Caroline, legitimate daughter of the peer, acknowledged the relationship. Washington could rest assured that Jacky was not consorting with 'Store boys', as he had suspected he was doing in Annapolis. George and Martha soon became regular visitors to Mount Airy; the Calverts, and Sir Robert and Lady Eden with them, visited at Mount Vernon. The elder Misses Calvert were company for Patsy. Now that Jacky was consorting with suitable company and attending steadily to his books, Washington could even hope that his ward might be brought to some understanding of 'the mathematics . . . than which', he had reminded Boucher in July 1771, 'so much of it at least as relates to surveying, nothing can be more essentially necessary to any person possessed of a large landed estate, the bounds of some part or other of which is always in controversy'.[26]

Unfortunately no more studying was to be done in the backwaters of Maryland than had occurred in bustling Annapolis. By early January 1773 Washington was determined to dispatch his stepson in March to one of the colonial universities. He favoured 'the Philadelphia College' over King's College in New York and Princeton in New Jersey. It had equal standing with the others, he believed – 'and being nearer', he told Boucher, 'is more agreeable to his Mother'. George had no intention of sending Jacky to William and Mary College in Williamsburg: 'the Inattention of the Masters, added to the number of Holidays, is the subject of general complaint . . .'[27] There was another motive for sending the boy out of the colony. Boucher appears to have warned Washington that Jacky was showing a tendresse for the eldest Miss Calvert. Boucher was direct in his reply of 19 January: 'It is certainly expedient to remove Mr Custis to some place of public education, and speedily.' He reverted to verbosity when pressing for King's College, and for New York as a more suitable situation for a young gentleman than Philadelphia. New York, 'generally reckoned the most fashionable and polite place on the Continent', was in addition, he wrote, inhabited by people of rank and fortune, attracted 'strangers of distinction' and was the headquarters of the military.

Boucher won the day for King's College, New York. The college President, Dr Myles Cooper, was a scholar, he wrote, who had 'completed his Education by a ten or twelve Years Residence in Oxford'. He brushed aside the city's great distance from Mount Vernon with a claim that, given Jacky's record to date, strains credibility: 'He may write every week, from one place as well as the other [Philadelphia] . . .'[28] President Cooper wrote more soberly in March with the terms and conditions of enrolment, expressing local prices in terms of the Spanish silver dollar.

'Our Tuition is only five pounds – one Dollar passing for 8 Shillings – New York Currency,' Cooper observed. The sterling equivalent of a Spanish dollar, given in a New York almanack for 1771, was 4 shillings, 7 pence. 'Room-rent four; and Board, including Breakfast, Dinner and Supper, at the Rate of eleven Shillings a week, for the Time each Student is actually in College. These, (saving Firewood, Candles & Washing which must be had every where) are the principal Expenses . . .'[29] The household at Mount Vernon prepared to send its prodigal son on his way in May, so that he might be in New York in time for Commencement in June. And then the prospective undergraduate set all the plans at disarray. Washington wrote to Benedict Calvert on 3 April: 'I am now set down to write to you on a Subject of Importance, & of no small embarrassment to me. My Son in Law [stepson] & Ward, Mr Custis, has, as I have been informed, paid his Addresses to your Second Daughter, & having made some progress in her Affections, required her in Marriage.'[30]

It was not, in short, the eldest Miss Calvert to whom Jacky had formed an attachment. He had – furtively – proposed marriage to her younger sister, Eleanor, or 'Nelly', who was only fifteen. How the secret engagement had come to light, whether by his confession or other means, is not clear. His future as well as his honour and the young woman's virtue now hung in the balance, while his stepfather, his mother and her father scrambled to find a solution to the vexed affair. For such a practical and orderly pair as George and Martha Washington, the unorthodox circumstances of Jacky's wilful engagement were hard to bear. Washington informed Nelly's father, Benedict Calvert, in his letter of 3 April 1773, that he would urge Jacky 'with the warmth that becomes a man of honour' – though his ward had proved no gentleman to date – 'to consider himself as much engaged to your daughter as if the indissoluble knot was tied . . .' But he was firm that marriage – 'an event, on which his own peace, and the happiness of another is to depend' – must follow only on Jacky's completing his course – 'two or three years' – at King's.[31]

Other schoolmates and friends of Jacky's might – and did – marry young. But Washington, as ever, had different ideas for his ward, writing: 'I do not conceive that he is capable of bestowing that due attention to the important consequences of a marriage state, which is necessary to be done by those who are inclined to enter into it.' Not the least of the responsibilities he had himself assumed on marriage had been the guardianship of his troublesome ward. He now gave Calvert an outline of Jacky's wealth. The young man's estate comprised 15,000 acres on the Pamunkey and York, 'good part of it adjoining to the City of Wmsburg, & none 40 Miles from it', and town lots in Williamsburg. He owned, besides, 'between two and three hundred Negroes', and 'about 8 or ten thousand pounds', either upon bond – out at loan – or in the hands of merchants, with Martha's dower portion to follow upon her death.

Washington made no mention of the Dunbar suit. It had earlier been expected to come on in the General Court in 1772, but now hung fire. It was, Washington wrote suavely of Jacky's estate, 'upon the whole, such a one as, you will readily acknowledge, ought to entitle him to a handsome portion [dowry] in a wife'. George did not insist on an heiress for his ward, but he did wish to know what dowry Jacky could expect from his bride. He wrote to Calvert, 'as I know you are full able' – Mrs Calvert had been an heiress – 'I should hope . . . that you would also be willing to do something genteel by your daughter'.[32]

Nelly's father, in his reply on 8 April, hastened to agree with almost all Washington's sentiments and proposals. Only at the prospect of doing 'something genteel' by his daughter did he rebel. With ten children to provide for, he wrote blithely, he could offer 'no very great fortune'. In common with half Virginia, he had hopes for the issue of a claim 'depending', or pending, which might alter this state of affairs.[33] But Calvert's claim, he made Washington aware, was against the estate of the late Lord Baltimore, of whom he was the illegitimate offspring. It was a claim, as Washington and he both knew, unlikely to succeed.

The Washingtons would have to be content with Nelly's beautiful brown eyes and pink cheeks, as seen in a miniature of a later date, in the place of a fortune. The stain of Benedict Calvert's illegitimate birth at least was no great issue. He had long served, in Annapolis, on the Governor's Council. On Nelly's mother's side the girl's pedigree was unassailable. Moreover Boucher, writing from Annapolis – also on 8 April – offered this sop. He described Jacky's fiancée as 'the most amiable young woman I have almost ever known. I know her well and can truly say', he added, with Martha in mind, 'she is all that the fondest parent can wish for a darling child.'[34]

Nelly's youth, and her giddiness in acceding to Jacky's reckless suit might have made a thoughtful mother wary. But Martha was blind where Jacky and Jacky's best interests were concerned. She may even have felt some sympathy with Jacky when he apparently confessed that he had been unable to apply himself 'with earnestness' to his studies for a full year, 'owing to the impression of this passion'.[35] Washington, too, termed Nelly, in a letter to Burwell Bassett, 'a girl of exceeding good Character'.[36]

If Jacky – and indeed Martha – hoped that his engagement to Miss Calvert might be an obstacle to his residence at King's, they were disappointed. In late April the Calverts and their two eldest

daughters paid a visit of some days to Mount Vernon. In early May
Jacky was permitted two nights at Mount Airy. On the 8th, just over
a month after news had broken of the illicit engagement, Jacky and
Washington headed north, in company with Governor Eden, who
had a horse running at the Philadelphia Jockey Club meeting. Fond
though Jacky was of his home comforts, the attractions of Mount
Vernon and even Mount Airy may have paled beside the splendid
entertainments that he and his stepfather enjoyed in Philadelphia
and on their way to New York. Alexandria, Annapolis and even
Williamsburg were pygmy towns compared to Philadelphia, where
the streets were handsomely built and laid out with great regular-
ity, with broad pavements and good lighting and patrols after dark.
Dinners and breakfasts at Governor Richard Penn's palace, assemblies
and balls, evenings at the Jockey Club and race meetings occupied a
week of their time. With visits to acquaintances in New Jersey, it was
not till 24 May that Washington and Jacky reached New York, their
final destination.

The city consisted of between two and three thousand houses
and occupied an area about a mile by a mile and a half at the
southern tip of Manhattan Island. William Tryon occupied the
Governor's Palace in the Battery, the fort dominating the seaward
end of the city. A gilded equestrian statue of King George III
adorned Bowling Green, the public place that lay between the fort
and a thoroughfare known as the Broadway. General Thomas Gage,
Commander-in-Chief of British forces in North America, directed
the British regiments which were charged with quelling political
unrest. Washington had served with Gage on Braddock's expeditionary force in 1754. Now he dined with the British commander
and attended an 'entertainment' given by merchants at 'the sign
of the Bunch of Grapes', a tavern, to mark Gage's departure for
England on leave. He attended 'the play' on 28 May – *Hamlet*, in
this instance, and a farce. Washington's principal concern remained
his stepson.[37]

Jacky, on enrolling in King's, which occupied a handsome site on
lower Broadway, adopted the gown that marked out Dr Cooper's
scholars, and took possession of two chambers, in one of which his

slave servant, Joe, slept. His stepfather wrote to the college President on 31 May: 'If, contrary to my expectation, you should find him inclined to run into any Act of extravagance, you will be so good by your friendly admonitions to check the progress of it.'[38] Jacky embarked on a programme of papering and furnishing his rooms, and wrestled with 'Mathematicks, Languages, moral and experimental Philosophy'. For exercise, he rode into the pastoral land on Manhattan that lay north of the Broadway.[39] Washington himself headed south for home, and reached Martha and Patsy at Mount Vernon on 8 June.

Death and Adjustment

. . . the lowest ebb of Misery.

On 11 June, soon after Washington returned from settling his ward in New York, Nelly Calvert arrived after dinner – with an attendant, Miss Read – to pay an extended visit at Mount Vernon. The day had been, as Washington observed in his diary, most unseasonable: 'Cloudy & exceeding cold. Wind fresh from the northwest, & snowing.' Cool weather and occasional rain obtained during the first days of Nelly's stay. It did not prevent the household attending service two days later at Christ Church, the new brick church in Alexandria funded through the purchase of pews by the Washingtons and other parishioners. A large party rode over to the grist mill on the 17th, Washington transacted business with numerous visitors, and by degrees a southerly wind blew in. The weather turned warm, and then 'clear, calm and exceedingly hot'. The summer party ebbed, then swelled on the 18th when Washington's brother John Augustine and his wife, Hannah, came to stay. They brought with them their daughter, Jane, and two younger children. Though rain threatened, none fell.

The next day – 19 June – was 'very warm, and clear, wind being southerly'.[1] Seventeen-year-old Patsy, rising from the table about four o'clock, was 'in better health and spirits than she appeared to have been for some time'. So her stepfather wrote to her uncle Bassett the following day. He continued his narrative: 'soon after which, she was seized with one of her usual fits, & expired in it, in less than two minutes without uttering a Word, a groan, or scarce a sigh.'[2] Hannah Washington and 'other witnesses' to Patsy's death scene – possibly Jane Washington, fourteen at this time, and Nelly Calvert – were later to expand Washington's bald account. They told how swiftly he was at his stepdaughter's side: 'before they could realize the event' – that Patsy was not limp but lifeless – 'he [Washington] knelt by her and prayed most fervently, most affectedly, for her recovery'.[3] His entreaties were to no avail. In his letter to Bassett of the 20th, Washington reflected that this sudden, silent death had 'removed this Sweet Innocent Girl into a more happy, & peaceful abode than any she has met with in the afflicted Path she hitherto has trod'.[4] The fits which had plagued Patsy's life for five long years and the courses of medicine which had failed to cure them were at an end.[*] After the death of Betsy Bassett, aged fourteen, earlier this year, Washington had counselled her father: 'the ways of Providence being inscrutable . . . resignation, and, as far as the strength of our reason and religion can carry us, a cheerful acquiescence to the d[iv]ine will is what we are to aim at'.[5] Martha was not so philosophical, as her husband recognized, writing now to Bassett: 'This Sudden, and unexpected blow, I scarce need add, has almost reduced my poor Wife to the lowest ebb of Misery.'[6]

The Washingtons' shock and grief, the need to inform Patsy's brother in New York of his sibling's death, the consternation among the house party at Mount Vernon – all were secondary, in the summer heat, to the need for burial. The very next day, with a coffin procured from Alexandria and draped with a black pall, Patsy was laid to rest in the Washington family vault near the house, the Reverend Lee Massey officiating. There seems to have been no thought of translating Patsy's remains to Queen's Creek graveyard on Parke Custis land. There her elder siblings Daniel II and Fanny, who had died so

---

[*] Even today, post-mortems offer no explanation of SUDEP – Sudden Unexplained Death in Epilepsy. It is given as the cause of death in 7.5 per cent of all deaths from epilepsy and in 15 per cent of those with intractable epilepsy. Respiratory, cardiac and cerebral factors are thought to be involved. Cardiac arrest, as here, without warning or prefatory seizure, is common.

long before, were buried with their father. Patsy had grown up at Mount Vernon, and her coffin took its place beside that of Washington's brother Lawrence.

In the days that followed, George William and Sally Fairfax, who had known Patsy since she first came north with her mother and Jacky in 1759, were much with the Washingtons. But soon the Washingtons were to suffer a further real, if lesser, loss. In August the Fairfaxes, so long tied to the Washingtons by propinquity and friendship, vacated Belvoir and sailed for London, where George William meant to pursue a lawsuit in Chancery. They were never to return to Virginia.

In the wake of Patsy's death, the John Augustine Washingtons left and Benedict Calvert came with his elder daughter to fetch away Nelly and Miss Read. George and Martha continued to stay close to home. On the day of Patsy's funeral, Washington, citing bereavement, had written to cancel a tour to prospect for land in western Virginia that he was to have undertaken with Governor Dunmore. Both he and Martha were in deep black. Fifteen months of deep, half and second mourning lay ahead, as was prescribed for the death of a child. Washington ordered from London a 'genteel Suit of Second Mourning, such as is worn by Gentlemen of taste, not those who are for running into the extreme of every fashion', as well as a 'genteel mourning sword, with belt, swivels, etc.'[7] Martha required a 'Black Silk Sacque & Coat' with '1 Suit of fashionable Linnen to wear with it (containing 2 Caps)' and '1 handsome Fan proper for Second Mourning'.[8] It would appear, in addition, that the Fairfaxes were deputed, on their arrival in London, to order 'mourning rings', possibly containing Patsy's hair. These were, no doubt, to be distributed among the girl's friends and relatives.[9]

Such material provision against the needs of the year to come was more easily effected than coping with other adjustments to the sudden loss of Patsy. Her costly wardrobe, her spinet and songbooks remained at Mount Vernon, sad souvenirs of her short life. The parrot which the invalid acquired shortly before her death would be a familiar sight in the outdoor aviary for decades. Washington, who judged his wife much in need of the 'balmy consolation' of her relations, hoped that Martha's mother would make her home with them. He told his brother-in-law Bassett he wished he was 'Master of Arguments powerful enough to prevail upon Mrs Dandridge . . . she lives a lonesome life (Betsy being married)'.[10] (Martha's sister Betsy had, on marrying John Aylett, moved away.) 'Lonesome' though her life might be, Mrs Dandridge remained at Chestnut Grove, and Martha's brother William farmed the smallholding. In the autumn the Washingtons themselves, with Jacky their companion, went south to Eltham and Williamsburg. Among other business, Washington now submitted the Guardian Accounts for the last time. Jacky had turned eighteen and would nominally have control of his fortune. Patsy Parke Custis's share of her father Daniel's estate – mostly bank stock in England – was meanwhile divided between her mother and brother.[11]

Upon receiving in New York the news of his sister's death, Jacky wrote to Washington in early July that he had, 'like a Woman', given himself up entirely to melancholy for several days. He wrote on 5 July to condole with his mother and, separately, to offer his step-father advice on how best to mend his mother's spirits: 'I think the only and most effectual means to remove from her mind the impressions of my poor sister [is] to carry her from home for some considerable time, for everything at Mount Vernon must remind her of her late loss.' He would willingly, he wrote, command lodgings in New York.[12]

Washington may have hesitated to disturb Jacky's studies. With the prospect of marriage ahead, it would seem that the young man was exerting himself academically. He told his mother: 'I assure you that I have done as much or more in 2 months than in the eight Months before.' His sober programme, Martha heard, included early attendance at chapel, 'a little Breakfast, to which I sit down very contentedly', and two periods of study during the day. Besides this, he announced, he dined with the professors – '(a liberty that is not allow'd any but myself)' – and attended prayers at six. The college day being then 'broak up', the model student thereafter allowed himself a measure of amusement.[13] Jacky's tutor, John Vardill, wrote from New York in September, praising his pupil's industry.[14] Jacky was still committed to his studies when he came home in October for the holiday. Before the party set out south for Williamsburg, Washington ordered from London on his stepson's account books including James Beatty's *Essay on Truth* and Thomas Reid's *Inquiry into the Human Mind.*[15]

At Eltham in November the Washingtons, mourning Patsy, found common cause with the Bassetts, who had lost two daughters in the one year. Washington dispatched business in Williamsburg. There were also, it seems, going by his journal entries and by a letter he wrote to President Myles Cooper in December, a series of meetings with Jacky's kith and kin on the subject of Jacky's wish to leave college and proceed to matrimony. On the Dandridge side, besides Bassett himself, Martha's brother Bartholomew Dandridge of Pamocra and Benjamin Harrison of Berkeley – brother-in-law to Bassett – may have offered advice. A visit to Westover on the James River may also have elicited counsel from its master, William Byrd III, kin to Jacky on the Parke Custis side.[16]

If Washington investigated the contents of the books that he had ordered in October for Jacky, when they arrived the following spring, we may be very sure that Jacky did not. Nor did he return to New York and to his studies. In mid-December 1773 Washington wrote to President Cooper from Mount Vernon: 'at length I have yielded, contrary to my judgment, & much against my wishes, to his quitting College . . .' Jacky had disappointed his stepfather's hopes for him, but Washington was a realist. He cited Jacky's 'own inclination – the desires of his mother – & the acquiescence of almost all his relatives' as being forces against which he did not care to 'push' his opposition too far. Allowing that, with Patsy's death, Jacky truly was 'the last of his family', Washington wrote to Cooper in New York that he had 'submitted to a Kind of necessity'.[17] What tussles occurred between Washington and Martha over Jacky's future this autumn, what pleas on either side for understanding were uttered, we do not know. But the die was cast, and Washington was not a man to repine. The upshot was that Jacky had got his way and was to embark immediately on the marriage to Nelly Calvert that his stepfather had so wished him to postpone. That ceremony concluded, groom and bride could at least begin forthwith to increase the Parke Custis stock. It remained to be seen what kind of plantation owner Jacky would make. In the meantime, Washington would offer advice on the management of the Parke Custis estates. Jacky and Nelly, of no fixed abode, would live for the moment between Mount Airy and Mount Vernon.

The marriage itself was effected easily enough. In January 1774 Washington advanced Jacky £24 to buy 'wedding clothes' and a further £37 for other nuptial expenses.[18] With his cousin Lund for company, Washington set out after an early dinner on 3 February to attend the ceremony, which took place that evening at the bride's home. Still in mourning for her daughter, Martha remained at Mount Vernon.Two days later, after 'much other company' had joined in festivities at Mount Airy, Washington was home again 'for a late dinner'.[19]

Jacky was settled after a fashion. This spring, visits from 'Mr and Mrs Custis' – and numerous Calverts – feature in Washington's journal. But he was to write to Dr Cooper in New York in April: 'the young gentleman' – Jacky – 'since his marriage has been a good part of his time in Maryland'.[20] Jacky had recommended to his mother, following Patsy's death, that she 'submit with Patience to the divine will'.[21] Her habit, anyway, was to read devotional works before rising and before settling for the night. The loss of her son to Mount Airy, as well as Patsy's death, both affected her. George, in his early forties, was as tireless and strong as a man half his age. He hunted and shot with Dr Rumney and Bryan Fairfax, George William's younger half-brother. He rode daily the full round – thirty miles – of the estate. Impatient with others' rate of work, he had a habit, in the fields, of seizing from overseers, hirelings and slaves their implements in order to show them how best to achieve what he sought.

News came early in January 1774 of a remarkable recent response to the Tea Act, a new law of the previous May. East India Company – taxed – tea, of which there was a surplus, was being offered cheaply in the colonies, so as to undercut other merchants' and smugglers' tea. Should colonists purchase it, it was arguable that they implicitly recognized the right of taxation without representation. Protesters – some dressed as Native Americans – boarded a British merchantman in Boston harbour on 16 December 1773, and dumped its consignment of the tainted tea in the water. Washington, far away, was occupied with George Mason and other vestrymen, furnishing a newbuilt parish church at Pohick. It fell to the master of Mount Vernon to import 'a Cushion for the Pulpit . . . and Cloths for the Desks & Communion Table of Crimson Velvet with Gold Fringe'.[22] While he deplored the Tea Act, Washington had no sympathy for the destruction of property.

In April the Bassetts came to stay for two weeks with their eldest son, Billy, and Fanny, aged six. With them the Washingtons went to observe the herring and shad being hauled in down at the fishing grounds, a spring ritual and an extremely productive enterprise. (Washington earned £100 this year from the 'fishery'.) Following the Bassetts' departure, a 'boat race and barbecue' at Johnson's ferry ushered in the early summer.[23] When George and Martha set out for Eltham and Williamsburg, where he was to attend the House of Burgesses in May, there seemed no reason to suppose that the even tenor of life at Mount Vernon would ever alter greatly.

The first days that the Washingtons were in the south in May 1774 were uneventful. Washington came and went between Eltham and Williamsburg, addressing local issues in the House of Burgesses. He pressed, at the request of prominent Alexandria merchants, John Carlyle among them, for 'a more effectual method to prevent the raising of Hogs and suffering them to run at large [through the town], also Goats and Geese'.[24] He dined at the Governor's Palace with Lord Dunmore. The previous autumn, when Martha had accompanied him south, both she and her sister Nancy at Eltham had both been in mourning for their daughters. This June, both Washingtons and both Bassetts – with 'Mrs Dandridge', either Martha and Nancy Bassett's mother or their brother Bart's wife – made an excursion 'by water' from Eltham.[25] Their destination was Pleasant Hill on the Mattaponi River, once the seat of John Robinson, Speaker and Treasurer of Virginia. After a long career as Speaker and Treasurer, his equally long embezzlement of public funds was discovered by Burgess Richard Henry Lee. The house, sold after Robinson's death 1766, when he was found to be £100,000 in debt to the colony, included a neat brick mansion and terraced gardens descending to the water. It had come on the market again the previous year. There was a silver lining to the death of Patsy – namely, the £16,000 'money on bond', or in stock in London and Virginia, that comprised her estate. Washington, on Jacky's behalf, invested his stepson's half share in the purchase of Pleasant Hill and of another plantation adjoining Parke Custis lands. If Jacky did not choose to repair the White House in New Kent County, which had been disused since Martha and the children left it fifteen years before, this was a fine gentleman's property – and one close to Williamsburg – in which the young Parke Custises could settle.

The other £8,000 from Patsy's estate devolved on Washington as disposable property, and formed a sizeable addition to the Parke Custis dower portion already in his control. He wrote in November 1773 to Cary and Co. in London, regarding £1,650, the dower share of the cash with them formerly assigned his stepdaughter on her father's death: 'as I would choose to discharge my Debt to you, I would apply her [Patsy's] money in the Bank to that purpose, provided I can sell out without loss'.[26] He flattered himself that this sum, once realized, would expunge what he owed the agents. He had no need to acquire more land on the Potomac (he now owned 6,500 acres). George and Martha could apply the remaining funds to the 'mansion' at Mount Vernon, and they embarked on an ambitious programme of alterations and extensions. Private quarters with a separate staircase and entrance were soon built to the south. They comprised, above, a large bedchamber, serving Martha also as a boudoir during the day, and below, for Washington's sole use, a library. A 'New Room' – a large reception room, two stories high, planned for an extension to the north – and a piazza, or portico, to the east, affording shade and views, were slow in the making.

Lund Washington was to complain of Lanphier, the joiner from Alexandria whom his cousin had employed to do much of the work: 'he mouths & talks in such a way that I do not understand him – I mean as to the dimensions of the Palisades – Sills, rails, Posts, & different Heights'.[27] The Washingtons admired the elaborate ceilings at Millbrook, the home of Washingtons sister Betsy and of her husband Fielding Lewis in Fredericksburg. George was to borrow the 'stucco man', an indentured servant, from his brother-in-law to decorate ceilings and walls at Mount Vernon. He took an inordinate length of time to achieve his effects. This August the first of two sales of contents was held at Belvoir, which George William Fairfax had resolved to rent out during his prolonged absence in England. Washington purchased, possibly for the new bedchamber, a 'mahogany chest and drawers' from Sally Fairfax's bedchamber. He also bought a 'mahogany sideboard', and '12 chairs and 3 window curtains from the dining room'.[28] If he intended these for the 'New Room', as seems likely, it would be long before they could be publicly admired. The work at the northern end was not to be completed for a decade.

The Washingtons had paused at the Lewises' at Fredericksburg on their way south in May, so that Washington could give up the title deeds of Home House, the farm there, where he had grown up – and where his mother had lived till lately – to Dr Hugh Mercer. Mercer had arranged to buy the farm for £2,000 in Virginia currency in five instalments.[29] Washington's mother, Mary, had been persuaded to move into a house that he had bought her on Charles Street in town, close to her daughter Betty, at Millbrook. With the sale of Home House, Washington was freed of a property – his inheritance from his father – whose upkeep had long been an encumbrance and a cause of occasional dissension between him and his mother, who owned the slaves and livestock.

Another longstanding sore, though, was not fully healed. Following the treaties of Fort Stanwix and of Lochaber in 1768 and 1770, which established a proclamation line further westward, the acres promised to those who had joined the Virginia Regiment in 1754 had at last, in 1772, been apportioned. This was thanks in large part to the efforts of Washington himself, who had chaired many reunions of the veterans and petitioned the different governors of Virginia in turn.

Washington had received 18,500 acres himself, and had bought up claims from other officers for a further 5,600.

An influential group of investors in London, the Pennsylvanian agent Benjamin Franklin among them, had been in discussion for some years with the government to obtain a grant of twenty million acres. They hoped to form a new colony, to be named Vandalia, south of the Ohio. As Washington had pointed out to successive governors of Virginia, Vandalia, should it come into being, would encompass the acres due the Virginia Regiment veterans. It would threaten, in addition, the lands not as yet granted but promised by the 1763 Royal Proclamation to all colonial veterans of the French and Indian War.

Nothing had been settled when the Washingtons headed south in May. In principle, they were the richer for the death of Patsy and following the apportioning of the bounty lands. In the spring Washington had embarked on his plan of embellishment at Mount Vernon, confident that the inheritance from Patsy would pay off the debt to Cary. But the plantation economy was as always subject to the vagaries of the climate. In May, the estate finances suffered an unforeseen setback, as he told Robert Cary on 1 June 1774. A vicious frost, accompanied by snow, had destroyed 'the better half of more than one thousand acres' which Washington had 'growing in Wheat'. Washington wrote from Williamsburg to enquire if his flour, which was of good quality, would command a good price in London. He offered Cary the opportunity – 'if our Commerce with Great Britain is kept open (which seems to be a matter of very great doubt at present)' – to sell, on commission, a hundred or two hundred barrels at a time.[30]

There was all of a sudden every reason for Washington to express doubt about the continuance of commercial relations between mother country and Virginia – and indeed between Britain and its other American colonies. In the week of 22 May news that a Boston Port Bill had passed into law in March had reached Williamsburg. The Act decreed that the Massachusetts Bay harbour was to be closed from 1 June – the date on which Washington wrote to Cary – until the colonial city had made reparation to the Customs Office and to the East India Company for the destruction of the tea in December. The Virginian capital had been in an uproar ever since. Washington was to write to George William Fairfax, nine days after the closure took place: 'the cause of Boston – the despotick Measures in respect to it, I mean – now is and ever will be considered as the cause of America (not that we approve their cond[uc]t in destroying the Tea) . . . we shall not suffer ourselves to be sacrificed by piecemeal . . .'[31]

Continental Army

. . . the Crisis is arrived when we must assert our Rights . . .

Some of the younger Virginian burgesses were swift to respond to what they judged to be an iniquitous Act. While Martha and George were dining in Williamsburg with Attorney General John Randolph on 23 May 1774, Patrick Henry, Thomas Jefferson and others met and 'cooked up', to use Jefferson's words, a resolution. Possibly George Mason, who was for once in the city, was present and encouraged them. At their instigation, Robert Carter Nicholas moved in the House next day that Wednesday 1 June, the date Boston harbour was to close, should be observed in Virginia as a 'day of fasting, humiliation, and prayer', in the pious hope that divine intervention might avert the 'heavy calamity which threatens destruction of our civil rights, and the evils of civil war'.[1] When this incendiary resolution was carried without a dissenting voice, a modicum of calm was restored to the city.

Though fasting and prayer were a peaceful response to what the malcontents termed 'despotic measures', they proved unacceptable to Governor Dunmore. He entered the House on 26 May and, condemning the resolution, curtly dissolved the assembly. Washington had breakfasted with the Governor at the latter's country house that very morning. 'This dissolution was as sudden as unexpected,' he was to write to Fairfax in England the following month.[2] He and other burgesses and their wives were due to attend a ball to be given at the

Governor's Palace the following day to welcome Lady Dunmore, who had only recently arrived in Virginia. The ball took place as though no quarrel between Dunmore and the burgesses existed. But Washington did not hesitate to join more than eighty others who gathered earlier in the day at the Raleigh Tavern, as they had done once before when dismissed.

The makeshift assembly agreed to support the Bostonians with an Association, a body given greater weight when a circulating letter arrived two days later from that northern city. Its inhabitants begged those of other colonies to join with them in a general non-importation agreement directed at the East India Company as well as at the British government. It was resolved in Williamsburg that the burgesses should return home for consultation and gather again on 1 August in Williamsburg at a Convention, to further discuss the agreement proposed. On 1 June, besides writing to Cary and Co., Washington fasted and attended church. George Mason, in advance of the date, had sent word home to Gunston Hall that, if Fairfax County supported the call to prayer, his elder children should attend church in mourning.

Given the previous failure of non-importation agreements, a cynic might have predicted that the other business proposed at the Raleigh Tavern would not amount to much. This was not to be the case in the summer of 1774. There was a new spirit abroad – a general perception that there was a need for co-operation among the disparate colonies. This was pithily expressed, on 7 July, on the masthead of Paul Revere's Boston newspaper, the *Massachusetts Spy*. Reviving Benjamin Franklin's famous print of 1754, *Join, or die*, he altered the segmented snake of that earlier image to form a conjoined serpent, representing all the colonies united. A month later, George Washington would present to the August Virginia Convention what became known as the 'Fairfax [County] Resolves'. These, too, were an expression of the need for co-operation.

The Resolves, or resolutions, passed in committee in July in Alexandria, were at once an embryo bill of rights and a clarion call for a Congress of delegates from all the colonies. That Congress, it was hoped, would consider how better to preserve those rights.[3]

George Mason's was the legal mind that framed the Fairfax Resolves in the Northern Neck, Washington the man of action who took them south. With extraordinary efficiency, it was agreed in August at the Virginia Convention and at similar assemblies in other colonies that such a Congress as Washington proposed to the Convention should be held in early September in Philadelphia. Washington was among the seven delegates chosen to attend from Virginia. At the end of August, Edmund Pendleton and Patrick Henry, who were also chosen, broke their journey at Mount Vernon, where they spent two nights. George Mason was also of the company. A letter from Pendleton, a moderate and a lawyer, gives an interesting account of Martha, their hostess – alternately gracious and steely:

> I was much pleased with Mrs Washington and her spirit. She seemed ready to make any sacrifice and was cheerful, though I knew she felt anxious.
>
> She talked like a Spartan mother to her son on going to battle. 'I hope you will stand firm – I know George will,' she said. The dear little woman was busy from morning until night with domestic duties, but she gave us much time in conversation and affording us entertainment. When we set off in the morning, she stood in the door and cheered us with the good words, 'God be with you gentlemen.'[4]

Not all on the Potomac were as radical as George and Martha. George William Fairfax was sympathetic to the 'cause' but remained absent in England. Washington had failed to convert George William's brother, Bryan Fairfax of Towlston Grange at Great Falls. Fairfax advocated the resumption of addresses, memorials and petitions to the Crown and Parliament. Threats, he wrote, had proved useless in the past. Washington replied heatedly: 'the Crisis is arrived when we must assert our Rights, or Submit to every Imposition that can be heaped upon us; till custom and use, will make us as tame, & abject Slaves, as the Blacks we Rule over with such arbitrary Sway'.[5] Here was a Virginia plantation owner writing with empathy of the slave workforce; there was provision in the Fairfax Resolves for the abolition of the slave trade. Martha was urging on her husband and his fellow delegates to rebel. The question was, how far would the Virginians go to assert the 'rights' of which Washington wrote?

In Philadelphia the Virginian delegates were much to the fore at the Congress, which met in Carpenters' Hall over the course of seven weeks. All of the colonies bar Georgia were represented, and Edmund Pendleton presided as Speaker. He and the six other Virginians were reckoned by one present to be sociable, sensible and spirited. This was not the case with all the delegates. Strangers to each other, 'not acquainted with each other's language, ideas, views, designs', they were characterized by the Massachusetts lawyer and delegate John Adams as 'jealous of each other – fearful, timid, skittish'.[6] Patrick Henry, holding out for one vote per colony, won popularity when he declaimed on September 6th, 'I am not a Virginian but an American.'[7] Richard Henry Lee's more substantial and Ciceronian speeches were also admired. Though Jefferson was not a delegate, he had penned and published at Williamsburg a pamphlet, *A Summary View of the Rights of British America*, which was widely discussed. Of all the Virginians, George Washington may be said to have aroused most curiosity. The Connecticut merchant and delegate Silas Deane wrote to his wife on 10 September of his fellow delegate's commanding height, his 'easy, soldier like air and gesture', and his honourable conduct in the French and Indian War. Deane also referred to a story which, though fiction, was current at the Congress. Upon hearing in the House of Burgesses of the Boston Port Act, he reported, Washington offered to 'raise and arm, and lead one thousand men himself at his own expense, for the defence of the country, were there need of it . . . His fortune is said to be equal to such an undertaking,' Deane added, knowing nothing of his hero's financial worries.[8]

George served on no committee during the Congress, which wound up with a broad agreement not to import British goods after 1 December 1774, to export no goods to Britain after 10 September 1775, and to meet again the following May of 1775. The company with whom he lodged and dined during the Congress were committed to the cause. They included, besides delegates from his own colony, prominent citizens of Philadelphia – the two Drs William

Shippen, Sr and Jr, financier Thomas Willing, merchant Thomas Mifflin and lawyer Joseph Reed.[9] Washington was as resolved as any other delegate that resistance must in future meet any government transgression. On 9 October 1774, he made his position clear in a letter to a fellow officer from his Virginia Regiment days: 'it is not the wish or interest of that government [the colonial assembly of Massachusetts] or any other upon this continent separately or collectively, to set up for independence'. But if they faced 'the loss of those valuable rights and privileges which are essential to the happiness of every free state', was it to be wondered that they should defend themselves against such an 'impending blow'? It was his opinion, he wrote, that 'more blood will be spilt on this occasion' – if the British government pushed matters 'to extremity' – 'than history has yet furnished instances of in the annals of North America'.[10]

In Alexandria Washington and George Mason had taken early steps to ensure that Fairfax County would be well defended, should the need arise. By September, a Fairfax Independent Company had been organized. Volunteer officers included Dr Rumney, Robert Hanson Harrison, a young lawyer in the town, Washington himself, Lund and Jacky. In other regiments there was a good deal of latitude allowed in the matter of uniform, and some officers wore plain brown coats. Such was not the case in the Fairfax Independent Company. Washington's own suit of regimentals, and those for Lund Washington and for Jacky – a 'regular Uniform of Blue, turn'd up with Buff [parchment yellow]' – were tailored that autumn.[11] A waistcoat and breeches of the latter shade and white stockings completed a uniform later known as 'buff and blue'. For 'the men', as other ranks were known – and for officers on foraging expeditions – hunting shirts, roomy, all-weather wear, were prescribed. Each member of the company was to acquire, besides a stock of gunpowder, 'a good Fire-lock and Bayonet, Sling Cartouch-Box, and Tomahawk'. In January 1775 a committee recommended that companies across the county organize and obtain, at general expense – they suggested a poll tax of three shillings – a quantity of gunpowder.[12] Mason's knowledge of the law made certain that these companies assumed no further appearance than that of the local militias authorized, since first settlement of the colonies, to protect homes and ensure public safety.

Washington was emerging as an important figure in the Virginian resistance movement. He advanced money for the immediate purchase of ammunition, and in mid-March 1775 he inspected volunteers at Dumfries, on his way to Richmond, where the second Virginia Convention was to be held, far inland from Williamsburg. At that assembly, which met at St John's Church on 23 March, Patrick Henry proposed that the whole colony be put immediately 'into a posture of defence'. His exhortation to those assembled passed into legend: 'We must fight!. . . Is life so dear, or peace so sweet, as to be purchased at the price of chains or slavery? Forbid it, Almighty God! I know not what course others may take, but, as for me, give me liberty or give me death!' Though there were those like Robert Carter Nicholas who urged delay, the vote in favour of arming the colony was decisive.

Henry and Washington made two of a committee of twelve appointed to bring in a plan for 'embodying, arming and disciplining such a number of men as may be sufficient for that purpose'.[13] These numbers were to include companies of footsoldiers sixty-eight strong. Counties on and east of the fall line – the set of rapids and waterfalls in the rivers of Virginia that prevented craft from travelling further upstream – were, in addition, to supply one cavalry troop or more of thirty men. Williamsburg lawyers worked to frame all such measures as defensive, so as to fall within the law. Just how closely Washington was engaged in this arming of Virginia appears from a letter he wrote, on 25 March, to his brother John Augustine, praising the latter's efforts in training an 'Independent Company'. Washington offered to review and command it, as he was to review and command an independent company forming in Richmond County. He declared: 'it is my full intention to devote my life and fortune in the cause we are engaged in, if need be'.[14]

With extraordinary rapidity, and even before the Second Congress could meet at Philadelphia in May, events occurred almost simultaneously to test Washington's expressed devotion to 'the cause'. Early on the morning of 21 April in Williamsburg, British marines, under orders from Lord Dunmore, began secretly to remove all the gunpowder in the city magazine to the *Magdalen*, an armed schooner lying in the James River. They had removed fifteen half-barrels before they were detected, and thereafter continued despite the alarm. The schooner then delivered its load to the *Fowey*, an armed man-of-war anchored off Norfolk.

Civilized uproar developed in Williamsburg. The city fathers requested the powder's return, affecting to believe a slave uprising, such as occurred periodically, to be imminent. Dunmore, referring to a nameless 'insurrection in a neighbouring county', asserted that he had sequestered the powder in the city's own interests.[15] The truth was, as everyone knew, that Dunmore feared that one or more of the many independent companies now forming would seize it. In fact, his action provoked those very volunteer forces. Dr Hugh Mercer and others in Fredericksburg wrote to Washington on 26 April that their Company intended to march, 'properly accoutred as light horsemen', on the colonial capital.[16] They aimed to seize whatever military supplies remained in the magazine.

Mercer and his fellow volunteers were dissuaded from this hasty action. In the meantime news came from Massachusetts, a colony which the British government had declared in a state of rebellion in February. Patriot – and British – blood had now been spilt. In the early hours of 19 April, a column of British infantry, 700 men strong, had marched on a village, Concord, some sixteen miles west. Their orders, from General Gage in Boston, were to search homes there for military stores. The troops were intercepted at Lexington, six miles short of their destination, by local militia who refused to disperse when ordered by the British to do so. The front ranks of the British column fired and killed eight of the men opposing them. When the troops moved on to Concord, some soldiers conducted the search, as required. But others, at the North Bridge over the river that gave its name to the settlement, were beset by Concord minutemen and militia from other areas who had come to join the fray. In an exchange of musket fire both militia and infantry suffered losses. The British troops, disconcerted and alarmed, rejoined their comrades and began the long march back to Boston. Reinforcements from the town bolstered their number, but local militia pursued them all the way, taking advantage of the scrub and undergrowth to disguise their positions. At the end of the day, a total of seventy-three British soldiers and forty-nine Americans lay dead. The local militia, moreover, were in triumphant possession of Boston Neck, the isthmus connecting the harbour town to Roxbury. The British troops in the city were penned in, and Boston was under siege. It was an extraordinary outcome to a day that had begun with routine orders for a search for powder.

From Philadelphia, where he had proceeded at the beginning of May to take his place as a delegate at the Second Congress, Washington, on 31 May, wrote a long account of the events of the 19th to George William Fairfax. He ended: 'Unhappy [though] it is . . . to reflect, that a Brother's Sword has been sheathed in a Brother's breast, and that, the once happy and peaceful plains of America are either to be drenched with Blood, or Inhabited by Slaves. Sad alternative! But can a virtuous Man hesitate in his choice?'[17] George's choice of language would resonate with Fairfax, a Virginia landowner though now resident in England. Though Washington foresaw that events might bring a rift between him and his boyhood friend, his duty as a 'virtuous man' led him onward.

At the outset of the Second Congress, held in the State House, the mood following Lexington and Concord was very different from that which had obtained at the first. 'There never appeared', wrote delegate Richard Henry Lee on 10 May to his brother William Lee in Virginia, 'more perfect unanimity among any set of men than among the delegates . . .'[18] A letter of 3 May from Dr Joseph Warren was read to the assembly on the 11th. It imparted the news that his 'Provincial Congress' – the Provincial Convention of Massachusetts – had authorized the raising of 13,600 men in that colony. They constituted, he wrote, 'a powerful army, on the side of America . . . the only means left to stem the rapid growth of a tyrannical ministry'.[19]

At this warlike Congress Washington adopted the uniform of the Fairfax Independent Company, and was much in evidence. He was made chairman of a 'ways and means' committee, created to supply the colonies with ammunition and military stores and to report immediately. News came that British ships were making for the Hudson. There was the fortifying of New York to consider, and companies to be raised for its defence. Some American officers – Benedict Arnold from Connecticut among them – had, against all odds, seized Fort Ticonderoga at Lake George. The cannon and mortars captured should be moved south and stored, Congress directed. Washington offered counsel to delegates untried in military matters. 'Colonel Washington', wrote John Adams to his wife, Abigail, on 29 May, 'by his great experience and abilities in military matters, is of much service to us. Oh, that I was a soldier!'[20]

For all these preparations, though the assembly was committed to aiding the patriots besieging Boston, the question of whether to take up the arms currently being amassed elsewhere against the mother country continued to be debated. After a time, the immensity of the action projected as much as the volume of correspondence with their colonial assemblies back home wearied the delegates in Philadelphia, who were, by and large, still reluctant to credit the King, rather than his ministers, with the measures that oppressed them. A day of fasting and prayer was accordingly prescribed for 20 July, in the hope that the Almighty would inspire the King 'with wisdom to discern and perceive the true interest of all his subjects, that a speedy end, may be put to the civil discord between Great Britain and the American colonies without further effusion of blood . . .'[21]

The militia besieging the British in Boston were no 'despicable rabble', General Gage wrote home. 'In all their wars against the French they never showed such conduct, attention, and persever-ance as they do now.'[22] But General Artemas Ward, in command of the Massachusetts forces, had no jurisdiction over militia from other parts of New England who had joined the siege. An American high command, supplies, powder and troops were desperately wanted.

A letter from the Massachusetts Convention was laid before Congress on 2 June. It suggested 'the propriety' of the assembly in Philadelphia taking on the 'regulation and direction' of the army now collecting from different colonies, as it was for the general defence of 'the right of America'.[23] It was a bold step. The militia in the differ-ent colonies had previously answered to no common authority.

Congress, on the 14th, agreed to the Provincial Convention's request, and authorized, in addition, the raising of ten companies of 'expert riflemen' in Pennsylvania, Virginia and Maryland. They were to be employed as light infantry 'under the command of the chief officer of the army' before Boston. The American Continental Army, composed of officers and men drawn from all thirteen colonies and answerable to Congress, was thus born.

It became a matter of urgency to appoint a 'chief officer' of this new army.[24] Next day, the 15th, it was proposed that 'a General be appointed to command all the continental forces, raised, or to be raised, for the defence of American liberty'.[25] John Adams declared in the State House that he had 'but one gentleman' in his mind for that important command – a gentleman from Virginia, 'very well known to all of us', an experienced officer of 'independent fortune'. Washington rose and left the chamber.[26] He was to write to Martha on 18 June: 'You might, and I suppose did perceive, from the Tenor of my letters, that I was apprehensive I could not avoid this appointment.'[27] The resolution that he be appointed was carried by unanimous vote. He returned to the State House the following day to accept the position of Commander-in-Chief. Expressing his unworthiness for this 'extensive and important trust', he declined the pay that had been voted him: 'no pecuniary consideration could have tempted me to have accepted this arduous employment, at the expence of my domestic ease and happiness'. He requested only that Congress would meet his expenses of which he would keep an 'exact account'.[28] To Martha, in his letter of the 18th, he wrote: 'You may believe me, my dear Patsy . . . I should enjoy more real happiness and felicity in one month with you, at home, than I have the most distant prospect of reaping abroad, if my stay was to be Seven times Seven years.'[29]

The Commander-in-Chief, it was decided, should come to the aid of the 'patriots' before Boston with a 'Continental army' of 15,000 men. Generals, engineers, artillery officers were hastily named and their pay agreed. Congress, approving the issue of a new currency, to be known as the Continental dollar, payable in Spanish dollars, put into circulation $3,000,000. Three days before he set off, Washington wrote to resign his command of the Fairfax Independent Company and of other volunteer troops in Virginia: 'I have launched into a wide & extensive field, too boundless for my abilities, & far, very far beyond my experience.'[30] On 17 July, John Adams wrote of the new commander to Abigail, 'The liberties of America depend upon him in great degree.'[31] But Washington knew that Martha depended on him too.

'I shall feel no pain from the Toil, or the danger of the Campaign,' he wrote to her in his letter of the 18th: 'My unhappiness will flow, from the uneasiness I know you will feel at being left alone – I therefore beg of you to summon your whole fortitude & Resolution, and pass your time as agreeably as possible – nothing will give me so much sincere satisfaction as to hear this, and to hear it from your own Pen.'[32] A day later he wrote to Burwell Bassett, to entreat him to visit Martha often and invite her to Eltham. He instructed Jacky to keep his mother company and enliven her spirits.[33] The subject was much on his mind. He wrote to his brother John Augustine on the 20th: 'my departure will, I know, be a cutting stroke upon her [Martha]; and on this acct alone, I have many very disagreeable Sensations'.[34]

Alone at Mount Vernon, Martha Washington must reassert the habit of independence she had last known as a young widow. She must manage fears and anxieties consequent on her husband's appointment to a dangerous command. In addition, with Lund Washington's help, she must manage the estate, a domain till now the object of George's assiduous care. There were good grounds for her husband's anxiety on her behalf. Neither Washington could have suspected just how resilient Martha would prove to be in the years to come.

BOOK TWO

The General and 'Lady Washington', 1775–1783

Taking Command, 1775

*I have sent an invitation to Mrs Washington
to come to me . . .*

Washington had told Martha, in his letter of 18 June 1775, that, should she wish to take up residence in their house in Alexandria while he was in Massachusetts, he would direct Lund Washington to build a kitchen and other offices lacking there. If, on the other hand, she inclined to spend time among her 'Friends below', he encouraged her to do so. 'My earnest, & ardent desire', he wrote, 'is, that you would pursue any Plan that is most likely to produce content, and a tolerable degree of Tranquillity . . .' There was, understandably, a degree of self-interest in this: 'it must add greatly to my uneasy feelings to hear that you are dissatisfied, and complaining at what I really could not avoid'. Martha chose to remain at Mount Vernon, for the time being. She would soon become a grandmother – and Jacky a father – if Nelly Calvert Custis's accouchement in late August or early September was successful. She had no thought of leaving her home until after this interesting event, but projected a visit to her 'Friends below' thereafter.

With his letter of the 18th Washington had enclosed a will drafted to his direction in Philadelphia by a fellow delegate, the lawyer Edmund Pendleton. 'I had not time to do it before I left home,' Washington told Martha. Then, he had been a delegate off to attend a congress. Now he was commander of a new army embarking on a campaign against experienced British regiments and risking death. Though news of a battle for Bunker Hill in Boston on 17 June had not reached Philadelphia when he wrote, casualty figures would sober Congress when first reports later arrived. The patriot forces were rumoured to have accounted for many hundreds of British regulars, but some among the rebels too had lost their lives.

If the arrival of her husband's last will and testament did not necessarily increase Martha's 'tranquillity', at least she was forearmed, should she become a war widow. Washington hoped the provision made for her was agreeable. He had included 'the Money for which I sold my own land [Home House, Fredericksburg] (to Doctor Mercer) in the Sum given you, as also all other Debts [owed by others to Washington]'. What he himself owed, he wrote, was 'very trifling', his debt to Cary excepted. He added that even that would not have amounted to much, 'if the Bank stock had been applied without such difficulties as he [Cary] made in the Transference' – from the Guardian Accounts to Washington's own. The previous year, legal documents that Washington and Martha had signed to facilitate the sale of Patsy's stock had been rejected by the directors of the Bank of England. New documents were not to be signed, nor the stock sold, till after hostilities had ceased. The outbreak of war between mother country and colonies also rendered moot all further action on the part of John and Joseph Dunbar Parke, residents of the British West Indies. Jacky's inheritance, and Martha's dower portion, were safe from foreign depredations.

In a much later will Washington was to leave his whole estate to Martha for the term of her life.The will that Washington made now in 1775 has not survived. From the above, it seems likely that he left Mount Vernon – a family property – and his other land immediately to one of his brothers – probably John Augustine Washington, who had cared for Mount Vernon in the 1750s. Should Washington perish in combat, Martha's Parke Custis inheritance would, of course, revert to her, including the inheritance from Patsy. She would be a rich woman in control of her own fortune as she had been once long before. It seems probable that it was intended she should make a home away from Mount Vernon, either looking to Jacky to provide a home on his Parke Custis estates or buying a property herself on the Potomac.

It is little wonder, in short, that Martha was to resist all entreaties, however well meaning, to get her to abandon a home that might not be hers for long. In the meantime she had the satisfaction of knowing that, hard pressed as Washington might be with military preparations, he understood the importance of other obligations. 'P.S.', he added to his letter of 18 June, 'Since writing the above I have received your Letter of the 15th and have got two suits of what I was told wa[s] the prettiest Muslin [for neckerchiefs]. I wish it may please you – it cost 50/. a suit that is 20/. a yard.'[1]

Early in the morning of 23 June, though surrounded by company come to take leave and within a few minutes of leaving Philadelphia, Washington wrote again: 'My dearest . . . I could not think of departing from it [the city] without dropping you a line . . .' With Charles Lee and Philip Schuyler, newly appointed major generals by Congress, he was about to set out north to take command of the army at Cambridge. The First City Troop, a company of light horse – mounted troops who could serve as cavalry or, dismounted, as infantry – had been raised in Philadelphia the previous year. They would form his escort on the journey. A crowd including all the delegates from Massachusetts then in Philadelphia were readying to accompany him on horseback, in carriages, and on foot to the bounds of the city. Washington's full concentration was for the moment given to this letter to his wife: 'I go fully trusting in that Providence, which has been more bountiful to me than I deserve, & in full confidence of a happy meeting with you sometime in the fall . . . I retain an unalterable affection for you, which neither time or distance can change, my best love to Jack & Nelly, & regard for the rest of the Family concludes me with the utmost truth & sincerity, Your entire Go: Washington.'[2]

Once the accompanying wellwishers had dropped away, Washington and his party proceeded north with haste and reached New York on 25 June. When they left for Cambridge the following day, Schuyler, who had served as a delegate to Congress and, in his time, as a colonial officer, remained behind. His task was to command

and order the American forces assembling in his native city. Washington's respect for Schuyler shows in the formal 'Instructions' he issued prior to departure: 'Your own good Sense must govern in all Matters not particularly pointed out, as I do not wish to circumscribe you within too narrow Limits.'³ Washington was all the more eager to come to the aid of the patriots besieging Boston, having read on the day of his arrival in New York a full account of the confused conflict at Bunker Hill on the 17th.

Many Bostonians had by this time left their city for towns and villages inland. In 1774, Gage had been appointed military Governor, and had dissolved the legislature. Patriots outside the city, in response, had founded the rebel Massachusetts Provincial Convention or Congress. Gage, with an army 40,000 strong, and men-of-war and smaller vessels in Boston harbour, could occupy the city indefinitely. The patriots, meanwhile, were guarding positions along eight or nine miles of shore and coastline.

Patriot leaders learnt of British plans to break out of the city and subdue western Massachusetts. On the night of the 16th, in consequence, they stealthily occupied and fortified two positions on the Charlestown peninsula – Bunker Hill and Breed's Hill. The latter position was directly above Charlestown and commanded views of Boston's northern shore opposite. Confusion reigned in the city next morning, when the British discovered the patriots' occupation of ground they had themselves expected to occupy in the following days. Two experienced generals, recently arrived from England – Howe and Clinton – with another, Burgoyne, led attacks that followed.

The conflict, during which the British destroyed Charlestown by fire, ended with the patriots retreating. But they were elated by the good showing they had made. The British had possession of Boston and the peninsula alone, and at great cost in lives. Nevertheless, the patriot forces were hard pressed for all supplies, lacked gunpowder, and, above all, direction. The rebel Provincial Congress wrote to Congress on 20 June: 'if a commander in chief over the army of the United Colonies should be appointed, it must be plain to your honors, that no part of this continent can so much require his immediate presence and exertions, as this colony'.⁴

When he arrived on 2 July at Cambridge Washington was in no danger of underestimating the difficulty of guarding 'a semi-circle of eight or nine miles'. As he wrote to his brother John Augustine later in the month, the British, from their central position in Boston and with the fleet in command of Boston Bay could 'bend their whole force . . . with equal facility' against any of the Continental – American army – positions.[5] At the outset he had to do everything himself. He supplied Congress with 'returns' for the different regiments, namely, the number of officers and men in each. He rendered account of the supplies each regiment had of clothing, foodstuffs and – most importantly – guns and powder. He inspected the different outposts and regiments. Slowly some of the burden lifted. In mid-July, at his request, Joseph Trumbull, son of Governor Jonathan Trumbull of Connecticut, was appointed Commissary General of Stores and Provisions. In August Washington appointed Philadelphia merchant Thomas Mifflin, originally one of his aides-de-camp, to the post of Quartermaster General. A Commissary of Artillery was appointed. Dr John Morgan, a leading Philadelphia physician, was given direction of a new army hospital and medical department.

Washington's instructions from Congress were to take command of a united army. But first the disparate militias and volunteers before Boston must be amalgamated. As an initial step, he made three grand divisions of the army. Within days of his arrival at Cambridge, he dispatched Charles Lee north to take command at Medford. He sent Artemas Ward, formerly in command of rebel forces in Massachusetts, to Roxbury. At Cambridge, he himself guarded against British incursions across Charleston Neck.

Within a couple of weeks of his arrival in Massachusetts, Washington had moved from makeshift headquarters in Harvard College to 'the Vassall house'. This elegant mansion, above the Charles and close to Cambridge Common, was on Brattle Street, a road generally known as Tory Row. When disaffection was rife in the town the previous year, the owner of the house, Henry Vassall, had, in common with several other Cambridge Tories, fled north to Nova Scotia. A patriot regiment from Marblehead had more recently occupied the dwelling. Washington now kept a ledger – as faithfully as he had ever kept Guardian Accounts for Jacky and Patsy – titled, 'The United States . . . in account with General Washington'. It shows that payment was made for cleaning the Vassall house before his arrival.[6] A steward – Ebenezer Austin – was appointed and furnished with £10 a week to supply the establishment.[7] A 'French chef' was located to cater to the needs of the Commander-in-Chief and any guests.[8] The military 'family' – as Washington's aides-de-camp and secretaries were known – also dined at this table. Philadelphia lawyer Joseph Reed served as the new commander's principal secretary.

At Cambridge Washington found, as he wrote privately in late July to his brother John Augustine, 'a mixed multitude of People here, under very little discipline, order, or Government'.[9] The democratic spirit in which Yankee officers mingled with men, he believed, was in part responsible. Washington, a Virginian to the bone as well as a former British officer, exhorted, threatened and cajoled throughout the month of July and August. Slowly distinctions between officers and other ranks and some measure of discipline and order were established. Washington corresponded with consummate tact with Congress, with the Massachusetts Provincial Congress and with other assemblies. He favoured his cousin Lund, however, on 20 August with his private opinion of the army which now numbered – 'including sick, absent, etc' – some 16,000 men: 'Their Officers generally speaking are the most indifferent kind of People I ever saw.' He had already cashiered a colonel and two captains for cowardice at the recent conflict at Bunker Hill. Nevertheless, he had some ground for optimism: '. . . I daresay the Men would fight very well (if properly Officered) although they are an exceeding dirty & nasty people.'[10] In one of his first 'General Orders' he exhorted officers to 'keep their Men neat and clean; to visit them often at their quarters, and inculcate upon them the necessity of cleanliness, as essential to their health and service'.[11] When Washington himself rode through the camps, he was clean-shaven and his buff and blue uniform, distinguished by a blue sash, was immaculate.

There was a wide variation in the attire of those the commander surveyed. Some regiments wore hunting shirts, others brown coats with coloured facings. There was not as yet any official Continental uniform, no telling who was a subaltern and who a sergeant. Washington acted on 23 July to order badges of distinction to be worn: 'Field Officers may have *red* or *pink* colour'd Cockades in their Hatt: the Captains *yellow* or *buff*...'[12] By the time he wrote to his cousin at Mount Vernon in August, the Commander-in-Chief had at least accomplished some important tasks. His General Orders of the 5th read: 'The Regiments of the several provinces' – the term newly coined to describe the American colonies – 'that form the Continental Army, are to be considered no longer in a separate and distinct point of view, but as parts of the whole Army of the United provinces.'[13] The lines of defence were complete, but the British showed no inclination to 'come out' of Boston or form their own fortifications above the ruins of Charlestown. 'We do nothing but watch each other's motions all day at the distance of about a Mile...' Washington wrote to Lund, 'every now and then picking off a straggler when we can catch them without [outside] their Intrenchments.' In return, the British wasted 'a considerable quantity of Powder' cannonading the Continental lines – powder, wrote Washington, that 'we should be very glad to get'.[14]

Their own stores at present would furnish no more than nine rounds a man, the commander told John Hancock, President of Congress, on the 4th. This was a state of affairs that he wished to keep a profound secret. 'Relief both speedy and effectual' was essential. The vital importance of securing gunpowder and arms from other colonies was a constant refrain in his letters to the President. In May, Hancock had been elected, in succession to Peyton Randolph, President of the Second Continental Congress. This role, for which there was no fixed term, was designedly limited. Hancock acted as moderator of Congressional debates and undertook official correspondence. During important business all Congress was adjudged a Committee of the Whole, and Hancock ceded his place to an appointed chairman.

The Commander-in-Chief was prescient in his call for supplies. Though news of it was not to reach Cambridge till the beginning of November, the King issued a Proclamation for Suppressing Rebellion and Sedition in London on 23 August, in response to the events on Bunker Hill. British officials were ordered 'to use their utmost endeavours to withstand and suppress' disorder in Massachusetts and in any other colony where inhabitants were in 'open and avowed rebellion'.[15] George III had refused days earlier to look at the petition that the Continental Congress had crafted on 6 July, affirming loyalty and expressing a wish to avoid conflict. This olive branch from the rebel assembly had admittedly followed fast upon their Declaration of Taking up Arms of the previous day.

In August in Boston the British were already looking ahead to wintering in their current quarters, contracting for 'quantities of coal', as Washington told Hancock. He had therefore set about securing fuel, clothing and cover for his own army as best he could.[16] Huts, winter-proofed, were slowly replacing those of boards in which the majority of troops were originally billeted on Cambridge Common and elsewhere. But his thoughts turned too to Martha and Mount Vernon. He had become alive to the danger that Martha might be in from one who had formerly been a friend and with whom they had often dined when in Williamsburg – Lord Dunmore, Governor of Virginia.

Dunmore had beaten off in May the threatened assault on his Williamsburg palace by Hanover County patriots en route to Congress, headed by Patrick Henry. In early June, he concluded that further residence in Williamsburg was unsustainable. A patriot youth, attempting to break into the town magazine and seize powder there, triggered a booby trap and was killed. Dunmore, who had ordered the trap to be set, attracted widespread condemnation. Different counties of Virginia raised militia, and armed independent companies streamed into the town. Under cover of night on 8 June, the Governor and his family took ship for Yorktown, where they stayed on board in the harbour. Here Dunmore remained, refusing to return to Williamsburg and sending his wife and children home to England.

Patriots feared that Dunmore meant to attack Williamsburg and establish martial law. Detachments of a foot regiment, recruited from General Gage in Boston, served the peer as a marine force. An attempt, which nearly succeeded, was made to seize him in early July, when he paid a rash visit upriver to his farm, Porto Bello. It was hoped he could be forcibly returned to the Governor's Palace and made to resume his gubernatorial duties. But Dunmore had his own ideas. With his 'boiled crabs' – as the *Virginia Gazette* dubbed his scarlet-coated companions – and in a small fleet, he sailed south-east for Norfolk. From this port in the Hampton Roads he directed many successful raids up and down the Chesapeake Bay over the course of the summer, seizing arms and supplies from patriot houses and burning townships.

Perhaps inevitably, rumours circulated that Dunmore intended to sail up the Potomac and kidnap Martha from Mount Vernon. They reached Washington, and, on 20 August, he wrote to Lund: 'I can hardly think that Lord Dunmore can act so low, & unmanly a part, as to think of seizing Mrs Washington by way of revenge upon me.' The passage of letters between Mount Vernon and Cambridge was as slow and erratic as rumour was swift to spread. Washington calculated that his wife would be mostly out of Dunmore's reach 'for 2 or 3 Months to come'. He had Nelly Calvert Custis's accouchement at Mount Airy and Martha's projected visit 'down country' in mind. During that time the fortunes of war, he wrote, might make her removal 'either absolutely necessary, or quite useless'. Should danger threaten more immediately, he told Lund to 'provide a Kitchen for her in [the town house in] Alexandria, or some other place of safety elsewhere for her and my Papers'.[17]

Martha had no intention of altering her plans. Burwell Bassett, who visited Mount Vernon in late August, made no mention, in a letter to Washington of the 30th, of any concern for her safety. His news was all of the third Virginia Convention, chaired by Peyton Randolph, which had been meeting in Richmond. In accordance with the demands of Congress, they had established a Committee of Safety to take the place of royal government in the province, formerly the colony of Virginia. They had agreed to print £350,000. They had approved the raising of two regiments, one of them to be headed by Patrick Henry, and comprising 1,450 men. In addition they had directed that each of sixteen districts in the province should equip

500 men to be called minutemen, and to be 'nearly under the same regulations as the Militia of England'.[18]

All over the Continental seaboard conventions and congresses were taking similar measures. In Fredericksburg Washington's brother-in-law Fielding Lewis was establishing the first Virginian gun manufactory. Everyone, be they young or old, farmer or merchant, appeared to want to fight. Even Congress President John Hancock had written to Washington in July: 'I am Determin'd to Act under you, if it be to take the firelock & Join the Ranks as a Volunteer.'[19] Boston merchant Hancock was to remain Congress President till October 1777, when Henry Laurens, rice planter from South Carolina, succeeded him. Only thereafter did Hancock take up arms, as senior Major General in the Massachusetts militia. At Mount Vernon, as Lund Washington was later to inform his cousin, Martha said repeatedly that she would go to her husband in camp if he allowed it.

In Cambridge Washington was taking advantage of the stalemate between the two armies. He sent some detachments to reinforce Schuyler's forces in New York and others to supplement expeditionary forces against British garrisons in Quebec and Montreal. Peyton Randolph sent word from Virginia on 6 September: 'We heard upon the road that Mrs Washington was very well. She was in Maryland to visit Mrs Custis, who has got a girl.'[20] News of family affairs – Martha's first grandchild did not survive long – and about estate matters was at a premium. Lund swore that he enclosed a letter from Martha with one of his own by the post each week. Washington was as insistent in turn that he wrote home to his wife and cousin every week. The Continental postal service was newly established, and Washington blamed, in a letter to his brother Samuel, 'the infernal curiosity of some of the Scoundrel Postmasters', for the delay or loss of his private correspondence. His secretary, Joseph Reed, upbraided Benjamin Franklin, now Postmaster General, on the subject in late September. Washington wrote to Samuel on the 30th: 'I am distressed exceedingly in my business, not being able to get any directions home in respect to matters that are referred to me from thence.'

Despite the efforts of Reed in Cambridge and Franklin in Philadelphia, the correspondence between the husband and wife and agent remained problematic. Some letters reached the recipient six weeks after they had been committed to the post. Others travelled swiftly. Some never arrived. Not only did the management of the Mount Vernon estate suffer in consequence, but Washington minded the lack of connection with his wife, for so long his daily companion. In his letter to Samuel he imagined Martha's time as hanging 'heavy and lonesome' upon her and begged his brother to visit her: 'her Situation gives me many a painful moment'.[21]

A letter of 5 October from Lund Washington to his cousin in Cambridge was not wholly reassuring about the danger Martha faced at Mount Vernon from Lord Dunmore and his marine force. ''Tis true many people have made a Stir about Mrs Washingtons Continuing at Mt Vernon,' he admitted. Some in Alexandria had earlier expressed concern, and now others joined in. The 'people of Loudon' (Loudoun County), he wrote, talked of sending a Guard to conduct her up into Berkeley in western Virginia, 'with some of their principal men to persuade her to leave this & accept their offer'. Moreover, Washington's brother John Augustine had written to Martha, 'pressing her to leave Mt Vernon'.

Martha stood firm. Lund wrote: 'she does not believe herself in danger, nor do I'. He added: 'Without [unless] they attempt to take her in the dead of Night they would fail, for 10 minutes' notice would be Sufficient for her to get out of the way [by road].' It is plain that Lund did not relish the task of having to persuade Martha to leave her home, should it become necessary: 'I have never Advise'd her to stay nor, Indeed, to go.' Colonel Bassett, who had been visiting, he wrote, thought her in no danger.[22] Washington responded with the practical suggestion that the merchants and gentlemen of Alexandria block the Potomac with *chevaux de frise*, defensive obstacles, so that Lord Dunmore could not proceed upriver.

Relations between Martha and Lund were sometimes strained, and tempers frayed during the absence of the lord and master of the house, as several of the agent's letters to his cousin reveal. Martha

alone had entry to his study and kept the keys of Washington's desk.
She also alone seems to have handled his account books and papers.
Lund applied to her when dealings with estate workmen, tradesmen,
local merchants, or those from further off required it. When one
supplicant, Bennet Jenkins, wanted payment for pursuing claims in
the west on Washington's behalf, Martha searched for the chit showing the sum owed him. 'Mrs Washington Could not find it – I wanted
to put the man off,' wrote Lund to Washington on 15 October, 'but
he murmured & thought it hard not to be paid after coming twice
such a distance for it.' Jenkins had already been turned away once by
Washington, demanding certification that the man had not been paid
by others. 'I was obliged to pay,' Lund ended dismally, a common
ditty in his accounts of clashes with claimants.[23]

At least in this encounter Martha and Lund had acted in unison.
They were not so amicable in the days before she left to go 'down
country' with Jacky and Nelly. Lund was no longer sanguine, by the
end of October, that Mount Vernon would escape the attention of
Lord Dunmore's troops. He wrote to Washington on the 29th: 'from
the accounts I get from you and what we are daily having here, it
looks like lost labour to keep on with our Building – for should they
[those parts of the mansion being altered] get Burned, it will be
provoking – but I shall keep on until I am directed to the contrary by
you'. In the circumstances, Martha had consented, Lund wrote to
the General, to pack the account books and papers that her husband
kept in his study in a trunk. This could be swiftly moved to a place
of safety in case of need. The agent then advised her that she 'should
be carefull to tie the papers in Bundles & put them carefully in'. He
supposed she had done so, Lund wrote, but could not say for sure.
Martha had chosen to do her packing in privacy. She did graciously
consent to leave Lund the key of her husband's study but did not tell
him if there were any 'papers of consequence' in the desk there. He
was resolved, he wrote stiffly, unless it became absolutely necessary,
not to 'look into any part of it, or in any other part of the Study,
without her being present'.[24]

Lund felt all too keenly the responsibility of managing the estate
during his cousin's absence and in these times of war. The First

Continental Congress had forbidden the export of grain as of 10 September this year. Wheat was nowadays the principal crop at Mount Vernon. With a glut on the American market, its price would inevitably fall. Moreover, continuous rain and harsh winds made ploughing and sowing this autumn difficult. Work on the house and garden undertaken with the inheritance from Patsy was nowhere near complete. The 'stucco man' from Fredericksburg was at work for long weeks which lengthened into months, ornamenting the dining-room ceiling. Lund, conscientious, careworn, urged on artisans, overseers, slaves, but the lack of a master was apparent to all. Martha was impatient for the 'stucco man' to start work on the bedchamber in the new southern addition to the house, so that she could 'get into it' that winter. Lund wrote on 15 October: 'if the sides is done in plain Stucco, it will not take him long'.[25]

While Martha stayed 'down country' – first with Fielding and Betty Lewis at their home in Fredericksburg and then with the Bassetts at Eltham – Lund longed for his cousin to return. He had written at the beginning of October: 'I hope to have the pleasure of seeing you this Winter, for, Whether Things are made up or not, I suppose you can Leave the Army in Winter.'[26] On Sunday 22 October he had his answer in the shape of a budget of letters, written on the 2nd, 7th and 9th of the month, from his cousin in camp. Not only would Washington not be coming home, but he wished his wife to join him in Cambridge. No attempt, given the scarce resources of the Continental forces, could be made at present to attack the British. The siege would continue through the winter with the idea of mounting an attack in the spring. The commander wrote to his brother John Augustine on the 13th: 'seeing no great prospect of returning to my Family & Friends this Winter, I have sent an Invitation to Mrs Washington to come to me . . .' He explained that he had laid a 'state of the difficulties' – notably, inclement weather – 'which must attend the journey before her, and left it to her own choice'.[27]

Lund Washington, responding to his cousin on 29 October, had no doubt that Martha would accept her husband's invitation: 'she has often declared she would go to the Camp if you would permit her'.[28] He expedited George's letters to her at Eltham. Martha, with Jacky and Nelly, did not leave that place till 6 November – a delay Lund thought, a week later, 'rather ill judge'd'.[29] She had, however, already settled much by the time she reached Mount Vernon. Jacky and Nelly and Washington's nephew, George Lewis, aged eighteen, were to travel with her to Cambridge. His father, Fielding Lewis, informed Washington that, at the gun manufactory he had established in Fredericksburg, he hoped to have fifty men producing twelve guns a day by the New Year. He begged Washington to find a position with emolument for his son, when once young Lewis reached headquarters: 'I am in hopes you will find him diligent in whatever duty is required of him.'[30]

Mount Vernon became a hive of activity as news spread that the Commander-in-Chief's wife was set to join him in the north. 'This House has been so Crouded with company since Mrs Washington came home', Lund wrote to his cousin on 14 November, 'that I fear many things is left undone that should have been done before she left home.'[31] Martha was unsuccessful in some business she did attempt. 'Mrs Washington could not find any list of your Rents,' Lund was to write to his cousin on the 24th. Leases on Washington and Parke Custis property would be up for renewal in the new year. 'I must endeavour to make out a list from the Leases, & will see if any part of them can be Collected.'[32] Even with a rent-roll there was no guarantee all the tenants would pay up. Virginia planters, farmers and merchants had all suffered, following the recent embargo on exports of tobacco and wheat. Nevertheless, leading merchants in Alexandria, and others who sat on the Fairfax County Committee of Correspondence, were eager to help 'the deserving poor of Boston'. Like other such bodies recently formed elsewhere, the Committee, twenty-five strong, provided a measure of government for the county and raised local issues in correspondence with Congress. They had already shipped flour and beans to Massachusetts. Now they presented Jacky with £53 13s 3d for Washington to distribute as he saw fit.[33]

The conflict that a few months before had been confined to the siege in Boston Bay and to operations in Canada was spreading. News of George III's Proclamation for the Suppression of Rebellion and Sedition spurred on both Government and patriot forces. In

Virginia Dunmore rallied an unexpected force to the British flag. In a Proclamation of his own, on 14 November, he declared martial law in Virginia and offered freedom to all slaves and indentured servants of patriots, capable of bearing arms, in return for military service. He termed the regiment he instituted Lord Dunmore's Ethiopian Regiment, in flowery allusion to the African blood of many of those who answered his call. From Mount Vernon one slave ran away to join up and gain his freedom, and took his wife, a cook, with him. A painter, an indentured servant, also went. Every precaution had always been taken in the colony to prevent armed uprisings by slaves against their masters. Now arms were in the hands of these slaves and being wielded on behalf of the British. Furthermore, the loss of each adult male slave to Dunmore represented, to their owner, a loss of as much as £100 Virginia currency. Sentiment against Dunmore and the British hardened among the Virginian planters accordingly.

Lund and Martha had a final passage of arms before she departed for Cambridge, with Jacky and Nelly, on 14 November. Lund gave an account of it to his cousin in the letter that accompanied Martha to camp: 'In your Letter you speak of Mrs Barnes' – Washington's cousin – 'staying here in the Absence of Mrs Washington', wrote Lund to his cousin, 'to assist in taking care of the Family'. The 'Family' in this instance denoted the household and included those servants and slaves who manned it. 'Mrs Washington seems to think it will not answer . . .' Those few words express much. As a result, 'what to me is very disagreeable', wrote Lund, he must assume, in addition to all his other duties, 'that of Housekeeping'.[34] Milly Posey, Patsy Parke Custis's earlier friend, was, with Martha's approval, appointed to aid Lund in managing the mansion.

Armed with estate accounts and letters, and with an escort of 'good gentlemen' as far as Baltimore, Martha and her companions departed north for Philadelphia. Joseph Reed had left off acting as Washington's secretary so as to attend to his legal practice there, muster-master Stephen Moylan taking his place. Washington wrote to his former secretary on 20 November: 'I expect her Horses will be pretty well fatigued; as they will, by the time she gets to Philadelphia, have performed a journey of at least 450 Miles – my Express finding her among her friends near Williamsburg 150 Miles below my own House.'[35] An 'express' – a letter conveyed by a rider rather than in the post – was the most expensive as well as the swiftest method of carriage.

When Martha reached the Pennsylvanian capital next day, she soon became aware that she was now a person of public interest. 'I don't doubt but you have seen the figure our arrival made in the Philadelphia paper,' she was to write to a correspondent in Alexandria.[36] Shortly after her arrival, John Adams wrote on 25 November from the city to his friend Mercy Otis Warren in Massachusetts: 'you will soon know the person and character of his [Washington's] lady. I hope she has as much ambition for her husband's glory as *Portia* and *Marcia*' – sobriquets for his wife Abigail and for Mercy herself – 'have, and then – the Lord have mercy on the souls of Howe and Burgoyne and all the troops in Boston!'[37] He wrote prophetically. Martha Washington was soon to show herself redoubtable in the Continental cause.

Besieging Boston, 1775–1776

... a number of cannon and shells from
Boston and Bunkers Hill ...

In November 1775, Martha and her companions stayed only a few days in Philadelphia, Joseph Reed and his wife Esther acting as their hosts, before resuming their journey north to Massachusetts. That stay was bedevilled by a spirited argument that developed between some of the Virginian delegates and a caucus of city fathers and Massachusetts Congressional delegates, who included Sam Adams. The former were keen to mark the presence in the town of the wife of the Commander-in-Chief, their fellow Virginian, and planned a ball, to be held on the evening of 24 November at the New Tavern. It was expected that President Hancock's wife as well as Martha would attend. The malcontents argued, with some justification, that such a meeting would run counter to the Eighth Article of the 1774 Congressional Association.

This Eighth Article discouraged 'every species of extravagance and dissipation', including 'exhibitions of shows, plays, and other expensive diversions and entertainments'.[1] In Philadelphia, a Committee of Inspection and Observation enforced the Association, and Christopher Marshall, a member of this body, came to hear of the projected ball on the afternoon of the day it was to take place. Hoping to find President Hancock at the State House at the end of the Congressional day, he met instead Sam Adams, the influential delegate from Massachusetts with whom he had become friendly. Marshall expressed his objections to the ball as well as 'some threats thrown out' of public commotion and of damage to the tavern, should the ball take place. The populace, it would seem, saw no reason why Congress should dissipate when they were deprived of their own habitual assemblies. The Committee had recently proscribed both spring and autumn fairs.

Adams agreed to seek out Hancock and beg the President to 'wait on Lady Washington to request her not to attend or go this evening'. Hancock accepted the task, and Marshall triumphantly informed the ball managers that the entertainment was not to proceed. 'Lady Washington,' as Marshall dubbed her, was having a somewhat weary time of it. She was first visited at the Reed house by John Hancock. Then Marshall and other members of the Committee of Inspection and Observation required audience with her. Before proceeding to inform her of the cancellation of the ball, they expressed at some length the 'great regard and affection' in which they held her, as well as 'the General', her husband. Martha, according to Marshall, received the ambassadors 'with great politeness', thanking the Committee for their kind care and regard 'in giving [her] such timely notice' of the proscription. She assured them that 'their sentiments, on this occasion, were perfectly agreeable unto her own'.[2]

Benjamin Harrison of Berkeley, one of the Virginian delegates and a chief correspondent of Washington's during the early stages of the war, was not so easily satisfied. Furious with Samuel Adams for using his influence to stop the ball, he burst in on Marshall and the Bostonian while they were at dinner that evening. Harrison was probably one of the ball managers and he declared the assembly 'legal, just and laudable'. A heated argument developed. Harrison remained unconvinced by his opponents' arguments. Commented Marshall with satisfaction, 'as he came out of humour, he so returned . . .'[3]

Harrison, brother-in-law to Burwell Bassett and a wealthy planter, was unquestionably an ardent patriot. But he littered his conversation with profanities and obscenities, and aroused Yankee ire in Congress. John Adams condemned him as 'an indolent, luxurious, heavy Gentleman, of no Use in Congress or Committees, but a great

Embarrassment to both'.[4] The prosperous Boston merchant John Hancock was more forgiving, and appointed the Virginian, a veteran of the French and Indian War, to a range of Congressional military committees. Harrison may have been especially keen to honour Martha, given the recent publication in the British press and in America of an intercepted letter he had written to her husband. In the published letter a spurious paragraph was inserted, referring to 'pretty little Kate the Washer-woman's Daughter over the Way, clean, trim and rosey as the Morning'. The paragraph writer continued with an account of how 'Harrison' was deprived of the 'golden glorious opportunity' that was offered when the girl appeared at his door. Had he not been interrupted by the advent of another female whom 'Harrison' dubbed a 'cursed Antidote to Love', he would have 'fitted' Kate 'for my General against his return'.[5]

The original letter contains no such paragraph, but many delegates, the Adams cousins included, believed the paragraph was genuine. Virginians had a reputation for loose and extravagant living. Of the Virginia delegates, John Adams respected only Richard Henry Lee, with whom he exchanged views on the future government of America. That there might be other kinds of Virginians, that Washington was a virtuous husband as well as a commander of merit, was still to emerge. At least Martha's ready acquiescence in the matter of the ball created a favourable impression. Of the fracas in Philadelphia she made no mention when she wrote to Elizabeth Ramsay in Alexandria, merely saying, following her departure north on 26 November with two companies of light horse as an escort: 'I left it in as great pomp as if I had been a very great somebody.'[6]

In the crucible of Philadelphia politics Martha had undergone something of a transformation. She left Mount Vernon a Virginia planter's wife. Now she was 'the amiable consort of his Excellency General Washington', or even, as Christopher Marshall had dubbed her, 'Lady Washington'. The first ship in commission in the recently established Continental navy was purchased in the month Martha passed through Philadelphia. The following spring a row galley, *Lady Washington*, joined the fledgling fleet.

Martha had received the Congressional President and given audience to the Philadelphia sub-committee. These individuals, as much as her military escort on leaving the city, had left her in no doubt that she was indeed 'somebody' in these bewildering and unprecedented revolutionary times. That the term 'Congress' denoted no meeting of minds, even among those who came together as delegates from the same colony, she was also now aware.

Martha had been confident all her life, and she accepted the new attentions as part and parcel of Washington's command. As Miss Dandridge, she had charmed old John Custis. As 'the widow Custis', she had corresponded with London tobacco agents. As Mrs Washington, she had made a new life far from home in northern Virginia. In the past few months she had adamantly refused to leave Mount Vernon despite reports of possible kidnap. She had dealt with her husband's accounts and rents and guarded her home and her husband's papers and possessions against all comers, be they his cousin Lund or Mrs Barnes. But all this she had done as a private individual. Now she embarked on a life in which every action of hers would be closely watched – and judged.

'This is a beautiful country, and we had a very pleasant journey through New England, and had the pleasure to find the General very well,' she wrote from Cambridge to an Alexandria correspondent at the end of December.[7] With General Horatio Gates's wife, Betsy, and her companions from home, she had reached headquarters on the 11th of that month. Martha made no mention of her husband's earlier frustrations and anxieties, but they had been manifold, not least in the matter of his aides-de-camp and secretaries. Washington had written to Reed in Philadelphia on the 20th, begging him – to no avail – to return to the 'family'. The commander was, at Cambridge, well supplied with willing young men who could ride, act as couriers and deliver oral orders. General Charles Lee was to deride the secretarial capabilities of these energetic centaurs: 'you might as well set them the task of translating an Arabick or Irish Manuscript as expect that they should in half a day copy a half sheet of orders'.[8]

Washington wrote of aide-de-camp George Baylor that he was 'not, in the smallest degree, a penman'.[9] He was initially chary of

Robert Hanson Harrison, who had abandoned the law in Alexandria to serve as his secretary. By late January 1776 he was living on terms of 'unbounded confidence' with the young man and his other principal secretary, Stephen Moylan.[10] Whatever their shortcomings, Martha took a lively interest in the young men who attended on her husband, who lived with them and Jacky and Nelly, and who dined with them and other guests at headquarters.

In advance of Martha's arrival at Cambridge, Moylan had sent for limes, lemons and oranges from a cargo on board a British brig inbound from Antigua. The vessel, heading 'for the use of the army and navy at Boston', had been captured and was soon to be added to the fledgling Continental fleet. 'The General will want some of each, as well as the sweetmeats and pickles that are on board, as his lady will be here today, or tomorrow . . .' wrote the secretary.[11] On 11 December Ebenezer Austin, the steward at the Vassall house, recorded in his cash book that 'ten baskets of oysters', for which Martha had a fondness all her life, were purchased. Though the army lacked powder and shirts, Austin's accounts show that the Massachusetts Bay and its hinterland supplied the household with ample quantities of fish, roast and boiled meats, gammon and 'fowls'. Purchases that he made following Martha's arrival at the Vassall house – a dozen 'cups and saucers' – may reflect her wish to dispense, even amidst the administrative mayhem at headquarters, genteel hospitality.[12]

The presence of fellow Virginians was undoubtedly congenial to Martha in this unfamiliar New England town and in this military context. She informed Miss Ramsay, her Alexandria correspondent, in her budget of news on 30 December: 'Your friends Mr [Robert Hanson] Harrison and [David] Henley [another aide and Alexandria resident] are both very well and I think they are fatter than they were when they came to the camp.' She added: 'the girls may rest satisfied on Mr Harrison's account. He seems too fond of his country to give his heart to any but one of his Virginia friends.' Aides-de-camp in search of romance at headquarters laboured anyway under this disadvantage: 'there are but two young ladies in Cambridge, and a very great number of gentlemen, so you may guess how much is made of them'. Martha dismissed them: 'but neither of them is pretty, I think'.[13]

Coincidental with Martha's arrival in Cambridge had been that of two exotic travellers, Messieurs Emmanuel de Pliarne and Pièrre Penet, Frenchmen respectively from Cap François, a trading post on the island of Hispaniola, and from Nantes, a busy port in France. As they spoke no language but French – and, in the case of M. Penet from Nantes, Latin – conversation with the Washingtons, who had neither language, was restricted. Their proposals, however, were welcome. Without the knowledge of the French government, they wished to supply the Continental army with arms and ammunition from France and with other supplies from the Caribbean in return for tallow, tobacco and other American goods.

Washington directed the foreign adventurers on to Congress to meet with the Secret Committee of Correspondence, which had recently been established to explore support in Europe. Benjamin Harrison and Benjamin Franklin were among its members, as was wealthy New York lawyer and delegate John Jay. Martha had a good return for her Cambridge hospitality, when the adventurers wrote to Washington to offer bounty. Secretary Moylan translated the letter from the French: 'Deign, Sir, we pray you, to prevail on Madam Your Lady, to accept of Some of the Fruits of our [French West Indian] Colonies, to which we have added, one bottle of Martinique Liqueur – two bottles of Ratafia, three [left blank in translation] of fruit preserved in brandy – one dozen of Oranges, and fifty Small Loaves of Sugar.'[14]

The French colonial produce was pressed into immediate service. In occupied Boston, British general Henry Clinton inhabited John Hancock's fine house on Beacon Hill. Meeting houses were made riding schools, and churches became barracks. Bostonians who had fled the city and Massachusetts patriots all came calling at the Vassall house. One cleric and his wife who came calling on 19 December were 'Treated with oranges and a glass of wine', and urged to stay to dine.[15] Washington's mood during the first weeks Martha was with him was sombre. Enlistments for the New Year stood at only 5,253 on the day she arrived in camp. A month earlier there had been more than 14,000

troops enlisted, but Connecticut troops who had performed bravely at
Bunker Hill had recently disgraced themselves. Having pledged to
remain till the New Year when new troops would enlist, they made for
home at the end of November, when their service officially ended.
Some departed even before the month was up, taking with them arms
and blankets badly needed for those still in camp.

Writing of this 'scandalous conduct' to Hancock in Philadelphia
in early December, Washington stated that he had called in 5,000
Massachusetts and New Hampshire militiamen as a stopgap measure. But he stressed that 'the Same defection is much to be apprehended,
when the time of the Massachusetts Bay, New Hampshire, & Rhode
Island Forces are expired' – on 31 December.[16] If more troops did not
come in at the New Year, the diminished Continental army would
find it hard to withstand the British, should they launch an attack in
January.

During anxious days at the end of 1775 the Washingtons dined out
at the quarters occupied by 'Old Put', as Major General Israel Putnam
from Connecticut was known. This veteran of the French and Indian
War and hero at Bunker Hill had command of divisions between
Prospect Hill and the Charles River, but proved powerless to prevent
his countrymen making for home.

George and Martha dined out, too, at Medford with General
Charles Lee, a Continental offcer, once of the British army, well
known to both Washingtons. Lee had engaged Washington at
Mount Vernon over New Year in discussions about American
independent companies. He also borrowed a sum of money so as
to travel to his next port of call. This was a debt which he had not
to date repaid.[17]

Washington valued Lee's military record in Europe as well as in
America, and was well aware that the presumptuous officer believed
his experience should have secured him the post of Commander-in-
Chief. Abrasive, eccentric and foul-mouthed, Lee, however, was not
the kind of man to endear himself to Congress.

Washington's Adjutant General, Horatio Gates, was another
professional soldier who might have aspired to become Commander-
in-Chief. Twenty years earlier, Gates, like Lee and Washington – and,

indeed, Thomas Gage, till lately in command of the British forces in Boston – had taken part in the ill-fated Braddock expedition. Unlike Washington, Gates had served in the French and Indian War until its close, and thereafter in Minorca during the wider conflict. But, like Lee, Gates was an Englishman and, like Lee, had served in America as a regular British officer. Admittedly, since 1772 he had been living, with his wife, Betsy, in western Virginia. Lee, too, had recently been peregrinating around America. Notwithstanding, neither man's greater military experience nor current residence could vanquish Washington's trump card as Commander-in-Chief of the Continental army: he was American born and bred. Though he had so wished for a regular commission, his service in the colonial forces in the French and Indian War was now a badge of honour.

Betsy Gates was a seasoned army wife and a pleasant companion at headquarters who accompanied Martha on numerous outings. Nelly Custis, who might have been of their party, was apparently still 'getting well', following the earlier loss of her child.[18] She appeared infrequently, much later apparently confessing that the 'bombs' that came over the river from the British had alarmed her greatly.[19] Martha confirmed in her letter to Miss Ramsay in late December 1775 the existence of these missiles: 'some days we have a number of cannon and shells from Boston and Bunkers Hill', she wrote, 'but it does not seem to surprise anyone but me. I confess I shudder every time I hear the sound of a gun.' But her enthusiasm for 'the cause' – and her curiosity – overcame any fears she might have had for her personal safety. She made an excursion to Prospect Hill, which Putnam's forces had taken in June. From that eminence Martha 'took a look at poor Boston and Charleston', as she informed Miss Ramsay. The latter settlement, which the British had torched, was in ruins, with 'only a few chimneys standing in it'. There seemed to be a number of very fine buildings in Boston, wrote this eyewitness from afar. How long they would stand, she added, 'God knows'. Of the harbour she had a clear view, and could see the British pulling up all the wharves for firewood. 'To me that never see [saw] anything of war, the preparations are very terable [terrible] indeed,' she confided.

But she endeavoured, she wrote, to keep her fears as much to herself as she could.[20] In this she was successful. 'Lady Washington' appeared calm, just as her husband's public utterances gave every indication that he expected a successful outcome. This was far from the case.

Not the least of the troubles to contend with was an epidemic of smallpox which developed in and around Boston. Dr Morgan supervised the inoculation of all troops who had not had the disease. His wife Mary, who had come with him to Cambridge in November 1775, was much at headquarters while her husband was occupied. She wrote later to her own mother that Martha and Nelly had been 'as a mother and sister' to her, 'Mrs Gates the same'.[21]

Meanwhile Congress had been slow and parsimonious in answering Washington's call for funds. He wrote to Hancock on Christmas Day 1775: 'The Gentlemen by whom you Sent the money are arrived. The Sum they brought, tho' Large, is not Sufficient to answer the demands of the Army, which at this time are remarkably heavy.'[22] He informed, cajoled and exhorted Congress by turns. The clothing sent to Thomas Mifflin, Quartermaster General, was not sufficient to put half the army into regimentals, he wrote on New Year's Eve. He hoped they would sanction his decision to re-enlist those 'free negroes' who had already served in the Continental army. He had feared that, if they were dismissed, they would seek employment with the enemy forces.[23] No issue was too small for him to consider. He wrote of the need to continue the butter allowance to the troops. Always in the guise of a respectful servant, he pressed Congress to respond. The stark truth was, as he wrote to Hancock on New Year's Eve, the army that would enlist the following day, 1 January 1776, numbered 9,650 men. Congress in June had authorized the raising of 20,000.

Washington's task in these days would have overwhelmed a commander with fewer organizational skills. 'It is not in the pages of History perhaps, to furnish a case like ours,' he was to write to Hancock in Philadelphia on 4 January 1776, summarizing his burden, 'to maintain a post within Musket Shot of the Enemy for Six months together, without [powder]'.[24] He had to disband one army and, at the same time, recruit another. The same day he wrote in similar vein to Reed at Philadelphia: 'For more than two Months past I have scarcely immerged from one difficulty before I have plunged into another – how it will end God in his great goodness will direct, I am thankful for his protection to this time.'[25]

Before Martha's arrival Washington had, on several occasions, observed, at the 'meeting house' in Harvard Square, the Puritan form of worship that most held to in New England. Christ Church, the Anglican church on Cambridge Common, had lost both minister and parishioners when the occupants of Tory Row vacated the town in 1774. It had of late been used as a barracks for Virginia and Maryland riflemen. With their passage into winter quarters, the church on the Common, though battered and with a broken organ, resumed its former function on at least one occasion. Aide-de-camp Colonel William Palfrey wrote to his wife on 1 January 1776: 'What think you of my turning parson? I yesterday [New Year's Eve], at the request of Mrs Washington, performed divine service at the church at Cambridge. There was present the General and lady, Mrs Gates, Mrs Curtis [Custis], and a number of others, and they were pleased to compliment me on my performance.' Martha had made a good choice of her 'parson'. In civilian life Palfrey had been an able adjutant to John Hancock in his mercantile business in Boston and was now in demand as a competent aide-de-camp. Currently serving General Lee, he was soon to be purloined by Washington. 'I made a form of prayer, instead of the prayer for the King, which was much approved,' he wrote.[26]

The 'Prayer for the King's Majesty', in the 1662 Book of Common Prayer, increasingly presented a difficulty. Sunday after Sunday, ever more disenchanted with the monarch, the Washingtons and other Anglican patriots in America responded 'Amen' to the following: 'strengthen him that he may vanquish and overcome all his enemies . . .'[27] The earlier belief that the King was innocent, that his ministers were responsible for crimes against the colonies, was fading. Palfrey's prayer effectively substituted Washington for the King as the focus for prayer: 'Be with thy servant, the Commander-in-chief of the American forces. Afford him thy presence in all his undertakings; strengthen him, that he may vanquish and overcome all his enemies; and grant that we may, in thy due time, be restored to the enjoyment of those inestimable blessings we have been deprived of by the devices of cruel and bloodthirsty men, for the sake of thy Son Jesus Christ our Lord.' The assembled company appreciated the rousing and seditious prayer, and Martha asked if she might have it. 'I gave it to Mrs Washington . . . and did not keep a copy, but will get one and send it you,' the gratified aide told his wife on 2 January.[28]

To the relief of Washington, the British in Boston, now under the command of General William Howe, did not attack. The American regiments slowly filled and, in General Orders, Washington named the new force 'in every point of View . . . entirely Continental'. A measure of relief – even hilarity – was felt by all in camp when the British mistook a new-minted standard for a flag of surrender.[29] But such emotions were short-lived. Copies of the speech that the King had given in London on the opening of Parliament on 26 October circulated early in the New Year: 'The rebellious War now levied is become more general', the speech read in part, 'and is manifestly carried on for the Purpose of establishing an independent Empire . . . It is now become the Part of Wisdom and (in its Effects) of Clemency, to put a speedy End to these Disorders by the most decisive Exertions.' The speech told of the increase of the naval establishment, of ground forces, and of offers of support from foreign allies. An expeditionary force would soon be dispatched across the Atlantic. The monarch was confident of victory, and the speech ran on: 'When the unhappy and deluded Multitude, against whom this Force will be directed shall become sensible of their Error, I shall be ready to receive the Misled with Tenderness and Mercy.'[30] Enclosing a copy of the document, Washington wrote to Hancock on 4 January: 'It is full of rancour & resentment, and explicitly holds forth his Royal will to be, that vigorous measures must be pursued to deprive us of our constitutional rights & liberties . . . Majesty', he reflected bitterly, was 'a name which ought to promote the blessings of his people & not their oppression.'[31]

On the 7th Washington asked John Adams, who was then at Watertown, to share 'pot luck' at headquarters.[32] It was anticipated that the British expeditionary force would strike first at New York. The commander wished to dispatch Charles Lee from Massachusetts to shore up defences there. Washington established, with Adams, that the original scope of his commission from Congress – to take command of the army at Cambridge – had widened. He was Commander-in-Chief of the Continental army, wherever it was posted. Washington duly dispatched Lee. The possibility of British reinforcements from England rendered the security of the Boston Bay area perilous. Mercy Otis Warren, wife of James, newly President of the Massachusetts Provincial Congress, wrote to Martha, offering a safe haven at Watertown, further inland. In reply – in the third person – Martha was polite but firm. 'If the exigency of affairs in this camp should make it necessary for her to remove, she cannot but esteem it a happiness to have so friendly an invitation as Mrs Warren has given.'[33] For the time being she remained at her husband's side.

In mid-January Washington wrote to Reed of experiencing 'many an uneasy hour when all around me are wrapped in Sleep'. At a council of war on the 8th it was agreed that the New England colonies should be called on to supply thirteen regiments of militia to reinforce the new Continental army. Even before they could be mustered, on New Year's Eve news came of disaster at Quebec. Besieging the Canadian city, American General Richard Montgomery had been killed, and his fellow General, Benedict Arnold, severely wounded. Accordingly, three of the new regiments forming were diverted north to aid in the continuing siege. Ammunition in the American lines facing Boston was in no greater supply than troops. Were he to overcome the innumerable difficulties he faced, Washington averred, 'I shall most religiously believe that the finger of Providence is in it, to blind the Eyes of our Enemys; for surely if we get well through this Month, it must be for want of their knowing the disadvantages we labour under.' He was determined to attack, as soon as the harbour froze over and troops could traverse the ice from Dorchester and Roxbury to Boston.[34]

George Washington wearing the uniform of the colonial Virginia Regiment. Painted by Charles Willson Peale at Mount Vernon in 1772.

Martha Dandridge Custis two years before she married George. Painted in 1757 by John Wollaston.

ABOVE LEFT: Mount Vernon, aerial photograph, showing the distinctive piazza and extensive grounds high above the Potomac.

RIGHT: View of the mansion from the north showing the servants' hall. Painted in 1857 by Eastman Johnson.

ABOVE RIGHT: Mount Vernon, looking south, c. 1802. Watercolour by William Russell Birch.

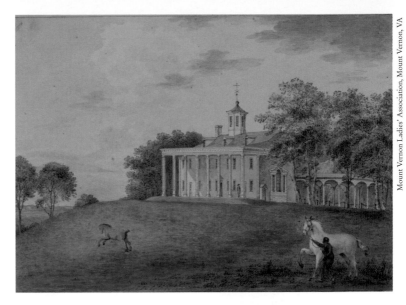

Both portraits by Charles Willson Peale, 1772, Mount Vernon Ladies' Association, Mount Vernon, VA

Patsy Parke Custis at about sixteen.

Jacky Parke Custis at seventeen.

National Gallery of Art, Washington

Presidential home life with Martha's grandchildren by Edward Savage, 1798.

John Trumbull's depiction of Washington at Verplanck's Point, 1782.

Washington resigns his commission, Annapolis, 1783. Martha, shown here in the gallery, in fact awaited him at Mount Vernon. Painted by John Trumbull.

Martha, painted by Peale at her husband's request, during the presidential years in Philadelphia.

Gilbert Stuart's famous portrait of 1797 shows Washington renouncing a third term.

Washington sought support and aid wherever he might find them. Towards the end of the month, he and Martha dined at Thomas Mifflin's in Cambridge. Six or seven Cagnawawa sachems (chiefs) and warriors were of the company and pledged support. The New Englanders present were somewhat at a loss. The Commander-in-Chief was familiar, from colonial military service and earlier, with the customs of Native Americans. He introduced John Adams, who was in the company and now of the Massachusetts General Court, as a member of the 'Grand Council'. The visitors looked on the lawyer with new respect.[35]

Martha continued resilient, whether at her husband's side on social occasions or overseeing the various needs of the household at the Vassall house. 'Nelly Custis . . . I believe, is with child,' she wrote to her sister Nancy Bassett at the end of January. Nelly was indeed in the early stages of pregnancy, and would in due course give birth in Virginia to a second child in August. Cautious following the early death of Nelly's first child the previous summer, Martha wrote, 'I hope no accident [miscarriage] will happen to her in going back.' She continued: 'I have not thought about it much yet. God knows where we shall be.' She supposed there would be 'a change' in the military situation soon but when she could not pretend to say. The winter continued mild, she added: 'the rivers have never been frozen hard enough to walk upon the ice since I came here'.[36]

Freezing weather in February brought the ice for which Washington had waited so impatiently – 'some pretty strong Ice from Dorchester Point to Boston Neck and from Roxbury to the Common', he informed Hancock. Troops could now attack the town from the south. He advocated a 'bold & resolute Assault upon the Troops in Boston with such Men as we had'. But a council of war, including the generals on his staff, voted against attack. Washington argued that this was the best recourse they had, when they neither had nor could expect enough powder to initiate 'a regular Cannonade & Bombardment'. The council opposed him. Knowing that 'the eyes of the whole Continent' were fixed on Cambridge, in 'anxious expectation of hearing of some great event', he could only wait for men and powder, uneasily aware that with the spring tides British reinforcements could sail at will into Boston Bay.[37]

At least the Continental army was now supplied with ordnance – sixty tons of cannon and mortars from Fort Ticonderoga, which patriot forces had seized in the spring. Henry Knox, a Boston bookseller turned artillery man, had supervised the transport of this heavy booty on ox-drawn sleds. He reached Cambridge, three hundred miles to the south, on 27 January. Five days later, he and his wife, Lucy Flucker Knox, received a formal – if ungrammatical – invitation, in the handwriting of George Baylor, whom Washington had dubbed 'no penman': 'Thursday evening, Feby 1st. The General & Mrs Washington, present their compliments to Colonel Knox & Lady, begs the favor of their company at dinner on Friday, half after 2 o'Clock.'[38] Washington grew to count on Knox, above all others, for strategic advice. But Henry and Lucy, though so much younger – Henry was twenty-five, Lucy, twenty – also became friends with George and Martha. Impetuous, headstrong Lucy was beguiling. An heiress, she had flouted the wishes of her father, a prominent government official in Boston, when she married bookseller Henry. But the young Knoxes – both of them tall and broad – were well matched. Both were enthusiastic patriots, both loved literature – and both enjoyed the pleasures of the table, as their wide girth evidenced.

Cannon was useless without gunpowder, but by degrees small parcels of it arrived in camp. Washington was cautiously optimistic in a letter to Burwell Bassett of 28 February: 'We are preparing to take possession of a post' – Dorchester Heights – '(which I hope to do in a few days – if we can get provided with the means) which will, it is generally thought, bring on a rumpus between us & the enemy, but whether it will or not – time only Can show.'[39] To Reed nine days later he wrote with justifiable pride: 'On Monday Night [5 March], I took possession of the Heights of Dorchester with two thousand Men under the Command of General Thomas.' To divert attention from their night-time entrenchments on the hill, he added, 'we began on Saturday night [the 3rd] a Cannonade and Bombardment' of Boston itself. This, 'with Intervals, was continued through the

Night. The same on Sunday. And on Monday a continued roar [of cannon] from Seven O'clock till day light was kept up between the Enemy and us.'

Howe, fully occupied with an artillery defence of the town, paid no heed to the heights across the bay to the south. Henry Clinton, his second-in-command, had sailed for the Carolinas to assess military opportunities there. Washington and Thomas had 'upwards of 300 teams in motion at the same Instant carrying on our fascines [brushwood to fortify the position] & other materials to the Neck', and the moon was 'Shining in its full lustre' all night. But only as day broke on the Tuesday morning, the 6th, did the British come to notice the occupation.[40] American observers saw every sign that the British in the town had been cast into utter confusion by both the bombardment and the fortification of the Heights. Would they now 'come out' and attack?

It was an outcome that Washington declared he would welcome and which, it seemed at first, might occur. Knox's cannon from Dorchester Heights were out of range of British cannon in Boston. Howe aimed to take the position with a thousand troops launched by sea. A violent storm, however, brewed up on the afternoon of the 6th, and drove his transports, with troops on board, back to base. Thereafter, there was every sign that the British were making haste to evacuate Boston. There was, in short, to be no attack, no battle. Washington had to be content with the seizure of Dorchester Heights as a 'great event'. In the days that followed, Knox wrote from headquarters to Lucy, who had recently given birth to their first child elsewhere in Massachusetts: 'certain it is they [the enemy] are packing up & going off bag & baggage'. The destination of the transports and troops, on their departure, was uncertain. 'If to New York, my Dear Lucy must prepare to follow them,' Knox wrote with youthful energy. 'As we are Citizens of the World, any place will be our home & equally cheap.'[41]

In his letter to his wife, Knox voiced anxiety that the government forces would reduce their hometown to a 'pile of rubbish' before leaving. The British duly demolished the castle and fortifications and rendered some artillery useless before they withdrew on 17 March.

But Washington, who toured Boston as soon as the enemy had departed, found that damage to the town was less extensive than he had feared. He told President Hancock on the 19th: 'your house has receiv'd no damage worth mentioning. Your furniture is in tolerable Order and the family pictures are all left entire and untouch'd.'[42] The British sailed for Halifax in Nova Scotia, where Howe was to await reinforcements from across the Atlantic. Washington, however, had no idea where the enemy was headed. Fearing that they meant to make for New York, he dispatched Continental troops south under Putnam to bolster the forces there led by Lee. Philip Schuyler, in New York, was still nominally in charge of the northern department, but he was now an invalid. Brass padlocks and 'a trunk' appear in the Vassall house accounts under the date 1 April 1776. The Washingtons, with much of the Continental army remaining in Massachusetts, would soon themselves leave for New York.[43]

Before she left Cambridge, Martha received a visit from Mercy Otis Warren, who had, in January, offered her asylum. Mercy did not stay to dine, though 'much urg'd'. On this occasion Mrs Warren, a devastating critic, noted of Nelly Calvert Custis that 'a kind of Languor about her prevents her being so sociable as some Ladies'. Nelly was pregnant, admittedly, but she was indeed very passive in character. Martha, far from langorous, sent the Washington 'chariot' for her new friend next day, and together they toured the 'Deserted Lines of the Enemy And the Ruins of Charleston'. Mrs Warren wrote this encomium of her new friend to Abigail Adams: 'her affability, Candor and Gentleness, Qualify her to soften the hours of private Life or to sweeten the Cares of the Hero and smooth the Rugged scenes of War'.[44]

When the Washingtons embarked on their journey south to duties at headquarters in New York, Mercy was not alone in feeling she had lost a friend in Martha. Dr Morgan remained in Cambridge to tend to the sick, and his wife missed Martha's company. But Martha's focus, for all her care of friends, family and members of staff, remained, as it had been ever since they married, her husband. When he was content, so was she. 'I am happy . . . to find, and to hear from different Quarters, that my reputation stands fair – that my Conduct hitherto has given universal Satisfaction,' Washington, on the point of leaving Cambridge, wrote to his brother John Augustine.[45] Within a few months, with his conduct under scrutiny and his reputation under fire, Martha would be more than ever needed to 'soften the hours of private Life . . . and smooth the Rugged scenes of War'.

New York and Philadelphia, 1776

. . . the place shall not be carried without some loss . . .

Washington reached New York on 13 April 1776, in company with his new aide William Palfrey, secretary Stephen Moylan and General Horatio Gates. Martha, travelling more slowly with her pregnant daughter-in-law and Jacky, arrived four days later. Three years earlier young Parke Custis had enjoyed a privileged existence at King's College, under the supervision of President Myles Cooper. The city was much changed now. A new Revolutionary Committee of Safety was in power, while Royal Governor William Tryon hovered in a British man-of-war in the harbour. All but five regiments of those that Washington had commanded at Cambridge were now stationed in the city. King's College was closed, and served as an army hospital. Dr Cooper himself, condemned for publishing tracts arguing that opposition to the Crown constituted treason, had taken ship for England, never to return.

The Washingtons established themselves in an elegant house on Richmond Hill, a mile and a half north of the city, belonging to Abraham Mortier, British army paymaster. New Yorker Mary Smith was employed as housekeeper and kept the accounts. Caleb Gibbs, an officer with the 14th Continental Regiment from Marblehead, Massachusetts, captained a company known as 'the guard', formed in March to protect the chief from attack. Yankee Gibbs himself was cheerful and capable, but some of the men under him proved irksome.

Though proud of their duty, they were not quick to perform it and consumed rather more than their fair share of food and drink.

Facing the Hudson, the Mortier property offered views of the New Jersey shore opposite, of the city southward and of farmland northward. The grounds included a large enclosed flower garden, shrubs and venerable oaks. There was little time for the Washingtons to enjoy these amenities together. The commander, whether at work here or at his official headquarters on Broadway in town, was overseeing the completion of fortifications to the city. Charles Lee, who had begun this work, was now in the south with orders to combat Clinton in the Carolinas. Washington reconnoitred, in addition, Staten Island and Long Island. His aim was to see all the places where Howe and his forces might possibly land. No matter where the British troopships which had earlier left Boston harbour might be currently located, their goal, in the opinion of the American commander, was New York. Wherever he was located, the General was, with his aides, engaged in correspondence. As at Cambridge, he pressed Congress for more arms, more men and more money.

Washington wrote from New York to President Hancock in Philadelphia on 23 April, pleading for an increase in pay for Robert Hanson Harrison, acting secretary, and other aides-de-camp. The letter attests to the burden of business undertaken at headquarters: 'nothing but the zeal of those gentlemen who live with me and act in this capacity for the great American cause and personal attachment to me, has induced them to undergo the trouble and confinement they have experienced since they have become members of my family. I give into no kind of amusements myself, consequently those about me can have none, but are confined from morn till eve hearing, and answering the applications and letters of one and another . . .' This work would, he expected, only increase as the business of the 'Northern and Eastern departments' passed through his hands.

'If these gentlemen had the same relaxation from duty as other officers have in their common routine,' he continued, 'there would not be so much in it, but to have the mind always upon the stretch – scarce ever unbent – and no hours for recreation, makes a material odds.'[1] By way of recompense, three days later his aides received the rank of lieutenant-colonel. If their minds were 'always upon the stretch – scarce ever unbent', how much more so was that of their commander.

Early in May Washington wrote again to Hancock: 'The designs of the Enemy are too much behind the Curtain, for me to form any accurate opinion of their Plan of Operations for the Summers Campaign; we are left to wander therefore in the field of conjecture . . .'[2] It had by now emerged that Howe and his forces were massed at Halifax in Nova Scotia. There was no doubt in Washington's mind that the British meant to gain control of the Hudson and thus isolate New England. It was anyone's guess whether they intended, proceeding up the St Lawrence, to advance down the Hudson on New York. They might instead sail down the coast, attack the city, and advance up the river. He had written to Hancock on 26 April: 'for anything we know, I think it not improbable they may attempt both . . . if they have men'.

The difficulties that Washington had faced, overseeing the siege of Boston, were as nothing to the oppressive responsibilities that were now his as Commander-in-Chief of the continental army. Word from Lee in the south came sporadically. There were not men enough to defend successfully the approach to the Hudson in the north and to garrison New York as well. Nine regiments had perforce been dispatched to Canada, where Continental troops were battered by disease as much as by the British army. There were those far off in Congress who clamoured for more troops to be sent north, advocating that Washington himself take the northern command. But he had made his position clear on the 26th: 'I Could wish indeed that the Army in Canada should be more powerfully reinforced, at the Same time I am Conscious, that trusting this important post (which is now become the Grand Magazine of America)' – New York – 'to the handful of men remaining here is running too great a risque . . .' Securing the Hudson was also of vital importance. 'I cannot at present advise the Sending any more troops from hence.'[3] As ever, Washington declared that he remained the servant of Congress and would do its bidding.

Though he continued to believe that the British would strike at New York, Washington was aware that he courted disaster, were Howe instead to launch all his forces down the St Lawrence. Martha remained behind at the Mortier house when her son and daughter-in-law left at the end of April for Virginia and Mount Airy, where Nelly would have her accouchement later in the summer. Jacky Parke Custis, for all his faults, was alive to the profound affection that existed between his mother and stepfather. He wrote from home, in June, that, in Martha, George had the one person who could 'alleviate the Care and Anxiety which public Transactions may occasion'.[4]

Martha had it in mind to undergo, in Philadelphia, inoculation for smallpox. The city boasted several physicians of repute who specialized in the procedure. 'I doubt her resolution,' wrote her husband Washington to his brother John Augustine on 29 April. No doubt he recalled Martha's fears where her son's inoculation had been concerned.[5] But when he was called to Congress to discuss the military options a month later, Martha went as well. Her motive in seeking inoculation at Philadelphia is clear from the June letter that Jacky wrote to Washington, following the conclusion of the operation: 'She can now attend you to any Part of the Continent with pleasure, unsullied by the Apprehensions of that Disorder . . . Your happiness when together will be much greater than when you are apart.'[6]

Martha had been bold this April, in going with Mrs Warren into the ruins of Charlestown, an area where smallpox had festered over previous months. In Virginia, too, the disease had broken out in January. Patriots rejoiced at the deaths of more than 300 emancipated slaves and indentured servants, and numerous British officers and sergeants, in Lord Dunmore's Ethiopian Regiment. Smallpox proved still more inimical to the Continental forces besieging Quebec. Over half of the 1,900 men there were diseased. The siege was raised in May, and the Continentals retreated south to Ticonderoga, pursued by British regulars. If Martha was determined to follow her husband wherever the vagaries of war should lead him, her inoculation was a very necessary measure.

President Hancock and his wife inhabited a large and airy house on Arch Street in Philadelphia. Hearing of Martha's resolution to take lodgings, while in that city, on Chestnut Street, Hancock wrote to Washington: 'Mrs Hancock will esteem it an Honour to have Mrs Washington inoculated in her House . . . I am informed Mr Randolph has not any Lady about his House to take the necessary care of Mrs Washington.'[7] Benjamin Randolph, master craftsman, sold cabinetwork and chair work at the 'Sign of the Golden Eagle'. He rented out rooms at the same establishment. Delegates to Congress – including Washington himself the previous year – were Randolph's clients of late. Though there was no other 'lady about his house', Martha had no need of one. As a Virginia lady, she travelled with her own maids – favoured house slaves from Mount Vernon. Her husband had at his various headquarters as 'body servant' or valet Billy Lee. This slave had, at home, among much else, accompanied his master out hunting. While Washington, lodging elsewhere, embarked on a slew of meetings with Congress, Martha was infected with the pox at Chestnut Street on 23 May, the day she arrived in Philadelphia.

Washington was – privately – disappointed by his dealings with Congress. The representatives of whole provinces were still 'feeding themselves upon the dainty food of reconciliation', he wrote on 31 May to his brother John Augustine. Rumours, widespread, that Britain was sending across the Atlantic commissioners bent on peace were acting in the House as 'a clog' to preparations for the defence of America. Washington wrote of his belief that 'the Idea was only to deceive, and throw us off our ground'. The only 'Commissioners' he believed in were the mercenaries from Hesse-Cassel and other German principalities hired by the British government who, according to intelligence, were sailing to America to swell the regulars there.[8]

The commander followed the progress of his wife's inoculation with anxious care from his own Philadelphia lodgings at Benjamin Randall's. Martha showed some bravery in being inoculated – probably by Dr William Shippen Jr – immediately on reaching the city. Most doctors – profitably – had their patients follow a regimen for weeks preceding the administration of the pox, with several weeks of isolation and convalescence to follow. Jacky's inoculation in Baltimore, on which Boucher had made detailed reports, had followed such a pattern. But Shippen and other physicians were fast moving to a belief that neither preparation nor prolonged convalescence was needed. Washington wrote to Burwell Bassett on 4 June that Martha was 'like to have it very favourably, having got through the Fever and not more than about a dozen Pustules appearing (this being the 13th day since the Infection was received)'.⁹ Five days earlier he had written to his brother John Augustine. Martha had thought it prudent to enclose no letter to her sister-in-law – 'notwithstanding', wrote her husband, 'there could be but little danger in conveying the Infection in this Manner'.¹⁰ Martha conformed to convention in abstaining from letter-writing while infectious. It was still widely believed that paper as well as clothes and other materials could carry the disease. She kept at least one appointment, when others would have convalesced. She and Washington both acceded to President Hancock's wish that they sit for three-quarter-length portraits to Charles Willson Peale, and gave the artist a sitting apiece.

In more peaceable times Peale had painted Washington in colonial uniform, as well as Jacky and Patsy, at Mount Vernon. Now, making a name for himself in Philadelphia, the ambitious young artist portrayed Washington in regimental buff and blue and against a background recalling the triumphant siege of the spring. Both portraits in oil – of the Commander-in-Chief and of his consort – were on show in Peale's studio on Arch Street through the summer and attracted the attention of delegates and citizens. Mezzotints of the companion images went on sale and were widely disseminated. These went some way to satisfy a public in this new America eager to know more of their chief General and his consort. Though Washington's portrait in oils survives, that of 'Lady Washington' has vanished. The engravings show her with pearls in her hair, standing, with one elbow resting on a monumental table. She wears a loose gown with billowing sleeves. A tail of brown hair is pulled forward over one breast.¹¹ The overwhelming impression is, if pleasing, also sober. It is implied that this is a woman given to grave reflection. A pilastered wall and classical view glimpsed through the window behind her lends something of the antique to the composition.

In the general confusion that reigned about the part that women might bear in an independent America, it became fashionable in learned circles to look to erudite or patriotic women of the Roman republic for models. Delegate John Adams was to write to his wife, Abigail, in August: 'In reading history, you will generally observe, when you light upon a great character, whether a general, a statesman, or philosopher, some female about him, either in the character of a mother, wife, or sister, who has knowledge and ambition above the ordinary level of women, and that much of his eminence is owing to her precepts, example, or instigation, in some shape or other.'[12]

Despite the nod to the antique in Peale's portrait of Martha, she hardly fits with Adams's model. She had no 'knowledge and ambition above the ordinary level of women' in the narrow sense. She read devotional literature at the beginning and end of each day. When she was at leisure, the books she liked were novels. Washington's 'eminence' was not owing to her exhortation. And yet she was supremely important to him. Theirs was not, in short, a marriage on the virtuous Roman model that so appealed to Adams and other contemporaries. Something of Martha's own confident and attractive personality emerges from the mezzotints. She appears sure of herself and at her ease, unrestrained by others' classical notions.

Martha, who was far more interested than her husband in the art of portraiture, also sat this summer for a miniature, which survives. Four years earlier, when Patsy still lived and before war had come to America, Peale had created a luxurious image for her son.[13] Everything about this new image is sober and realistic. Martha's hair is powdered but otherwise without ornament, and her dress is dark. At her neck she wears a thin ribbon, and her chin is now doubled, her face more rounded and her bosom plumper. Though she smiles, her eyes are watchful, and her mouth strained.

The simple gold frame of this miniature is worn and thin. Washington, according to legend, carried his wife's miniature with him during the war. If such was the case, this was probably the image in question. Martha had a matching miniature by Peale of her husband. His long head and pink cheeks are like those in the artist's full-scale paintings, where Washington is a General in action. The mood here is pensive. The royal blue sash, mark of office, is a flare of colour in an otherwise quiet portrait. This keepsake Martha, too, is said to have had with her throughout the war.[14]

Both Washingtons were in Philadelphia when they learnt from John Augustine, delegate to the Virginia Convention, of dramatic events in that cauldron of revolution, Williamsburg. On 15 May the Convention had approved a resolution directing its delegates to the Continental Congress to introduce a motion of independence. A further resolution was also carried unanimously. It called for a Convention committee to be appointed and prepare a declaration of rights and a 'plan of government' or constitution for an independent Virginia. Washington wrote to his brother, on 31 May, that he was very glad to hear of 'so noble a vote'.[15] In mid-June George Mason, author of the Fairfax County Resolves, was to introduce in Williamsburg the declaration of rights he had composed. The preamble to Mason's Virginia declaration began : '. . . That all men are by nature equally free and independent and have certain inherent rights . . . namely, the enjoyment of life and liberty . . .'[16]

With a copy of this document to hand, Thomas Jefferson worked in Philadelphia on a document that would assert independence for all thirteen colonies. At the end of May Washington's mind was, instead, on the planned Constitution. 'To form a new Government', he wrote to John Augustine, 'requires infinite care, & unbounded attention . . . My fear is, that you will all get tired and homesick, the consequence of which will be, that you will patch up some kind of Constitution as defective as the present.' This should be avoided, he urged. The framework of the Constitution was intended to 'render Million's happy, or Miserable . . . a matter of such moment cannot be the Work of a day'.[17]

The delegates in Williamsburg were in no mood for long deliberations. The provisional assemblies of other former colonies were eager to be first to declare independence. Following a few fervent weeks of business, Virginia was to be third to declare – on 29 June – and to approve a constitution. George and Martha Washington became citizens in an independent state, a commonwealth, and ties between the former Old Dominion and Britain were declared 'totally dissolved'.[18]

Washington left Philadelphia in early June. He planned to await Howe and his forces in New York, where he presumed the enemy's grand efforts would be centred, now they had control of Canada. Before setting out, he told his brother, on the 4th, that he anticipated a 'very blood[sic] Summer of it' in the north.[19] But he did not anticipate the enemy's early arrival. Accordingly Martha, who remained behind in Philadelphia, intended to join her husband soon.[20] She was apparently 'in fine spirits' when she dined, a week after Washington's departure, at President Hancock's Arch Street home. The times were stirring. Richard Henry Lee had galvanized even the most sluggardly delegates to Congress when he proposed this motion on the 7th: 'That these United Colonies are, and of right ought to be, free and independent states'.[21] John Adams seconded him. In the debates that followed, some delegates proved more determined than others in the pursuit of liberty from the mother country. The arguments were not yet concluded when Martha set out for New York.

Soon after her arrival there the Washington household on Richmond Hill was thrown into sudden confusion.[22] A considerable number of Loyalists remained in the city, though others, like their Massachusetts brethren, now avowed their fidelity to the Crown in England or in more peaceable parts under British rule. On the 23rd the New York authorities arrested Mary Smith, housekeeper at the Mortier house, on suspicion of being involved in a Loyalist plot to take the city. This left the commander of the Continental army, as he told Colonel James Clinton in Albany, 'entirely destitute, and put to much inconvenience'.[23] Clinton, Washington directed, was to search out a Mrs Thompson in the Albany area, who was recommended as a fit person to supply Smith's place. Elizabeth Thompson was located and hired. Though over seventy when she arrived at the Mortier house, she was to act as housekeeper in many different headquarters during the war. Caleb Gibbs took over the keeping of the household accounts.

On 29 June – the same day that Virginia became a commonwealth – fifty sail, bearing the first of General William Howe's troops, arrived in New York waters. The ladies of the Continental command were dispatched, in consequence, out of the city the following day. Only days after she had journeyed from Philadelphia, Martha was bound there once more. By 1 July, 130 sail, with an estimated eight or nine thousand troops, were off Sandy Hook. Howe swiftly occupied Staten Island, as Washington, powerless to prevent it, had guessed he would. News that the British had arrived in New York, if nothing else, secured, in Philadelphia, universal approval, on 2 July, for Lee's resolution. Two days later, 'The unanimous Declaration of the thirteen united States of America', the statement of independence that Jefferson had crafted, was adopted.

Washington, writing from New York on 10 July, informed President Hancock that he had 'caused the declaration to be proclaimed before all the army' under his immediate command – 'the expressions and behaviour of both officers and men testifying to their warmest approbation of it'.[24] Some ebullient troops pulled down a statue of George III on Bowling Green, an act that the commander condemned in passing next day. He had matters of greater moment to occupy him. On the 12th a flagship was sighted. Aboard was Admiral Lord Howe, in command of the British fleet off the American coast, as his brother was of the army amassing on Staten Island. Washington, writing an account of enemy activity to his own brother John Augustine on the 22nd, observed that more ships were 'popping in'. He guessed – correctly – that German mercenaries were on board. The Crown had hired from Hesse-Cassel and other small German principalities regiments to supplement the British forces sent against the American rebels. No attack, Washington surmised, would take place until all reinforcements had arrived. Time alone would show what kind of opposition the Continentals offered. 'The men appear to be in good spirits,' he wrote, but he presumed New York would soon be in enemy occupation: 'if they [the men] will stand by me the place shall not be carried without some loss . . .'

Washington laboured to put New York and Long Island into a 'posture of defence'. Martha, by contrast, was in residence at Germantown, a summer resort above the Schuylkill River popular with Philadelphia society and – of late – of delegates to Congress.

She lodged with Virginia delegate Thomas Nelson of Yorktown and his wife. Washington told his brother that Martha thought of returning home to Mount Vernon: 'there is little or no prospect of her being with me any part of this Summer'.²⁵ Her grandchild's coming birth might have lured her home. The marauding 'Ethiopians', commanded by Lord Dunmore, were now greatly reduced in number by smallpox, and the force had ceased to represent any threat in Virginia. She remained, however, at Germantown, where she would have early news of action at New York, through July and August.

Though all were anxious about the outcome in the north, life in the resort was pleasant, and intelligence from Virginia as well as from New York easy to come by. Martha dined at The Hills, the elegant country retreat of Robert Morris, Philadelphia financier. Virginia delegate, Benjamin Harrison, whose language so outraged John Adams, was another of her hosts. News came that Lord Dunmore was gone from Virginia waters at last. The piratical earl had sailed, with his few remaining troops, for New York. Jacky wrote from home on 21 August of 'everything being quiet (which I think is the best news) since Dunmore left us'. He had heard that the Earl was 'dead of the flux (I wish it may be true)'.²⁶

In New York Washington was waiting, and his spies were watching, for the British and Hessians to launch an attack from Staten Island. As 'another revolving Monday' came round on 19 August, Washington told Lund at Mount Vernon that he was at a loss to account for the delay: 'they are in possession of an Island only, which it never was in our power, or Intention to dispute their Landing on . . . this is but a small step towards the Conquest of this Continent'.²⁷ Moreover, he argued, the enemy must be aware that the American forces were being – if slowly – augmented as the weeks passed. Over a week later, when Washington wrote to Martha, stalemate still obtained.

From Pennsylvania Martha sent her sister Nancy Bassett at Eltham a budget of news next day: 'My dear sister, I am still in this town and no prospects at present of my leaving it. The General is at New York. He is very well and wrote to me yesterday.' In consequence she could inform her sister that Dunmore had joined Howe at New York.

Another division of the Hessians was expected 'before, they think, the regulars will begin their attack'. She added, 'some here begin to think, there will be no battle after all'.

Martha glossed over the failure, on 16 August, of Continental row galleys, including *Lady Washington*, and fireships, to destroy enemy vessels on the Hudson. She wrote to Nancy that one of the Continental fireships had grappled with a British ship of war 'ten minutes, but she got clear of her . . . Our people burnt one of the tenders.' She continued, 'I thank God we won't want men – the army at New York is very large, and numbers of men are still going. There is at this time in the city [Philadelphia] four thousand on their march to the camp . . .' For all her martial vigour, Martha longed for the battles to come to be concluded: 'I do, my dear sister, most religiously wish there was an end to the matter that we might have the pleasure of meeting again . . .' The elder sister admonished the younger: 'I don't hear from you as often as I used to do at Cambridge . . .'[28]

If Nancy was an infrequent correspondent, Jacky wrote from Mount Airy on 21 August with compliments to Mr and Mrs Nelson and very welcome news: 'I have the extreme happiness at last to inform you that Nelly was safely delivered this morning about five o'clock of a fine daughter . . .' He wished his mother had been present to see 'the strapping hussy'. The 'other little one' – the daughter who had lived briefly the previous year – was 'a mere dwarf', he declared, beside this one. 'Her clothes are already too small for her.' Jacky could not pretend to say who the child – to be christened Elizabeth and known during youth as Bet, then as Betsy and later as Eliza – resembled. 'It is as much like Doctor Rumney' – the family physician and Washington's fellow sportsman – 'as anybody else,' he wrote. 'She has a double chin something like his, in point of fatness.' He went on to write rhapsodically of her 'fine black hair and eyes. Upon the whole I think it is as pretty and fine a baba as ever I saw.' If he would never be the sober man of business and learning that his step-father had hoped for, Jacky assumed the roles of husband and father willingly. 'Poor Nelly has had a very indifferent time', he wrote of his wife; '. . . the pleasure her daughter gives her compensates for the pain she has suffered.'[29]

In New York Washington continued to write regularly of estate matters to Lund at Mount Vernon. He wrote on 26 August that he 'most ardently' wanted the northern extension to the house covered in and completed, 'if you should be obliged to send all over Virginia, Maryland and Pennsylvania for nails to do it with'. He was eager for the New Room – as the large reception room this extension would furnish was always known – to be constructed. Uncharacteristically he encouraged Lund to act for himself, if only in the matter of where best to sell flour: 'you know I shall not disapprove of anything you do (although it should not turn out well), as I am persuaded you mean to do for the best'. It is unlikely that Lund, a natural lieutenant, was cheered by this expression of – limited – confidence in him. But the General was oppressed, when he wrote, by his duties to 'the noble cause we are engaged in'. The British had at last made a move, and 'a pretty considerable part of their force' had landed on Long Island. These troops were now encamped within three miles of the Continental lines there that General Nathanael Greene commanded.

Only a wood and some broken ground lay between these opposing forces. In New York, Washington thought the British show of strength on Long Island might yet prove a feint. They had sufficient troops still on Staten Island to attack the city. He hesitated to commit more men to Greene. 'A few days more, I should think, will bring matters to an issue one way or another,' he told Lund on the 26th; '. . . victory, if unfortunately it should decide in favour of the enemy, will not be purchased at an easy rate'.[30]

The General proved a poor prophet. The very next day the British struck on Long Island. Aided by information that the Continentals had left a strategic eastward pass undefended, they secured an easy victory. In this first engagement between the United States of America and the army of their former overlord, two Continental generals – Lord Stirling and Sullivan – as well as 600 troops were taken prisoner. In driving rain Washington watched from afar on horseback, helpless to affect the disastrous outcome. Only in the retreat from Long Island to Manhattan, which took place under cover of darkness, on the night of 29 August did Washington prove effective as a General. The 9,000 troops under his command gained and crossed the East River successfully.

Washington apologized to President Hancock, on the morning of 31 August, for a delay in informing him of the retreat. For forty-eight hours he had hardly been off his horse and had never closed his eyes till he reached New York. He was thus, he regretted, 'quite unfit to write or dictate' till now.[31] Within days it became clear that further mortification and humiliation was to be his lot. Intelligence came that the British intended to 'enclose' the American forces on Manhattan, taking up a position at the northernmost part of the island and securing the harbour to the south with their ships. At a council of war on 7 September the painful decision was taken to evacuate New York. The new aim was to establish 'strong posts' on the upper part of the island and on the Jersey shore opposite.[32]

From new headquarters in Harlem Heights, Washington wrote to his cousin Lund that all comfort and happiness eluded him: 'such is my situation that if I were to wish the bitterest curse to an enemy on this side of the grave, I should put him in my stead with my feelings . . . I see the impossibility of serving with reputation, or doing any essential service to the cause by continuing in command, and yet I am told that if I quit the command, inevitable ruin will follow from the distraction that will ensue.' He told his cousin, 'I never was in such an unhappy, divided state since I was born.'[33]

Martha could no longer linger in Pennsylvania. All hope of rejoining her husband was extinguished with British occupation of New York. Now they would be eager to overcome Washington's forces on the Hudson and sweep through New Jersey, with Philadelphia their next goal. She set out southward, bound for home.

Retreat to the Delaware, 1776–1777

I think the game is pretty near up . . .

In Philadelphia, Martha had depended on the constant comings and goings of delegates and army officers between that city and New York for delivery and receipt of her correspondence with her husband. Were Washington to have been wounded, taken prisoner or fallen in a skirmish or battle, she would soon have heard while she was in the home of Congress. With Jacky her escort, Martha arrived home in early autumn 1776. At Mount Vernon, remote from the theatre of war, the weekly post must serve as a less reliable conduit for the couple's letters. Intelligence about the fortunes of the Continental forces would be hard to come by, as would be news of any injury to their Commander-in-Chief. Martha was, like every patriot, anxious about the dangerous situation obtaining in New York, but the safety of her husband was paramount.

The General had already had a narrow escape. British troops landed at Kips Bay on the East River on 15 September. They harassed Continental soldiers who were in the midst of the planned retreat northwards. Washington was to write to his brother Sam in early October of the 'dastardly behaviour of part of our Troops' under attack. Two brigades ran away, and left the Commander-in-Chief, with his aides-de-camp, exposed 'in the field'. He might easily have been killed. Though they succeeded in making their way to the new headquarters at Harlem Heights, this experience was fresh in his mind when Washington wrote to Lund on 30 September. A tirade followed the ominous words, 'If I fall . . .' He wished it to be known that, 'under such a system of management as has been adopted', he had not had 'the least chance for reputation'.[1]

He was smarting from the loss of New York, and stung by Congress's refusal to allow him to burn the city prior to the retreat. It now provided, he wrote, 'warm and comfortable' barracks and an impregnable base for the British army and fleet. A fire had broken out south of King's College subsequent to Howe's arrival and destroyed much of the surrounding area. The British commander, fearing arson, responded by placing the city under martial law. Governor Tryon was made a Major General and dispatched to subdue Connecticut.

In a further letter to Lund on 6 October Washington blamed the new government of the United States for its failure of nerve. Even after declaring independence, they had clung to hopes of a reconciliation with Britain. Lord Howe, whom he termed a 'thorough paced courtier', in the guise of Peace Commissioner, had fuelled these unrealistic expectations. In consequence, week by week, month by month, Congress had hesitated time and again to vote the funds necessary for the defence of America.[2]

Washington had no high opinion of the different militia pressed into service for periods as short as six weeks in return for a bounty. He wrote, from his headquarters on Harlem Heights, to Samuel on 5 October that they were 'eternally coming and going without rendering the least Earthly Service'.[3] He had long urged on Congress – most lately in a letter to Hancock of 2 September – the need for a 'permanent, standing Army – I mean one to exist during the War'.[4] Still, men were engaged for twelve months only. He told Lund on 30 September that he would not undertake to say whether 'the unfortunate hope of reconciliation was the cause' of the refusal of Congress to entertain his scheme, 'or the fear of a standing army prevailed'. He had low expectations for the future: 'if the men will stand by me (which, by the by, I despair of), I am resolved not to be forced from this ground while I have life'. A few days would, he thought, determine the point, 'if the enemy should not change their plan of operations'.[5]

At Mount Vernon Martha had returned to a home substantially improved since she had left it nearly a year earlier. She now had the use of a new master bedroom in the southern extension. When Washington should come home, a study below awaited him. Further works were complete at this end of the house, now conveniently connected by a colonnade to a new kitchen and storeroom. The northern end of the house was still a building site. For all Washington's impatience, the double-storey New Room was not yet finished, and work was still ongoing to complete the northern colonnade, hall for visitors' servants, and gardener's house.

In August, while waiting for Howe to make a move, Washington had sent Lund detailed directions for a 'grove of Trees' to be planted 'at each end of the dwelling'. Close to the new bedroom and study were now planted a variety of saplings. Washington wanted 'all the clever kind of Trees (especially flowering ones) that can be got, such as Crab apple, Poplar, Dogwood, Sasafras, Lawrel, Willow (especially yellow & Weeping Willow)'.[6] Locust trees were in due course to be planted to the north, adjoining a new walled garden, now in place. This planting must wait till the area was no longer littered with building materials.

Lund continued to steward the plantation with anxious care. When an attack by Lord Dunmore and his regiment on Alexandria had seemed imminent this January, he had written to Washington: 'I am about packing up your China Glass &c. into Barrels, & shall continue to pack into Casks, Whatever I think should be put up in that way, & other things into Chests, Trunks, Bundles &c.' Mount Vernon neighbours had offered to store the Washington rum in their cellars. 'The Bacon, when it is sufficiently smoakd, I think to have put up in Cask with Ashes.' If necessary, he could then remove it, 'together with some Pork which I have already put up into Barrels', to a place of greater safety. Distractedly he wrote, 'these are dreadfull times to give people so much trouble and Vexation . . .' In his opinion, in which his correspondent and Mrs Washington did not necessarily concur, 'Fighting and even being killd, is the least troublesome part.'[7]

The following month Lund wrote: 'I have had 300 Bushels or more of Salt put in to Fish Barrels which I intend to move to muddy Hole Barn. If it Should be destroy'd by the Enemy, we shall not be able to get more . . . and our people must have Fish.'[8] Every year, during the spring running of shad on the Potomac, the barrels that he named were filled with fish and salt and emptied over the winter. Dried fish was a staple foodstuff for the plantation slaves. Their master, who could choose what he ate, was partial to it.

Now that the threat Dunmore had represented to Virginia had gone, Martha could enjoy her china and glass with impunity in the newly established Commonwealth of Virginia. Lund tried as best he could to execute Washington's minute instructions. The chimney-piece in the northern annexe should be 'exactly in the middle of it', the commander wrote on 30 September from headquarters in Harlem Heights, 'the doors and every thing else to be exactly answerable and uniform – in short I would have the whole executed in a masterly manner'.[9] Though Lund served his cousin as best he could, he had ambitions of his own – to purchase 'a small Farm in some part of the Country where the produce of it wou'd enable me to live, and give a Neighbour Beef, & Toddy'.[10] He had been far too busy to contemplate finding such a property while both Washingtons were away. He was no less busy now that Martha was returned.

Where the young Parke Custises would ultimately settle, with Martha's granddaughter, baby Bet, was by no means fixed. The White House in New Kent County, Jacky's place of birth, would pass to him only on his mother's death. In July Washington had written to Jacky, encouraging his acquisition of some land on the ground that it was contiguous to 'a large part of your Estate, and where you will probably make your residence'.[11] He referred to Pleasant Hill, the country seat in King and Queen County, which he had bought, on his ward's account, three years earlier. But Jacky made no move to set up home there. His heart belonged in northern Virginia, and this June he wrote to his stepfather: 'It pleased the Almighty to deprive me at a very early Period of Life of my Father, but I can not sufficiently adore His Goodness in sending Me so good a Guardian as you Sir; Few have experience'd such Care and Attention from real

Parents as I have done. He best deserves the Name of Father who acts the Part of one.'[12] By now Jacky, fond to a fault, was also almost as much attached as Nelly to her family in Maryland. For the time being the young couple moved with indifferent ease between Mount Vernon and Mount Airy. For Martha, Jacky and Nelly afforded welcome companionship, and their child, diversion from anxiety about Washington.

Martha was as ever hospitable. The dining room with its new stucco ceiling was much in use, following tireless attention by Lund Washington the previous winter to a problematic chimney, which served this and other rooms. He wrote to Washington, then at Cambridge with Martha, that the fireplaces 'really smoked so Bad that the walls looked as bad as any negroe Quarter, and the Smoke from the cellar came into the other Rooms'.[13] Lund saw Martha's many visitors and even her disposition to charity primarily as a drain on the corn supply at the plantation. The stables already housed five horses for her chariot, as well as seven horses that Jacky kept at the house. There were besides, Lund's own riding horse and numerous mares and wagon horses requiring fodder. The agent was to write to his cousin dolefully: 'these, added to the Visitors' Horses, consume no small Quantity of Corn'.[14] On 17 January 1776, he wrote that they had killed 132 hogs: 'They, with the Fattening Beeves [beef cattle] ate 247 Barrels . . . You will ask me what we are going to do with so much meat. I cannot tell. When I put it up, I expected Mrs Washington would have lived at Home, if you did not.' He added in justification: 'Was I to judge the future from the past consumption, there would have been a Use for it. For I believe Mrs Washingtons Charitable disposition increases in the same proportion with her meat House.' In consequence, he declared, there had been no surplus the previous fall to feed hired harvesters: '& she can tell you, there was very little Salt Provision in the House for Servants, &c., all this fall Past'.

Lund lamented, in this letter of 17 January, 'I am by no means fit for a House keeper, I am afraid I shall consume more than ever, for I am not a judge how much should be given out every Day – I am vex'd when I am called upon to give out Provisions for the Day.

God Send you were both at Home – and an End to these trouble-some times.'[15] Lund might baulk at the alms Martha gave and the entertaining she did. Now she was home, she also supervised the spinning women at their wheels, and made the daily distribution of salt, supplies and medicine.

Elsewhere in Virginia Fredericksburg was unrecognizable from a year earlier. In addition to the gun manufactory funded by Fielding Lewis, there was now an arsenal, naval dockyards and a hospital for soldiers, marines and seamen. October saw, with concomitant festivities, the General Assembly of the new Commonwealth of Virginia meet for the first time in Williamsburg. Martha's brother Bartholomew Dandridge was a Councillor of State. Patrick Henry was ensconced as Governor in the palace that Lord Dunmore and other British peers and commoners had formerly occupied. But Martha remained on the Potomac in northern Virginia. The incom-ing post on Thursdays to Alexandria sustained her with newspaper accounts of the war's progress and with letters from her husband. The outgoing post on Sundays offered an opportunity to convey both fortitude and fears to him.

Washington had written to Lund at the end of September: 'I am resolved not to be forced from this ground while I have life.'[16] He was very much alive when forced by the British from Harlem Heights in mid-October. He regrouped with his troops at White Plains, north of Manhattan Island in New York, where he hoped to withstand attack by General Howe. A letter that he wrote to Martha from here on the 25th was among other correspondence from headquarters that fell into the hands of the British three days later. A careless dispatch rider, in whose charge it was, stopped at a Pennsylvanian public house, which also served as post office. In the 'bar room' of the inn, in a district inhabited by numerous Loyalists, he opened his 'bundle'. Extracting a letter which required forwarding, he stepped out of the inn for a moment, leaving the other correspondence on a table inside. As Hancock informed Washington by express the same day: 'on his return the whole of his Letters were carried off & no person could give any account of them . . . he is here without a single Letter'.[17] The dispatch rider was incarcerated, the publican deprived of his office of postmaster, and the bartender closely questioned. The stolen corre-spondence reached British headquarters, as all at headquarters and in Congress had supposed it would. General Howe, now Sir William Howe, Knight of the Bath, sent back to Washington his letter to Martha of 25 October. The covering note, written on 11 November, ran: 'I am happy to return it without the least Attempt being made to discover any Part of the Contents.'[18] Washington told Hancock three days later: 'I conclude that All the Letters which went by the Boston Express have come into his possession.'[19]

He was correct. The 'bundle' had reached Howe on 5 November, and his private secretary, Ambrose Serle, made notes on the content of the letters. The Continental officers were, Serle observed, '(to use Mr Washington's own Words) *dreaming, sleepy-headed*" Men'. The American commander had also written that discord existed between 'the Eastern & Southern Colonists', and that the Province of Massachusetts Bay, in particular, could raise neither men nor money. In short, Serle summarized in his diary in December, the General and his military 'family' entertained 'the strongest Fears, respecting their Success, and of the Consequences of a Disappointment'.[20]

When Serle made his notes, the Continental troops were long gone from White Plains. The 'strongest fears' of those at headquarters had proved justified. On 28 October – the same day that the 'bar room' incident took place in Pennsylvania – Howe attacked Washington's troops. Though the battle was inconclusive and a large-scale exchange of prisoners followed, Washington abandoned the position, and made for 'General Greene's quarters' at Fort Lee on the New Jersey shore. With him, he wrote to Hancock on 14 November, came 'the whole of the troops' – bar one garrison – 'belonging to the States which lay South of Hudsons River and which were in New York Government'. New York might be lost to the Continentals. New Jersey would not fall if the men, quartered at Brunswick, Amboy, Elizabethtown, Newark and about Fort Lee – Washington's own location – were ready to 'check any incursions the enemy may attempt in the neighbourhood'.

Washington left 3,000 troops at Fort Washington, on an eminence above the Hudson, on Manhattan island, and opposite Fort Lee.

Nathanael Greene, whom Washington trusted, believed that the former position could be held against enemy attack. It had sufficient cannon and range to do useful damage to British shipping in the river. Washington was irresolute. 'The movements and designs of the Enemy are not yet understood,' he told Hancock.[21] He thought the enemy might well succeed if they attempted to invest the fort. Later, Washington was to acknowledge to Joseph Reed, who was with him at Fort Lee, that there was 'warfare in my mind and hesitation', as he sought to find a way forward.[22] But he gave no order to evacuate the Manhattan garrison.

Next day the British and Hessians seized the fort and took prisoner the majority of the garrison – 2,858 men comprising Maryland and Virginian regiments, militiamen and Pennsylvanian battalions. Reed, who had succeeded Gates as Adjutant General in the summer, wrote to Charles Lee six days later: 'General Washington's own Judgment seconded by Representations from us would, I believe, have saved the Men & their Arms but unluckily, General Greene's Judgment was contrary. This kept the Generals Mind in a State of Suspence till the Stroke was struck – Oh! General – an indecisive Mind is one of the greatest Misfortunes that can befall an Army.'[23]

Now the British had control of the Hudson, retreat from Fort Lee was inevitable. News, on the 19th, that barges were bearing British general Lord Cornwallis and 5,000 troops to the New Jersey shore hastened the evacuation. At Hackensack, Washington tallied for Hancock the British gains: 'the whole of the Cannon that was at the Fort, except Two twelve Pounders, and a great deal of baggage – between Two & three hundred Tents – about a Thousand Barrels of Flour & other Stores in the Quarter Master's department'.[24] With the approach of winter, the loss of the tents was especially regretted by both officers and men.

In Reed's letter of 21 November, which Washington never saw, the Adjutant General called on Lee to hasten to New Jersey: 'I have no Doubt, had you been here, the Garrison at Mount [Fort} Washington would now have composed a Part of this Army . . . every Gentleman of the Family, the Officers & soldiers generally have a Confidence in you . . . All Circumstances considered, we are in a very awful &

alarming State, one that requires the utmost Wisdom & Firmness of Mind.'[25]

Cornwallis continued to press, and the Continentals to retreat before him. From Newark, Samuel Blachley Webb, a new aide at headquarters, wrote to Commissary General Joseph Trumbull: 'You ask me [for] a true Account of our Situation . . . I can only say that no lads ever showed greater activity in retreating than we have since we left You. Our Soldiers are the best fellows in the World at this Business.'[26]

On 30 November from New Brunswick, a new refuge, Washington addressed the President of Congress: 'It was the opinion of all the generals, who were with me, that a retreat to this place was requisite and founded in necessity.'[27] The vanguard of the British army had entered Newark as his rearguard left it.

At New Brunswick, also, with the enemy within two hours' march, Washington read Lee's bombastic reply of 24 November to Reed. The General lamented 'that fatal indecision of mind which in war is a much greater disqualification than stupidity or even want of personal courage . . . eternal defeat and miscarriage must attend the man of the best parts if curs'd with indecision . . .' Lee ruminated, 'to confess a truth I really think our Chief will do better with me than without me . . .'[28]

Lee, it was known, believed he should be Commander-in-Chief. He was needed to defend Philadelphia. But Washington was less forgiving of Reed, his former secretary, to whom he forwarded Lee's missive. 'Having no idea of its being a private letter', he wrote, assuming it would be 'upon the business of your office', he had read the 'Contents . . . which neither inclination or intention would have prompted me to'.[29]

The enemy were advancing. More Continental troops were going off home, the term of their service expiring. Washington was as dogged in retreat as ever, gaining first Princeton, then, on 2 December, Trenton. Thomas Paine, Anglo-American newspaperman, was with Washington's army on this sorry march through New Jersey. He described 'both officers and men' as 'greatly harassed, and fatigued, frequently without rest, covering, or provision'. With reference to the Commander-in-Chief, he wrote ecstatically: 'There is a natu-ral fannels [tabernacle] in some minds, which cannot be unlocked by trifles, but which, when unlocked, discovers a cabinet of forti-tude.'[30] During these desperate months there was one consolation for Washington. Congress had at last heeded him, and directed in October that the states raise a 'standing army', comprising eighty-eight regiments, to serve for the duration of hostilities. Furthermore, now that the United States were independent, there was the hope that the French King, Louis XVI, and his ministers, inimical to British interests, would look kindly on their cause, and on their quest for foreign arms and regiments.

Washington's initial aim at Trenton, in which he succeeded, was to convey his small army over the Delaware to the Pennsylvania side of the river, taking with him or burning all boats and barges in moor-ings on the New Jersey side. The pursuing British and Hessians – at more than 10,000 men, an apparently insuperable adversary – had no option but to wait till the river froze. When it did, as it surely would, they would as surely cross and attack.

An urgent plea to Philadelphia for men at the end of November had resulted in 2,000 townsmen volunteering to form a city mili-tia. With those volunteers, among them artist Charles Willson Peale, the Continental army at the Delaware now stood at 5,000 men. But, across the river, Hessians were quartered in the garrison at Trenton. British soldiers were camped on the New Jersey river banks opposite 'above & below us . . . for fifteen Miles', Washington told Lund on 10 December. The enemy could at any time cross the river at several different places and attack the smaller American force; 'vigilance' was the only defence.

Washington was not optimistic. It was, he wrote to his cousin, 'next to impossible to guard a Shore for 60 Miles with less than half the Enemys numbers'.[31] Martha's brother Bartholomew Dandridge, Councillor of State, was to give vent the following month in Williamsburg to the feelings of many patriots of standing in the new Commonwealth of Virginia. It was 'astonishing and will hardly be credited hereafter', he told his brother-in-law warmly, 'that the most deserving, the most favorite General of the 13 united American

States, should be left by them, with only about 2500 Men, to support the most important Cause that mankind ever engaged in against the whole Power of British Tyranny'.[32]

Washington, following eighteen months of dealings with Congress and provincial governments, was inured to the procrastination and irresolution of both. He was aware that he sank in the esteem of so many, if not that of his friends and family in Virginia, with every retreat he made. Stolidly, steadily he worked to increase the numbers on the Pennsylvania shore.

Though the atmosphere at headquarters was highly charged, Washington wrote calmly to Lund of planting 'Holly trees' or 'young & strait bodied Pines' on the 'Circular Banks' at Mount Vernon. He had no time, nor anyone to spare, to send the horses he had promised – 'Mrs Washington must therefore make the old greys serve her a little while longer.' While unwilling to buy expensive 'Linnen for the Negros', he held that 'they certainly have a just claim to their Victuals and cloths, if they make enough to purchase them'. A week later the commander resumed his letter. Headquarters was now a farmhouse 'ten miles above the falls'. So far they had prevented the enemy from crossing the Delaware, he wrote. 'How long we shall be able to do it, God only knows, as they are still hovering about the River.'

With the British and Hessians so close to Philadelphia, Congress had taken the decision on 12 December to remove south to Baltimore. They hastened their departure on learning that General Charles Lee had been taken prisoner at a Basking Ridge tavern, where he was lodging. 'Unhappy man!' wrote Washington four days later, 'taken by his own imprudence!' Following information from a Loyalist, a party of British light horse rode through the night and carried off the prize 'in high triumph, and with every Mark of Indignity – not even suffering him to get his Hat, or Surtout Coat'.

Disaffection and 'want of spirit & fortitude', Washington told Lund on 17 December, reigned in the Jerseys. 'In confidence . . . as a friend', he advised his cousin, 'look forward to unfavorable Events, & prepare accordingly. In such a manner, however, as to give no alarm or suspicion to any one.' Washington's papers at Mount

Vernon, he directed, should be readied for dispatch westward to Samuel Washington in Berkeley County – 'in case an Enemy's Fleet should come up the River'. A week earlier he had written that the 'old greys' must serve Martha. Now, with flight in mind, he was at pains to see that she had a 'very good set' for her chariot. With Mercer he sent southwards two 'exceeding good Horses . . . Young, the lightest of the two Bays is an exceeding tough, hardy horse as any in the World, but rather lazy – he will do well for the Postilion before'.[33]

To his brothers John Augustine and Samuel Washington, the commander wrote nearly identical letters next day : 'I have no doubt but that General Howe will still make an attempt upon Philadelphia this Winter – I see nothing to oppose him in a fortnight from this time.' The terms of almost all the troops would then expire, except those of some much fatigued regiments from Virginia and Maryland. 'In a word my dear Sir, if every nerve is not strained to recruit the New Army with all possible Expedition, I think the game is pretty near up . . .'[34]

Washington had written to Martha from Philadelphia in June 1775 on his election as Commander-in-Chief. He had written to her when they were parted on many occasions since. According to his and Lund's testimony, the General never failed to enclose a letter for her when he wrote to his cousin at Mount Vernon. When Mercer bore these confidential letters south, in that case, and at this time of crisis, a letter for Martha went too.

It was a time of national crisis, and one in which information, especially in the south, was at a premium and swiftly disseminated, however unreliable or out of date it might be. From Williamsburg, on 20 December 1776, William Fitzhugh of Chatham, a member of the new Virginia legislature, wrote by 'a very indifferent fire by candlelight and with a very weak eye' to inform his uncle, Landon Carter, 'The accounts yesterday from Philadelphia are bad indeed. The enemy within a few miles of that city and our worthy General Washington flying before them with a few fatigued and shattered troops.' Fitzhugh expected soon to hear that Philadelphia was in ashes or occupied by the enemy. 'If the latter, I fear almost a total disaffection will be the consequence, and if the former what a loss must America sustain.' Wrote this wealthy man, 'I would with pleasure part with my last shilling to procure my liberty.'[35]

The 20th brought about a change in the fortunes and dispositions of the armies. Continental reinforcements arrived, and Howe ordered his troops into winter quarters. Washington took the decision to launch a surprise attack on the garrisoned Hessians. He wrote to Reed on the 23rd, 'Christmas day at night, one hour before day, is the time fixed upon for our attempt on Trenton. For Heaven's sake keep this to yourself, as the discovery of it may prove fatal to us.'[36]

Two nights later, in freezing weather, Washington assembled 2,500 troops at McKonkey's Ferry on the Pennsylvania bank of the Delaware. Officers, men and ordnance were embarked in flat-bottomed boats for the New Jersey shore. He later informed Hancock: 'the quantity of Ice, made that Night, impeded the passage of Boats so much, that it was three o'clock before the Artillery could all be got over, and near four, before the Troops took up their line of march'. Though it was now snowing hard, the Continentals rapidly covered the nine miles that lay between the ferry on the New Jersey shore and Trenton. They surprised the sleeping Hessians before light dawned on the 26th. In a short engagement, they took more than a thousand of the German mercenaries prisoner, and escorted them back across the river.

For once Washington was satisfied with his officers and men: 'their Behaviour upon this Occasion, reflects the highest honor upon them. The difficulty of passing the River in a very severe Night, and their March thro' a violent Storm of Snow and Hail, did not in the least abate their Ardour. But when they came to the Charge, each seemed to vie with the other in pressing forward . . .'[37] Any patriots who still questioned the General's skills as a commander were soon silenced. On the night of 2 January 1777, Washington outmanoeuvred Sir William Howe, who was advancing on Trenton, and took Princeton on the 3rd. Howe, now nineteen miles away from Philadelphia when he had been as close as six, relinquished his plan to seize it.

From Pluckemin on the 5th, on his way to Morristown, New Jersey, Washington wrote an account of the victory at Princeton for Hancock. He dispatched his letter 'open' for Robert Morris at Philadelphia to read and forward to Baltimore. Though the fighting was brief, it had been bloody. In one mêlée Hugh Mercer, Fredericksburg apothecary turned brigadier general, was savaged with seven bayonet thrusts after his horse had been killed from under him. 'One of these wounds is in his forehead, but the most alarming of them are in his belly,' wrote physician Benjamin Rush, who attended Mercer at the Princeton field hospital.[38] Washington was on his way to Morristown, which he deemed the place 'best calculated of any in this quarter, to accommodate and refresh' the army.[39] He could send only messages of support to the officer who had once supplied so many nostrums for Patsy Parke Custis. Fatally wounded, Mercer was to die in agony on 11 January.

At Pluckemin Washington waited for nearly a thousand troops to arrive who could not 'through fatigue and hunger' keep up with the main body of the army.[40] In Hackensack in November Thomas Paine had written in his pamphlet *American Crisis*: 'These are the times that try men's souls.'[41] The recent victories were brittle. The Pennsylvanian militia had left their blankets at Burlington. Many on the icy roads were 'entirely barefooted', Peale, at Pluckemin, wrote in his diary. He got a raw hide to make these men moccasins, 'but made a bad hand of it, for want of a proper needle or awl'.[42]

Robert Morris in Philadelphia had occupied a crucial role since Congress's departure for Baltimore in Maryland. He and a few others, remaining behind, formed an Executive Committee with the authority to forward supplies to Washington and fulfil other much needed services. In addition he himself made loans to Washington which were applied, in particular, to the payment of bounties for troops who stayed on beyond the end of their prescribed service. In his covering letter of 5 January to Morris, accompanying his dispatch to Hancock, Washington added: 'Your sending the Inclosed [letter] for Mrs Washington to the Post Office (if in time for the Southern Mail) will much oblige, Dear Sir, Your Most Obedient servant . . .'[43]

The fortunes of Washington's wartime correspondence with Martha and Lund continued vexed. From Morristown, over a week later the commander was to beg the Philadelphia financier, as a favour, to obtain at the post office and forward to him – 'as opportunity offers' – such letters as came 'by the southern mail . . . A Letter or two from my Family are regularly sent by the Post, but very irregularly received, which is rather mortifying, as it deprives me of the consolation of hearing from home on domestic matters.'[44]

How early Martha knew of her husband's transformative victories at Trenton and Princeton, and that he was safe and, if much harassed, well, is unclear. But Washington replied later in January to a letter of Jacky's of the 7th: 'Providence has heretofore saved us in a remarkable manner, and on this we must principally rely. Every person, in every State, should exert himself to facilitate the raising and Marching the New Regiments to the Army with all possible expedition.' He wrote matter-of-factly, discussing New England regiments, of 'that hunger, & thirst after glory which spurs on . . . to distinguished Acts'.[45] His own hunger for glory was slaked for the time being. He wanted instead pledges from the different states of recruits for the 'standing army' – eighty-eight regiments in all – now forming and which, come the summer, he would command. From Williamsburg his brother-in-law Bartholomew Dandridge wrote in January: 'I have the pleasure to inform you that the business of recruiting goes on well, and that we have a fair prospect of raising our new Regiments in good time.'[46] Owing to pressure of business, Bartholomew had not seen his sister Martha. John Augustine Washington visited his sister-in-law at Mount Vernon and sent the General, on the 24th, a pleasing account of her. Above all, Washington wanted his wife with him. In February, the British were established in New York and in Rhode Island. Martha's residence at Morristown became feasible.

Some years later, submitting 'Lawful' wartime accounts to Congress, Washington would include 'Mrs Washington's travelling Expenses in coming to and returning from my winter quarters annually . . . The money to defray which being taken from my private purse and brought with her from Virginia.' He wrote: 'in the commencement of them' – when she first travelled to join him in Cambridge – these expenses 'appeared at first view to wear the complexion of a private charge', and he was in doubt about 'the propriety' of charging them to the public account. But, he noted, he was obliged by 'the embarrassed situation of our [national] affairs' continually to postpone the visit home that he 'every year contemplated between the close of one campaign and the opening of another'. He had ended by judging Martha's travelling expenses, 'incidental thereto and the consequence of my self-denial', 'just with respect to the public' and 'convenient' with respect to himself. In the accounts he submitted, he included an account for sixty-one-odd Continental dollars, comprising Mrs Washington's journey to Morristown 'when the army lay there'.[47]

On 6 March 1777 he wrote impatiently to 'The Commanding Officer' in Philadelphia: 'Being informed that Mrs Washington was to set out from Virginia for Philadelphia on Monday the 24th Ultimo [February], I presume she must be, e're this, in that City . . .'[48] Martha's journey from Mount Vernon to Morristown, with Jacky her escort, had been far from smooth. When she passed through Baltimore, she found some members of Congress packing up the lodgings that they had occupied while Howe threatened Philadelphia. The roads were busy, and Philadelphia itself in a state of some chaos as other, more prescient delegates made haste to secure quarters. Martha lodged in the city, as she had the previous year, at Benjamin Randolph's on Chestnut Street. On 15 March the *Continental Journal* informed its readers that 'His Excellency' had 'the satisfaction of his amiable lady's company'. Martha had arrived at Morristown that day. At Cambridge and at New York the Vassall house and the Mortier house had provided elegant lodgings, and there had been families of standing in the locale for company. At Morristown headquarters was the tavern on the green, and the military 'family' formed the principal society.

Washington had been dangerously ill shortly before Martha reached headquarters, and was still recovering. Samuel Washington, far away in western Virginia, had earlier requested a portrait of his absent brother. George growled in return on the 15th: 'two insurmountable obstacles offer themselves – the want of a Painter – and, if a Painter could be brought hither, the want of time to Sit'. Should Sam ever get 'a Picture of mine, taken from the life', he wrote, it must be when he was 'remov'd from the busy Scenes of a Camp'.[49]

In a time of privation at camp, Washington thanked Hancock on the 29th for a 'valuable present of Fish . . . nothing could be more acceptable'. But even such small pleasures were a distraction from the stern work to be done. 'The Genl. tho' exceeding fond of Salt Fish', he continued, 'is happy enough never to think of it unless it is placed before him, for which reason it would give him concern if Mr Hancock should put himself to the least trouble in forwarding any to Camp on his Acc't.'[50] He had information that the British in New York were embarking an expedition of 3,000 men, and conjectured Philadelphia to be its object.

Severe difficulties faced Congress and the Commander-in-Chief, as the 'standing army' of the United States struggled to fill its ranks. Washington told his brother Sam in early April that the troops were coming in 'exceedingly slow'. Whether from 'an unwillingness in the Men to Enlist, or to the Idleness and dissipation of the Officers, and their reluctance to leave their friends & acquaintance', he could not say: 'it looks to me as if we should never get an army assembled'.[51] Though the military situation was not to improve, Washington's spirits slowly revived, following his wife's arrival at headquarters.

Morristown and Brandywine, 1777

*Mrs Washington is excessive fond of
the General and he of her.*

The Washingtons savoured their reunion at Arnold's tavern in Morristown in the spring of 1777. It was now nine months since they had last been together, at the elegant Mortier house in New York. The evenings in New Jersey over which she now presided were more domesticated, the company less varied. Later this year one of their number wrote of being 'Authorized', in a dream, to grant the General, prey to every kind of care in Pennsylvania, 'two Months' leave of absence, or the Alternative of Sending for Mrs Washington, a generous glass of wine on your Table & riding more or less on horseback almost every dry day!'[1] With Martha came familiar news from a home that Washington had now not seen for nearly two years. She had a way of keeping conversation flowing among those around her, a conversation to which Washington could contribute or not as he pleased.

At Morristown, Nathanael Greene, the commander's trusted deputy, took stock, on 8 April, of the relationship between husband and wife. He informed his young wife, Caty – Catharine Littlefield Greene – who was at home in Rhode Island: 'Mrs Washington is excessive fond of the General and he of her. They are very happy in each other.'[2] These were strong words, 'excessive fond', an expression more normally applied to a demonstrative couple recently matched and still a little foolish with love. The Greenes themselves, married barely a year before Nathanael went off to the war, were just such a couple. This spring Nathanael and Caty Greene's baby daughter in Rhode Island became another namesake of Mrs Washington. When Martha was in Cambridge the previous year, a baby in Dunstable, Massachusetts had endured a very patriotic christening. In a dress of buff and blue, with a 'sprig of evergreen' on her head 'emblematic of his Excellency's glory and provincial affection', she was given the name Martha Dandridge.[3]

The Washingtons, in contrast with the Greenes, had been married nearly twenty years. Greene was by upbringing a Quaker, and the Washingtons' courtly Virginia manners may have confounded him. While Washington was implacable and stern in the exercise of his public duties at Morristown, he was apparently happy to be affectionate in private.

In June 1775, when called upon to command the United armies, he had told Martha that he would enjoy 'more real happiness and felicity in one month with you, at home, than I have the most distant prospect of reaping abroad . . .' He had written of 'the uneasiness I know you will feel at being left alone . . .'[4] But it was Washington who stood in need of the very 'fortitude and resolution' he had recommended to Martha. In the days after he had crossed the Delaware and won victories at Trenton and Princeton, he wrote to Martha not once but several times, hungering for her presence at that momentous time. When at Mount Vernon, Martha had the consolation of Jacky's company together with that of Nelly, a new grandchild to admire, and friends and neighbours to call upon. Her husband had to withstand, alone, separation from the wife who, for nearly twenty years, had been so inextricably linked with his life at the home that he loved passionately.

Martha had never made any bones about her devotion to her husband. A Virginia matron, writing home in May from Morristown, noted of the Commander-in-Chief: 'his Worthy Lady seems to be in perfect felicity while she is by the side of her Old Man as she calls him'.[5] Though dressed in buff and blue and aged forty-five, General

Washington in 1777 still had the patrician good looks and strong, sinewy figure that had distinguished the younger soldier in a blue coat faced with red who had come wooing her on the Pamunkey. In Virginia, where the Washingtons were so long established as a couple, Martha's fondness for her husband had escaped remark. In the close confines of headquarters, where were gathered so many from states where very different manners obtained and even some from Europe, this passion came under scrutiny, and – an engaging anomaly in so level-headed a personage – attracted attention. The following January, a French officer, the Marquis de Lafayette, was to write home confidently of Martha from Washington's headquarters in Pennsylvania. Though he knew her only by reputation, he told his wife that Mrs Washington was 'a modest and respectable person, who loves her husband madly . . .'[6] It was an unlooked-for, if welcome, concomitant of the war that Washington so appreciated Martha's worth. Perhaps for the first time in all their long marriage, he yearned for her when she was absent and delighted in her company when she was present.

Martha's stay at headquarters, for all that, was likely at any point to be truncated. General Howe and the troops under his command were recuperating from the autumn campaign at Brunswick and on board transports at Amboy. These troops, 10,000 in number, were 'well Officerd, well disciplined, and well appointed', Washington wrote to Robert Morris on 2 March 1777. The Continental army, ranged across New Jersey in opposition to the enemy, numbered at best 4,000 men – 'raw Militia, badly Officered, and ungovernable'. Washington was convinced that Howe would seek to strike at Philadelphia as soon as the weather favoured an assault. 'All the heavy Baggage of the Army – their Salt Provisions – Flour – Stores – & ca – might go round by Water,' he conjectured. 'With what propriety . . . can he miss so favourable an opportunity of striking a capital stroke against a City from whence we derive so many advantages, the success of which wou'd give so much eclat to his Arms, and strike such a damp upon ours?'[7]

Once Howe made the move that Washington was convinced was inevitable, Martha must return to Virginia, while the Continental army, however inadequate, proceeded to defensive positions in Pennsylvania. Meanwhile, headquarters in Morristown was lively, though Arnold's tavern on the green was a modest establishment. Caleb Gibbs continued to command the General's guard, and continued, too, a faithful steward of the household accounts, while Mrs Thompson kept house. Sixteen-year-old Thornton Washington, Samuel Washington's eldest son, was convalescing following inoculation against smallpox. Once he had recovered, the boy was to proceed home to Charles Town, Virginia, and enlist as ensign in a regiment recently raised.

There were several aides who were new to the military 'family' since Martha had last inhabited her husband's headquarters – in the salubrious Mortier house on the Hudson in New York. Alexander Hamilton, a young graduate of King's College, New York, originally from the West Indies, had distinguished himself as a young artillery officer at Princeton, covering the Continental retreat with a barrage of fire. Since the New Year he had proved himself an invaluable letter-writer for the commander at Morristown. Tench Tilghman was proving a reliable assistant secretary who took over much of Harrison's work. Though son to the Crown Attorney General of Pennsylvania, he had enlisted at the outbreak of hostilities. Since the previous autumn, he had been serving, in a voluntary capacity, as aide to the commander.

With Hamilton, Tilghman and other aides, Washington was at work to provision the officers and men currently serving, to augment the army, and to plead the case to Congress for an improved hospital department. This April, Dr William Shippen Jr, in Philadelphia, was to assume full powers as Director General of a reorganized hospital department with innumerable sub-divisions and provision for a 'flying hospital', or field hospital. In addition, when Martha joined him, Washington was still overseeing an emergency project that he had initiated in February: mass inoculation of the army. He wrote on 5 February to Hancock: 'The small pox has made such Head in every Quarter that I find it impossible to keep it from spreading thro' the whole Army in the natural way. I have therefore determined, not only to inoculate all the Troops now here, that have not had it, but shall order Docr Shippen to inoculate the Recruits as fast as they come in to Philadelphia.'[8]

It was imperative that the British should not learn of the medical procedures taking place at Morristown. Though the mass inoculation was ultimately successful, at any one time many hundreds of troops lay invalid. Washington had chosen his winter headquarters well. The inhabitants of Morristown and its neighbours, settlements protected by the Watchung Mountains to the east and by the Ramapo Hills running north, were strongly Presbyterian and favoured the 'rebel' cause.

No word apparently reached the British of the weakened health of the Continental troops. During Martha's first weeks at headquarters the church on the green in Morristown and the church in nearby Hanover were still serving as crowded, makeshift hospitals. Washington and Nathanael Greene sought to maintain good relations with the population through the intercession of the ministers of both parishes. General Orders to the army included directives each Sunday for troops to attend divine service if in town – services were held outside while the churches still served as hospitals – and for regimental chaplains to deliver sermons to those cantoned further off. Washington told Hancock on 14 March that there were about a thousand troops under inoculation at Morristown, Princeton and elsewhere: 'the whole of our Numbers in Jersey fit for duty at this time, is under Three Thousand. These (981 excepted) are Militia & stand engaged only till the last of this Month.'[9]

The churches in Morristown and Hanover slowly emptied of invalid soldiers. Encouraged by the success of the experiment, following an outbreak of smallpox in the Mount Vernon area this spring Washington gave orders for the 300 slaves on the plantation to be inoculated. In Morristown and Hanover, nevertheless, the graveyards filled. The majority of the local inhabitants had rejected all offers of inoculation, and whole families died from the disease, as the Bills of Mortality for these months show.

Congress had voted Washington, in October and December 1776, the authority to raise and officer a number of new regiments. Aide George Baylor, who had the glory of bearing the Hessians' captured standard to Congress in Philadelphia, raised a regiment of light horse in his native Virginia. Young Thornton Washington, Washington's nephew, and his cousin George Lewis, now a captain, joined a regiment headed by Colonel Charles Minn Thurston. Washington instructed both Baylor, in Williamsburg, and Thurston, in western Virginia, to inoculate the troops as fast as they came in. He wrote in April to Governor Patrick Henry that smallpox was 'more destructive to an Army in the Natural way, than the Enemy's Sword . . . I shudder when ever I reflect upon the difficulties of keeping it out . . .'[10]

Difficulties faced Washington wherever he turned. Congress was resistant to his pleas for a more ready response to his demands for cash to pay the troops. Demurrals from relatives, friends and patriots in Virginia who had been counted on to supply officers for the new regiments included an account of a mother's lachrymose opposition to her son's enlistment under Baylor. Washington replied in April: 'a Mother's tenderness and Fears too often interpose, & check the ardour of our Youth'.[11] If Jacky Parke Custis was in his mind, the young man was still a valuable escort for his mother between Mount Vernon and headquarters. There remained, also, the task of fathering an heir for the Parke Custis estates. When once he had delivered Martha to Morristown this March, Jacky returned to Virginia and resumed his conjugal duties with enthusiasm. By the late spring Nelly was pregnant again.

Washington's forces continued weak and small in number. Recruiting officers in all states met with a tepid response from those they canvassed. Stories of hardship at the front from those returned had their effect on some. Fear of harsh treatment at the hands of the British if captured, and pessimism about the outcome of the war, disinclined others to commit to the patriot cause. Unaccountably, however, Howe made no decisive move towards Philadelphia. At the beginning of April Washington wrote to Hancock: 'By the latest accounts from Brunswick, it looks as if the Enemy were projecting an embarkation, they have been stripping the Buildings of Boards and cutting small Timber and transporting them from Brunswick to Amboy. It is imagined this is to build Berths in their Transports.'[12]

He believed the British would soon make by water for Delaware Bay. But the activity slowed and no embarkation took place.

Slowly Continental troop numbers augmented and Washington, with generals Nathanael Greene and Henry Knox, began to feel greater confidence in the army's ability to resist a British attack. The spring weather afforded opportunities for outings. New Yorker General, William Alexander, played host at his estate at Basking Ridge, fifteen miles away. An enterprising soldier of fortune, he was generally addressed as Lord Stirling, though his claim to the earldom of that name had been unsuccessful. He and his wife and their daughters – 'Lady Mary' and 'Lady Kitty' – enjoyed an aristocratic life at the estate, and stocked an 'English park' with deer. A profitable ironworks and money that 'Lady Stirling' had inherited from her father, Philip Livingston, Lord of Livingston Manor, Albany, helped to fund this splendour.

Lady Stirling's nephew, New Jersey Governor William Livingston, and his family, had fled the British, and also lodged at Basking Ridge. They joined the Washingtons and the military 'family' in afternoon riding parties. Mrs Bland, wife of a Virginia colonel, wrote home to a sister-in-law: 'At such times General Washington throws off the Hero – and takes on the chatty agreeable companion – he can be down right impudent sometimes – such impudence, Fanny, as you and I like.' The Theodorick Blands visited at headquarters 'twice or three times a week by particular invitation – Every day frequently from inclination'. Caleb Gibbs, by Martha Bland's account, was 'a good natured Yankee who makes a thousand Blunders in the Yankee stile and keeps the Dinner table in constant Laugh'.

Martha, providing tea and conversation to visiting officers and their ladies, members of Congress and provisional assemblymen, forged close links with her husband's aides who were, according to Mrs Bland, 'all polite sociable gentlemen who make the day pass with a great deal of satisfaction to the Visitors'.[13] Francophone Alexander Hamilton, in particular, was invaluable when numerous French officers without a word of English appeared at headquarters. With these foreigners came letters of introduction from Silas Deane in Paris, whom Congress had deputed to seek from the French government financial aid and arms for the cause. Washington – who had not a word of French – was reliant on others to explain to these enthusiasts that there was no regimental command to offer them.

Martha sometimes took a hand in domestic affairs, as is evident from an item in the accounts for April: 'To cash paid for vegetables which Mrs Washington bought'.[14] Usually the supervision of the household at Morristown, as at all headquarters, was a matter for those paid from the public purse. In early May, Caleb Gibbs, captain of the commander's personal guard, procured at Philadelphia cloth, buttons and trimmings. New breeches and waistcoats were to be tailored in Morristown for Will Lee, the Mount Vernon slave who valeted for the commander. Two pounds of 'scented best' hair powder for Martha and a chest 'to put public papers in' were among other acquisitions which included loaf sugar, green tea, pepper, lime juice and bacon. Washington wanted Gibbs to find in the city a steward or a man of experience who had been employed 'as a butler in a gentleman's family'. Such a major domo might check the lower servants at headquarters in their 'extravagance and roguery, in making away with liquors, and other articles laid in for the use of the family'. Though Washington's jaundiced view of the lower servants' probity did not alter, Martha interfered at this time to good effect. Mrs Thompson, who had until recently served as housekeeper, had been let go. 'Mrs Washington wishes I had mentioned my intention of parting with the old woman, before her, as she is much in want of a housekeeper,' Washington told Gibbs on 1 May.[15] Mrs Thompson returned, made the Washingtons' quarters relatively comfortable, and aided different stewards and cooks, over the next several years, in serving up dinners for as many as thirty. Fowls, both turkeys and chickens, eggs, veal and mutton were staples at the headquarters dinner table.

In late May the Washingtons parted. Martha, under the escort of Tench Tilghman, proceeded to Philadelphia, where she would stop on her way home. Washington moved to new headquarters at Middlebrook, a village on the north bank of the Raritan. The 18,000 British troops that Howe commanded at New Brunswick and Amboy lay a few miles south-east. The Continentals were well placed, ready to march northwards if Howe made a bid to join General Burgoyne's forces on the Hudson, or southwards if Philadelphia proved to be Howe's objective. There were between seven and eight thousand troops in all under Washington's command, forty-three regiments in all. Greene, Stirling and others commanded five divisions. Furthermore, Washington could count on militia to the north or to the south to irritate the British forces, as gadflies will annoy a bull.

On an earlier visit to Philadelphia, Martha had acceded to the wish of city fathers that a ball in her honour be cancelled. Now, the Pennsylvania General Assembly resolved to make her an extraordinarily handsome present – 'a very handsome round Bottom Crane Neck Coach made of the very best materials'. This ornamental carriage, previously property of colonial Lieutenant Governor Richard Penn Jr and intended only for processional use, was not a very practical gift, given the vast distances that Martha travelled to be with 'his Excellency'. Notwithstanding, she 'politely accepted' the vehicle, which was appraised at a value of £457 18s 6d sterling, when a committee presented it to her on 14 June. It was to serve, they informed her, as 'a small testimonial of the sense the Assembly have of his [His Excellency General Washington's] great and important services to the American States'.[16]

Other assemblies and institutions were eager to honour 'His Excellency' and 'Lady Washington, his amiable consort'. Following the British evacuation of Boston in March 1776, Congress had authorized a medal to be struck, 'George Washington before Boston'. Harvard University conferred an honorary degree on the General, whose earlier education had been truncated. Martha's arrival in Williamsburg early in August was saluted, according to the *Virginia Gazette*, with 'the fire of cannon and small arms', and she was presented with a 'golden emblematic medal', as testimony of the high regard in which the General Assembly held Washington, 'illustrious defender and deliverer of his country'. The Mayor bestowed on the General, 'through his lady', the freedom of the city.[17]

There were elaborate celebrations in Philadelphia on 4 July to mark the anniversary of the day on which the states had declared independence the previous year. Thirteen volleys of guns and as many peals of bells were repeated many times. In the afternoon companies of sailors performed aerial displays on the rigging of vessels in the Delaware. The evening was marked by a 'general illumination'. Citizens set candles in the windows of their houses, and bonfires were lit in the streets. Washington, the man charged with guarding the cause of these celebrations, was confounded by Howe's intentions. The British General had evacuated the Jerseys, embarking the troops he commanded for Staten Island. Washington and the officers about him believed the enemy meant to sail up the Hudson and join with British General Burgoyne in an attack on Fort Ticonderoga. In an attempt to forestall this, Washington marched his troops north through mud and driving rain and over inhospitable country. Discipline and 'manual exercise' – drilling with weapons – were his watchwords, particularly the former, as he stressed, before setting out on 6 July: 'discipline, more than numbers, gives one army the superiority over another'.[18] Sheltering in a log house in the Clove, a wild and narrow pass in the Hudson Highlands, dining on rough rations and with his aides sleeping on the floor around his bed, the General may have wondered how long his troops would submit to the discipline he advocated.

While in Orange County, New York, on 15 July, Washington learned of what he described as 'an Event of Chagrin & Surprize not apprehended, nor within the Compass of my reasoning'.[19] The forts of Ticonderoga and Mount Independence had been ceded to Burgoyne on the 5th without the Continental command making any effort to defend them. Other intelligence was disturbing. Howe and his troops had boarded transports, and remained in New York harbour, off Sandy Hook. Washington wrote to Hancock on the 25th, 'The amazing advantage the Enemy derive from their Ships and the command of the Water, keeps us in a State of constant perplexity and the most anxious conjecture . . .'

The British might yet sail up the Hudson, or instead make for the south and sail up the Delaware to attack Philadelphia. They might even, he suggested, sail towards that city in a 'deep feint', only to turn away. Washington recommended to Hancock that militia 'of the neighbouring counties' in Pennsylvania be called upon. Should the British make a 'sudden and rapid push' for the city, the militia could at least retard and check enemy operations 'till other succours can arrive'.[20] He himself and the Continental army he commanded adopted positions on the New Jersey bank of the Delaware. From there they could respond to an attack either on Philadelphia or on Putnam's forces in the north.

The call to action came on 31 July. Washington wrote to Jonathan Trumbull Sr, Governor of Connecticut: 'At half after nine O'Clock this morning, I received an express from Congress advising – that the Enemy's Fleet consisting of two hundred and twenty eight were at the Capes of Delaware yesterday in the fore noon.'[21] By that evening he was lodged in the City Tavern in Philadelphia. The Continental regiments he commanded – 11,000 strong – were encamping between Germantown and the Schuylkill Falls, five miles north of the city.

The Marquis de Lafayette, graduate of an elite French military academy, had recently come out to America to volunteer for the Continentals. He described the troops as ill armed and ill clothed, and many of them, as he described it, almost naked. 'The best clad wore hunting shirts, large grey linen coats common in the Carolinas.'[22] Their knowledge of military tactics was, he observed, rudimentary. It was not made trial of immediately. Intelligence came on 1 August that Howe and his shipborne army had sailed away again, their destination unknown. Forgetting that he had earlier suspected Howe capable of a 'deep feint', Washington railed to Governor Trumbull: 'the conduct of the Enemy is distressing beyond measure, and past our comprehension . . . nobody doubted but that Philadelphia was the immediate object of their expedition, and that they would commence their operations as soon as possible'.[23]

While the whereabouts of the British fleet were unknown to Washington, he had at least the satisfaction of hearing news of Martha in Virginia. Her brother Bartholomew Dandridge wrote to him from Williamsburg on 22 August to say that Martha was 'in perfect health' at Eltham with the Bassetts, where there was something of a family gathering.[24] Jacky, too, wrote from Williamsburg, with news in early August that the harvest promised 'a plentiful crop' at Washington's land in Frederick County and throughout the state.[25] In a further letter, of 11 September, Custis was bursting with plans for his future and that of his young family. He meant to sell the plantation on the Mattaponi that Washington had purchased on his behalf, following Patsy's death. Jacky cited, among the estate's drawbacks, 'an insufferable quantity of mosquitoes'. He was also hoping, in the next election to the General Assembly, to be selected as delegate for New Kent County. Towards that end he was taking steps to repair the White House on the Pamunkey, where he had been born. It wanted, in his optimistic view, little but whitewashing and plastering. An annexe 'with two good rooms above and below stairs' would make the Parke Custis house 'very comfortable though not elegant, and we shall have room to entertain our friends who will favour us with their company'. Should he be elected a delegate, he wrote earnestly, he meant to serve 'on true Independent Principals to the best of my abilities'.[26] Martha added a fond but matter-of-fact postscript: 'My love, the silver cup I mentioned to you in my letter by the last post – W[eigh]t 113 oz.'[27] The vessel to which she referred is not identifiable.

Though Jacky expressed buoyant confidence in his stepfather, on the very day he wrote Washington suffered the first of several defeats. Howe and his army had at last disembarked. Landing near Head of Elk in Maryland, they marched north-east. In Pennsylvania the Brandywine River lay between them and Philadelphia. The same day that Jacky wrote, 11 September, Washington and his generals offered battle at Chadd's Ford and at contiguous crossings of the river. But Howe and troops under the command of Lord Cornwallis outwitted and outflanked the Americans and crossed at unguarded fords to the north. Battle ensued around a tavern and around a Quaker meeting house within whose walls Friends prayed, undeterred. Over the course of the day the British gained the advantage. Retreating to Chester, Washington wrote to Hancock: 'we have been obliged to leave the enemy masters in the field'.[28]

Plans for a reprisal on 17 September foundered. Severe rain the previous night rendered the arms of the Continental troops, Washington told Thomas Nelson, 'unfit for use, and destroyed

almost all the Ammunition in the men's pouches'. The enemy continued to advance on Philadelphia. 'It is probable some of their Parties
have entered the City,' Washington wrote, 'and their whole Army
may, if they incline to do it, without our being able to prevent them.'
The Continental troops' 'distress for want of Shoes' was, he added,
'almost beyond conception', and rendered both 'operations' and
pursuit 'impracticable'.[29]

The British were indeed in possession of the Pennsylvania capital.
Lord Cornwallis was the first of the British to enter the city, on 26
September, to the triumphant accompaniment of fife and drum. The
population usually numbered 40,000, but he found only a quarter of
the inhabitants in residence. The Pennsylvania Assembly had
adjourned to Lancaster. Congress, pausing only briefly there, had
reconvened still further west and out of reach of the enemy at York,
Pennsylvania, on a tributary of the Susquehanna River.

Though the British held Philadelphia, Washington launched, on
the 4th of the month, a surprise attack on a British garrison, 9,000
strong, in nearby Germantown. This engagement, he later told his
brother Samuel, 'had every appearance (after a contest of two hours
and 40 Minutes) of deciding in our favour'.[30] But visibility was much
reduced by the clouds of artillery smoke as well as by foggy conditions. Two American columns were on the point of driving out the
British in separate attacks. 'Unhappily', Washington wrote on the
fifth to Congressional delegate Benjamin Harrison, '. . . each took
the other for fresh troops of the enemy, and retreated precipitately'.[31]
A thousand Continental troops, he later told his brother John
Augustine, were killed or wounded, or had deserted. The enemy had
suffered too: 'the hospital at Philadelphia and several large meeting
houses are filled with their wounded . . . In a word it was a bloody
day – would to Heaven I could add that it had been a more fortunate
one for us.'

Washington's reputation, the 'honour' he held so dear, could gain
little from such encounters. But he was busy, supervising the defence
of forts on the Delaware still in American hands. General Horatio
Gates, newly commander of the army in the north, enjoyed more
success. Burgoyne and 6,000 British and Hessian troops surrendered

to him at Saratoga, New York on 17 October. The north was in American hands. Washington, imparting this 'important and glorious news' to John Augustine next day, deemed the surrender a 'signal stroke of providence'.[32] The British General and his troops would now be embarked for Europe, and lost to Howe. Washington was perturbed that Gates had sent him no word of the victory. He had instead to rely on unconfirmed reports and copies of Gates's communications to Congress. But the parlous situation to hand was uppermost in his mind.

From Mount Vernon, on the 26th, Jacky wrote: 'from the favourable reports circulating among us, I am in hopes shortly to hear that Howe is in the same situation with Burgoyne'. Jacky had it in mind to transact numerous land bargains with his stepfather, and hoped Washington might soon be free to come home. He had been checked by his mother in one transaction he had earlier proposed. Washington himself was agreeable to his stepson's renting Claiborne's, a dower property with good grazing in King William County. The affair must be postponed, Jacky told Washington: 'Mamma seems to have some objections to renting it during her life. When I first wrote to you I thought she had no objections, but since I received your letter, I have talked to her on that subject and it does not appear to be perfectly agreeable to her.'[33]

Washington had deferred to Martha in much of her children's upbringing. In the matter of the Parke Custis lands that came to her second husband by marriage, it would appear she had a veto and was not afraid to use it. 'It is not my wish to let it for any longer term than your Mama inclines to,' the commander confirmed in due course.[34] Should Washington predecease Martha – and it was not improbable that on some 'bloody day' soon he might fall – Mount Vernon would pass to Washington kin. For good reason she wished her husband only to rent out for his own life a property a short distance upriver from the Bassetts at Eltham. Upon its reversion to her, it might afford a comfortable dower house across the Pamunkey from the White House in New Kent County.

If Howe should remain at large, Jacky wrote on 26 October from Mount Vernon, he himself would have the 'pleasure of visiting camp'.

He hoped he and his stepfather could transact other business there.[35] Washington informed his brother Samuel, on the 27th, that Fielding Lewis had bought him some lots at Warm Springs: 'it was always my intention to become a proprietor there if a town should be laid off at that place'. As commander and not as land speculator, he ended his letter: 'The situation of the two armies is shortly this – the enemy are in Philadelphia – and we hovering round them, to distress and retard their operations as much as possible.'[36]

Martha, writing from Mount Vernon on 18 November to her sister Nancy Bassett, confirmed her husband's activities: 'The last letter I had from the General was dated the 7th of this month – he says nothing has happened since the unsuccessful [British] attack upon our forts on the Delaware.' Martha's two nephews, Burwell Junior and John, who had been inoculated with the smallpox at Mount Vernon, were now returning home. She told her sister that they had been 'exceeding good boys indeed and I shall hope you will let them come to see me whenever they can spare so much time from school . . . the doctor's charge is very high but I did not say a word – as he carried the children so well through the smallpox'. In other family news, she wrote that her daughter-in-law and granddaughter had been 'over the river' – at Mount Airy in Maryland – for the past three weeks. 'Jack is just come over – he tells me that little Bet is grown as fat as a pig.'[37]

Days later in Pennsylvania Washington wrote to John Augustine with less cheerful news. The enemy had taken Forts Mifflin and Mercer on the Delaware, and removed the *chevaux de frise* in the river that had previously obstructed their shipping. Now 'their provisions, stores, etc' could come upriver, and the British could be expected to winter in Philadelphia. He himself was now looking for a winter cantonment for the Continental troops. Attack on the British in Philadelphia for the moment was out of the question. The Continental troops were exhausted by the gruelling marches, counter-marches, attacks and retreats that had marked this punishing summer and autumn campaign. Moreover, they still desperately wanted clothing, shoes and food. Congress – in exile at York – lacked the wherewithal to supply these necessities.

Washington settled in December, for a winter cantonment, on an area known as Valley Forge, a maze of disused ironworks twenty miles north-west of Philadelphia at the mouth of Valley Creek on the Schuylkill. The terrain was such that they could at least fend off any surprise raid. At Valley Forge they must regroup and recover, in preparation for further campaigns. Ragged force though they were, this army must withstand, in the new year, attempts by the British in Philadelphia to march on Congress in York and win new territory elsewhere.

Martha told her brother-in-law Burwell Bassett on 22 December, 'he cannot come home this winter but as soon as the army under his command goes into winter quarter he will send for me. If he does, I must go . . .' Washington and the army under his command had in fact reached Valley Forge two days earlier. Martha's letter was one of condolence. Following invalid years, her beloved sister Nancy – 'the greatest favourite I had in the world' – had died. Martha wrote wistfully to widower Bassett, who was mourning his heir, Billy, as well 'I have often wished that fortune had placed us nearer to each other'. She then ventured a suggestion: 'My dear sister in her lifetime often mentioned my taking my dear Fanny' – the Bassetts' ten-year-old daughter – 'if she [Nancy] should be taken away before she grew up.' She made this offer to her brother-in-law: 'If you will let her come to live with me, I will with the greatest pleasure take her and be a parent and mother to her as long as I live.'[38] If her husband did not call for her, if Bassett acceded to her request, Martha could come and fetch her niece early in the New Year. She waited only for the birth of a new grandchild, expected imminently, and for her daughter-in-law's recovery.

Over the holiday period Martha was hospitable. Lund Washington complained to Washington on Christmas Eve: 'you, sir, may think (as everyone would) that in your absence we live at a less expense than when you are at home but it is the reverse, it is seldom that this house is without company – our stable always full of horses'.[39]

Nelly gave birth on New Year's Eve 1777 to another daughter, Martha Parke Custis, to be known as Pat, and later as Patty. But Martha did not go south to Eltham to fetch her niece. The call had come from Washington for her to join him. Jacky wrote to his stepfather in mid-January 1778, apologizing for not escorting his mother, 'Nelly will not be in such a situation as I could leave her.' One of his toes, besides, Jacky noted, was not recovered from 'an ugly frost bite I got some time ago'.[40]

Washington replied at the beginning of February: 'Your Mamma is not yet arrived, but if she left Mount Vernon on the 26th Ultimo as intended, may, I think, be expected every hour.' He added, aware of the danger of his letter falling into enemy hands: 'We are in a dreary kind of place, and uncomfortably provided.'[41] Conditions at Valley Forge were, in fact, not far from desperate, as Martha discovered upon her entry into camp on 5 February.

Valley Forge, 1777–1778

No bread, no soldier.

Four days after his arrival on 19 December 1777 in remote Valley Forge, Washington had issued this warning to Henry Laurens, newly President of Congress. Unless 'some great and capital change' occurred in the commissary, or provisioning department, he advised, 'this Army must inevitably be reduced to one or other of these three things. Starve – dissolve – or disperse, in order to obtain subsistence in the best manner they can.' The troops, numbering 12,000 and wintering by the Schuylkill, were 'as often without Provisions now, as with them'. Looking ahead, he added: 'what is to become of us in the spring, when our force will be collected, with the aid perhaps of Militia . . .?'[1] Some months later he gave a vivid picture of the hardship endured during the initial weeks at Valley Forge: 'men without clothes to cover their nakedness, without Blankets to lay on, without Shoes, by which their Marches might be traced by the Blood from their feet . . . Marching through frost & Snow, and at Christmas taking up their Winter Quarters within a day's march of the enemy, without a House or Hutt to cover them till they could be built & submitting to it without a murmur.'[2] He listed, for Congress, in December 1777, numerous supplies that had been lacking since Brandywine, among them soap and vinegar. He added, 'The first indeed [soap] we have now little occasion for', few men having more than one shirt and some 'none at all'.[3]

Washington established headquarters in a fieldstone house above the Schuylkill, a quarter of a mile from the tents that the officers and men, some 12,000 strong, occupied on their arrival. Aide Timothy Pickering wrote to his wife that they were 'exceedingly pinched for room', but the General considered the arrangements adequate. He had an upper bedchamber. The secretaries and aides bunked in smaller rooms on the same storey. Conditions were luxurious compared to the cabins that the troops, in squads of twelve, set about making, according to Washington's specifications: 'fourteen by sixteen each – sides, ends and roofs made with logs, and the roof made tight with split slabs – or in some other way – the sides made tight with clay – fire-place made of wood and secured with clay on the inside eighteen inches thick, this fire-place to be in the rear of the hut – the door to be in the end next the street . . . The officers' huts to form a line in the rear of the troops . . .'[4]

Over the next six weeks this 'hutting' was accomplished. When Martha arrived at headquarters, a great city of log cabins, affording winter shelter, had been erected above the banks of the Schuylkill. Provisioning the army, however, early on an anxiety, was now in crisis. In late January 1778 Washington had castigated the different branches of the 'Commissary's Department', source of food, forage, transport and much else for the troops. He was 'supplying the army from hand to mouth (if I may be allowed the phrase), scarcely ever having more than two or three days provisions beforehand'.[5] General Greene, offering thoughts on the reform of the army this month, confirmed the bleak outlook: 'People begin to think coolly, they compare their condition in the field with that at home. The situation of their families, & their future prospects grow into objects of importance.'[6] Officers were reluctant to renew their commissions, and desertion by the hungry men they commanded was increasing.

When Martha joined her husband in camp on 5 February, he was oppressed by these difficulties. He had also recently been subject to what he called, in January, 'insidious attacks' and 'injurious' insinuations.[7] Few – and Washington was not among them – had failed to make the comparison between the British surrender to Gates at

Saratoga in October 1777 and his own loss of Philadelphia. Members of Congress and officers – some said, Gates himself – were among those who campaigned behind closed doors to have the successful General replace the current Commander-in-Chief. An anonymous printed letter, headed 'Thoughts of a Freeman', lauded Gates, criticized Washington and ended with the charge: 'That the people of America have been guilty of Idolatry by making a man their god – and that the God of Heaven and Earth will convince them by wofull experience that he is only a man.'[8]

Tench Tilghman wrote from Valley Forge to Robert Morris on 2 February: 'I have never seen any stroke of ill fortune affect the General in the manner that this dirty underhanded dealing has done. It hurts him the more because he cannot take notice of it without publishing to the world that the spirit of faction begins to work among us.'[9] The young Marquis de Lafayette, at headquarters, scoffed at those in Congress who criticized Washington. They were, in his view, 'Stupid men who, without knowing a Single word about war, undertake to judge You . . . make Ridiculous Comparisons; they are infatuated with Gates without thinking of the different Circumstances, and Believe that attacking is the only thing Necessary to Conquer.'[10] But the Commander-in-Chief himself became prey to doubt about his powers of leadership. He wrote to President Laurens on 31 January, 'My Heart tells me it has been my unremitted aim to do the best circumstances would permit; yet, I may have been very often mistaken in my judgment of the means, and may, in many instances deserve the imputation of error.'[11] He detailed to a Congressional committee in camp the many obstructions to success that threatened his army and made recommendations for their removal. When the committee reported back to York, their first-hand testimony to the strains under which Washington was operating had their effect. Gradually, agitation to replace Washington with Gates died away. Alexander Hamilton opined to New York Governor George Clinton on February 13 that a 'Certain faction' – he dubbed it a monster – had unmasked its batteries too soon.[12] But, when Martha arrived in camp, the attacks were still fresh in the minds of all. Benjamin Harrison, in Virginia, averred to Robert Morris on the 19th that only duty had kept Washington from resigning: 'The general is fully informed of all these cabals, they prey on his constitution, sink his spirits . . . He well knows bad consequences would follow his resignation, or he would not leave it in the power of the wicked and designing thus to insult him . . .'[13]

The day after Martha's arrival on 5 February, Washington wrote to Jonathan Trumbull, Sr, Governor of Connecticut: 'There is the strongest reason to believe, that its [the army's] existence cannot be of long duration, unless more constant, regular and larger supplies of the meat kind are furnished, than have been for some time past.' He urged 'those in the purchasing line' in Connecticut to forward supplies of cattle. Similar letters went to the governors of other states.[14] He informed the Commissary General of Purchases, on 7 February, that the 'occasional deficiencies in the Article of provisions', so often severely felt, were now 'on the point of resolving themselves into this fatal crisis – total want and dissolution of the army'. The 'spirit of desertion among the soldiery' was alarming, he added: the 'murmurs on account of Provisions are become universal'. He dreaded mutiny.[15]

The cold, and the damp earth on which the men slept in the huts, had other ill effects. Three thousand men were invalid that month, dysentery and malaria among their complaints. Local farmhouses were pressed into service as makeshift isolation wards for smallpox patients. 'Our men are falling sick in numbers every day', General Anthony Wayne told Thomas Wharton on the 10th, 'contracting vermin and dying in Hospitals, in a condition shocking to Humanity, & horrid in Idea.' Hundreds of men, he wrote, had 'not a single rag of a shirt, (but are obliged to wear their waistcoats next their skins & to sleep in them at nights) . . .'[16] Many were without shoes and could neither make foraging expeditions nor successfully skirmish with the British in the country between the camp and Philadelphia. Everywhere, in short, there were signs of distress. Horses were dying for want of forage, and carcasses littered the camp.

For lack of central organization in the wake of the autumn campaigns, wagons and teams, with tools and regimental weapons, were scattered haphazardly all over Pennsylvania and New Jersey. The Congressional committee, in camp to observe conditions, reported on 12 February, 'Not less than three thousand spades, and shovels, and the like number of tomahawks have been lately discovered . . . in the vicinity of the camp.'[17]

The troops at Valley Forge made a pitiful if valiant picture. Teams of men patiently yoked themselves to little carriages of their own making and loaded wood or provisions on their backs. A gallows humour developed among officers and men reduced to mounting guard in blankets, for lack of a coat and breeches; to drilling with muskets rusted with rain and lacking bayonets; and to eating 'fire-cake', a patty of flour and water baked in the ashes of camp fires when no other rations were forthcoming.

In these days of suffering Washington was a highly visible commander, riding daily with his aides between the log huts. But Francis Dana, chairman of the Congressional committee, noted on the 15th that, on average, 'every regiment had been destitute of fish or flesh four days. On Saturday evening they received, some, three-fourths, and others, one half pound, of salted pork a man – not one day's allowance.'[18] Discipline in the camp, always fragile in the Continental army, was in danger of breaking down. Officers were daily court-martialled for seizing bread from their men – or whisky or shoes. On the 18th some of the troops received rations of a quarter of a pound of meat; some, none. Mutiny and desertion threatened more than ever. 'No bread, no soldier', went the cry.[19] Common soldiers protested their plight to General Washington himself at headquarters.

There were at Valley Forge no afternoon riding parties for Martha and her 'old man' as there had been the previous spring at Morristown. Washington was occupied with his aides and generals until they joined Martha at dinner at three. Thereafter Washington and his aides – Tench Tilghman, Hamilton and John Laurens among them – fell to business again, before joining Martha and other company. The Washingtons were alone together only at night, before the rigorous routine began again with morning.

No trace of self-pity appears in the animated letter that Martha directed, a month after her arrival in Valley Forge, to Mercy Otis

Warren in Cambridge. She conceded that the General's quarters at Valley Forge were 'very small'. But she added appreciatively, 'he has had a log cabin built to dine in which has made our quarters much more tolerable than they were at first.' She hoped and trusted that all the states would 'make a vigorous push' early in the spring, 'thereby putting a stop to British cruelties and afford[ing] us that peace liberty and happiness which we have so long contended for'. It had given her, she wrote with martial fervour, 'unspeakable pleasure' to hear that General Burgoyne and his army – prisoners-of-war, awaiting embarkation for Europe – were 'in safe quarters in your state'. She added, 'Would bountiful Providence aim a like stroke at General Howe, the measure of my happiness would be complete.'

Martha's description of conditions in camp on 7 March was bland: 'The general is camped in what they call the great Valley on the banks of the Schuylkill. Officers and men are chiefly in huts, which they say is tolerable comfortable. The army are as healthy as can well be expected in general.'[20] The truth, not to be expressed in correspondence that the enemy might acquire, was less palatable. More than 2,500 men died at Valley Forge from frostbite, dysentery, malaria and smallpox during the six months the army was encamped there. Interception of correspondence across state lines was common. It was essential that Howe and the British in Philadelphia should not learn of the ravages that lack of food and other necessities had wrought on the army.

'Total want', or famine, and dissolution of the army, which Washington had earlier dreaded, did not take place. At the end of March there were still men unshod and others without shirts. There was still no straw for bedding, and there were to be days of short rations ahead. Many of the civil departments of the army continued in disarray. Congress was slow to act on the recommendations for reform that the committee at Valley Forge urged upon the assembly. But the governors to whom Washington had written made determined efforts to respond to the army's need for provisions, and a competent Commissary General for Purchases was appointed. The commander also prevailed on Nathanael Greene to take on the duties of Quartermaster General. Greene oversaw the refurbishment of thousands of stands of arms in readiness for a new campaigning season. He also led successful foraging expeditions far afield. As spring came to Pennsylvania, at headquarters a monotonous February diet of veal, fowl, cabbage and turnips expanded in the course of March to include fresh pork, beef, cheese and oysters.[21]

A few weeks after Martha's arrival, a Prussian officer, Baron Friedrich von Steuben, had appeared at Valley Forge. His role, with Congressional approval, was to be Inspector General of the army, or drillmaster. Employing a comical mixture of French and pidgin-English imprecations, he forced parade-ground discipline on the army. Von Steuben, with his secretary, Pierre Du Ponceau, became a regular guest at dinners at headquarters. Du Ponceau later recorded of their relations with the commander: 'We visited him also in the evening, when Mrs Washington was at headquarters. We were in a manner domesticated in the family.' At these gatherings, he added, 'Every gentleman or lady who could sing, was called upon in turn for a song.'[22] Other foreign volunteers, too, many of them French, made their way to headquarters. The Washingtons could rely on Lafayette, on Alexander Hamilton, raised in the French West Indies, and on Francophone Caty Greene, who joined her husband at camp in March, as interpreters. New aide John Laurens, President Laurens's son, who had been educated in Europe, and James Monroe, linguist aide-de-camp to Lord Stirling, were other magnets for foreign visitors.

While Washington was at work during the day, Martha had established an upper sitting room of her own. In April some Quaker ladies from Philadelphia came to headquarters, seeking clemency for the husband of one of their number. He had been charged with selling supplies to the British. Following the usual 'elegant dinner', Washington considered Henry Drinker's case, while Martha entertained the ladies upstairs some hours. Though the commander's Washington's verdict was not favourable to the ladies' cause, they appreciated their civil reception by his wife. Elizabeth Drinker described Martha as a 'sociable, pretty kind of woman'.[23]

Such gatherings of ladies, though they be sober Quakers, in the upper sitting room were rare. Elias Boudinot, a Morristown acquaintance, now Commissary of prisoners-of-war, declared Martha in April 'almost a mope', for want of 'a female companion'.[24] She was indeed much alone, though numerous officers' wives dined at headquarters with their husbands. Lucy Knox, Henry Knox's wife, whom Martha liked, was in New Haven, Connecticut, with her young daughter and only reached Valley Forge in late May. The Stirling ladies were never close to Martha. Caty Greene, in her early twenties, took up residence with her husband at Moore Hall, some distance from headquarters. This house, better than his cabin at camp, could accommodate the press of business that came his way, now that Greene was Quartermaster General. Young Mrs Greene was 'saucy', by her own confession – and, some said, more than that with her husband's colleague, General Anthony Wayne. She was a general favourite, but she was no confidante for Martha.

Nevertheless, Martha remained stoutly at her husband's side. In Virginia, as a result of both births and deaths, her world was undergoing significant changes. Her mother, Frances Dandridge, had recently moved from Chestnut Grove, long her residence, after her elder son, William, drowned there. Frances was now the pensioner of her younger son, Bartholomew, elsewhere. With her sister Nancy's death and this removal of her mother from the Dandridge family home, Martha's ties to New Kent County sensibly lessened.

Martha appears to have been stoical concerning Jacky's plan to forge a life among the squirearchy on the Pamunkey. Neither her son nor her daughter-in-law were as much with Martha as they had been before starting a family. Nelly was now 'so much confined with her children', Martha told Mercy Otis Warren in March 1778, 'that she stays altogether with them'.[25] Jacky had always doted on his elder daughter, who had dark Parke Custis good looks. He had dubbed her 'Miss Bet' and thought her, when she was not yet two, 'very saucy and entertaining'. Pat, 'the most good natured, quiet little creature in the world', with her mother's fair colouring, he wrote to his mother in April, had initially been 'a disappointment' to him. He had hoped for a son and heir. But a few months after her birth he was partisan: 'I could not have loved it better if it had been a boy.'[26]

Content to be at her husband's side, while Jacky and Nelly lavished affection on their children in Virginia, Martha burnished Washington's image as commander to some purpose. She paid $56 to Charles Willson Peale, who delivered to her on 16 February a 'picture' of her husband, and, the following month, '2 miniatures' of His Excellency.[27] These miniatures, unlike full-scale portraits in oil, were eminently portable. Visible emblems of Washington's status and no bigger than the palm of a hand, they could be displayed and shown and copied in Congress and in camp.

Martha was not always satisfied with her husband's portraits and was not afraid to say so. In March, John Laurens, acting as her secretary, expressed dissatisfaction with a recent likeness that an aide-de-camp to the Austrian volunteer Baron de Kalb had taken: 'Mrs Washington has received the Miniature, and wishes to know whether Major Rogers [the artist] is still at York – the defects of this Portrait, I think, are that the visage is too long, and old age is too strongly marked in it.' Amateur artist Nicholas Rogers had complained of Washington, as a sitter, that he had a 'remarkable dead eye'. Young Laurens conceded, 'Altho' his Countenance when affected either by Joy or Anger is full of expression – yet when the Muscles are in a state of repose, his eye certainly wants animation.'[28] Washington's impassive gaze was on many occasions, when another might have shown signs of frustration, of great utility to him.

Martha was not only a fierce guardian of her husband's image. She, who had never doubted him, was a recipient for confidences he could make to no one else. Hamilton, Lafayette and Laurens, devoted though they were to the Commander-in-Chief, were young and sometimes rash. His senior aide, Fitzgerald, and Harrison and Tilghman were conscientious copyists and messengers. With Nathanael Greene and Henry Knox, both excellent officers, Washington fruitfully discussed the progress of the war, the strategy, and the needs of the army. But he had known all these officers and aides for, at best, a very few years. With Martha, his wife and close companion of nearly two decades, he could speak of a future after the war. With Martha he could share his frustrations at being kept from home and from the management of the property which meant so much to him. He concluded a long list of instructions to Lund Washington in a letter of 28 February: 'nothing but your having the charge of my business, and the entire confidence I repose in you, could make me tolerable easy. To go on in the improvement of my Estate in the manner heretofore described to you – fulfilling my plans – and keeping my property together, are the principal objects I have in view during these troubles.'[29]

Lund Washington toiled on and on in his cousin's absence. He was eager to have work on the front of the house finished, and scaffolding taken down, before Martha should return. But, as usual, local craftsmen were laggardly. 'Of all the worthless men living Lanphier is the greatest,' he wrote on 22 April. 'No art or temptation of mine can prevail on him to come to work, notwithstanding his repeated promises to do so.' Until this joiner finished making the window in the pediment, the scaffolding must remain.[30]

This was not Lund's only concern. Washington, in March, directed him to sell two unsatisfactory slaves, Bett and Phyllis, to new masters, if the women were willing to go. Neither sale was successful. Bett was to have gone, for £200, to 'a man living in Botetourt city'. Her mother, Lund wrote in early April, appeared 'so uneasy about it', and Bett herself 'made such promises of amendment', that he 'could not force her to go with the man'. Phyllis, whom Lund offered for £200 to another man, 'was so alarmed at the thoughts of being sold, that the man could not get her to utter a word of English, and therefore he believed she could not speak'. This transaction, too, failed.

Lund suggested he sell at public auction these two slaves and a third – Orford – and 'pay no regard to their being willing or not'. He intended coming to camp soon, when he would see his cousin's instructions. Lund awaited the annual spring run of shad on the Potomac. Some of the fish, when netted and dried, was destined for sale to the army, following Congress's orders for 'a quantity of shad to be cured on this river'. Some, he would keep, for the use of 'our own people'.[31]

At Valley Forge the Washingtons lived on sociable terms with many European volunteers – Lafayette, Du Ponceau, de Kalb and von Steuben among them. In their countries, medieval serfdom was now long forgotten, though slave labour still drove the economies of the French West Indies, where Alexander Hamilton had grown up. Lafayette openly voiced his distaste for the oppression of 'negroes' in America and for the public auctions at which they were often sold. John Laurens, the son of a Carolina plantation owner, had been educated in London and Geneva. He begged his father, Congressional President Laurens, to cede him 'a number of your able-bodied men slaves'. It was his intention, wrote John, to form from this 'untried source' – slaves from the different southern states – a black light horse regiment 5,000 strong. He argued that slaves' 'habits of subordination, patience under fatigues, sufferings and privations of every kind' would serve them well as soldiers. At the same time, he argued, they would embrace military service with enthusiasm – a 'proper gradation between abject slavery and perfect liberty'. The Commander-in-Chief, he reported, had given a cautious welcome to the project, though expressing concern for the financial loss it would constitute to the Laurenses estate: 'He is convinced that the numerous tribes of blacks in the southern parts of the continent, offer a resource to us that should not be neglected.'[32] President Laurens squashed his son's proposal as an 'eccentric' notion. But Washington's willingness to countenance such a venture was part and parcel of the direction his thinking was taking.

Since December 1776 'free negroes' had been encouraged to enlist in the Continental army, and hundreds served in the militia of different states. In late winter 1778, when Rhode Island had few recruits to offer the army, Washington gave tacit encouragement to a plan to recruit slaves in the state. The slaves were to be 'absolutely made free', and entitled to all the wages of any Continental soldier enlisting. The masters were to be compensated at a rate of £120 'for the most valuable slave', and in proportion for those of lesser value.[33]

In more populous Virginia, no such scheme was suggested. Lord Dunmore's Ethiopian Regiment, which slaves had run away to join, still rankled with plantation owners. Moreover, Washington would have regarded £120 as a low return for 'property', when even women slaves went for more. Nevertheless, he had long regarded the slave workforce at Mount Vernon as 'stock' expensive to maintain. Clothing, rice, rum and shoe leather were the least of it. Doctors' and midwives' bills were a constant drain on the estate. Above all, overseers in every 'quarter' were required to threaten a labour force reluctant and lacking in incentive to work. When he could, Washington paid hirelings to supplement the less than satisfactory efforts of his 'negroes'. In August 1778 he was to write to Lund of a new plan he had conceived. He had it in mind to barter, for land that he wished to acquire, 'Negroes (of whom I every day long more & more to get clear of)'. He wrote of other acreage: 'For this Land also I had rather give Negroes – if Negroes would do. For, to be plain, I wish to get quit of Negroes.'[34]

There is no evidence that Martha shared Washington's wish to 'get quit of negroes' or his repugnance about selling them at public auction. Bett, Phyllis and Orford were all sold at auction the following year. A Mount Vernon peopled by waged workers was as yet as much a pipe-dream as was John Laurens's plan for the regiment of black light horse. For Martha, the dower slaves were property, like the land at Claiborne's, in which she had a life interest. On her death she fully intended that those slaves who survived her would revert to the Parke Custis estate.

As slaves were subject to their masters and mistresses, so was their comfort subject to the wishes of their owners. This February Washington's mother in Fredericksburg had required a slave, Silla, to be sent to her from Mount Vernon. 'I believe she will be very unwilling to go,' wrote Lund on 18 February, 'she having cooper Jack for a husband, and they appear to live comfortable together.' In March he wrote of Jack: 'He cries and begs, saying he had rather be hanged than separated.'[35] But Mary Washington's comfort was paramount, and go to Fredericksburg Silla surely did. Meanwhile Washington's body servant, Will Lee, and Martha's maids – house slaves from Mount Vernon – served their master and mistress at Valley Forge.

In early April Charles Lee, on parole and soon to be exchanged with a British officer, was received in camp with full honours. The general's earlier foolhardiness in venturing so near the enemy at Basking Ridge as to be captured was passed over. By the approaching exchange of prisoners, Washington would gain an experienced general who could play a part when the enemy again began their military operations. Washington 'received General Lee as if he had been his brother', and escorted him to headquarters where Martha was waiting. Following an 'elegant' dinner in the log annexe, Lee was assigned a room 'back of Mrs Washington's sitting room, and all his baggage was stowed in it . . .'[36] The allocation of this chamber in the cramped house was a mark of favour. Washington also assigned to Lee command of the right wing of the army in due course. If he thought that, by these attentions, he had propitiated his volatile subaltern, he was mistaken.

The high command of the Continental army, soon to include Lee, held numerous Councils of War this spring at Valley Forge. On each occasion they judged it inadvisable to launch an attack on Philadelphia. They would wait, rather, until the British moved against them or, indeed, against American positions on the Hudson. Von Steuben continued to drill officers and men, Knox, to train the artillery, and Greene, to muster supplies of horses, wagon teams and tents for the field. But across the Atlantic the British government was working to suppress American rebellion, while in Paris, Benjamin Franklin and other envoys were pressing Louis XVI and his government to support the patriot cause.

The same day that Lee received his full exchange, Washington wrote: 'The enemy are beginning to play a game more dangerous than their efforts by arms . . . They are endeavouring to ensnare the people by specious allurements of peace.'[37] Copies of draft Parliamentary Bills which reached Valley Forge on 18 April made clear that Lord North, the British Prime Minister, was sending peace commissioners to offer terms to Congress at York.[38] These emissaries were to offer pardons and more equitable taxation to the American 'rebels' in exchange for a cessation of hostilities.

For all that the former colonies named themselves states, statehood would be officially conferred upon them only when final ratification of Articles of Confederation, signed the previous November, took place. Notwithstanding their unofficial standing, from when they were first mooted these Articles provided a serviceable framework for national and international government. Virginia had promptly ratified the Articles in December, and most of the other former colonies soon followed suit. Final ratification by Congress was to take place only in March 1781, Maryland being the last province or state to approve them. The emissaries must fail if Congress held firm to these Articles, which set the United States of America on the path to a stable and independent footing. There were those within Congress and without, however, who wavered at the thought of peace.

In a highly charged atmosphere at camp, welcome news from Europe was received. Evading British navy ships, the *Sensible*, a French frigate of thirty-six guns, had docked at Casco Bay in Maine. Passenger Simeon Deane, brother to one of the United States' three commissioners in Paris, bore dispatches for Congress. Treaties of commerce and alliance between France and America had been signed in the French capital in February. Louis XVI's government was assembling a fleet and troops to come to the aid of the United States of America. The victory of Gates at Saratoga had done much to persuade the French to recognize the new nation across the Atlantic.

At Valley Forge, so recently the scene of hardship and deprivation, a 'grand military fete and jubilee' took place on 7 May. The chaplain attached to the 'Jersey service' – the regiments from New Jersey – preached at a service which George and Martha, with other officers and their wives, attended. Thereafter Washington reviewed the whole army, and dined in public with all its officers, while a military band played. 'Long live the King of France' was among the toasts made. When the commander took his leave, 'there was a universal clap, with loud huzzas' and 'a thousand hats tossed in the air. His Excellency turned round with his retinue and huzzaed several times.'[39] Opponent Sir William Howe had resigned as British Commander-in-Chief and sailed for England later that month. General Washington, whose spirits had recently sunk so low, whose leadership had been doubted, was restored to grace.

Philadelphia and Middlebrook, New Jersey, 1778–1779

His Excellency and Mrs Greene danced
upwards of three hours . . .

The time had nearly come for Washington and Martha to part once more. To Washington's chagrin, the French Admiral the Comte d'Estaing did not arrive in American waters in time to give battle to the British fleet while they occupied the Delaware. Reacting with alarm to reports of the new alliance, the British in Philadelphia embarked nearly all their baggage and stores. Washington surmised that Clinton, recently knighted and newly British commander in America, planned to make for the Hudson Highlands. There, the enemy would hope to take American posts before auxiliary French troops arrived to bolster the Continental numbers. News of the Franco-American alliance had revived Congress. Those delegates who had earlier favoured making terms were now among the foremost to reject the offer of peace the British commissioners now brought to Pennsylvania.

While Martha headed south to Mount Vernon, Washington's own intention was to force an engagement on Clinton before the British forces could reach the Hudson. On 18 June, the commander informed Congress at York that, upon receiving news of the evacuation of Philadelphia early that morning, he had 'put six brigades in motion' to follow the enemy. Three marched off under Lee at midday, the others followed in the afternoon.[1] The next morning, at five o'clock, Washington himself departed with the rest of the army.

On the 24th, at Hopewell, New Jersey, Washington decided to attack the enemy, an intention in which his generals supported him – bar Lee, who declared himself strongly opposed to such a plan. Indeed, Lee gave up the command of the advance divisions to Lafayette, only to demand it back a day after the Marquis pressed forward. Washington wrote to the volatile General on the 26th: 'it is not in my power fully to remove it [the command of the detachment sent forward] without wounding the feelings of the Marquis de Lafayette'. He placated Lee with the command of the 'whole advanced body'.[2]

Two days later Washington, with the main army, was advancing towards Monmouth Courthouse, where the British and Hessians were encamped. But the morning of 28 June had an 'unfortunate and bad beginning', as Washington later informed his brother, John Augustine. Suddenly, three miles from the Courthouse, General Lee and his advance troops, 6,000 of them, appeared. They were fleeing General Cornwallis and the enemy, who were pressing hard upon their rear.

What followed owed much to the American commander's leadership, though he wrote modestly about the role he played: 'the disorder arising from it [this retreat] would have proved fatal to the Army, had not that bountiful Providence, which has never failed us in the hour of distress, enabled me to form a Regiment or two (of those that were retreating) in the face of the Enemy, and under their fire . . .' Washington arrested the flight of enough troops to form a body of men to repulse the oncoming British. He limited his engagement with Lee to an angry exchange, then sent the General to the rear, and later had him court-martialled. 'In the Morning we expected to renew the Action,' he told John Augustine, 'when behold! the enemy had stole off as Silent as the Grave in the Night after having sent away their wounded. Without exaggerating,' Washington concluded with satisfaction, 'their trip through the Jerseys in killed, Wounded, Prisoners, & deserters, has cost them at least 2000 Men & of their best Troops.'[3] He ordered, in celebration of the second anniversary of the declaration of independence, on 4 July, a firing of cannon and a *feu de joie*, or rapid rifle salute, of the whole line on the Brunswick side of the Raritan.

The pitched battle at Monmouth Courthouse represented America's last effort in the cause of independence unaided by a foreign power. As ever, following an engagement, the Commander-in-Chief had been punctilious in assuring his wife that he was safe. Major General Benedict Arnold, Military Governor of Philadelphia since the British had abandoned the city, wrote on 30 June to Washington, 'I received your Excellency's Favour of yesterday, at 10 o Clock this morning with the Letter Inclosed for Mrs Washington which I dispatch'd immediately by Express. I beg leave to present your Excellency my Congratulatory Compliments on the Victory you have obtained over the Enemy.'[4]

Martha had returned to Mount Vernon earlier that month, Lund Washington acting as her escort from Pennsylvania. She found her son newly a delegate to the Virginia General Assembly in Williamsburg. Though Jacky had earlier intended to offer himself for New Kent County, when he meant to reside there, the attractions of his birth-place had palled. Instead, he and George Mason had been elected in April by the 'gentlemen of Fairfax', the property holders of Fairfax County. 'I never wished anything more in my life than to settle in this county,' he averred to Washington on 11 May. 'I know the people, they are better disposed than any part of Virginia.' He was satis-fied, he went on, that he would live happier there, 'than in any other part'. He added blithely that communication with the Parke Custis lands in the south, as they lay on the water, would be 'very easy, and not attended with great expense', whenever the Chesapeake Bay was open for shipping.[5]

Jacky, looking about for a home to buy, settled on Abingdon, a plantation twelve miles north of Mount Vernon and upriver of Alexandria. It belonged to a Fairfax County neighbour, Robert Alexander, and Washington deemed it in May 'a pleasant Seat & capable of improvement'.[6] He later wrote that his stepson's residence at Abingdon would be 'an agreeable measure to your Mother – and a pleasing one to me'.[7] The price of the estate was, Jacky admitted, 'very extravagant' – £12,000. His stepfather agreed, but remarked: 'as you want it to live at – as it answers your's & Nelly's views – I do not think the price ought to be a capital object with you . . .' Jacky had determined to sell some parcels of his estates on the York and Pamunkey. Washington urged, on 26 May, that any money secured by these sales should be 'immediately vested in the funds, or laid out in other lands . . .' He warned his stepson: 'if this is not done be assured, it will melt like Snow before a hot Sun, and you will be able to give as little acct of the going of it . . . Lands are permanent – rising fast in value – and will be very dear when our Independency is established, and the Importance of America better known.'[8]

Jacky made a very bad bargain, including paying Alexander, at the expiration of twenty-four years, the principal – £12,000 – 'with compound interest'. He wrote to Washington on 15 July, 'Nothing could have induced me to give such terms, but the unconquerable desire I had to live in the neighbourhood of Mount Vernon and in the county of Fairfax.' He intended, he wrote, to sell much of the estate he had inherited, leaving only some profitable tracts in King William and New Kent which could be looked after by a single manager.[9]

Though he apologized for 'intermeddling', in his response of 3 August, Washington did not allow Jacky's profligacy to pass without comment: 'let me entreat you to consider the consequences of paying compound Interest . . . I presume you are not unacquainted with the fact of £12,000 at compound Interest amounting to upwards of £48,000 in twenty four years'. He suggested that Jacky sell the entire Parke Custis holdings in the south, advising him: 'depend upon it, while you live in Fairfax you will get very little benefit from an estate in New Kent or King William, unless you have much better luck than most who have plantations at a distance'.[10] He instanced Bryan Fairfax and other Mount Vernon neighbours as landowners possibly disposed to sell Jacky tracts contiguous to Abingdon.

There was only so much that Washington in White Plains could do to advise the young Virginian. The Franco-American operation in America was under strain. After French troopships arrived in July at Sandy Hook, a project that Admiral d'Estaing formed to attack New York foundered: the Sound proved too shallow to allow the French men-of-war passage. A joint attack on Newport, Rhode Island, on 9 August, in which the Comte d'Estaing and his fleet acted in uneasy concert with General Sullivan and American troops, enjoyed no greater success. A storm brewed up before the French fleet could engage with enemy shipping. The *Languedoc*, the French flagship, was badly damaged, and the admiral insisted on sailing away to have it repaired in Boston. Sullivan and his fellow officers were left to repine and expostulate that the Comte's retreat was 'derogatory to the honour of France'.[11]

Tempers rose high. American volunteer Lafayette was in Boston, about to take ship across the Atlantic, hoping to return to America, with a French commission. He begged d'Estaing to attempt a new joint operation, but the Admiral refused. A battle later in August, when Rhode Islander Nathanael Greene came to Sullivan's assistance, was inconclusive, and the British remained in control of Newport. When d'Estaing's fleet was repaired, it headed south to the West Indies, eventually to prosecute war against the British there. It had hardly been an auspicious beginning to the French alliance.

More welcome at White Plains than all this news was the gift of a fine chestnut horse, property of Thomas Nelson of Yorktown. The patriot, determined that his favourite mount should go to war, sent an accompanying note to Washington: 'He is not quite reconciled to the beat of Drums, but [with] that he will soon be familiarized.'[12] The American commander wrote to thank the donor for this new horse, which he named 'Nelson'. He was pragmatic about the Franco-American alliance: 'The arrival of the French Fleet upon the Coast of America is a great, & striking event; but the operations of it have been injured by a number of unforeseen & unfavourable circumstances – which, though they ought not to detract from the merit, and good intention of our great Ally, has nevertheless lessened the importance of their Services in a great Degree.' Washington mused: 'I do not know what to make of the enemy at New York.' If their stay there were not from necessity – 'proceeding from an inferiority in their Fleet – want of Provisions – or other causes, I know not' – it was, he wrote, 'profoundly mysterious, unless they look for considerable reinforcements and are waiting the arrival of them to commence their operations. Time will show.'[13]

A month later the British designs were no clearer. Washington marched the army in mid-September to Fredericksburg, New York. From vantage points here it could, as needs be, support posts on the Hudson or, alternatively, defend French ships in Boston harbour from attack. In pursuit of the enemy, the troops endured a wearying series of autumnal marches and counter-marches up and down the North River.

In the early autumn Jacky paid a visit to headquarters and secured Washington's consent to the sale of almost all of the dower lands. Claiborne's only was excepted. Jacky aimed to sell the land he owned there outright as well, all but the White House estate. In return for the loss of the dower land income, Jacky was to pay to his step-father – and his mother, if she survived her husband – an annuity of £2,100 in silver coin. The payment and value, in paper dollars, of this annuity were, over the course of the following years, to be the subject of altercation between debtor and creditor. For the moment Washington only urged Jacky to reinvest his gains in land: 'our paper currency is fluctuating . . . by parting with your lands you give a certainty for an uncertainty . . .'[14] Meanwhile Martha had made her own visit of inspection to Claiborne's in the summer. She found fault with a great deal and gave specific orders, all of which she reported to her husband. On 27 October he wrote to reproach James Hill, manager of the diminished Parke Custis estates: 'I have understood that, till Mrs Washington was at my Plantation at Claiborne's in August & directed or rather advised the Beeves [cattle] and Corn to be Sold, no steps were taken to do it; in short, that you were very seldom at or gave yourself much trouble about the Plantn.'[15]

Not only did Martha direct 'beeves and corn' to be sold in Washington's absence, she insisted that Jacky rent the property from Washington and take it in hand himself. Burwell Bassett, at Martha's wish, appraised land, slaves and stock at Claiborne's, so as to find a rental value that would be fair to his brother-in-law and to Jacky. Washington wrote to Bassett from Fredericksburg on 30 October: 'Mrs Washington in a late letter informs me that you have been so

obliging as to assure her that you would readily render me any services of this kind in your power.' He offered his brother-in-law in
thanks one of the 'choice Bull-calves . . . descended from Mr [John]
Custis's English bull' at Claiborne's. Martha's insistence that the
farm be retained is striking. The whimsical young Parke Custises
now seemed settled at Abingdon. On her husband's principle of land
for land, should she face widowhood, she could parlay Claiborne's
for a home near them.

Washington at Fredericksburg anxiously examined spies' accounts
of British movements. 'We still remain in a disagreeable state of
suspense respecting the enemy's determinations,' he told Bassett.
There were 'circumstances and evidence' leading to suspicions that
the British meant to evacuate New York. 'A few days must, I think,
unfold their views . . .'[16] Four days earlier he had written irritably to
his brother John Augustine: 'If I was to hazard an opinion upon the
occasion, it would be, that they do not leave it this Winter. If I was
to be asked for a reason, I should say because I think they ought to
do so they having almost invariably run counter to all expectation.'
Looking ahead, he continued: 'I begin to despair of seeing my own
home this Winter, & where my Quarters will be, I can give little acct
of at this time.'[17]

Martha wrote on 2 November to her brother Bartholomew
Dandridge that she was 'very uneasy', having 'some reason to expect
that I shall take another trip to the northward. The poor General
is not likely to come to see us, from what I hear – I expect to hear
certainly by the next post.' If she were to be so happy as to stay at
home, she added, 'I shall hope to see you with my sister [-in-law]
here as soon as you are at leisure.' Their mother, who now lived with
her son, had been very ill. 'I wish I was near enough to see you and
her,' Martha wrote to Bartholomew, and she sent love to 'my sister
Aylett'. Their younger sister, Betsy, had recently lost her husband
and both her sons. She enclosed, in 'a bundle for my mama', a pair
of shoes for 'little Patty', her brother's daughter and her namesake:
'there was not a doll to be got in the city of Philadelphia, or I would
have sent her one'.[18] She would soon have ample opportunity to
make further purchases herself in that metropolis. Shortly after she

wrote this letter, Washington deputed his senior aide, Virginian John Fitzgerald, to oversee Martha's journey north as far as Philadelphia. By the time she arrived in that city, the commander hoped to have determined where the army would winter.

At home, life at Mount Vernon was comfortable and full of small pleasures. Nelly was expecting again, and Jacky was occupied with readying Abingdon for occupation in the New Year. Martha's journey to Philadelphia was not easy. She was delayed on the road when the springs of her travelling carriage were found wanting. Earlier repairs to this chariot had not been entirely satisfactory, and Washington had hoped to acquire a new carriage. Merchant John Mitchell, who served under Greene as a Deputy Quartermaster, cast about for one in Philadelphia without success: 'none of them appears to me fit for your service or such as would please Mrs Washington. They are all carriages which have been long used and refitted up to serve the purchasers that now own them.' Four days later Mitchell offered a chariot, 'Mrs Montgomery's', for £750. It was, he wrote, 'the best to be got here, and as reasonable as can be expected from the very extravagant price of every article and the folly of people in general giving into these prices'.[19] Though Washington declared an interest in acquiring this handsome vehicle, Martha ended by travelling in her own untrustworthy chariot. On hearing that new springs had been dispatched to her on the road, Washington begged Mitchell for news of her arrival in Philadelphia. The commander still did not know when his winter quarters would be fixed. He had, therefore, 'under the uncertainty of her stay in the city,' politely declined Mitchell's offer that Martha lodge with him and his wife. He cited 'the trouble of such a visitor (for more than a day or so) being too much for a private family'.[20] Wherever either Washington went now, august and stately addresses and visitations from the great and good were to be expected. Mitchell, instead, was commissioned to obtain for Martha 'good lodgings' and see to it that her horses be stabled.

Washington was now satisfied that the British did not mean either to evacuate New York or to mount a winter assault on his army. The activity in the city in October had proved preliminary to the dispatch of a convoy with troops to the south, Sir Henry Clinton commanding.

As yet ignorant of their precise destination, Washington must rely on General Benjamin Lincoln, American commander in the south, to make the best defence possible of Charleston and Savannah, both in American hands. In late November, he ordered the army under his own command into winter quarters.

Washington had determined that he and his military 'family' would winter, with seven of the thirteen brigades that constituted the army in the north, at Middlebrook, New Jersey. He was pleased with what he found when he arrived there on 11 December. The location of the winter cantonment on the Raritan River allowed for an easy chain of supply from Philadelphia. Immediately to the north rose the heavily wooded Watchung Mountains which afforded a liberal source of timber for hutting the army.[21] Greene had secured as headquarters a number of rooms in a house about four miles west of the main camp. Its owner, Philadelphia merchant John Wallace, remained in occupation, somewhat inconveniently, of other rooms. At Pluckemin, still further west, Henry Knox took up residence and mounted cannon in an artillery park. The flat Raritan plain was ideal ground for drilling, and a Grand Parade – or parade ground – was easily accommodated, as well as lodgings for Baron von Steuben. Greene and his wife Caty rented a house at Bound Brook, on the eastern bank of the Raritan. It was a world away from the rigours and hardship that had characterized the previous winter cantonment at Valley Forge. 'The soldiers are very comfortable,' wrote Nathanael Greene to John Hancock on 20 December.[22] All that was wanted, from Washington's point of view, was the domestic comfort that his wife represented.

It was to be several months before 'Lady Washington' came to Middlebrook. In the latter half of December her husband was summoned to Philadelphia, where she was now lodged. A Congressional Committee of Conference, numbering Henry Laurens among its members, was charged with consulting the General about a Canadian expedition, which the French were urging, and about campaigns to succeed the winter encampments. Evading militia, light horse and others who had hoped to greet him, Washington slipped into the city on 22 December, and was reunited with Martha.[23] Their residence – until 2 February 1779, when they left together for

Middlebrook – was the town house on Chestnut Street close to the State House which Laurens and his wife occupied.

Laurens had recently resigned as President, in turbulent circumstances, and New York lawyer John Jay served in his place. All Philadelphia flocked to the house on Chestnut Street, seeking to fête and honour the southern delegate's illustrious guests. Washington, however, was much in conference at the State House.²⁴ He was of John Jay's mind, that French ambitions in Canada were to be checked. Not all agreed. John Laurens wrote privately to his father, Henry, that he hoped no heed would be paid in Congress to the Marquis de Lafayette's romantic visions of heading north in command of an allied expedition: 'He lays down as self-evident that Canada cannot be conquered by American forces alone: that a Frenchman of birth and distinction at the head of four thousand of his countrymen, and speaking in the name of the Grand Monarque, is alone capable of producing a revolution in that country.'²⁵ But some in Congress favoured an expedition, so as to please the French; still somewhat amazed by the alliance itself, they were nervous that Franklin, recently joned by John Adams in Paris, might yet fail to ratify the treaty. A recent public breach between Arthur Lee and Silas Deane, lately American commissioners in France, had damaged Congress's standing, not only in France but also in Spain and Holland whose friendship – and resources – America sought. In the unsettled atmosphere, there were those in Philadelphia who held that it would be unwise to deny America's new ally its Canadian ambitions.

Besides, there were few in Philadelphia who were not impressed by Monsieur Conrad-Alexandre Gérard, Louis XVI's Minister Plenipotentiary to the United States of America. Upon his arrival in the city in July, installing himself in a commodious house in Market Street, he had lavished entertainment on delegates and on city dignitaries. The forms and protocol on which Gérard insisted as due a representative of his royal master awed these citizens. Many of them inhabitants of meagre lodgings, they were hard pressed to reciprocate. But they made the attempt, spending hundreds of pounds on banquets in taverns. The presence of General and 'Lady' Washington in the city, and the advent of Christmas and New Year festivities, only drove the populace to new heights of extravagance. Early in 1779 Nathanael Greene, who came from Quaker stock, reported that he sat down to a dinner in the city which boasted 160 dishes.[26]

The dinners 'abroad' to which the General and Martha were constantly bidden left the commander in no good humour. He was to tell General Schuyler in February that he had enjoyed 'few moments of relaxation' while in Philadelphia.[27] Even visits to Robert Morris and his wife, with whom the Washingtons dined on 4 January, were not entirely comfortable. The Laurenses, their hosts, and the Morrises were on opposite sides of the Deane–Lee controversy. But these dinners afforded Martha – pragmatic, sociable and tasteful – good reason to patronize Simpson's tailors and other modish emporia, if not as extensively as she had two summers before, when prices were lower. Philadelphia was also a good source of children's toys. She told Jacky and Nelly in March 1779 that she had a 'pretty new doll' for her eldest grand-daughter, Bet.[28]

On Twelfth Night – 6 January 1779 – two evenings after they had dined with the Morrises Washington was for once in good humour. He and Martha attended a ball at the elegant home of Samuel Powel, former Mayor of the city, and his wife, Elizabeth Willing Powel. Benjamin Franklin's daughter, matron Sarah Bache, was of the company, and some days later wrote to her father in Paris, of her conversation with the General: 'he told me it was the anniversary of his marriage. It was just twenty years that night.'[29]

Washington proved himself so able in meetings with the Committee of Conference that, before the new year, he had won his object. There was to be no invasion of Canada attempted. Discussions about other campaigns to come were protracted, but ended again with Washington's will prevailing. For want of money, operations, except against marauding Indians in the west, should be defensive. He was well aware that his stock had risen following his powerful performances in committee, but he inveighed against the public mood when he wrote, late in December, to Benjamin Harrison, now a State Councillor in Virginia, 'If I was to be called upon to draw A picture of the times – & of Men – . . . I should in one word say that idleness, dissipation & extravagance seems to have laid fast hold of most of them . . . Party disputes & personal quarrels are the great business of the day whilst the momentous concerns of an empire – a great & accumulated debt – ruined finances – depreciated money & want of credit . . . are but secondary considerations & postponed from day to day – from week to week as if our affairs wore the most promising aspect . . .' He continued:

> In the present situation of things I cannot help asking – Where is [George] Mason – [George] Wythe – [Thomas] Jefferson, [Robert] Nicholas – [Edmund] Pendleton – [Thomas] Nelson – & another I could name [Benjamin Harrison himself]?. . . Your Money is now sinking 5 pr Ct a day in this City . . . And yet an assembly – a Concert – a Dinner, or Supper (that will cost three or four hundred pounds) will not only take Men off from acting in but even from thinking of this business, while a great part of the Officers of your army, from absolute necessity, are quitting the Service and the more virtuous few, rather than do this, are sinking by sure degrees into beggary & want.

Washington added soberly: 'I feel more real distress on acct of the present appearances of things than I have done at any one time since the commencement of the dispute . . .' As he had done before when matters seemed hopeless, he would trust in 'Providence'.[30] Either 'Providence' or his haranguing had its effect in one quarter. Harrison and Nelson, among others, resumed office as delegates to Congress in the spring.

Besides Congressional calls on his time, Washington had to receive delegations from numerous bodies with addresses. That of the magistrates of the city ran in part: 'you have defeated the designs of a cruel invading enemy, sent by the unrelenting King and Parliament of Britain to enslave a FREE PEOPLE. By the vigilance and military prowess of your Excellency and the brave Army under your command, we now in this city enjoy PEACE FREEDOM and INDEPENDENCE; and we hope, worthy Sir, that you will see the same compleatly established throughout the Thirteen United States, which will redound immortal honour to you, Sir, and to your country for so great and good a man.'[31] If they did not match this florid prose, Alexander Hamilton and others of Washington's 'family' with him in Philadelphia became adept at framing suitable responses for the General to deliver.

In January, the Supreme Executive Council, with Joseph Reed at its head, requested of Washington his full-length likeness, to be taken by Charles Willson Peale, for their council chamber. In addition, Peale had commissions for portraits of the commander from both M. Gérard, who wished to send one to His Most Christian Majesty, the King of France, and from Don Juan de Miralles, the Spanish agent in Philadelphia, who had his own royal master in mind. Though Martha appears to have been an enthusiast for the project, for once Washington escaped a duty he disliked. Owing to pressure of other business, sittings were deferred.

The commander was, by 29 January, fretting to leave Philadelphia, citing, in a letter to President Jay, the 'many inconveniences to the common business of the army' that his long stay in the city had occasioned.[32] Jay did not acquiesce in his request without extracting his pound of flesh. With the Washingtons' departure set for 2 February, the previous morning the General and Jay visited artist Pierre Eugène du Simitière at his house. The commander, the artist noted, 'condescended with great good nature to sit about three-fourths of an hour' for a profile in black lead, 'form of a medal'.[33] Du Simitière profited from the sitting with a number of engravings. The delegates and populace of Philadelphia continued to feud and feast. George and Martha departed, as planned, the following day and on 5 February reached Middlebrook.

Correspondence with his cousin Lund at Mount Vernon and with Jacky over the course of this winter had brought Washington no solace. Before he left for Philadelphia, he had written to Lund, 'I am afraid Jack Custis, in spite of all the admonition and advice I gave him against selling faster than he bought, is making a ruinous hand of his Estate.'[34] He had touched then on the depreciation of current money, or Virginia money, as the paper bills now issued by the Commonwealth of Virginia and denominated in pounds, shillings and pence, were indifferently known, against the Spanish silver dollar.* Pondering, in Middlebrook, on 24 February 1779, the sale of his slaves 'at public vendue', or auction, Washington was irresolute: 'if these poor wretches are to be held in a state of slavery, I do not see that a change of masters will render it more irksome, provided husband & wife, and Parents & children are not separated from each other, which is not my intention to do'. But the depreciation of the currency was yet again paramount in his mind. Being at such a distance, he could not judge when the 'tide of depreciation' had turned, and it was the optimum time to sell. It was a point of such nicety, he wrote, that the longer he reflected upon the subject the more at a loss he was. Before the war an adult male slave of working age might have commanded a price of a hundred pounds. While his cousin agonized at headquarters, Lund had, in January, sold on his behalf nine slaves including Phyllis, Bett and Orford, for a total of £2,303 19s.[35]

At Middlebrook, where George and Martha remained from February till early June 1779, the weather was consistently mild and moderate. The hutting and the heavily wooded site afforded the troops a degree of comfort and warmth. But the depreciation of the currency had alarming consequences both for the provisioning of the current army and for the recruiting of future regiments. Washington wrote to President Jay towards the end of April: 'a waggon-load of money will scarcely purchase a waggon-load of provisions'.[36] A week later he wrote to New York delegate, Gouverneur Morris, referring to the reluctance of both officers and men to soldier for the beggarly sum that was their pay: 'Our army, as it now stands, is but little more than the skeleton of an army; and I hear of no steps that are taking to give it strength and substance.'[37]

Martha shared others of his anxieties with Jacky and Nelly, writing from Middlebrook in March: 'all is quiet in this quarter. It is from

---

* Like everyone else, the American Commander-in-Chief avoided, when he could, transactions in the Continental dollars issued by Congress. While Virginia currency depreciated alarmingly against the Spanish dollar, the Continental dollar was rapidly becoming all but worthless. In 1779 $115 Continental currency had had a value of a hundred dollars cash. In May 1779 $1,215 Continental currency secured the same sum. A year thence a hundred Spanish dollars would be equivalent to $4,600 in Continental money.

the southward that we expect to hear news. We are very anxious to know how our affairs are going in that quarter.'[38] A British expeditionary force from New York had launched a successful attack on Savannah late the previous year, and General Lincoln feared for the patriot garrison at Charleston.

At Middlebrook, as in other winter encampments, Washington had officers of the different regiments on duty to dine at his table together with his chiefs of staff, his aides and secretaries and other guests. Now that Martha was with him, Lucy Knox and Caty Greene, living close by at Pluckemin and Bound Brook respectively, were often of the party. When Massachusetts army surgeon John Thacher dined at the Wallace house on 25 February, no hint of the difficulties facing Washington was vouchsafed. Searching in his host's countenance for 'some peculiar traces of excellence', Thacher found it 'fine, cheerful, open' and expressive in conversation. But, writing of the 'veneration and respect' and even love that Washington commanded, he added: 'He is feared even when silent.' Washington's silences could unnerve the most confident. In conversation, Thacher further observed, 'a placid smile is frequently observed on his lips, but a loud laugh, it is said, seldom if ever escapes him'. The General, he noted, while attentive to all, left his guests 'after the compliment of a few glasses'. The Washingtons were adept and efficient hosts and, unlike at Philadelphia, could retire at leisure. Of Martha, Thacher remarked that she was uncommonly dignified as well as affable, if displaying 'no striking marks of beauty'. He heard, too, from the 'Virginia officers' that she was honoured for her benevolence and charity, ever 'seeking for objects of affliction and poverty that she may extend to the sufferers the hand of kindness and relief'. Thacher went away with exactly the degree of confidence in the commander that these dinners were designed to engender.[39]

There was, in fact, a new energy about Washington. Following his impressive performance before the Committee of Conference, Congress had effectively ceded to him direction of the grand strategy of the war. A year earlier this had been the province of Gates and an obstructive Board of War. Now the General, with 'Lady Washington' at his side, and the Knoxes and Greenes willing accomplices, embarked on a series of successful enterprises in the rustic setting of the Raritan valley. They convinced Congress that in Washington should also be vested the power to conduct direct joint operations with the French in America. The first of these enterprises was a vastly expensive entertainment, a belated celebration of the first anniversary of the alliance with France, that Henry Knox hosted on 18 February in the academy at the artillery park at Pluckemin. Knox later described the occasion to his brother with some pride: 'A most genteel entertainment given by self & officers – everybody allowed it to be the first of the kind ever exhibited in this state at least – three to four hundred gentlemen and above seventy Ladies – all of the first ton in the State.'[40] Fireworks and elaborate allegorical transparencies – large scenes painted on glass or translucent cloth, back-lit – occupied a part of the evening, and Washington led off the dancing with Lucy Knox. Washington, meditating further entertainment, sent to Mitchell in February for a service of 'Queen's china' (Queen's ware), the creamware from England off which they dined when en famille at Mount Vernon.[41]

As was intended, private accounts as well as newspaper paragraphs giving details of this distinguished compliment to France inclined M. Gérard in Philadelphia to take a kindly view of the American high command. At Middlebrook the Washingtons and the 'family' and other officers and ladies got up another, more private, entertainment. General Greene wrote to a friend on 19 March: 'We had a little dance at my quarters a few evenings past. His Excellency and Mrs Greene danced upwards of three hours without once sitting down. Upon the whole we had a pretty little frisk.'[42]

News came in April that M. Gérard himself, together with Don Juan de Miralles, had accepted Washington's invitation to review the army at Middlebrook. Though the review was deferred until 2 May, Henry Laurens was one of many from Philadelphia who made a point of travelling to New Jersey to be among the company on the day. On a stage erected in a 'spacious field', Martha, Lucy Knox and Caty Greene, pre-eminent among the other ladies, took their places. The whole of the army was paraded 'in martial array' on the field. Thirteen cannon then signalled the approach of Major

Henry 'Light Horse Harry' Lee – cousin to the Lees of Stratford Hall – and his dragoons. Behind, followed Washington, his aides, the 'foreign ministers', or envoys, and their retinue, and general officers. Once these dignitaries had reviewed the ranks and received full military honours, they joined the ladies on the stage, while the army performed wondrous 'field manoeuvres and evolutions, with firing of cannon and musketry'.[43]

If the review impressed upon the Europeans that the American army was a credible fighting force, it was only a lure. During the conferences and dinners that followed, Washington wished to return to the project of joint operations with the Comte d'Estaing and his fleet, which had come to such a resounding halt the previous summer. He wished also to pay proper respect to the Spanish agent, de Miralles. Though it was not news as yet to be shared with the public, he knew from President Jay that Spain aimed to ally with France against Great Britain, with the object of recovering Gibraltar and other territories lost in the Seven Years War. Under the terms of the proposed treaty, Spain would enter the American war as France's ally.

Martha, it would appear, struck Don Juan's fancy during the foreign envoys' stay in Middlebrook. From Philadelphia he was to shower her, in proper diplomatic fashion, with luxuries from Havana and other Spanish possessions. Washington's conversations with Gérard also bore fruit. When the Minister Plenipotentiary wrote home to the French Foreign Minister, the Comte de Vergennes, for the first time he praised an American. With Washington, he favoured rekindling the joint operations with the Comte d'Estaing's fleet.

Those whose friendship the Washingtons sought would not always be as suave as Gérard and Don Juan. The outlandish and ragged appearance of some Delaware Indian chiefs, who this same month came to pay their respects to Washington while en route to Philadelphia, provoked much mirth in Middlebrook. But the commander treated them with as much courtesy as he had the Europeans and led them on a review of the troops. Their support would be crucial in summer operations against the British and Indians in the west, which he had entrusted to John Sullivan.

At last Washington heard that the British had come out of New York and were heading up the Hudson. He had to move fast to defend West Point and other key positions on the river. Martha left for Virginia, Washington was to tell a Mount Vernon neighbour later in the month, 'so soon as I began my march from Middlebrook', that date being 3 June.[44] The couple could not know the time or place of their next meeting. They could pride themselves on having restored to some degree, on the Raritan plain, the reputation of America in the eyes of the world that was France and Spain.

The Hard Winter: Morristown, 1779–1780

. . . so extremely cold, that there was no living abroad . . .

Should the British take West Point and other American garrisons on the Hudson, patriot forces would be denied the easy access to militia, troops and supplies that New England currently afforded. Washington had no option but to strike camp and march north. He took with him a ring, set with a tiny and fanciful image of Martha in Elizabethan ruff and hood. While still at Middlebrook, he wrote on 28 May to Major Nicholas Rogers, now a colonel and creator of the quaint souvenir: 'Difficult as it is to strike a likeness on so small a scale, it is the opinion of many that you have not failed in the present attempt.' He added drily: 'The dress is not less pleasing for being a copy of antiquity. It would be happy for us, if in these days of depravity the imitation of our ancestors were more extensively adopted – their virtues would not hurt us.'[1]

Washington later admitted to his brother John Augustine that he was 'illy enough prepared, Heaven knows', in the month of June 1779, to defend the Hudson against British attack.[2] Ammunition, provisions and wagons for the journey were lacking. Troops in the different winter cantonments were dispersed over a wide area, and would have to rendezvous in the north. Washington feared, moreover, that the British troops might yet double back and launch an assault on New Jersey, with Philadelphia their ultimate aim. He ordered government stores and vital papers in that city to be moved to secure locations. The pleasant conditions in camp these months past, however, and the discipline that von Steuben had introduced had had their effect. The army he led was now in comparatively good spirits.

Martha was escorted southward by her husband's principal secretary, Colonel James McHenry. They appear to have followed a circuitous route. Both American and British commanders at different times meditated kidnap of their enemy counterparts and of key enemy generals. Irrespective of the anxiety he himself would undergo, her husband was aware that the capture of 'Lady Washington' – Martha was by now firmly ensconced in American minds as a high personage of irreproachable patriotism – would sap the morale of citizenry as well as of soldiers. It must at all costs be avoided. Unharmed, Martha arrived at Mount Vernon in late July. Her grandchildren, newly ensconced with their parents at Abingdon, now numbered three: Nelly had given birth in March to another daughter. Jacky, though a fond father, was still in want of an heir.

The young Parke Custises were struggling to establish a comfortable home. Nelly had not been in good health since she gave birth this year. At some point following Martha's return, it would seem that she took over the care of her infant granddaughter, Eleanor Parke Custis. An English nurse, Mrs Anderson, and the baby became resident at Mount Vernon. The elder two Parke Custis children, Bet and Pat, remained with their ailing mother and their father at Abingdon. Jacky was not finding the responsibilities of home ownership easy. He was to complain to his stepfather in December of 'the great load of family business which demands my utmost attention . . . I have been, ever since I settled here, struggling with every inconvenience that a person could meet with, in coming to a plantation in every respect out of order and in want of every necessary house . . . the master's eye is necessary in most things.' An ambitious project to drain some swampy ground caused him infinite trouble, but Jacky, optimistic to the last, concluded: 'I flatter myself with having in a few years one of the best meadows in the state.'[3]

Far away in the north, while the American army was still some way from the Hudson, grim news reached Washington. The British had captured key garrisons, Stony Point and Fort Lafayette, on either bank of the Hudson. Washington wrote to Philip Schuyler on 9 June: 'We have the mortification to be spectators of this and . . . to see it out of our power to counteract a measure, from which we must experience many inconveniences.'[4] He established headquarters later in the month at New Windsor, six miles above West Point, a stronghold he intended to defend against all comers. Following the loss of the garrisons, festivities in camp, to mark the third anniversary of independence, were muted.

Within days Washington learned that British generals William Tryon and Thomas Garth had sailed up Long Island Sound, plundered New Haven and burned the public stores on 6 July. Three days later they burnt Fairfield, Connecticut, and, on the 11th, Norwalk. Houses, barns, stores, the church, the meeting houses, schoolhouses, courthouses and jails alike were torched. The monetary value of what was lost was immense. The mood of even the most fervent patriots in the eastern states was soured. Washington asked General Anthony Wayne to assess the 'practicability' of an assault on Stony Point: 'If it is undertaken, I should conceive it ought to be done by way of surprise in the night.'[5] A laconic entry in the commander's accounts records the success of Wayne's enterprise on the night of the 15th: 'To expenses in reconnoitring the enemy's post at Stony Point previous to the assault of it, and on a visit to it after it was taken . . . £10.10'.[6] The recapture of the garrison raised spirits dramatically. Five days thereafter President Jay addressed Washington in the following terms: 'General Wayne's coup de main occasions as much joy as the barbarous conflagrations of the enemy excite indignation. The former, I hope, will lead to further successes, the latter to retaliation and resentments favourable to our independence.'[7]

Over the summer the American commander oversaw the strengthening of fortifications at West Point, and in addition worked with the Board of War to standardize uniforms in accordance with regulations for the army that von Steuben had recently issued. His attention never drifted far from the dangers of campaigns to come.

He wrote, on 1 August, to Edmund Randolph in Virginia that they laboured under the effects of 'two of the greatest evils that can befall a state of war, namely, a reduced army at the beginning of a campaign which, more than probably, is intended for a decisive one, and want of money, or rather a redundancy of it, by which it become of no value'.[8] The term of no fewer than 8,000 troops who had enlisted for three years in 1777 would expire in May 1780. It was difficult to persuade officers or men to re-enlist, when their livelihoods at home were threatened by an ever depreciating currency and when negligible army pay was no lure. But discussion of these deficiencies, both in Congress and in state assemblies, was often heated and ill tempered, and more often than not productive of stasis. In Philadelphia Henry Laurens and Robert Morris lamented the political divisions in Congress. In Paris the French government was disturbed by reports of these differences. At West Point Washington and his 'family' and staff corresponded with all parties concerned and urged action to secure men, money, arms, powder and stores.

Provisions at West Point – which Washington named caustically 'this happy spot' – in the summer were in short supply. Having invited ladies to dine at headquarters in August, he asked Dr John Cochran, surgeon-general of the army, to forewarn his wife, who would be of the party. The plates off which they would eat, once tin, were now 'iron', from constant use. Nor would the meal be lavish. There was generally 'a ham (sometimes a shoulder) of bacon, to grace the head of the table', he wrote, and 'a piece of roast' to adorn the foot. It was probable, Washington conceded, that the cook would have 'a mind to cut a figure', and offer beefsteak pies or dishes of crabs. But this menial had recently chanced upon the discovery that 'apples will make pies' and, 'amidst the violence of his efforts', might substitute fruit for meat.[9] If the commander's humour was heavy, his hospitality in trying circumstances could not be faulted.

While she was at Middlebrook in March, Martha had told Jacky and Nelly that it was 'from the southward' that they expected news.[10] In October disastrous intelligence from Savannah reached Washington at West Point. D'Estaing and fleet – with a French general and troops on board – had appeared in late September off the coast of Georgia. In the expectation that the French admiral would head north, Congress urged the 'middle and eastern States' to furnish Washington and the foreign fleet and army with 'men and provisions'.[11] D'Estaing, however, turned his ships towards Savannah. American General Benjamin Lincoln hurried from Charleston to join him. On 9 October they made a joint assault on the British lines, which failed miserably, and in the wake of the disaster the French fleet and army withdrew once more to the West Indies. All thought of a joint attack with Washington on New York was now in abeyance, and Lincoln returned to Charleston.

Martha, resident in Virginia, was reliant on correspondence with her husband at headquarters in the north for firm news of campaigns in other southern states as well for accounts of his own travails. Erroneous reports in the *Virginia Gazette* of the campaign in the south raised others' hopes. Jacky wrote to Washington on 7 October, two days before the disastrous attempt on Savannah, to congratulate him on the Comte d'Estaing's 'important success in Georgia', declaring himself 'very sanguine in my expectations of a glorious close to the war this campaign, and in seeing you in Fairfax this winter'.[12]

Martha no doubt was a good deal less sanguine. Besides, there were troubles at Mount Vernon this summer and autumn to oppress her. A long drought in northern Virginia engendered a poor harvest at the plantation, and the finances of the estate were less than sound. Following Williamsburg legislation designed to cure the currency crisis, Washington was offered in his absence by debtors a shilling or even sixpence in the pound. Furthermore, a British proclamation in June had offered the slaves of 'rebels' everywhere their freedom and even land, should they cross to the enemy lines. A good many slaves were not slow to seek their liberty. Though none had as yet fled Mount Vernon, the *Virginia Gazette* was crowded with advertisements from other plantation owners giving details of runaways.

News from Europe trickled through to Washington at West Point. He learned in October that, following 'improvident delay' in Congress, applications for 'clothing and military stores' had been dispatched to the French government only in the late summer. It was to be hoped that Laurens's son John, now secretary to Benjamin

Franklin, Minister Plenipotentiary at the court of Versailles, could expedite the applications. The earliest that these foreign cargoes could arrive was the following January or February. Henry Laurens asked, 'Can the several [American] states supply the necessary wants and in proper time for saving our brave fellow citizens from another Valley Forge scene?'[13]

John Adams had left Paris for London, with orders to initiate negotiations for treaties of peace and commerce with Britain, should that government recognize the United States as 'sovereign, free and independent'.[14] No great expectations of success attended Adams's embassy. Its aim was to persuade Europe that the United States were fighting a defensive and just war.

Don Juan de Miralles, for his part, sent Washington an enormous sea tortoise and lemons from Havana, and confirmation of reports that Spain had declared war against England. John Jay, who had ceded his place as President of Congress to Samuel Huntington of Connecticut so as to negotiate with Madrid, would, with luck, persuade the Spanish government to come into the American war as well. Washington, thanking de Miralles on 16 October for the intelligence and for the gifts, was sure that his wife would receive 'with gratitude and pleasure' Don Juan's compliments, which he would convey in his next letter to her: 'you stand high in her estimation'.[15]

Martha had good reason to fear 'another Valley Forge scene'. But she was set on joining her husband, wherever he might settle for the winter, and eager to travel, as Washington noted in a letter to John Mitchell, 'before the roads get bad and weather severe'. He asked Mitchell to hire 'lodgings in some genteel (but not a common boarding) house in Philadelphia'.[16] By the end of the month Mitchell had secured apartments at 'the late Mr Israel Pemberton's house' – Clarke Hall – which included 'a handsome front parlour, a good bed chamber, kitchen and rooms for servants'.[17] On 10 November Washington told an officer in Fredericksburg, Virginia that Martha was setting out 'immediately' for the north.[18] Jacky and Nelly must fend for themselves and Lund take pains to ensure that no slave escaped to an alluring enemy. Though Martha exchanged the privacy and comfort of her Virginian home for what would no doubt be, in due course, rude lodgings and severe weather at headquarters, she did not hesitate. It was enough that her husband counted on her coming. The assiduous Mitchell promised her while she stopped at 'Mr Pemberton's house' in Philadelphia, 'some of the best tea, sugar, coffee, etc'. He volunteered further that he and his wife would do all 'to render her accommodations convenient and agreeable'.[19]

While still at West Point in late October, Washington took the decision to concentrate most of the army at Morristown, New Jersey. He knew the locality well from when he, Martha and the 'family' had occupied the tavern on the town green in the spring of 1777. The countryside would be a source of flour, among other essentials, though its price was exorbitant – £60 a hundredweight.[20] The army was weakened, following the recent dispatch of regiments to reinforce Lincoln's Southern army, and few new recruits were coming in to replace those whose enlistment was concluded. News that a large-scale embarkation was in preparation at New York, its likely object Charleston, forced Washington to consider sending a 'further reinforcement to the southward'. On 30 October he wrote to Greene, who was already at Morristown. The Quartermaster General was to lay out the ground at 'the position back of Mr Kemble's' – a wood known as Jockey Hollow, in the vicinity of Morristown. Given the likely future reduction of forces already weakened, it was now incumbent on the army, he advised, to 'seek a more remote position than we would otherwise have done'. Six hundred acres of timber at Jockey Hollow, in his estimation, would furnish log cabins to accommodate all. He ended by asking Greene to order him a late dinner the following day, when he would reach the township. He understood that headquarters were to be at Mrs Ford's.[21]

Just as Mr Wallace had done at Middlebrook, so the widowed Mrs Ford remained in her home, a mile or so east of the township, after it became headquarters for the army in the north. There was only one kitchen to accommodate both Ford domestics, who served their mistress and her two children, and army servants as well as cooks. An ancillary kitchen was begun, but the logs cut for it lay fallow on the ground. Winter came early this year to New Jersey, and there was little labour to be spared for the provision of such amenities.

Washington himself arrived on a day that the gathered regiments had suffered a 'very severe storm of hail and snow all day'.[22] Two weeks later army surgeon James Thacher wrote that snow on the ground at Jockey Hollow – 'this wilderness . . . where we are to build log huts for winter quarters' – was 'about two feet deep'.[23] The lack of shoes, blankets, tents and wagons – all long the subject of correspondence between Washington and Greene, on the one hand, and Congress and the states on the other – was much felt. Drillmaster von Steuben was later to write of the New York brigade, in particular: 'they exhibited the most shocking picture of misery I have ever seen, scarce a man having the wherewithal to cover his nakedness, and a great number very bad with the itch [scabies]'.[24]

Many officers as well as men slept on 'brushwood thrown together' on the frozen ground. In mid-December Washington addressed the governors of the former Middle Colonies – New York, New Jersey, Delaware and Pennsylvania – in strong terms. Unless aid was given swiftly, he warned them, 'there is every appearance that the army will infallibly disband within a fortnight'.[25] Supplies came fitfully if at all. Washington was to tell Philip Schuyler later that the soldiers ate 'every kind of horse food but hay'. The horses peeled bark off trees for sustenance. There were further snowstorms on the 16th and 18th and again on the 28th. The freezing conditions did not abate.

The army did not disband.[26] The soldiers continued to fell the oak and walnut trees around them. The log cabins multiplied, offering reprieve from the bitter conditions to more and more men who had been sleeping on the ground or under canvas. On 29 December, despite the snowstorm the previous day, Washington wrote that the work was 'nearly completed'.[27] The warmth and shelter of the huts were of inestimable value in raising morale, though so much else was wanting. Once again, it seemed, the army had endured and survived.

Before Martha's arrival, Washington had paid £15 'for a band of music' to play at headquarters on Christmas Day.[28] On the last day of the old year, she arrived at Mrs Ford's. Twelfth Night – 6 January 1780 – would see the twenty-first anniversary of the couple's wedding. In the short interval between New Year's Eve and that date, calamity again descended on the camp. A prolonged and violent snowstorm, during the night of 3 January, left the ground four feet and in some places six feet deep in snow. Several officers still under canvas had their marquees 'torn asunder and blown down' over their heads. 'Some of the soldiers were actually covered while in their tents and buried like sheep' beneath the enveloping powder, wrote Dr Thacher.[29] Blankets, baggage, stores had to be dug out. Roads within and outside the camp were impassable, not only rendering wagons useless but also cutting off Jockey Hollow from Morristown, headquarters and supply routes. 'For six or eight days it has been so extremely cold, that there was no living abroad,' wrote General Greene, during the days that succeeded the storm.[30] The freezing conditions continued. Officers and men alike, Washington told Schuyler on 30 January, were 'five or six days without bread, at other times as many days without meat, and once or twice two or three days without either'.[31]

The crisis was little less acute where the men's clothing was concerned. Many of them did their duty in the snow without benefit of shoes or stockings. Even breeches were sometimes lacking, a captain in Stark's Brigade writing, on 6 February, of 'many a good lad with nothing to cover him from his hips to his toes save his blanket'.[32] The ravages of the smallpox epidemic at Morristown in the spring of 1777, the cries of 'No bread, no soldier' at Valley Forge – where, at least, the winter had been largely mild – were expunged from the minds of veterans as the conditions continued. There appeared no sign, though the weeks and months passed, of a thaw. Washington was to remark in March: 'The oldest people now living in this country do not remember so hard a winter.'[33] An attempt in mid-January to take advantage of the freeze, cross the ice at Amboy over to Staten Island, and attack British troops failed dismally. The enemy had got word of the intended assault and repelled the Americans.

For once Martha failed to lift her husband's spirits. Washington was hard-pressed and irritable, and the conditions at the crowded Ford house were hardly conducive to repose and ease. He complained to Greene on 22 January, '. . . I have been at my present quarters since the 1st. day of Decr. and have not a Kitchen to Cook a Dinner in, altho' the Logs have been put together some considerable time by my own Guard; nor is there a place at this moment in which a servant can lodge with the smallest degree of comfort. Eighteen belonging to my family and all Mrs Ford's are crowded together in her Kitchen and scarce one of them able to speak for the colds they have caught.'[34]

He had been unusually curt and dismissive two days earlier in response to a letter from Jacky the previous month, requesting a deferral of the annuity payable on 1 January. An offer to pay him in 'paper money' elicited the response that his stepson might as well pay him in old newspapers and almanacs. If, as Jacky complained, he had been 'unfortunate' in his crops, Washington was sorry for it. The debt 'may lie till my wants, or your convenience, is greater', he conceded.[35] As Jacky may have calculated in making his request, there were matters of more urgency to occupy the commander than what was due him from his wayward stepson.

Washington's anxieties about the men in Jockey Hollow as well as about the southern campaign communicated themselves to Martha. For once she was to admit a kind of defeat, following her return to Mount Vernon, in a letter of 18 July to her brother-in-law Burwell Bassett: 'we were sorry that we did not see you at the camp. There was not much pleasure there [from] the distress of the army and other difficulties, though I did not know the cause. The poor General was so unhappy that it distressed me exceedingly.'[36] Washington thanked Robert Morris in Philadelphia at the beginning of February for a promised gift of wine: 'Should it arrive in good order, I shall be able to give my friends a glass of such as I could wish.' If Morris himself should do him 'the favour to partake of it' at Morristown, he would be most happy. On such red-letter days as a visit from a friend, Washington informed the financier, he felt the want of good wine. Otherwise, he wrote dourly, he had long resolved to be content with grog, 'should it even be made of North East rum, and drunk out of a wooden bowl, as the case has been'.

Martha joined him in grateful thanks for the Morrises' offer of hospitality, Washington added, should they this winter visit Philadelphia. For once, the Virginian who had, before the war, frequented dinners, balls, assemblies and race meetings – and enjoyed the best of wine – was to the fore. Washington admitted to an inclination for 'relaxation of this kind' and 'social enjoyments'. But he brought himself up sharply. Public duty and private pleasure being 'at variance', he continued, 'I have little expectation of indulging in the latter while I am under ties of the former. Perhaps', he ended on a dismal note, 'when the one ceases, I may be incapable of the other.'[37]

A visit to Philadelphia with Martha might, in fact, have increased his distress and certainly would have taxed her wardrobe, elegant though it was. While the men at Jockey Hollow wanted for food and clothes, in early March New Jersey delegate John Fell commented on the dissipation and extravagance in the city as 'beyond conception'. He added, 'The dress of the ladies in paying their visits is quite equal to the dress of the ladies that I have seen in the boxes in the playhouses in London, and their dress in general even along the streets resembles in a great degree the actresses on the stage.'[38]

Washington, nevertheless, knew the value of a good appearance. Late in March he ordered Mitchell to procure him a new chariot for four horses: 'please to have my arms and crest properly disposed of on the chariot. I send them for this purpose.'[39] Though, in Boston, George III's coat of arms was torn from the State House, Washington, like many other Americans, continued to appreciate some aspects of his English heritage. Just over a week later he added: 'it may not be amiss to ornament the mouldings with a light airy gilding'. The harness too should be ornamented. 'The pocket money which Mrs Washington has, and some I can borrow here', he wrote, would cover the costs, until specie from Lund Washington arrived.[40]

Though Martha had an 'unhappy' husband to comfort, she remained a consummate hostess. She took an interest, moreover, in all the military 'family', and she amused them when she named a tomcat 'Hamilton'. Her husband's young aide from the West Indies was notably amorous. This February, however, the taming of Alexander Hamilton ensued. Philip Schuyler's daughter Betsy came to stay in Morristown with her aunt and uncle, Gertrude and John Cochran. Miss Schuyler was an heiress, which was necessary, as Hamilton had no means or expectations. She was also pretty and intelligent. The

Washingtons, when dining with the surgeon-general and his wife, watched the romance develop with an indulgent eye. Martha on one occasion sent Betsy 'some nice powder' in return for 'very pretty' cuffs which she had received, and for which she was much obliged.[41] Philip Schuyler, persuaded by Washington's high opinion of his aide, and perhaps by Hamilton's oratory when he requested Betsy's hand in marriage, agreed in April to an engagement.

Entertainment of a more public kind occupied the Washingtons and the 'family' at headquarters on one occasion. Thirty-five subscribers, Washington heading the list, sponsored a series of assemblies, held at Arnold's tavern on the green. Quartermaster General Nathanael Greene wrote to Joseph Reed on 29 February: 'From this apparent ease, I suppose it is thought we must be in happy circumstances. I wish it was so, but, alas, it is not.' The currency was worthless, forage scarce and ammunition lacking. 'We have been so poor in camp for a fortnight, that we could not forward the public dispatches, for want of cash to support the expresses.'[42] Nevertheless, the freezing conditions and consequent difficulties which had absorbed so much of Washington's attention by degrees eased. Finally, the hard winter gave way to spring.

The Grand Parade at Jockey Hollow was clear of snow when the Chevalier de La Luzerne, new French envoy to the United States, visited headquarters in the latter part of April. Every effort was made to show him that the American army was an ally worth supporting. He was accorded, on his entry into camp on the 19th, full military honours, and treated thereafter to a battery of parades and cannon salutes. He was to be the guest of honour at a grand review to be held on the 24th. Though the parlous state of supplies and provisions was not hidden from him, de La Luzerne praised to Washington 'the good order and discipline of the troops'.[43] He expressed himself in a letter to the French government as convinced 'more than ever, of the very great advantage which the republic derives' from the services of its Commander-in-Chief.[44]

With de La Luzerne on the 19th had come Martha's admirer from Havana, Don Juan de Miralles. On the day of the grand review he was 'confined at headquarters . . . dangerously sick of a pulmonic fever'. While the Washingtons entertained de La Luzerne below, the exotic dignitary, who had courted and been courted by Washington and Martha to such good effect, languished in an upstairs room. De La Luzerne departed for Philadelphia. In the upper chamber Don Juan lingered between life and death. To the consternation of all, he died, far from his island home and family, on the afternoon of 28 April 1780.

Washington had the task of arranging a burial the following day. To satisfy Don Juan's family and the Spanish government, due honour must be accorded the deceased, though the coffin must lie in the Presbyterian church graveyard at Morristown, for want of a Catholic burial ground. As chief mourner with his aides and staff, the American commander followed the open coffin. Don Juan's corpse had been attired in tricorne and peruke wig and scarlet coat embroidered with gold lace. A costly watch, in addition, and 'a profusion of diamond rings' on the stiff fingers were among the valuables committed to the earth with the coffin, once a Spanish chaplain had commended the Don's soul to heaven. A guard was placed to prevent looting.[45] Washington had lost an enthusiastic supporter, though one who was never fully acknowledged by Madrid as its envoy to the United States. Don Juan's death, coldly viewed, paved the way for the Spanish government to send official representation to America.

It was virtually impossible, had Washington either energy or inclination, to keep his wife apprised of the many anxieties that oppressed him this winter and spring. While Miralles yet languished upstairs, the commander had written a private letter to his former aide John Laurens. Back from France, Laurens was now with General Lincoln and the 5,000 American troops who defended Charleston. Since early April 14,000 British troops had been besieging the town. Washington opined to Laurens that the loss of the town and garrison must soon occur, and that any attempt to defend them ought to be 'relinquished'. Being at a distance, Washington hesitated to give Lincoln the firm order to do so. A plea by Laurens that Washington himself head the army in the south elicited the admission that he should not 'dislike the journey'. But a Congressional committee was expected in camp. Besides, should Clinton and his troops take Charleston, the British commander would almost certainly return to harry the north, which must be at the ready to respond to attack. Though the 'dangerous crisis' in the south was much in his thoughts during subsequent weeks, he remained at Morristown.[46]

Unlooked for but wholly welcome during this anxious time was the news in early May that Lafayette had returned to America from France. He wrote from Boston harbour, on 27 April, that he was looking forward to being once more one of Washington's 'loving soldiers', and had 'affairs of the utmost importance' to communicate. He assured Washington that 'a great public good' would derive from the news he brought. On a personal note, before embarking, the Marquis had commissioned the Prince de Poix to 'put together a tea service', which he meant as a gift for Martha. It was, he instructed, to be 'very white, fine *Sèvres*, and the spoons of gold plate'.[47]

Lafayette reached headquarters at Morristown on 10 May. He informed Washington that six French ships of the line and 6,000 French troops, destined to leave for America in early April, should be in Rhode Island by June. They had orders to participate in joint operations with Americans to seize New York. This was the prize, above all others, that Washington wished to secure.

Lafayette left for Philadelphia to inform Congress and de La Luzerne of his news. But could the army in the north hold out until June? Would Charleston fall, as seemed all too likely? Could America provide supplies for an additional 6,000 French troops when it was hard put to it to supply its own army? With these questions and others Washington grappled. 'Providence', he told Lund Washington on 19 May, 'has always displayed its power and goodness, when clouds and thick darkness seemed ready to overwhelm us.' The hour was now come, he wrote, when they stood 'much in need of another manifestation of its bounty' – adding, as though to propitiate Providence itself, 'however little we deserve it'.[48]

Providence indeed appeared to have deserted the American army in the days that followed. Want of meat at Morristown since 21 May drove two regiments of the Connecticut Line to mutiny on the 25th. Though that revolt was efficiently suppressed by officers, Washington wrote the following day to Jonathan Trumbull, Governor of Connecticut, that there was not only no meat to feed the troops but no money to pay them. There was, as there had been before, a very real danger that the army might disband. Lafayette, when he returned from Philadelphia at the end of May to resume his place at Washington's side, wrote to Joseph Reed in Philadelphia: 'An army that is reduced to nothing, that wants provisions, that has not one of the necessary means to make war . . . however prepared I could have been to this unhappy sight by our past distresses, I confess I had no idea of such an extremity . . .'[49]

Strenuous attempts to make Congress and the states see the absolute necessity of supplying the troops with food and pay continued, despite an unhappy diversion. An extraordinary edition of the loyalist *Royal Gazette,* printed on 30 May, brought intelligence that Charleston had fallen to the British on the 12th. Others might wail and gnash their teeth. It was an outcome that Washington had expected. Now he must prepare for the return of Sir Henry Clinton. The British Commander-in-Chief sailed for New York on 5 June, leaving Lord Cornwallis to command troops in the south.

At Morristown the Washingtons soldiered on. But their tenure of the Ford house was to come to an abrupt end. While Clinton was still at sea on his way to New York, General von Knyphausen and British troops crossed during the night of 6 June from Staten Island to Elizabethtown Point. Next morning, they had advanced nearly as far as Springfield, only ten miles south-east of Morristown. Martha left promptly for Philadelphia, while Washington and the troops under his command were unexpectedly forced into action. By the afternoon of the 7th the American troops were skirmishing with the enemy, and successfully forced them back. During the British retreat a soldier shot dead a reverend's wife where she sat, surrounded by her children, at home in Connecticut Farms.

This atrocity, and the subsequent burning of Springfield, attracted much indignation in the patriot press. Washington could be thankful that the British had not penetrated Morristown, where the artillery as well as baggage and horses had remained. Suspecting that an attack on West Point was in the offing, he put the army under marching orders for the North River. While on his way there, he received the welcome news that Admiral Chevalier de Ternay and a French fleet had arrived at Newport. An experienced general, the Comte de Rochambeau was in command of the 5,000 troops aboard. Washington continued the journey north. Martha was making by stages for Virginia and home. They had both lived to fight another day.

Home and Headquarters, 1780–1781

. . . she reminded me of the Roman matrons . . .

Washington, on 11 July 1780, directed 'Light Horse Harry' Lee to dance attention on the French admiral and general at Newport, and impress 'every kind of refreshment the country affords; cattle, vegetables, etc for the use of our allies'.[1] Five days later the American commander addressed the Comte de Rochambeau directly, in a letter he entrusted to Lafayette. He begged the French general to consider 'all the information' this emissary gave and 'all the propositions he makes . . . as coming from me'. His chief wish, as he wrote to Rochambeau, was to 'fix our plan of operations, and with as much secrecy as possible'. Washington concluded, 'Impatiently waiting for the time when our operations will afford me the pleasure of a personal acquaintance with you, I have the honour, etc'.[2]

British naval superiority frustrated Washington's scheme for an allied attack on New York in the coming months. A second fleet with a division of French troops, 2,000 strong, with arms and armaments, was expected from Brest. While they awaited this aid, the American and French commanders separately endured numerous alarums and excursions. Clinton, returned from the south, made a move on Rhode Island. Washington countered by marching on New York. The British commander speedily returned to the city.

Constantly on the move so as not to exhaust any one district's supplies and enrage its inhabitants, Washington wrote to his brother

Samuel from 'Camp near Fort Lee' on 31 August: 'The flattering prospect which seemed to be opening to our view in the month of May is vanishing like the morning dew.' There was no sign of the French troops and ships expected from Brest. 'I despair of doing anything in this quarter this campaign . . . At best the troops we have are only fed hand to mouth and for the last four or five days have been without meat . . .'[3]

Within days the *Alliance* frigate brought bad news from France. The British had blockaded Brest. The ships and troops promised to America were penned in. With no prospect of taking New York while the British enjoyed naval supremacy in the Sound, Washington looked to campaigns in the new year to restore the country's fortunes. Much ceremony and professions of friendships at a meeting with Rochambeau in the latter part of September could not disguise this unpalatable fact. For the moment the allies were powerless to move against the British.

In the south Lord Cornwallis, whom Clinton had left in command, scored a notable victory over Horatio Gates at the battle of Camden. The British general was moving north, and was dangerously near the border of North Carolina with Virginia. If he and Clinton were to succeed in joining forces in the Chesapeake, they could rout the American army of the north. Washington placed little confidence in an act passed in the Virginia Assembly to raise 3,000 men. He told Jacky on 6 August: 'it is our misfortune to have such kind of laws (though most important) badly executed, and such men as are raised dissipated and lost before they join the army'.[4]

Troubles came daily. General Benedict Arnold, recently appointed to the command of West Point, was unveiled a traitor. He had been ready to hand the garrison to the British. Washington rejected the plea of the British Major John André, Arnold's accomplice, that, as an officer, he should be executed by firing squad. He had André hanged as a spy on 2 October. Arnold himself had escaped arrest, and led enemy troops south the following month. His former commander was relentless in his pursuit of the turncoat, whom he wished to see court-martialled.

There was general condemnation of Horatio Gates for the inadequate part he had played at Camden, and Washington directed

Nathanael Greene to take over the command in the south. It was an admirable appointment. Victories over the British were to follow, culminating in the defeat of Cornwallis at the battle of Guilford Courthouse, North Carolina the following spring. When the British general began a march northward into Virginia in April 1781, Greene lost the advantage, but he seized the opportunity to take back undefended positions in South Carolina.

Commenting, in early October 1780, on the 'inactive campaign' in the north drawing to a close, Washington wrote to General Cadwalader: 'I hoped, but I hoped in vain, that a prospect was displaying, which would enable me to fix a period of my military pursuits, and restore me to domestic life.'[5] On the cold, wet and tedious journey to a new encampment which followed, he informed the President of Congress on 7 October that there was not a drop of rum to be had for the men.

Martha had reached Mount Vernon in mid-July, and told her brother-in-law Bassett on the 18th, 'I got home on Friday, and find myself so much fatigué with my ride that I shall not be able to come down to see you this summer . . .' Sending compliments to Eltham neighbours, the rector of the parish church and his wife included, she asked that, instead, he would bring her niece Fanny to her, and indeed her nephews too. 'As soon as you can', she urged, already thinking ahead to her return to her husband. 'I suffered so much by going late that I have determined to go early in the fall before the frost sets in – if Fanny does not come soon, she will have but a short time to stay with me.'[6]

At Abingdon, Jacky was filling the house with fine furniture and company, but he still lacked a son. Nelly gave birth this year to twin daughters. They survived long enough to be mourned when they sickened and died. Jacky had now sired six children in all without a male heir living or dead among them. On one occasion, when his eldest daughter, 'Bet', later Eliza, was four or five, he responded carelessly and even cruelly, if her later recollection is to be believed. After a convivial dinner at home, he lifted her onto the dining table. He and Dr Rumney, who was among the guests, had the child sing 'very improper' ballads to amuse the company. When Nelly Calvert Custis came in to remonstrate, Jacky replied that 'his little Bet could not be injured by what she did not understand, that he had no Boy, & she must make fun for him, until he had'.[7]

Nelly retired, smiling, according to her daughter's recollection, who would think no ill of her father. Eliza Parke Custis's later imagination soared on wings when describing Jacky, early life at Abingdon, and those events of the war that she was old enough to remember. The lack of an heir undoubtedly kept Jacky from undertaking military duties. He served his country only as a member of the Virginia Assembly.

Eliza later affirmed that, when they were children, the Calvert family at Mount Airy favoured her younger sister Patty, who was as fair and peaceable as themselves. Of Martha, her paternal grandmother, she wrote: 'she had all that tenderness of manner which my father had, & when with her I was always in her arms'. Distance may have sugared her memory. Eliza recorded, too, times when she had stood by and seen Martha pack her travelling trunk: 'my heart was almost broke, when she was obliged to go to the Gen.rl, & I was always talking of her & wishing her return'.[8] To the lid interior of a trunk, she affixed a label recalling the high days when Martha returned with 'the many gifts she always brought for her grandchildren'.[9] To this extent Eliza's colourful testimony is corroborated: during her absences from Mount Vernon in the years of conflict, Martha was always at pains to acquire dolls and toys for the children back home.

Martha had expended much love on Jacky and on Patsy, who had required so much care. In her affections Fanny Bassett probably came before her Parke Custis granddaughters, though the youngest, Eleanor – or Nelly like her mother – was resident at Mount Vernon. Her daughter-in-law, Nelly, since becoming a mother, was less close to Martha. But a bond survived from when the two had earlier been affectionate, following Patsy's death and during the early years of the Parke Custises' marriage. Jacky warred with Washington for prime place in her affections. The looked-for birth of an heir to the Parke Custis estates might bring a new contender.

At the beginning of the year, for reasons of security, Thomas Jefferson, Governor of the Washingtons' home state, had transferred all public offices and the state assembly from Williamsburg to Richmond, further inland. From Mount Vernon Martha wrote in early August to urge participation in an unusual fundraising scheme on the Governor's wife, Martha Skelton Jefferson. The campaign, spearheaded by Joseph Reed's wife, Esther, had been launched while Martha was in Philadelphia in June, on her way home. In the *Pennsylvania Gazette*, on 21 June, 'American Women' in that state were urged to contribute funds so that Washington could 'procure to the army the objects of subsistence, arms or clothings, which are due to them by the continent'. Monies raised were to be regarded as an 'extraordinary bounty, intended to render the condition of the soldier more pleasant'.[10] On 4 July Esther Reed informed the Commander-in-Chief that '200,580 Doll. & £625.6.8 in Specie' had been donated. This amounted, 'in Paper Money' – that is, the depreciated Continental currency – to $300,634.[11] French ladies, as well as 'American Women', had contributed, Madame de La Luzerne chief among them. Lafayette pledged a generous sum on behalf of his wife the Marquise in France. Washington, though grateful, resisted suggestions from Mrs Reed that the sum raised be doled out in cash to the soldiers. Shirts, stockings and sobriety were called for in the current crisis. He informed her of these needs in courteous language.[12] Shirts and stockings, if not sobriety, he got.

Mrs Washington informed Mrs Jefferson that the ladies of Maryland were proving similarly generous. In her turn on 8 August the Governor's wife addressed the wife of James Madison, Sr, a wealthy Virginia planter and militia colonel. Mrs Jefferson felt justified, she informed Eleanor Madison, by the 'sanction of her [Mrs Washington's] letter in handing forth the scheme'. Next day the announcement of the campaign in the *Virginia Gazette* duly bore the name of the Governor's wife.[13]

In the locale of Mount Vernon, the 'American Ladies' vigorously set to their task of rendering the soldier's life pleasant. Collections were made at the different churches, following 'sermons suited to the occasion'. The ladies of Alexandria, 'under the lead of "Lady Washington"', it was later asserted, contributed $75,800. Martha herself gave $20,000, equivalent to £6,000. It was listed in October, in the account book that Lund kept at Mount Vernon, as 'Mrs Washington's Bounty to the Soldiers'.[14]

Whether at headquarters or at home, Martha, as wife of 'His Excellency', was courted. In September she thanked Arthur Lee, former Commissioner at Versailles, for 'an elegant piece of china'.[15] Gone was the servitude of the Old Dominion when Martha and George – and, before them, Martha and her first husband – sent to the china merchants of London for tea services and dinner plates. In the United States of America all things French were prized, and this gift was no doubt a souvenir of Lee's time in Paris. Martha placed no less a value, at a time when resources of all kinds were scarce, on a 'piece of net'. She informed Elizabeth Powel, the Washingtons' elegant friend in Philadelphia, that she was sending it to her by a Lee emissary – either Arthur himself, or another of the tribe: 'Mr Lee has promised to be careful of it and to deliver it himself.' Martha, closing, begged her compliments to 'Mr Powel'.[16]

Far to the north, at Preakness, her husband worked on with his 'family' – Alexander Hamilton, Tench Tilghman – and staff officers – Knox, Wayne, Robert Howe of North Carolina and Captain of Guard Caleb Gibbs – to secure an end to the war. In December, New Windsor, immediately north of West Point, became their new winter home. Though he had not seen his own home for more than five years, Washington could at least now look forward to the arrival of his wife.

Nathanael Greene, while on his journey from New Jersey to assume the command in the south, had stopped briefly at Mount Vernon with Baron von Steuben, engineer Du Ponceau and other officers. They had found Martha planning to leave for the north 'about the middle of this week'. If Martha was preoccupied by arrangements for that imminent and prolonged absence from home, she gave no sign of it. Hospitable and warm, she asked after Caty Greene, her companion in numerous winter headquarters, and promised to write to her. In a letter to Washington, Greene waxed lyrical about the commander's home: 'there is everything that nature and art can afford to render my stay happy and agreeable . . . I don't wonder that you languish so often to return to the pleasures of domestic life.'[17] Du Ponceau years later recalled that at dinner at Mount Vernon the 'table was abundantly served, but without profusion'. Afterwards, while others viewed the grounds, Du Ponceau sat in the parlour 'tête-à-tête' with Mrs Washington. He recorded: 'I shall never forget the affability, and, at the same time, the dignity of her demeanour. Our conversation was on general subjects. I can only remember the impression it left upon my mind . . .' Before the war Virginian Edmund Pendleton had likened Martha to a Spartan mother when she urged Washington to be bold at the forthcoming First Continental Congress. Du Ponceau rather thought of Martha as a woman from later antiquity: 'she reminded me of the Roman matrons of whom I had read so much, and I thought that she well deserved to be the companion and friend of the greatest man of the age'.[18]

While at Philadelphia, resting before her further journey north to New Windsor, Martha stayed with Joseph Reed, President of the Pennsylvania Council. The house was quiet. Reed was in mourning for his wife Esther, who, following her recent exertions to secure donations from 'American Ladies', had unexpectedly died. Martha did receive de La Luzerne, the French minister, who had at all costs to be propitiated. With him came the Marquis de Chastellux, bearing agreeable news. He had visited Washington in New Jersey in late November, and told of the commander's good health and apparent good spirits. De Chastellux took away an impression that Martha was 'about forty or forty-five, rather plump, but fresh and with an agreeable face'.[19] Martha would in fact be fifty the following June. Her energy as well as her pink and white complexion – and good white teeth, on which many remarked – remained youthful.

The Reed mansion was to be Martha's last taste of comfort for many months, following her arrival in mid-December in New Windsor. Washington derided this settlement above the Hudson as a 'dreary station'. Headquarters was a 'plain Dutch house', belonging to one William Ellison, just outside the village. But at New Windsor, the commander enjoyed the benefit of good communications by road and river with Congress, Rochambeau in Rhode Island and Greene in the south. Up a hill at Vail's Gate Henry Knox and other key officers occupied a more commodious stone house. Lafayette installed himself, with Washington's nephew George Augustine among his aides, in quarters across a creek.

Martha's arrival lightened Washington's mood. He wrote to Caty Greene in Rhode Island, enclosing a letter from her husband in the south: 'Mrs Washington, who is just arrived at these my Quarters, joins me in most cordial wishes for your every felicity; & regrets the want of your Company – remember us to my namesake – Nat – I suppose can handle a Musket.'[20] The Greenes had named their first two children after George and Martha. The birth of Nathanael, their fourth, had occurred in freezing Morristown this January.

Martha settled with apparent ease into the customary pattern of winter life in camp, though Washington told Lafayette their quarters were 'very confined'. Dinner – meat, chicken and vegetables, with pies and puddings to follow – was as ever the great event of the day at headquarters. Washington, as ever, was much in conference with his staff and, with the 'family', occupied in anxious correspondence. Martha found time, on Boxing Day, to write to Peale in Philadelphia. She asked that a jeweller set, 'neat and plain', and in matching bracelets, the miniatures of Jacky and Patsy that the artist had painted while her daughter still lived.[21]

Pay and clothing for the army at New Windsor and in winter cantonments elsewhere were equally lacking this winter. Early in January 1781 Washington dispatched Knox on a mission to the eastern states. He had orders to beg from the governors of each 'a sum equal to three months pay at least' for their troops and 'a complete suit of clothes . . . shirts, vests, breeches, and stockings to carry them through the winter'.[22] Knox was still on this thankless errand when Pennsylvania troops mutinied at Morristown. They raided the magazine for arms, and set off for Philadelphia, declaring they would 'demand a redress of their grievances from Congress'.[23] The mutineers, following negotiation at Princeton, desisted. No mercy was shown to New Jersey troops who were arrested the following month after they seized arms and marched. On Washington's orders, their leaders were executed.

News came that 1,600 British and German troops had embarked at New York, their destination almost certainly the south. Still more unwelcome was the information, which Washington conveyed to Greene on 2 January: 'Arnold commands.'[24] Greene wrote from Virginia to Alexander Hamilton at New Windsor that the Commander-in-Chief was adulated in his native state. Regrettably this veneration did not translate into a supply of men, clothing, provisions or arms for Washington's deputy. Cornwallis and his troops fortified southern positions and laid waste swathes of the Carolinas and of coastal Virginia. Greene could put up little defence. Washington took the decision to send Lafayette south with an auxiliary force consisting of 1,200 troops. At Head of Elk, Maryland, he was to combine forces with 1,200 French soldiers, who would come from Rhode Island by sea. Together they were to proceed to Virginia, to combat Arnold.

Washington's decision to give this important command to the young French Marquis, who was wholly unfamiliar with both the geography and the inhabitants of Virginia, was unpopular with many. Alexander Hamilton was one of several of the 'family' who yearned for action and for an end to the daily drudgery of drafting and copying. One day in mid-February high words ensued between Washington and Hamilton, after they had been working at correspondence together till midnight the previous evening. Hamilton kept the commander waiting a few minutes. Washington lost his temper, and Hamilton seized the moment to resign. Though Washington apologized immediately, the insulted aide kept to his resolution. Hamilton remained at headquarters until David Humphreys, a new amanuensis, arrived, and then secured, as he had long wished, command of a regiment.

So pressing was the need for communication with so many at this time that Martha herself turned secretary on at least one occasion: a February letter emanating from headquarters and bound for a clothier is in her handwriting. She may have been glad to pay a visit in March to Philip Schuyler at his elegant home in Albany. Dr John Cochran, Schuyler's brother-in-law and uncle to Betsy Schuyler Hamilton, was her escort.

Washington's plans for Lafayette and French troops to confront Arnold were doomed to failure. A British naval armament at the entrance to Chesapeake Bay drove the French transports back to their base at Rhode Island. In the wake of this intelligence, the American commander ordered the marquis to head south and combine with Greene in Virginia against Cornwallis. Private as well as public humiliation was the American commander's lot this spring. Towards the end of April, he and Martha learnt that a marauding British warship had threatened Mount Vernon from the Potomac below. Custodian Lund had offered its captain refreshments and provisions in a – successful – bid to preserve the estate. Washington told his cousin on the 30th : 'it would have been a less painful circumstance to me, to have heard, that in consequence of your non-compliance with their request, they had burnt my Houses, and laid the Plantation in ruins'.[25] Martha, too, was exacting, writing in the third person to Lund a month later: 'Mrs Washington will be glad to know if the cotton for the counterpanes was wove and whitened. How many yards was there of it? How many counterpanes will it make? She desired Milly Posey' – aide to Lunda – 'to have the fine piece of linen made white. How is Betty?' – slave, spinning woman – 'Has she been spinning all winter? Is [has] Charlotte' – [house slave, seamstress] – 'done the work I left for her to do?'[26]

If Martha was more than usually short with Lund, she had been suffering from what Washington described to Jacky, on 31 May, as 'a complaint in the Stomach, bilious, and now turned to a kind of Jaundice . . .' Though she was better than she had been, he wrote, she was 'still weak and low'. He added: 'As she is very desirous of seeing you, and as it is abt. the period for her returning to Virginia, I should be glad, if it does not interfere with any important engagements, if you could make her a visit.'[27] Jacky excused himself. Nelly had at last given him, on 30 April, a son and heir. George Washington Parke Custis, as the infant was named, was febrile in the early weeks of his life. His mother was unwell, as she had been following the birth of her third daughter. Jacky, an anxious husband and father, was reluctant to leave home.

Martha continued ill some weeks at New Windsor. In mid-June Washington returned to a loyalist donor gifts intended to be restorative, including oranges, lemons and limes, pineapples, orgeat and hyssop tea. No truck must be had with the enemy, however kind.[28]

When Martha left for home at the end of June, her health was still not firmly reestablished. Dr James Craik, Alexandria physician turned army surgeon, was provided as a suitable escort for the journey to a state that was rapidly becoming a cauldron of war.

Cornwallis and Lafayette and Greene were skirmishing and fighting over much of southern Virginia. The defences at Richmond, as Jefferson had feared, proved inadequate to resist British attack. Many of Martha's relatives and friends, including her brother Bartholomew and brother-in-law Burwell Bassett, saw their estates damaged in the course of the fighting. Mount Vernon and the Potomac region did not suffer. Martha resumed control of her own household and, with it, responsibility for her grandson. The child, known as 'Wash' or 'Washy', appears to have joined his elder sister Nelly in the Mount Vernon nursery, even before Martha reached home. Her daughter-in-law at Abingdon, it would seem, was once more, following childbirth, too ill not to relinquish care of her infant to others.

On the Hudson Washington concocted numerous plans with Rochambeau to take New York, all of which failed. In mid-August came intelligence that the Comte de Grasse, admiral of a large French fleet in the West Indies, had responded to a plea from Rochambeau for aid. With 3,000 infantry on board, commanded by the Marquis de Saint-Simon, an experienced general, de Grasse and the fleet were headed for Hampton Roads, a large natural harbour in south eastern Virginia. The time for a reckoning in the south had come, and Washington and Rochambeau, with their respective armies, headed swiftly south to bolster Lafayette's forces in the state.

The Marquis, encamped at Williamsburg, had skilfully backed Lord Cornwallis and the enemy into a defensive position at Yorktown, near the southern entrance to Chesapeake Bay. While heading south from Philadelphia, on 5 September, Washington learnt that de Grasse's fleet had arrived off Cape Henry, in Virginia, at the southern extremity of Chesapeake Bay. An opportunity offered to invest Yorktown and force a British surrender.

Washington had resumed writing a journal earlier in the year. 'Judging it highly expedient to be with the army in Virginia as soon as possible, to make the necessary arrangements for the Siege, & to get the Materials prepared for it,' he now wrote at Head of Elk, Maryland, 'I determined to set out for the Camp of the Marquis de la Fayette without loss of time . . .'[29] Leaving the northern army to make its way south under the command of Benjamin Lincoln, Washington pressed on. Leaving Baltimore early on the morning of 9 September, he was soon in the Commonwealth of Virginia, which had been a British colony when he had last left it. An entry in his journal is, though laconic, expressive of his pleasure in being, if briefly, at home: '9th. I reached my own Seat at Mount Vernon (distant 120 Miles from the Hd. of Elk). . .'[30]

One evening only the Washingtons had for some degree of private pleasure together. On successive days members of the military 'family' – Rochambeau, de Chastellux and others – arrived. Mount Vernon was, until the allied commanders and suites left for Williamsburg on the 12th, as much the scene of anxious conference as previous lodgings at Morristown or New Windsor. At this impromptu headquarters Washington dared to hope for victory ahead at Yorktown.

Victory on the York and Private Grief, 1781

General goes to Colonel Bassett's where
Mr Custis is very ill.

Though Washington's stay at home in September 1781 was brief and the time he could give to Martha negligible, the master and mistress of Mount Vernon could congratulate themselves that they had upheld the honour of Virginia, even in wartime conditions. Aide Jonathan Trumbull Jr was dazzled by the 'elegant seat and situation, great appearance of opulence and real exhibitions of hospitality and princely entertainment'.[1] George and Martha were used to the comforts of their home. She now faced once more the prospect of a husband absent on a dangerous mission. He must prove a master puppeteer of the forces converging on Yorktown. De Grasse's fleet and troops from the West Indies were at Cape Henry, and the Comte de Barras – replacing de Ternay, who had died – was expected with a squadron and troops from Rhode Island. Washington's immediate aim was to join Lafayette at Williamsburg as swiftly as possible.

Upon his arrival there, in mid-September, he urged hasty embarkation on his second-in-command, General Benjamin Lincoln, still at Head of Elk with the Continentals from the north: 'every day we lose now is comparatively an age; as soon as it is in our power with safety we ought to take up our position near the enemy. Hurry on . . . my dear General, with your troops upon the wing of speed, the want of men and stores is now all that retards our immediate opera-tions.' Cornwallis was daily improving his position at Yorktown, Washington added: 'every day that is given him to make his prepa-rations may cost us many lives to encounter.'[2] The British General had made his headquarters at a handsome brick mansion close to the main fortifications above the river, property of Thomas Nelson of Yorktown, now Governor of Virginia. Thomas Jefferson, disgusted by the enemy's easy reduction of Richmond, had declined to stand again. All around, British and Hessian troops were fortifying the town and numerous inland outposts, as well as Gloucester, across the James River.

De Grasse had no intention of remaining off the American coast beyond early November. No future joint attack on New York could be planned. On the credit side, Admiral de Barras's squadron bearing French troops and siege artillery from Rhode Island had now arrived. Allied plans for the siege of Yorktown and British surrender – a surrender to rank in terms of national humiliation with the Continental surrender of Charleston the previous year – could proceed.

At Williamsburg Henry Knox, in conclave with engineers du Portail and Gouvion, worked to assemble a heavy arsenal of siege artillery. Lincoln disembarked his Continental troops and stores, and French troops from Baltimore landed. Washington, on 23 September, informed Thomas McKean, the new President of Congress, that the allied forces expected to be in a few days 'before the enemy's works at York and Gloucester'.[3] Notwithstanding the lack of some supplies, including rum, which, he told Robert Morris, he deemed essential for the men's health and spirits, Washington recorded in his journal: '28th . . . we commenced our march for the investiture of the enemy at York.'

The column of troops – Americans preceding the French – was more than a mile long. According to plan, they separated at a given point so as to adopt, at the prescribed encampment before the enemy lines, a semi-circular formation – French troops to the left, Americans and militia to the right. Among these last was Thomas

Nelson of Yorktown itself and many other delegates to the Virginia Assembly, keen to play a part in the fray. 'The line being formed,' wrote Washington, 'all the troops, officers and men, lay upon their arms during the night.'[4] The following morning the American and French forces made the welcome discovery that the British had, under cover of darkness, abandoned all their exterior works. They had retreated within redoubts and within the walls of Yorktown. Allied troops took up positions in the earthworks the enemy had abandoned.

Operations must be conducted without the assistance of any shipping on the James River. De Grasse, notwithstanding the American commander's 'earnest solicitations', declined 'hazarding any vessels on that station'. The French fleet was at least in place in Lynnhaven Bay to prevent the British escaping out to sea. A week passed in which the opposing forces skirmished. American engineers, felling thousands of trees, built new earthworks and began to put their artillery in place. The British improved their defences and, as rations grew scarce, sent out foraging parties.

During the night of 6 October the first allied 'parallels', or trenches, 600 yards or so from the enemy works, were opened. Three days later, on the 9th, communication trenches between the parallels were open, advanced redoubts, or defensive emplacements, were complete, and allied batteries in place. That afternoon, Washington put a match to the first of the cannon, trained on the enemy's works, to open fire. Smoke and pungent gunpowder filled the air as six American 18- and 24-pounders, mortars and howitzers, and a French battery of four 16-pounders, six mortars and two howitzers, commanded by the Marquis de Saint-Simon, 'began to play'.[5]

The siege had begun, the British responded, and army surgeon James Thacher recorded in his journal: 'The bomb shells from the besiegers and the besieged are incessantly crossing each other's path in the air. They are clearly visible in the form of a black ball in the day . . . in the night, they appear like fiery meteors with blazing tails, most beautifully brilliant, ascending majestically from the mortar . . . to a certain altitude.' These missiles then descended to where they were 'destined to work their act of destruction'.[6] The Continentals and the French had the best of the contest, the more so when, as aide Tilghman noted in his journal, during the night of the 11th, 'the second parallel was opened within three hundred yards of the enemy's works with scarce any annoyance'.[7] Once this closer parallel was complete and batteries established, the allied artillery aimed to shell the beleaguered garrison into submission. Over the following two days work on this important trench was completed.

Martha had word of some of these doings from her son in a letter of 12 October, headed 'Camp before York'. Jacky had joined his stepfather before Yorktown a fortnight earlier. The birth of his son provided some degree of security for the family estates, but he did not, like other Virginia Assembly delegates, join the militia. On his way south, he stayed at Pamocra, his uncle Bartholomew Dandridge's plantation on the Pamunkey, and wrote of his maternal relations to his mother: 'They are very desirous of seeing you. My grandmother wishes you to bring down both Bet and Pat' – his eldest children – 'but I told her it would be too inconvenient for you to bring down both.'[8]

Jacky's role at headquarters was undefined. Henry Knox was later to write of him to Commissary General Clement Biddle: 'his patriotism led him to camp to participate in some degree of the dangers of his amiable and illustrious father'.[9] Custis could at least reassure his mother: 'the General, though in constant fatigue, looks well'. He made enquiries about slaves from Mount Vernon and Abingdon, who had run away to seek the freedom promised by the enemy, in return for military service. 'I fear that most who left us are not existing,' wrote the young planter. 'The mortality that has taken place among the wretches is really incredible. I have seen numbers lying dead in the woods, and many so exhausted that they cannot walk.' Jacky's own health, which had been of concern before he left Mount Vernon, was much better, he informed his mother, despite the 'change in lodgings'.[10] Though he filled the duties of an aide only to 'some degree', the young master of Abingdon slept, like Washington and the rest of the military 'family', under canvas.

Jacky brought with him to camp a letter to Henry Knox, entrusted to him by the General's wife, Lucy. Mrs Knox, pregnant and with a young son who clung to her in unfamiliar surroundings, had been Martha's guest at Mount Vernon since mid-September. Now Lucy's hostess was set to make an autumn pilgrimage to see relations. 'Her return is very uncertain,' wrote Lucy Knox to her husband Henry on 8 October.[11] Martha received, a few days later, as well as Jacky's missive of the 12th, a long letter from Washington. Lucy Knox, who had received no communication from her own husband, noted on the 16th with some wonder: 'he informs her of every manoeuvre, however trifling, which has taken place since the opening of the trenches'.[12]

Allowing for the special affection that bound husband and wife, the tenor of Washington's letter to his wife probably resembled in great part that of his wartime correspondence with his brothers and close friends not in the military line. It was now nearly thirty years since the publication of his 1754 *Journal*, which detailed his expedition into Ohio country and the French commandant's refusal to cede British territory. Then as now, and on occasions earlier in this war, Washington took pleasure in giving an account of operations, once concluded. That he wrote in such detail on the 12th is indication that he could see an end to the siege of Yorktown.

Following receipt of her husband's letter, Martha formed the intention to proceed, after first visiting her family in New Kent County, to Yorktown. Lucy informed Henry Knox, on the 16th, that her hostess, with Nelly Custis, was setting off the following day – 'in full expectation of being in camp very shortly'.[13] 'Bet' Parke Custis, now five, went too. Martha's movements, once she left Mount Vernon, are thereafter for some time undocumented. Disconsolate and heavily pregnant, Lucy passed her time at Mount Vernon with her young son, Harry. She told his father on the 23rd, that the boy ate 'hominy', or grits, 'like a true Virginian'.[14] A letter from Knox, dated 'Trenches before York, 16 October 1781', brought her cheering news: 'The night before last we stormed the enemy's two advanced works with very little loss – the fate of the enemy draws nigh.' Henry estimated that, in ten or twelve days, they would, 'with the blessing of heaven, terminate it [the siege]'.[15]

Heaven was kinder. The very next day the enemy beat a parley at ten o'clock in the morning. Cornwallis suggested a 'cessation of Hostilities for 24 hours', to see if commissioners could agree terms for the surrender of the British posts at York and Gloucester.[16] The British met humiliating Articles of Capitulation that the allies proposed with protest and procrastination. As all were aware, these 'articles' mirrored those to which the Continentals had submitted when Benjamin Lincoln surrendered Charleston. Cornwallis responded, on the 19th, to an ultimatum from Washington, and the vexed Articles of Capitulation were signed and in the American commander's hands by eleven o'clock that morning.

Three hours later, at two o'clock, the allied command awaited the surrender of the town. Marching in slow time to a British tune, over 7,000 British and German troops, now all prisoners-of-war, passed between the French and American lines. Their colours were unfurled, their muskets were reversed, and a field was made ready where they would lay down their arms.

With an array of Continental generals and staff officers, Washington, distinguished by his blue sash and mounted on Nelson, awaited Cornwallis. Rochambeau, other French generals and de Grasse with their suites formed another group. As the principal British officers reached this allied command, there was no sign of Cornwallis. The British second-in-command, Brigadier General Charles O'Hara, pleaded indisposition on his superior's behalf. Washington, without comment, gestured his own second-in-command, Benjamin Lincoln, forward, and stood aloof as the surrender was concluded.

For once the American commander was ebullient in his correspondence with Congress: 'a Reduction of the British Army under the Command of Lord Cornwallis, is most happily effected. The unremitting Ardor which actuated every Officer and Soldier in the combined Army on this Occasion, has principally led to this Important Event, at an earlier period than my most sanguine Hopes . . .'[17] The golden autumn victory on the Chesapeake in which the American and French had combined to such swift and devastating purpose did not fade easily from combatants' minds. At the end of the month Knox wrote to his wife at Mount Vernon: 'How is Hal [their young son, Harry]? Cannot you impress his memory so powerfully with the taking of Lord Cornwallis as to make the little fellow tell it to his children?'[18]

When the British Prime Minister, Lord North, was brought news in London of the American and French victory, he supposedly responded, according to testimony attributed to Foreign Secretary Lord George Germain: 'As he would have taken a [cannon or musket] Ball in his Breast . . . He opened his Arms, exclaiming wildly as he paced up and down the Apartment . . . "O God! It is all over!"'[19] Washington, preparing to head north for Philadelphia and winter quarters in New York, had no means of knowing what the British government's reaction would be. He was anxious that success at Yorktown should not cause Congress or the army to relax in their efforts to dislodge the British from New York and other strongholds. Indeed George III initially refused to allow that the American victory had been decisive, and the war continued.

In her letter of 23 October to her husband in camp, Lucy Knox at Mount Vernon wrote of her absent hostess: 'She will be just in time to dance at your ball' – a Yorktown Victory Ball, of which there was much talk, though it never took place – 'where I should like to be present.'[20] But Martha did not join her husband before Yorktown, nor when he departed for Williamsburg in early November.

As Washington was later to tell George William Fairfax, Jacky Parke Custis was 'taken sick at the siege of York'.[21] Henry Knox, in his letter of 11 November to Biddle, confirmed that his friend's ward 'contracted the seeds of his disease' at camp, though he did not state what that disease was.[22] 'Camp fever', or typhus, and malaria afflicted large numbers of the allied forces on the York, and hospitals in the field and in Williamsburg were crowded. Jacky was removed to be nursed and to convalesce at Eltham, thirty miles upriver. Martha and Nelly came to the Bassett house to be with him. Washington, once he had concluded a variety of business consequent on the British surrender, struck out north from Williamsburg on 5 November with a small suite including aides John Laurens and Jonathan Trumbull Jr.

That progress came to an abrupt halt the same evening at Bird's Ordinary, an inn only sixteen miles or so north of Williamsburg.

Trumbull wrote in his journal: 'General goes to Colonel Bassett's where Mr Custis is very ill.' The aides were unaccustomed to idleness when with 'the General', but no word, no direction or orders came from Eltham. '6th,' wrote Trumbull. 'Still at Bird's – nothing from Bassett's till noon . . .'[23] The following letter from Washington at Eltham, received at the inn about midday, broke the silence:

My dear Sir,

I came here in time to see Mr Custis breathe his last. About eight o'clock yesterday evening he expired. The deep and solemn distress of the Mother, and affliction of the Wife of this amiable young Man, requires every comfort in my power to afford them. The last rites of the deceased I must also see performed – these will take me three or four days; when I shall proceed with Mrs Washington & Mrs Custis to Mount Vernon.

As the dirty tavern you are now at cannot be very comfortable, and in spite of Mr [Laurence] Sterne's observation, the house of mourning [Eltham], not very agreeable, it is my wish, that all the Gentlemen of my family – except yourself – may proceed on at their leisure to Mount Vernon, & wait for me there . . . [Trumbull was directed to join the general at Eltham.] My best wishes attend the Gentlemen & with much sincerity & affection I remain –
Yr very Hble Ser.[24]

Jacky Parke Custis, hale and hearty so recently, roaming the woods around Yorktown, writing cheerfully to his mother in mid-October, was dead. Washington, informing Lafayette of 'this unexpected and affecting event', described Martha and Nelly Calvert Custis as in 'deep distress'.[25] While Jacky's mother and wife reeled, his stepfather, no less moved, made burial arrangements. For once private obligations were a priority, as he informed John Hanson, McKean's successor as President of Congress: 'an event which I met with at this place (very distressing to Mrs Washington) will retard my arrival at Philadelphia a few days longer than I expected, which I hope Congress will have the goodness to excuse as I am not conscious that any important public duty will be neglected by it'.[26]

During the night of 6 November Jacky's wasted body was dispatched to the 'family burying place' at Queen's Creek, close to Williamsburg. His sister Patsy's grave, where Martha sometimes walked, was in the garden at Mount Vernon. Jacky was to lie with his Parke Custis ancestors, with his siblings Daniel II and Fanny, and with his father. At the interment that followed next day Washington was chief mourner among those who assembled to mourn the young man named by Knox a few days later as 'the amiable Mr Custis'.[27] Three days later by stages the Washingtons, Nelly and five-year-old Eliza, all in mourning garb, left Eltham, and turned for home.

It was not a home where Martha could easily give way to grief. Mount Vernon was once more an army headquarters. The mansion was crowded with American aides and generals, copying, consulting, and awaiting the General's orders to head north. Congress waited at Philadelphia to hail the victor of Yorktown. From there Washington would head for winter quarters at Newburgh on the North River.

Martha might have remained at home, after her husband and staff were gone, and mourned her last remaining child in some degree of privacy. She might have wished to provide some degree of comfort for her daughter-in-law and grandchildren. Williamsburg lawyer Bartholomew Dandridge was, in the Washingtons' view, the natural person to act as his late nephew's executor and as administrator of the Parke Custis estates. George wrote to him from Mount Vernon on 19 November: 'The purchase of Alexander's Land will, I fear, be the most difficult and perplexing matter of all. I shall commence my journey for the Northward tomorrow. Mrs Washington goes with me.'[28]

Any consolation there was for Martha lay with George, who had shared her grief when Patsy died, who had stood in place of a father to her son. Washington was to tell a former aide, mourning his father, that he rarely attempted to console the bereaved. He was 'of Sterne's opinion', expressed in *Tristram Shandy*: 'Before an affliction is digested, consolation comes too soon – and after it is digested – it comes too late . . .' Washington also abjured fond recollections of the departed: 'it would only be a renewal of sorrow by recalling afresh to your remembrance things which had better be forgotten'.[29] Whether

Washington kept to these stern prescriptions in the case of his grieving wife, he himself was much affected by the young man's death.
Before proceeding to Pennsylvania, he replied to an address from
'Citizens of Alexandria', many of them friends of long standing: 'The
present prospect is pleasing, the late success at York Town is very
promising, but on our own Improvement depend its future good
consequences . . . A Relaxation of our Exertions at this moment may
cost us many more toilsome Campaigns, and be attended with the
most unhappy consequences.' He ended on a personal note: 'Your
condolence for the loss of that amiable youth Mr Custis, affects me
most tenderly. His loss' – as Fairfax County delegate – 'I trust will be
compensated to you, in some other worthy Representative. Amidst
all the Vicissitudes of Time or Fortune, be assured Gentlemen,
that I shall ever regard with particular Affection the Citizens and
Inhabitants of Alexandria.'[30] Martha had, as emblems of her own
loss, Jacky's and Patsy's miniatures, made by Peale and mounted
by a jeweller the previous winter. These images of Jacky, bursting
with health, and of his sister, forever wan, were to remain with their
mother until her death.

Uncertainty and Disaffection, 1781–1783

. . . this long and bloody contest . . .

The Washingtons took up residence in a handsome house on South Street in Philadelphia late in November 1781. Congress paid tribute on the 28th to the commander they had so often failed to fund and supply. The following month the French Ambassador, de La Luzerne, hosted an oratorio on 11 December. The addresses were endless, the visits and dinners inevitable. The 13th, a day set aside for prayer and thanks, was filled with so much ceremony as to leave little time for either. Washington, when not otherwise engaged, worked with the Secretariats of the Finance and War Departments to prepare for campaigns in the year to come. He and Martha were only to leave Philadelphia for Newburgh late in March 1782. Throughout the months in Pennsylvania, Washington warned – in Congress and outside of it – against 'languor and relaxation', following victory at Yorktown.[1] Peace – the word now whispered with increasing volume throughout the country – might well come. Until official intelligence came that treaties were signed at Versailles, it was his duty to try and regain Charleston in the south, and wrest New York from Clinton.

On Christmas Day 1781 George and Martha permitted themselves a measure of 'languor and relaxation', and dined with Robert

Morris and his wife, Mary. The following February the Comte de Rochambeau, wintering with the French army, wrote, on the 10th, of his intention to honour Washington's fiftieth 'anniversary' with 'a great ball' at Williamsburg the next day.[2] The American commander was appreciative of the honour done him, though he himself kept his birthday on the 22nd, New Style. He was less happy with one of several advances of age. His eyesight was faltering, and he needed spectacles for reading. By degrees, too, his chestnut hair was turning grey. The strain of being occupied, over so many years, for hours on end, in conference and correspondence, had had other effects. His pleasant smile, formerly commonplace, he now kept for a select few. Light conversation, with which he had earlier whiled away many evenings at home and elsewhere, was also at a premium. He was pensive and often silent in company. With Martha and a few intimates only his contracted features relaxed and took on their previous open cast. For all the want of exercise, his tall figure remained strong, his seat on a horse admirable. Whatever the future held, the Commander-in-Chief was fit for business.

Martha, like Washington, was changing physically. Her hazel eyes, white teeth and fine complexion were still attractive, but as she grew stout with age and acquired a pronounced double chin, her caps became larger and whiter, her clothes, though still of the best quality, plainer. Washington continued to admire his wife for her confidence and affable energy. For Martha there were resonances in the preamble to her husband's November remarks to the 'Citizens' of Alexandria: 'The great Director of events has carried us thro' a variety of Scenes during this long and bloody contest in which we have been for Seven Campaigns, most nobly struggling.' The different winter headquarters had indeed represented for Martha, who had never previously left Virginia and Maryland, 'a variety of scenes'. Sociable, curious, she had enjoyed that variety, and playing some small part in the 'long and bloody contest'.[3]

The usual tenor of life at winter headquarters resumed, upon the Washingtons' arrival in late March 1782 at Newburgh, on the Hudson. A small Dutch farmhouse, belonging to a Mr Hasbrouck, was their new temporary home. Lucy Knox, with her children, stayed with her husband Henry nearby, and was a frequent guest at head-quarters. The Washingtons were by now well used to the restrictions of camp life. A visitor later in the year complained of the dining room, formerly Mr Hasbrouck's parlour, that there was little vent for the smoke from the fireplace. A smaller room served as parlour, where the company assembled before dinner. This same visitor wrote, 'when the hour of bedtime came, I found that the chamber, to which the General conducted me, was the very parlour I speak of, wherein he had made them place a camp-bed.' During breakfast the following morning, the bed was folded up, and the erstwhile bedchamber became once more a parlour.[4]

A guest on another occasion was more easily satisfied. 'The dinner was good, but everything was quite plain,' George Bennet, an Englishman, recorded; 'we all sat on camp-stools and there was nothing to be seen about his [Washington's] house, but what every officer in the army might likewise have in his – Mrs W was as plain, easy, and affable as he was, and one would have thought from the familiarity which prevailed there, that he saw a respectable private gentleman dining at the Head of his own Family.'[5]

At Newburgh Washington continued to hold to the position that he had expressed to his former aide, Robert Hanson Harrison, the previous November: 'one thing we are sure of and that is, that the only certain way to obtain Peace is to be prepared for War . . .'[6] In London, Lord North's government had fallen this March. The ministers who succeeded him favoured an end to the expensive war with America, the King's wishes notwithstanding. Peace negotiations of an informal kind ensued in Paris between the British, the Americans and the French. Washington maintained his offensive stance, writing now, in early May 1782, to John Hancock, 'No Nation ever suffered in Treaty by preparing, even in the moment of Negotiation, most vigorously for the Field.'[7] A letter arrived in Newburgh a few days later from Sir Guy Carleton, who had succeeded Sir Henry Clinton at New York. He announced that he was 'joined with Admiral Digby in the commission of peace', but news, inconsistent with that declaration, followed. British Admiral Rodney had fought and defeated de Grasse off Guadeloupe in the West Indies.[8] Washington continued to propitiate de La Luzerne in Philadelphia and consult with Rochambeau, still in Virginia with the French troops.

Reports of the birth of a Dauphin to Queen Marie Antoinette in Paris offered Washington an opportunity to honour the French nation. In late May, the Washingtons were joined at an elegant dinner by 500 officers and their wives, and gentlemen of standing in the locality with their ladies. As evening fell, thirteen cannon fired a *feu de joie*, to general approval, and Washington led off the dancing with Lucy Knox.[9] Notice of these rude rejoicings on the Hudson may not have reached the Dauphin's sire and his ministers at Versailles, but Washington continued to stress to anyone with any influence at that place of power, that the war could not be won without French naval superiority.

In the second week of July Martha left Washington at Newburgh to return home. George Augustine, Washington's namesake and soldier son of his younger brother Charles, had been suffering from an intermittent fever. He was to recuperate at Mount Vernon, and Martha and he made the journey south together. She had written in wonder, on her way to the siege of Boston in 1775, that she was treated everywhere as though she were a great personage. Now she thought nothing of the honours she received everywhere on the road. Prints of Washington, against a background of cannon, drums and flags, and of Martha, garlanded with flowers, had been recently published at Boston. They served to increase the crowds who turned out to applaud either one of the celebrated couple when they passed. At Mount Vernon, a home she reached on 19 July, she was safe from crowds and official entertainment.

Though Martha was never an enthusiast for civic receptions, she was as eager as her husband to propitiate French officers. Soon after her return home she invited one of them, the Comte de Custine-Sarreck, who was in the district with his regiment, to dine with 'some officers' of his choice. The French officers, ten in number, appear to have admired the widowed Nelly Calvert Custis quite as much as the gardens and grounds. De Custine-Sarreck, owner of a celebrated porcelain factory in Niderviller in north-eastern France, presented his hostess with a tea and coffee service, decorated with her husband's monogram and emblems of glory. A proud Virginian matron, Martha might have been stung by the character that another of the French officers gave her: 'a woman of about fifty years of age; she is small and fat, her appearance is respectable. She was dressed very plainly and her manners were simple in all respects.'[10] The Washingtons were prepared to overlook any such condescension if the French would remain their allies.

Washington counted on Martha, at Mount Vernon, to offer hospitality to many in return for aid rendered him. He entrusted a letter for her later this year to a young Rhode Islander: 'My dearest, if this letter should ever reach your hands, it will be presented by Mr Brown, Son of a Gentleman of that name in Rhode Island, from whom I have received civilities, & to whom, or his connections, I could wish to make returns.' Merchant John Brown had played a leading role in patriot agitation before the war. 'As he [James, the son], has thoughts of going into Virginia I recommend him to your notice & attention. I am most sincerely & affectionately – Yrs Go: Washington.'[11] Brown did not, in the end, visit Martha, but the letter may serve as representative of many others which have not survived.

In New York state, Washington was uncertain what to do, and vexed by his own indecision. Following surrender at Yorktown, the British appeared to have abandoned offensive war in their former colonies. Further, in August 1782 they evacuated Savannah, Georgia. With Congress, the state assemblies and the rest of America, Washington guessed as best he could at the intentions of the London government. The American peace commissioners at Versailles seemed to have no better understanding of their British counterparts' strategy. Hope mingled with uncertainty. Adverse weather conditions forced the Commander-in-Chief in October to seek early winter quarters in Newburgh once more for the army currently under canvas elsewhere. He told Nathanael Greene on the 17th: 'despairing of seeing my home this Winter, I am now writing to her [Mrs Washington] to make her annual visit'.[12]

George Augustine was still invalid at Mount Vernon. In his place Dr David Stuart, Scottish émigré and Alexandria physician, escorted Martha north. Other wives, too, made arrangements to join their husbands in the familiar setting of Newburgh, Lucy Knox and Betsy Gates among them. Horatio Gates wrote: 'upon talking with The General [Washington], I have sent for Mrs Gates to keep me from Freezing this Winter . . . Mrs Washington is, I understand, upon the road'.[13]

Washington had the satisfaction of knowing that the army was better organized, disciplined and clothed now than it had ever been. He inspected the regiments closely and regularly. He – and Knox and Gates with him – were aware that the field officers were much agitated. No arrangements were yet in place for half-pay, the usual reward for military service, should peace come swiftly and, with it, the disbandment of the army. Despite all Washington's urging, Congress, absorbed in sifting intelligence from across the Atlantic, was reluctant to turn its attention to this issue. Every new development that seemed to tend towards a peace disturbed the officers at Newburgh, fearing to go without reward for their services. Rochambeau and Chastellux departed America late in the year to unite in joint operations with the Spanish army in Santo Domingo against the British. In January 1783 news came that the British had evacuated Charleston. Washington called Greene's forces north. Though he longed to strike against New York, the one remaining British stronghold, the protracted peace negotiations at Versailles might yet succeed and render such plans irrelevant.

Railing in February at the 'rugged and dreary mountains' that formed his immediate view at Newburgh, the American commander worked on daily with the 'family', continuing to press on Congress the need for half-pay for officers.[14] 'The temper of the army is much soured,' he had written to Virginia delegate Joseph Jones the previous December, 'and has become more irritable than at any period since the commencement of the war.'[15] Practical as ever, Martha looked ahead to the spring and summer. Washington ordered in January, at her request, six yards of 'very fine Jacanet Muslin', one and a half yards wide.[16] In March, she presented Henry Knox with two 'hairnets' – to confine his queue, or pigtail. She would have sent them long before, she wrote, 'but for want of tape, which was necessary to finish them and which was not obtained till yesterday'.[17]

The disaffection that Knox and Washington feared came to a head this month. An anonymous paper circulated among the field officers, sugggesting that, if the war continued, the army as a whole should desert and inhabit some unnamed wilderness. If a peace were brokered, the army should instead refuse to lay down its arms. Following swift intervention by Washington, representatives of each regiment met on the 15th in the Temple, a large hall in the cantonment. More pacific measures to secure the half-pay the officers sought, it was hoped, might there be agreed. Washington entered the hall and spoke for a few minutes. He begged the sullen officers not to take any measures that would 'lessen the dignity and sully the glory you have hitherto maintained'. Urging patience, he began to read aloud a recent letter from Joseph Jones. It detailed obstacles that lay in the way of meeting the army's due claims. Washington stumbled over the sentences, or at least affected so to do. Reaching into his pocket, he took out spectacles and put them on, saying: 'Gentlemen, you must pardon me. I have grown gray in your service and now find myself growing blind.'[18]

This remark, as much as Jones's explanations that Washington then read, had a salutary effect on the mood of the assembled officers. The government of the United States and its Commander-in-Chief survived this challenge to their authority. Such rhetorical devices could not be essayed twice. A letter from Lafayette at Cadiz of 5 February reached Newburgh two months later, anticipating official intelligence crossing the Atlantic to America. Preliminary articles of peace had been signed at Versailles on 20 January by Britain, France and Spain, making operative an earlier pact of November 1782 between the British Crown and the United States. Though peace treaties between the different combatants were yet to be signed, Britain had announced the cessation of hostilities on 4 February.

Cautious for so long, Washington could at last dwell on an end to war. Peace would signal a return to Mount Vernon. He and Martha could once more resume the characters of private individuals. Writing to the marquis on 5 April, Washington's thoughts were all of his future retirement. Once the treaties were ratified, he would promise the United States aid only 'as far as it can be rendered in the private walks of life'. His mind, he wrote, would at last be 'unbent'. He would endeavour to 'glide down the stream of life 'till I come to that abyss, from whence no traveller is permitted to return'.[19]

A few days earlier, George had been in an energetic frame of mind when denouncing the Articles of Confederation, the framework for government in America for much of the war. He wrote to Alexander Hamilton: 'No Man in the United States is, or can be more deeply impressed with the necessity of a reform in our present Confederation than myself . . . to the defects thereof, & want of Powers in Congress may justly be ascribed the prolongation of the War, & consequently the Expences occasioned by it.'[20] These impassioned words were not those of a man whose mind would be easily 'unbent', or who would succeed in gliding down any stream.

Peace on the Hudson, 1783

I now see the Port opening to which I have been steering...

On 18 April 1783, Washington ordered 'the Cessation of Hostilities' with the British truce to be proclaimed at Newburgh next day, anniversary of the actions at Lexington and Concord. Only after a 'general peace' – a lasting peace treaty – was signed and ratified, he stressed, would the British forces sail for home, and the American army be disbanded. It would, however, be 'ingratitude', he remarked, not to rejoice now, 'on such a happy day, a day which is the harbinger of Peace, a day which compleats the eighth year of the war'. He ordered, in celebration of the proclamation, 'An extra Ration of Liquor, to be issued to *every* man tomorrow, to drink Perpetual Peace, Independence and Happiness, to the United States of America'. [1]

The initial exultation in camp at the prospect of peace faded. The mood among the 'war men' – so Washington termed the soldiery still enlisted – grew ugly. [2] They made no distinction between the 'cessation of hostilities' proclaimed and a binding peace, and were vociferous in their demand for their discharge – with back-pay. On 22 April Washington told Alexander Hamilton that he had lately increased the Guard to prevent rioting. Officers met with 'Insults' when attempting to hold the fractious, homeward-looking men to their duty. [3] Two days later he wrote to aide Tench Tilghman, 'I can scarcely form an idea at this moment, when I shall be able to leave this

place; the distresses of the Army for want of money – the embarrass-
ments of Congress – and the conseqt delays, and disappointments
on all sides, encompass me with difficulties. . .' He envisaged himself,
not without justice, as a helmsman in national waters: 'as I now see
the Port opening to which I have been steering, I shall persevere till I
have gained admittance'.[4] He pressed Congress to send a committee
to camp with the aim of settling all accounts and releasing most of
the army early.

As summer succeeded spring on the upper Hudson, aides like
Tilghman, tired of the clerking and copying that constituted their
days at headquarters, were on extended furloughs or had left the
army to try their luck in political or civilian life. Washington turned
to Martha on several occasions in the spring to make fair copies of
letters he sent out to army colleagues, to Congress and to the states.
In July she worked with him to make a fair copy of his expenditures
on a recent journey, but she was not always fit for secretarial service,
as an old complaint recurred. 'Mrs Washington enjoys an incompe-
tent share of health,' the General wrote to George William Fairfax
on 10 July. 'Billious Fevers & Cholic's attack her very often, &
reduce her low. At this moment she is but barely recovering from
one of them.'[5]

Washington had been drawing up an account, to submit to
Congress, of his wife's 'travelling expenses, in coming to and returning from my winter quarters annually'. He had previously paid these
from his 'private purse', with money that Martha had brought to
headquarters from home. At the beginning of the war he had not
thought, he wrote, in an appendix to the account, to make what must
'at first view . . . wear the complexion of a private charge' into a
public one, but with the passage of years, owing to the 'embarrassed
situation' of national affairs, he had been obliged 'continually to postpone (to no small detriment of my private interest) the visit I every
year contemplated to make my family . . .' He had ended by judging Martha's travels to headquarters 'lawful', the term he employed
for public charges. He billed Congress for £1,064 1s od. Martha had
been a dauntless adventurer.[6] Some of the dwellings where she had
joined her husband – the Vassall house at Cambridge, Richmond Hill

in Manhattan – had been capacious and elegant. The Ford house at Morristown had been well appointed. More often than not – at Valley Forge, at Middlebrook and in Newburgh, where they now resided – the Washingtons' quarters were cramped and confined. Visitors slept in parlours, aides slept four to a room. Tin and pewter were dull on the dinner table, and there were stools for seats. Though she referred readily to the fatigue of her long and uncomfortable journeys, Martha never complained of conditions she endured in camp.

Washington wrote to his brother, John Augustine, on 15 June: 'I wait here with much impatience, the arrival of the Definitive Treaty; this event will put a period not only to my Military Service, but also to my public life . . .'[7] To while away the time, he had asked for histories of Charles XII and Peter the Great, and 'Wildman on Trees' to be sent to him.[8] He was as fractious and homesick now as any of the 'war men'. Lund at Mount Vernon received a reprimand, on the 11th, for failing to gather rents from his cousin's tenants in the west: 'you seem to have had an unconquerable aversion to going from home'. Washington shrank from the outcome of this neglect: 'worse than going home to empty coffers, and expensive living, I shall be encumbered with debt'.[9]

Though Martha might have returned home earlier to prepare Mount Vernon for peacetime occupation, she remained with Washington at Newburgh through the summer. In June George sent off, on her account, to a merchant in Philadelphia, for a piece of stuff to be matched. Mrs Washington, he wrote, required 'three yards of black silk like the enclosed; it is to repair old gowns, and consequently must be like them.' She would make and mend till she got home. He himself, in the same letter, wanted: 'for the purpose of Transporting my Books of record and Papers with safety . . . Six strong hair Trunks well clasped and with good Locks'.[10]

By the end of July Congress had adopted measures that Washington had advocated to calm the agitation at Newburgh, and a large part of the army had been disbanded. Washington was now called by Congress to Nassau Hall, Princeton, where the peripatetic body was in session to advise on the establishment of a permanent army. He had already set out his ideas on the subject in a lengthy memorandum, and had hoped to proceed directly from Newburgh to Mount Vernon, once news of the 'general peace' came. Yielding to the pleas of delegates, he declared himself, as ever, the servant of Congress. He took up residence with a small suite in a house they selected to serve as headquarters at Rocky Hill, some four miles from Princeton. After an interval Martha followed.

The army on the Hudson was now for others to manage. Life at Rocky Hill, in the placid Millstone river valley, was pleasant. A kind of holiday atmosphere ensued. It was an easy journey when Washington rode into Princeton to report to Congress. Delegates and Princeton dignitaries, anxious to savour the hospitality of the celebrated commander, rode out to this agreeable headquarters.

A young artist, William Dunlap, lodging near by, spent days producing an indifferent crayon portrait of the commander. He later reflected: 'I was quite at home in every respect at head-quarters. To breakfast and dine day after day with the general and Mrs Washington, and members of congress, and [be] noticed as the young painter, was delicious.'[11] Martha, too, gave the young man a sitting. A more distinguished artist, Joseph Wright, also came calling. He had been commissioned by Congress to produce an equestrian statue of the Commander-in-Chief for the national government's eventual home, wherever that should be. Some favoured Philadelphia, others thought of New York. (The project of the statue ultimately failed.) The portrait in oils that Wright made was thought by many who knew the American commander well to be extremely realistic. It shows a man who had, to use the General's own words, 'gone grey' in his country's service.

The Washingtons took advantage of Rocky Hill's propinquity to Philadelphia to deluge Clement Biddle, now a civilian once more, with orders – linen, nails, paint, blankets for the slaves – for Mount Vernon. George's nephew Bushrod Washington, who was a law student in the city, also received numerous commissions. The General was not flattering in his estimation of Bushrod's capabilities: 'As you are young in this business, take some Mentor as a guide to your enquiries.' The young man was to inquire of leading cabinetmakers after 'two dozen strong, neat and plain, but fashionable' dining-room chairs 'with strong canvas bottoms to receive a loose covering of check, or worsted'. Additionally he was to ask after the price and availability of French wines, olives, nuts, oils and 'blue and white china'. When the Washingtons were first married, they had sent to London for what they required. When they wished to protest against British taxation, they had turned to the domestic market. Now, aware of the need to renovate and refurbish after long years dedicated to public affairs, the couple looked once more to New York and Philadelphia. They also – at first timorously – investigated the luxury market in Paris. Washington wished to know 'whether French plate is fashionable and much used in genteel houses in France and England'. He and Martha had heard that 'the quantity in Philadelphia is large'.[12]

The Washingtons might stock Mount Vernon with French plate and wines, but word of a 'general peace' in Paris was still lacking. In early October Martha left Rocky Hill for the Potomac, before the roads and weather should deteriorate. Washington would follow, as he told Tilghman on the 2nd, 'as soon as the Definitive Treaty arrives, or New York is Evacuated by our Newly acquired friends [the British]. On the first there is little said. Of the latter a great deal, but scarcely the same thing by any two who come from there.'[13] The general opinion, he noted, was that the British would be gone by the end of the month.

Martha broke her journey at Philadelphia, where she stayed with the Robert Morrises and dined out with de La Luzerne and others. Her principal aim was to further equip Mount Vernon. She had brought £1,500 with her from New Jersey. She reimbursed Samuel Powel, who had paid for the two dozen chairs for the New Room, £136. Remaining at the Morrises' most of October, she purchased linens, china and carpets as well as household stores – medicines, nuts, pickles – and personal items – stays, caps, shoes. Her total expenditure was £650. Washington had told Biddle to defer choosing linens: Martha, on her arrival, would 'please herself in the quality' of different materials.[14] Washington wrote in October to Wakelin Welch, sole surviving partner of those at Robert Cary and Co. in London with whom he had dealt before the war. He wanted to know how his account, and that of his deceased ward, Jacky, stood with them.[15] Other Americans might now default on debts to London merchants that had been outstanding on the outbreak of hostilities. He would not be among them.

News – not unwelcome but unexpected – had come while Martha was still at Rocky Hill. Her daughter-in-law, Nelly, meant to remarry, and Alexandria physician David Stuart, who had formerly escorted Martha to Newburgh, was her intended. Stuart was an intelligent and educated man who lacked only fortune – which Nelly would supply – to play a part in the new America. Winsome Nelly would have a sober husband to manage the Parke Custis estate and act as guardian to Jacky's children. It was a match that promised well, though Nelly had made no mention of romance previously in letters to Martha. Washington told Lund that they had never expected that Nelly would spend the rest of her days a widow; Nelly now sought counsel through intermediary Lund. Washington declined to give any: 'A woman very rarely asks an opinion or requires advice on such an occasion, 'till her resolution is formed; and then it is with the hope and expectation of obtaining a sanction, not that she means to be governed by your disapprobation, that she applies.' He suggested she consider whether her suitor would likely prove kind and affectionate, and 'just, generous and attentive' to her children.[16]

Martha, at Mount Vernon, saw much of the new couple at Abingdon, after Nelly became Mrs David Stuart in late November 1783. If it was bittersweet for Jacky's mother to see his bride with a new husband, his children responding to a stepfather, she gave no sign of it. The Stuarts were assiduous visitors to the Washington home, not least because four-year-old Nelly Parke Custis and her younger brother still lived there. 'Wash' – sometimes 'Tub' – was now two and a half and bore a strong physical resemblance to his father as a child. His grandmother and mother thought him exceptional, and visitors found him promising.

At last, on 31 October, intelligence came to Rocky Hill that the peace treaty had been signed in September at Paris. Congress had decreed that the wartime army might, upon receipt of this news, disband. Two days later Washington issued a farewell address to the army. If his words lacked the pen of an Alexander Hamilton to shape them, they were at least sincere. He asked, with good reason, 'who has before seen a disciplined Army form'd at once from such raw materials?' Recommending the soldiers whom he discharged to a 'grateful country', he wished for those who had fallen for the cause 'the choicest of heaven's favours'.[17]

Before he himself could 'take his ultimate leave . . . of the military character', Washington must participate in the transfer of New York to civil – and American – government. Once Sir Guy Carleton had completed the evacuation by British troops in late November, Washington entered and took possession of the city that he had so ignominiously and hastily left seven years before. He then turned it over to patriot George Clinton, long the governor of New York State.

Addresses, conferences and formal dinners occupied Washington during ensuing days. 'The principal officers of the army in town' gathered on 4 December at the tavern kept by patriot Samuel 'Black Sam' Fraunces. They wished to bid the Commander-in-Chief farewell before he made for Annapolis, where Congress was in session and where he would resign his commission. The room in the tavern was too crowded to allow Washington passage among the officers. After having drunk with them, he asked each of them to come to him, where he was, and take him 'by the hand'.

The officer nearest him was Henry Knox, Boston bookseller turned artilleryman, and Washington's closest associate throughout the war. When Knox came up and extended his hand, his commanding officer spontaneously embraced him. Having apparently been surprised by emotion into this act, Washington embraced all the other officers, though many of them were unknown to him.[18] Of all the numerous officers who had composed his 'family' at different times, only John Laurens had died in battle – in a skirmish close to his home in South Carolina, shortly before the British withdrew from Charleston.

Punctilious servant of Congress to the last, on his arrival in Annapolis, Washington enquired if they wished his resignation to be effected by letter or in person at the State House. They chose the latter alternative, and named the 23rd. At a ball on the eve, the General 'danced every set', wrote one present, 'that all the ladies might have the pleasure of dancing with him, or as it has since been handsomely expressed, get a touch of him'.[19] In a crowded State House the following day Washington recommended his 'family' to Congress as deserving of reward. He relented in his opinion of that 'august body', under whose orders he had so long acted, so far as to bid it an 'Affectionate farewell'. But he expressed his main purpose pithily: 'I here offer my Commission, and take my leave of all the employments of public life.'[20]

Washington made one request of Congress, a month after he had reached home in time for Christmas with Martha. He wrote to the body's Secretary, Charles Thomson on 22 January 1783, begging for his commission, were it not to be needed by Congress: 'I should be glad to have it deposited among my own papers. It may serve *my Grand Children*, some fifty or a hundred years hence, for a theme to ruminate upon, *if they should be* contemplatively disposed.'[21] Thomson replied, the following month, that it had 'been in agitation' among members of Congress, even before receipt of this letter, to bestow the order 'in a gold box' upon the former Commander-in-Chief.[22] But no commission, in plain or ornate box, came to Mount Vernon. Washington's 'grandchildren' – he was thinking of Martha's as his own – would have to look elsewhere for 'a theme to ruminate upon'. Washington, a Virginia farmer once more, did not pursue the matter.

Martha was resolved not to stir again from home. She wrote in January to congratulate Mrs Boudinot, a friend from wartime New Jersey, on her return home to Elizabethtown after an 'exile' of seven years. They would not meet again, unless her correspondent should come to Mount Vernon: 'my frequent long journeys have not only left me without inclination to undertake another, but almost disqualified me from doing it, as I find the fatigue is too much to bear'. She had this advice for her friend: 'The difficulties and distresses to which we have been exposed during the war must now be forgotten.'

Making reference to Proverbs 3, she added: 'we must endeavour to let our ways be the ways of pleasantness and all our paths, peace'.[23] The Washingtons, however, so strongly united in the recent conflict, would find the way ahead in private life neither wholly pleasant nor peaceful.

BOOK THREE

After the War, 1784–1802

Mount Vernon, 1784–1786

You will see the plain manner in which we live . . .

It took Washington some time to adjust to civilian life. In February 1784, two months after returning home, he confided to Henry Knox: 'strange as it may tell, it is nevertheless true, that it was not 'till lately I could get the better of my usual custom of ruminating as soon as I waked in the Morning, on the business of the ensuing day; and [the better] of my surprize, after having revolved many things in my mind, to find that I was no longer a public Man, or had anything to do with public transactions'.[1]

Earlier that month the General had written to Lafayette in Paris: 'I am not only retired from all public employments, but I am retiring within myself . . .'[2] Determined to play no part in public life, however innocuous, he resigned from the Truro parish vestry. Wearing the grey coat of a 'Virginia farmer', he resumed his former long daily rides around the different quarters of Mount Vernon. He directed overseers, slaves and hirelings, for all the world as though he had never been away.[3]

He was, however, far from content. Everywhere he saw neglect to remedy. An examination of the accounts that Lund had kept while he was away brought him no satisfaction. He declined an invitation to be Lafayette's guest in France, citing 'the deranged situation of my private concerns, occasioned by an absence of almost nine years, and an entire disregard of all private business during that period'. During the war he had several times expressed a desire to visit Paris and Versailles. He feared that attention to his affairs now would 'put it forever out of my power to gratify this wish'.[4]

Martha had different obligations. In April her husband addressed Lafayette's wife, the Marquise: 'Mrs Washington . . . feels very sensibly the force of your polite invitation to Paris; but she is too far advanced in life, & is too much immersed in the care of her little progeny to cross the Atlantic.'[5] The General urged the young Parisian woman to come and see America, 'young, rude & uncultivated as it is'. In high Augustan style he wrote: 'You will see the plain manner in which we live; & meet the rustic civility, & you shall taste the simplicity of rural life . . .'[6]

A division of the Parke Custis children long in place, though provisional, had by now hardened into permanence. Nelly Parke Custis and her younger brother, Wash, Martha's 'little progeny', were Martha's responsibility at Mount Vernon. She established a routine for them and their nurse, as she had once directed the upbringing of her own children. The elder girls, Bet and Pat, now rising eight and seven, lived with their mother at Abingdon, but were often to be found at Mount Vernon. Martha told a New Jersey correspondent this January: 'My little family are all with me and have been very well till within these few days, that they have been taken with the measles.' The worst, she opined, was over: 'I shall soon have them prattling about me again.'[7]

Though never in robust health, the children's mother, Nelly Stuart, was to succeed in giving her new husband, David, more than a dozen children. If their mother had little time to offer Bet and Pat, their stepfather could advise on their suitable education. Stuart had studied languages as well as medicine in Europe before emigrating to Virginia. He was often of service to Washington, acting as an interpreter when foreign visitors came calling, and assisting with French correspondence.

The French Ambassador, de La Luzerne, when visiting Washington at Mount Vernon in April 1784, noted 'the great

Washington Crossing the Delaware. Washington's Christmas-night raid, 1776, immortalized in the mid-nineteenth century by Emanuel Gottlieb Leutze.

An imaginary depiction of contented field slaves and benevolent master at Mount Vernon. Junius Brutus Stearns, 1851.

Washington, seated, rests while Betsy Ross sews the American flag. Again imaginary. From J. L. G. Ferris's late-nineteenth-century *Pageant of History*.

Washington's love of dancing on show at a victory ball, 1781. Neither he nor Martha attended any such event. J. L. G. Ferris.

Washington and Lafayette at Valley Forge. J. W. Dunsmore, 1907.

The Prayer at Valley Forge. Painted by Arnold Friberg in 1975 to mark the bicentennial of the Revolution.

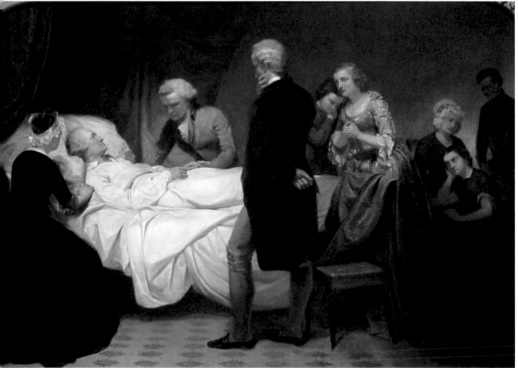

Washington on His Deathbed, by J. B. Stearns, 1851.

This eight-cent stamp (1902) was the first issued to honour a woman.

Martha was also, in 1886, the first woman represented on a silver dollar certificate.

George and Martha dolls, American, c. 1946.

Washington, himself a Mason, looms over President Harry Truman,
who is addressing Freemasons in the George Washington National
Masonic Memorial, Alexandria, Virginia, 1950.

© David Lit

The Washington Monument, Washington DC, at dusk, January 2006.

number of foreigners who come to see him'.[8] Strangers from all over America came calling too. The Supreme Executive Council of Pennsylvania had earlier suggested to Congress that an allowance be made to the General. Visitors, 'desirous of seeing the great & Good Man who has so eminently Contributed to the happiness of a Nation', would otherwise prove a great expense to him. Washington, characteristically high minded, scorned to accept any such subsidy.[9] Equally characteristically he complained of the huge drain on his personal finances.

In June 1784 Martha wrote to her sister-in-law Hannah Bushrod Washington that she hoped to pay her a visit, whenever it was convenient for 'the General' to leave home. For the moment there could be no thought of it: 'he has so much business of his own, and the public's, together that I fear he will never find leisure to go see his friends'.[10] The 'business of . . . the public's' to which she referred was something of a poisoned chalice.

Washington had presided the previous month in Philadelphia over the first general meeting of a chivalric association, the Society of the Cincinnati. Cincinnatus, a general in republican Rome, was twice called from his plough in Latium to lead the army at a time of crisis. Each time victorious, Cincinnatus afterwards slipped away to resume life as a farmer. The chivalric order given his name in 1783 by Knox and von Steuben aimed to render permanent 'the cordial affection' then subsisting among the officers serving in the war.[11] Membership was limited to those who had fought three years or more during the war, and was hereditary, so that the ideals of the revolution might ever be kept alive. French officers who had served in the war received honorary membership.

The proceedings of the first general meeting in Philadelphia proved turbulent. The hereditary principle underlying the Society was controversial, causing offence to many citizens proud of having espoused a republican cause. Others viewed this club of veteran officers as a potential threat to civil government. In May Washington managed with some skill to eliminate both hereditary element and 'political tendency' from the rubric.[12] They were subsequently reintroduced by branches in the different states.

Martha might regret that Washington had little leisure to accompany her on family visits, but she was a hardened planter's wife. She was later brisk with a niece who complained of her husband's preoccupation with business: 'if he does not attend to his affairs he will get nothing done, and if his people do not make bread, how will he be able to pay the taxes if nothing else is wanting?'[13]

Plenty of family visited Mount Vernon, by way of recompense. Samuel Washington's two sons were being educated, following their father's death, at their uncle George's expense in Alexandria. Another of the General's nephews, George Augustine Washington, formerly Lafayette's aide, was a firm favourite – not least with Fanny Bassett – but his health was poor. In the autumn he was dispatched to the West Indies, in the hope that a warmer climate would do him good.

Martha prized the company of some of their guests more highly than that of others, writing to her niece Fanny Bassett in August 1784: 'Tho I have never been alone since you left this [house], yet I cannot but say that I have missed your company very much.' She added, as if preparing for an ordeal, 'The General is still determined to set out the first of next month over the mountains.'[14] Before the war and until his death, in 1781, her son's careless affection and high spirits had sustained Martha during Washington's absences. The home in which he had grown to manhood was full of memories. The loss of her son was not one from which Martha recovered easily, but the small adventures of his children amused her. Referring to her grandson 'Wash' by an affectionate derivative, she wrote to Fanny: '. . . Tub is the same clever boy you left him. He sometimes says, why don't you send for Cousin?' Her niece should consider this a compliment. 'You know he never makes himself unhappy about absent friends.'[15]

Lafayette, still Washington's fervent admirer, crossed the Atlantic this summer. Crowds at New York, in New Jersey, and at Philadelphia mobbed the Marquis. His goal, however, was Mount Vernon. On his arrival in August, he found Washington, he wrote to the Marquise in France, absorbed 'in the routine of his estate'. Their meeting, he reported, was truly tender, adding: 'in retirement General Washington is even greater than he was during the Revolution. His simplicity is truly sublime, and he is as completely involved with all the details of his lands and house as if he had always lived here.'

The Custis children had been anxious to see if Lafayette resembled his portrait which hung in the house. 'The general has adopted them and loves them with great tenderness', the marquis wrote. Conversation at table centred on 'the events of the war'. In addition, Lafayette wrote home, he and Washington, after breakfast each morning, reviewed 'the past, the present and the future'.[16] Martha urged him to come again and bring with him his wife and 'whole little family'. Since she and her husband were 'both old', she said, the Lafayettes must not defer the pleasure such a visit would give.[17]

The following month Washington made a round trip of 680 miles, when visiting his lands west of the Appalachians, that might have tired a younger man. He admitted to disappointment, but not to especial fatigue, when he regained his home. He had hoped to extract rent due from tenants there. Some had pleaded inability to pay rent. Squatters occupied a portion of his lands. 'Land Jobbers & Speculators' were offering other properties, to which he had title, for sale at Philadelphia and even in Europe.[18]

In early December, following some last days together, Washington said his farewells to Lafayette, who was taking ship for France. As the Marquis's carriage was lost to view, the General questioned if that was the last sight he would ever have of his protégé. 'And tho' I wished to say no, my fears answered yes,' he wrote to Lafayette from Mount Vernon. Washington was, he wrote, 'now descending the hill' that he had been 'fifty-two years climbing'. On a marginally more cheerful note he ended: 'but I will not repine, I have had my day'.[19]

Martha at Mount Vernon might have taken leave to doubt that last sentiment. Following an inspection of the western Potomac that he made on his tour, Washington was promoting a scheme to make the upper reaches of the river navigable by bateaux, flat-bottomed transports. He argued that a Potomac Company should be incorporated for political as well as commercial reasons. Swift transport of soldiers to the western borders of Virginia and Maryland, and efficient portage of furs from the north-west to the Middle States, were both desirable.

Martha celebrated Christmas at Mount Vernon without her husband this year. Less than a year after he had resigned his commission at Annapolis, he was in the Maryland town again, once more a public servant. With two other Virginia commissioners, his task, in which he was successful, was to agree terms with three commissioners for Maryland. The Potomac Company slowly took shape.

Washington was less sanguine about his finances. He told George William Fairfax in February 1785, 'My accounts stand as I left them near ten years ago; those who owed me money, a very few instances excepted, availed themselves of what are called the tender Laws, & paid me off with a shilling & sixpence in the pound. Those to whom I owed, I have now to pay under heavy taxes with specie, or its equivalent value.'*

He had hoped, this winter, to 'overhaul & adjust' all his military papers. They were, he wrote, 'in sad disorder, from the frequent hasty removals of them, from the reach of our transatlantic foes, when their Ships appeared'. He was beset, however, by what he termed 'old military matters, with which I ought to have no concerns . . .' His opinion was none the less sought constantly. He was looking for an aide or secretary to whom he might delegate work: 'at no period of the War have I been obliged myself to go thro' more drudgery in writing, or have suffered so much confinement to effect it, as since what is called my retirement to domestic ease & tranquillity . . .'

Washington complained to Fairfax of having been additionally distracted by 'company' at the house this winter.[20] The visitors contiinued to come. He was to make an entry in his diary on 30 June this year: 'Dined with only Mrs. Washington, which I believe is the

---

* The 'tender laws', as the Currency Act of 1773 was commonly known, had made 'Virginia currency', paper bills, as well as gold and silver, legal tender for the repayment of debts. While he had been away at war, his debtors had paid Washington in these paper bills, also known as 'current money'. As mentioned, they depreciated to the point of being worth 1s 6d in the pound, their value only rising after the war, when three-quarters of the bills were withdrawn. Now, once more, only specie – gold or silver – was legal tender for repayment of debts. Washington reckoned he was the loser by £10,000.

first instance of it since my retirement from public life.'[21] Not only was this a call on his purse; he must expend on his guests' entertainment that commodity most precious to him, time. Both George and Martha were assiduous hosts. A Massachusetts entrepreneur, Elkanah Watson, suffered a severe cold while staying in January. Washington, a towering and awesome night-time visitor, appeared by his bed with a 'bowl of hot tea'.[22]

Martha oversaw the management of the household. The 'drudgery of ordering & seeing the Table properly covered – & things economically used', to employ Washington's words, was the business of the household steward.[23] A competent individual, Richard Burnet, was let go when he was to become a married man and thereby judged by his employers no longer suitable for the position. He was subsequently re-hired when substitutes were found wanting. A butler, Frank Lee, waited at table, and house slaves saw to the comforts both of the family and of visitors who stayed overnight.

Guests continued to arrive, with letters of introduction in hand. Benjamin Lincoln recommended British author Catherine Macaulay, once celebrated across the Atlantic for her *History of England* and now notorious for a recent marriage to William Graham, a young man twenty-six years her junior. The Grahams were resident at Mount Vernon ten days. Washington wrote subsequently to Richard Henry Lee: 'her sentiments respecting the inadequacy of the powers of Congress . . . coincide with my own'.[24] Martha, possibly less the focus of Mrs Graham's attentions, wrote of their guest to Mercy Otis Warren in Massachusetts: 'she now returns to make happy those whom she left'. The 'kind terms' of Mrs Warren's recent letter, 'added to the recollection of those days in which you honoured me with your friendship', filled Martha with 'agreeable sensations'. Her husband, she added, would never forget his friendship with 'General Warren' in Cambridge: 'It was among the first formed, and most lasting . . .'[25] The war was history now, 'the General' a veteran. The complex friendships, alliances, and even quarrels with officers, state officials and members of Congress that had obtained were now dissolved.

The previous December Martha's wish, expressed seven years earlier, to be 'a parent and mother' to her niece, Fanny, was fulfilled when Burwell Bassett consented to his daughter joining the household at Mount Vernon. Fanny's portrait, taken by an English artist this summer, is beguiling.[26] It was said of Fanny that to know her was to love her. Washington might have loved her more had she remained at home with her father, but he accepted her presence, as he accepted all that gave his wife pleasure.

Fanny's presence was more than acceptable to Washington's nephew, George Augustine, who had returned from the West Indies in the spring. In May the young man, aged twenty-two, obtained her father's consent to their marriage, though she was not yet eighteen. Washington wrote to Burwell Bassett, father of the bride, that it had ever been his maxim 'neither to promote, nor to prevent a matrimonial connection, unless there should be something, indispensably requiring interference in the latter . . .' Washington had earlier declined to give advice that Nelly Calvert Custis sought when intending to marry Stuart. 'Neither directly, nor indirectly,' he continued, 'have I ever said a syllable to Fanny, or George, upon the Subject of their intended connection . . .' However, he believed that their attachment to each other was 'warm, & lasting'. In consequence, he had 'just now' informed George Augustine – Martha broke the happy news to Fanny – that it was his wish that they should live at Mount Vernon.[27] Washington's nephew was happy to accept, and to accept the offer that he take the place of Cousin Lund as factor. Lund was far from being discomposed by this turn of events. Moving to a house nearby, with his wife of some years, he was at last his own master.

While George Augustine learned the trade of agent, Washington hired a secretary, William Shaw, a young man lately in business in Canada. His principal duties were to 'methodize' the General's papers, still in disarray, and undertake business on his patron's behalf abroad.[28] He was to devote a portion of his time to teaching the 'first rudiments of education' to four-year-old Wash and his sister, Nelly, aged six.

Though Shaw could attend to some business on his behalf, Washington himself was often absent from home on Potomac Company business. In October 1785 Martha wrote to excuse them

both from attending the wedding of John Augustine's son Bushrod
to a bride in Dumfries. She herself pleaded ill health. Washington's
'particular engagements' in coming weeks included attendance at the
'Board of Directors at Georgetown, the Great Falls, etc.'[29]

Another engagement detained him at home this month, though
she did not mention it. The renowned French sculptor Houdon had
been lured from Paris by Jefferson. He was to undertake a commission for the Virginia legislature – a portrait statue of Washington, to
be erected in the future Richmond Capitol. The cornerstone of this
building had just been laid by Governor Patrick Henry.

The arrival of Houdon with a bevy of assistants one October night
was unexpected. No one at Mount Vernon and none of the travellers had a word of each other's language. The commotion was little
less when the Parisian followed Washington on his rounds of the
estate. Houdon, if irritating, was a shrewd observer of Washington's
relaxed stance in the fields. Before the sculptor returned to Paris to
start work on the commission in earnest, he had the General lie on
his back on a large table in 'the white servants' hall'. Laying a sheet
over Washington's body, Houdon applied plaster of Paris to his face,
so as to make a life mask. Six-year-old Nelly Parke Custis, passing,
thought her 'Grandpapa' a corpse. Though reassured that he lived,
she retained a vivid memory of the scene into later life. 'Quills were
in his nostrils', she recalled.[30]

A more conventional event took place the same month at Mount
Vernon. Washington recorded in his diary for the 15th: 'After the
Candles were lighted George Augustine Washington and Frances
Bassett were married by Mr Grayson.' George and Martha, the
bride's brother Burwell Bassett Jr and the Lund Washingtons
looked on.[31]

William Shaw shirked his duties and proved an unsatisfactory
secretary and tutor. In November 1785, searching for a replace-
ment, Washington told George William Fairfax that he meant, in due
course, to provide Martha's grandson – 'a remarkable fine one', he
wrote – with a 'liberal education'. He sought: 'a classical scholar, &
capable of teaching the French language grammatically; the more
universal his knowledge, the better'. Wash was, he admitted, still
young. He himself, however, had need of 'a man of Letters & an

accomptant'. Such employment could usefully occupy the successful candidate, 'until attention should be more immediately required for his pupil'.[32]

Later that winter Benjamin Lincoln in Boston recommended a protégé, Tobias Lear, a sober New Englander and Harvard scholar, in his early twenties. In February 1786 Washington set out the terms on which the young man would live with the family at Mount Vernon. Lear would, he wrote, 'sit at my Table – live as I live – mix with the Company which resort to the Ho[use]. – and . . . be treated in every respect with civility, and proper attention'.[33] The appointment proved a great success. Lear was soon on good terms with all, and told a well-wisher in late July: 'I have every attention paid me by His Excellency and all the family that I can wish; the duty required of me is small, and agreeable.' He added, 'more than one half of my time is at my own disposal, which I employ in reading the Law.'[34] The General did not as yet rely on Lear as he later would.

Washington bought this summer, for $150, some 'Cincinnati china' that had been brought to the United States by the first American ship to enter the China trade. 'Light Horse Harry' Lee, who acted as Washington's agent, wrote, 'what renders this china doubly valuable & handsome is the order of the eagle engraved on it in honour of the Cincinnati – it has upward of 306 pieces'.[35] In Canton an enterprising member of the Society had had Chinese painters overlay the glaze with elements of the insignia of the order.

Washington relished this 'Cincinnati' dinner service as an appropriate, if expensive, souvenir of his command. Those years when he was the servant of Congress were growing distant now. He and Martha were apparently firmly established at home, though that home was a destination for all too many pilgrims and roost for passing travellers. Washington was to refer a year hence to Mount Vernon as 'a well resorted tavern'.[36]

Conventions and Elections, 1787–1789

. . . a tendency to sweep me back into the tide of public affairs . . .

Washington declined to attend a meeting of the Society of Cincinnati, due to take place in May 1787 in Philadelphia, on the grounds that he was now committed to a life of retirement. In March of this year, however, he wrote, with good reason, of 'a tendency to sweep me back into the tide of public affairs.' [1]

Washington's former protégé Alexander Hamilton, of New York, and James Madison, of Virginia, had earlier been foremost in calling for a Grand Convention of all the states to address the weaknesses in the Articles of Confederation. It was to be held this May in Philadelphia. The Articles provided Congress with no power to raise taxes: it could only request monies from individual states, and those requests were often ignored. The control that the states wielded over trade and commerce was often as punitive as that emanating from London, against which patriot Americans had rebelled. Madison and Hamilton were intent on establishing a federal government with a bicameral house, executive and judiciary. Both of them pleaded with Washington to attend the convention as a Virginia delegate who favoured their cause. In January 1784 he had written to Benjamin Harrison of the 'disinclination of the individual States to yield competent powers to Congress for a federal Government'. He deplored the states' 'unreasonable jealousy of that body & of one another'.[2]

At a preliminary convention in Richmond, Washington was named a delegate to the Grand Convention with Governor Edmund Randolph, Madison, Mason, Henry and two others. However, it looked for some time as though he would refuse to serve in May. He had always guarded his reputation like a dog its bone. It would cause grave offence to his former comrades, members of the Society of Cincinnati, he argued, if, having declined to attend their meeting, he attended instead the Grand Convention. At the end of March he yielded to Madison and Hamilton. However, he still had misgivings, as the letter he wrote on the 28th to Governor Randolph shows: 'there will be, I apprehend, too much cause to charge my conduct with inconsistency, in again appearing on a public theatre after a public declaration to the contrary . . .'³

Confident that Martha would be at her husband's side, the Robert Morrises begged the Washingtons to make their Market Street house their home while they were in the city. 'We will give You as little trouble as possible,' Morris wrote on 23 April, 'and endeavour to make it agreeable, it will be a charming season for Travelling, and Mrs Washington as well as yourself will find benefit from the Journey, Change of Air, etc.'⁴

Early in May the reluctant delegate replied: 'Mrs Washington is become too Domestick and too attentive to two little Grand Children to leave home . . .'⁵ When Jacky had been young, Martha had been too nervous about his health to leave him much, and fancied him at death's door when she went visiting. She expressed similar agitation about Wash, writing to Fanny Bassett Washington a year hence: 'I cannot say but it makes me miserable if ever he complains, let the cause be ever so trifling. I hope the Almighty will spare him to me.'⁶ There were others genuinely in need of her attention. This April Fanny Bassett Washington gave birth at Mount Vernon to her first child, a boy, whom they named George Fayette. Within two weeks, however, the child sickened. The Reverend Lee Massey, sent for to administer the rite of baptism, very soon officiated at the child's burial. Martha mourned with Fanny and consoled her.

In early May Washington prepared George Augustine for new responsibilities: 'Rid [rode] to the Fishing landing – and thence to

the Ferry, French's, Dogue run, and Muddy Hole Plantations with
my Nephew G.W. to explain to him the Nature, and the order of the
business at each, as I would have it carried on, during my absence at
the Convention in Philadelphia.'[7] But he still harped on his reluctance to serve at the Grand Convention, writing on the 5th to Robert
Morris: 'I can assure you, Sir, that it was not until after a long struggle
I could obtain my own consent to appear again in a public theatre.'
As often before, he wrote of his wish to 'glide gently down the stream
of life in tranquil retirement' towards what he now described as 'the
world of Spirits'.[8]

He and Martha were both aware that it was unlikely that his return
to public life would end with the closure of that assembly.

When elected Commander-in-Chief, Washington had told
Congress: 'I do not think myself equal to the Command I am
honored with.'[9] He was again humble when he was – unanimously –
elected, on 25 May, to preside over the Grand Convention. From the
chair, he reminded delegates of 'the novelty of the scene of business
in which he was to act, lamented his want of [better qualifications],
and claimed the indulgence of the House towards the involuntary
errors which his inexperience might occasion'.[10] Such declarations
only caused the Convention President's stock to rise. Washington
had, of course, extensive experience as a burgess and as a delegate to
the First and Second Continental Congresses. He had, besides, dealt
constantly with Congress and state assemblies during the war.

The battles in the chamber over which Washington presided were
fierce. There was a powerful anti-federalist lobby that included
the Washingtons' neighbour George Mason as well as Governor
George Clinton of New York. They held that only amendments to
the Articles of Confederation currently in force were required. The
federalists as staunchly favoured Madison's and Hamilton's plans
for a central government. By the end of July the latter had won the
day, and the framework of a constitution for the United States was
agreed. But there was still an array of details to debate.

During the months Washington spent in Philadelphia, when not
required in the State House he was unusually sociable. In town he
dined frequently in company with the Morrises. Morris's business

partner Thomas Willing, Willing's sister Elizabeth and her husband
Samuel Powel, and Gouverneur Morris were other hosts. Washington
attended numerous parties of pleasure at these friends' country villas.
Martha, occupied with her grandchildren, was far away, but he enjoyed
the company of his friends' wives. With Elizabeth Willing Powel, in
particular, a spirited woman ten years his junior, Washington, aged
fifty-five, was on excellent terms. He took her in his carriage, on two
occasions, to drink tea after dinner at Lansdowne, John Penn's home.
He wrote to her on 30 July, regretting that he could not form one of
a party for a production of Sheridan's *The School for Scandal* that
evening. About to depart on a fishing expedition with Gouverneur
Morris, the grave Washington was for once playful: 'The Genl can
but regret that matters have turned out so unluckily, after waiting so
long to receive a lesson in the School for Scandal.'[11]

Mrs Powel, in turn, sent him, in early September, an economical new device, a 'reflecting Lamp' for his hall. 'I well know your
Delicacy on the Subject of accepting the smallest Present even from
your best Friend,' she wrote. She hoped, nevertheless, on the score
of patriotism, that he would accept it. 'Your Example will, I flatter
myself, be always sufficient to recommend & establish the Use of
any Articles in America . . . The One sent is not of the ornamental
Kind, but simple & neat; but, with your Temperance & Aversion to
Ostentation, that will be no objection.' She signed herself, 'with great
Sincerity, dear Sir, Your affectionate Friend and very humble Servt,
Eliza. Powel'.[12] Washington replied the same day, 'Neat simplicity,
is among the most desirable properties of the one you have sent me,
but that which stamps the highest value thereon, is the hand from
which it comes.'[13]

Such flirtatious friendships between the sexes within the bounds
of marriages to others were not uncommon in Philadelphia. Mrs
Powel was on civil terms with Martha. But this correspondence with
Washington suggests a different order of intimacy.

On 17 September, the Constitution was adopted by the Convention.
On the point of setting out for home the following day, Washington
enclosed a copy of the document in a letter to Lafayette, naming
it 'the production of four months' deliberation. It is now a Child

of fortune, to be fostered by some and buffeted by others.' Article VII provided for further ratifying conventions to meet in each state. If nine or more of those conventions voted 'Aye', they would be bound by 'this constitution'. Washington continued: 'what will be the General opinion on, or the reception of it, is not for me to decide, nor shall I say any thing for or against it – if it be good, I suppose it will work its way good – if bad, it will recoil on the Framers'.[14]

Washington, on his return home, was soon once again the farmer: 'Friday 28th. Rid to the Plantns. at the Ferry – French's, Dogue run & Muddy hole – engaged in the same work at each.'[15] But for how long would he be permitted to remain at his plough? His name was widely canvassed as that of the only candidate of sufficient experience and standing to assume the executive office, when once the Constitution was ratified and elections were held. Gouverneur Morris wrote to him on 30 October: 'I have observed that your Name to the new Constitution has been of infinite Service. Indeed I am convinced that if you had not attended the Convention, and the same Paper had been handed out to the World, it would have met with a colder Reception . . . As it is, should the Idea prevail that you would not accept of the Presidency it would prove fatal in many Parts.' He argued: 'your great and decided Superiority leads Men willingly to put you in a Place which will not add to your personal Dignity, nor raise you higher than you already stand'.[16]

The Samuel Powels visited Mount Vernon in the autumn, and Mrs Powel took some trouble thereafter to secure some 'collars' that her hostess wanted for the Parke Custis girls, to improve their posture. In her letter of thanks, Martha, on 18 January 1788, begged the Powels to return: 'though we are not as gay as you are at Philadelphia, yet in this peaceful retreat you will find friendship and cordiality which, to one who does not go fully into all the gaieties of the city, will, I flatter myself, be quite as agreeable'.[17] Martha set her face resolutely against both urban pleasures and current affairs. In February she wrote to Fanny, who was lying in for her second child at Eltham, 'we have not a single article of news but politics which I do not concern myself about'. David Humphreys, a former aide of her husband's, she wrote, was at Mount Vernon, intent on writing a life of the

General. Bad weather had foiled a journey the two were to make on Potomac Company business. The Colonel, she wrote, 'thought himself quite as well by the fire side at Mount Vernon as he should be at the Shenandoah'.[18]

For all Martha's concentration on the pleasure of home and hearth, elsewhere five ratifying conventions in five states had met and voted 'Aye' to the Constitution. Soon news would come that Massachusetts had made a sixth in favour. Following ratification by Maryland and South Carolina in the spring, Washington read anxiously every dispatch from David Stuart, a delegate to the ratifying convention that met in Richmond in June. News came of victory in the Virginian capital, capped by news of ratification in New Hampshire four days earlier, on 21 June. The new Constitution now bound all these states, and New York, which shortly afterwards voted 'Aye'.

Friends and admirers of Washington's continued to beg him to serve as President or 'Chief Magistrate' of the United States, should he be elected. The latter term was used by many, in allusion to the range of powers the head of the executive branch of government would enjoy. 'I take it for granted, Sir,' wrote Hamilton on 13 August, 'you have concluded to comply with what will no doubt be the general call of your country in relation to the new government. You will permit me to say that it is indispensable you should lend yourself to its first operations – It is to little purpose to have *introduced* a system, if the weightiest influence is not given to its firm *establishment*.'[19]

Washington responded on 28 August, 'I can say nothing.' He explained that 'the event' – his election as President – might never occur. If it did, he continued, 'it would be a point of prudence to defer forming one's ultimate and irrevocable decision, so long as new data might be afforded for one to act with the greater wisdom & propriety'. He wrote, as ever, of his 'great and sole desire to live and die, in peace and retirement, on my own farm'.

A Congress of Confederation, in the autumn, made final arrangements for the new government. A bicameral legislature, with an upper house, to be known as the Senate, and a lower house, formally, the

House of Representatives – informally, 'the House' – was created. Washington had admitted to Hamilton in August that it might become at some point 'indispensable' to accept high office. At the same time he shared his fear that, in that case, 'the world and Posterity might probably *accuse* me of *inconsistency* and *ambition*'.[20]

The new year of 1789 brought elections for senators and representatives – and a date for the election of President and Vice President. There was at last an end to Washington's havering. He asked Madison in early January, 'Is there any safe, and tolerably expeditious mode by which letters from the Post Office in Fredericksburg are conveyed to you? I want to write a private & confidential letter to you, shortly, but am not inclined to trust to an uncertain conveyance, so as to hazard the loss or inspection of it.'[21]

The document that the General conveyed to this trusted political ally in February was a draft of the inaugural address he meant to give as President. He had at last, and well in advance of the actual election, made his peace with the doubts that had so long beset him. On 7 January he noted in his diary: 'Went up to the Election of an Elector (for this district) . . .' Dr Stuart was the successful candidate, one of twelve Virginian electors who would cast a vote on the 4th for Presidential and Vice Presidential candidates the following month. The new Senate would count the votes of all the states' electors. 'Dined with a large company on venison at Page's Tavern and came home in the evening.'[22]

Washington could have been forgiven for considering the venison in some measure funerary meats. He wrote to Knox on 1 April: 'my movements to the chair of Government will be accompanied with feelings not unlike those of a culprit who is going to the place of his execution: so unwilling am I, in the evening of a life nearly consumed in public cares, to quit a peaceful abode for an Ocean of difficulties, without that competency of political skill – abilities & inclination which is necessary to manage the helm'.[23]

On the 14th of that month, however, he was prepared and ready to depart when Charles Thomson, Secretary of Congress, arrived to inform him of his election as President of the United States. John Adams had been elected Vice President. The new President, elected, like his Vice President, for a four-year term, was to be inaugurated in New York on the 30th. There was no time to be lost, and Washington, with Thomson, left Mount Vernon on the 16th.

Martha was not shy with her opinion of these proceedings. Four days after her husband's departure she wrote to her nephew John Dandridge, 'I am truly sorry to tell that the General is gone to New York.'[24] That city was the – temporary – home of government. No. 3 Cherry Street, a town house, had been selected by Congress as a suitable Presidential residence and leased for an initial year at $845.*

Martha continued: 'When, or whether he will ever come home again God only knows. I think it was much too late for him to go into public life again, but it was not to be avoided.' She added tersely, 'Our family will be deranged, as I must soon follow him.'[25]

---

* Congress, in August 1785, had authorized the issuance of a new official and decimal currency, the United States dollar. As no mint was yet established, the currencies of different states and specie continued to circulate, and sums were quoted sometimes in dollars and sometimes in their equivalent in current money, denominated in pounds, shillings and pence.

New York Houses, 1789–1790

The President to accept no invitations . . .

On 30 April, 1789, large crowds gathered in Wall Street. High above them, on the balcony of Federal Hall, Washington took an oath of office on a Bible loaned from a local Masonic lodge: 'I do solemnly swear that I will faithfully execute the Office of President of the United States, and will to the best of my Ability, preserve, protect and defend the Constitution of the United States.' Immediately afterwards, indoors, the new President delivered to members of both Houses an inaugural address, which he had struggled to make concise.

His first words were of the home from which he had been called to office – 'a retreat which I had chosen with the fondest predilection, and, in my flattering hopes, with an immutable decision, as the asylum of my declining years . . .' He gave 'homage to the Great Author of every public and private good', expressing his long held conviction: 'No People can be bound to acknowledge and adore the invisible hand, which conducts the Affairs of men more than the People of the United States. Every step, by which they have advanced to the character of an independent nation, seems to have been distinguished by some token of providential agency.' Though he had quit the 'asylum' of Mount Vernon, Washington did not wish to gain by it: 'I must decline as inapplicable to myself, any share in the personal emoluments, which may be indispensably included in a permanent provision for the Executive Department.'[1] He would, as when he had commanded the army, submit to Congress his expenses only.

During his first days at Cherry Street, Washington found it difficult to give sufficient attention to official business. Tobias Lear, who fulfilled in New York the duties of private secretary to the President, described the house as being in a 'state of the greatest confusion – pulling down – putting up – making better & making worse'.[2] While alterations were being completed, Washington later recalled, 'Gentlemen, consulting their own convenience rather than mine, were calling from the time I rose from breakfast – often before – until I sat down to dinner.'[34]

It was resolved that afternoon gatherings, lasting an hour, on Tuesdays and Fridays would accommodate those gentlemen wishing to pay their respects to the President. The *Gazette of the United States*, the New York newspaper, announced, on 2 May: 'visits of compliment on other days, and particularly on Sunday, will not be agreeable to him'. Lear elaborated to George Augustine at Mount Vernon next day: 'this regulation is a very necessary & a very good one – it answers two valuable ends – it allows a sufficient time for dispatching the business of the office – and it gives a dignity to the President by not obliging him to expose himself every day to impertinent or curious intruders.'

The secretary was anxious to know how these arrangements were thought of, 'particularly among those who have not been friendly to the Government'. What said those 'of this description' who lived 'in your neighbourhood' – George Mason was a strong anti-federalist – '& also of other matters respecting the Govt & its Administration?' Lear told George Augustine: 'Your time . . . I know, is too much employed for you to investigate or to inform of these matters, and as the Ladies are very expert at this business – suppose Mrs Washington should do it?'

Lear's assessment of Martha's powers of persuasion is of some interest: 'I know of no person better qualified. Her very serious & benevolent countenance would not suffer a person to hide a thing from her, which would be kept from another, whose countenance did not say so much in their favour.' He added: 'Now I would give a great deal to be present when you inform Mrs Washington of this – or read it to her. If she ever put on a frown, it would be on this occasion – What does he mean! she will exclaim! Does he wish to make a spy of me? Who knows, if I should engage in this business, but that I might be brought before a high tribunal and accused of treason – and, Lord have mercy upon me! be executed . . .' Lear, George Augustine and others in the Washington circle had the utmost respect for the new President. With Martha, however, they could indulge – in private – in nonsense.

The secretary told George Augustine that the house on Cherry Street was now in order. Two footmen and a porter were engaged and in livery; there was a maid to make the beds. In short, the 'family' was as well settled as if they had been there twelve months. 'We have engaged Black Sam Fraunces as Steward & superintendent of the Kitchen' the secretary announced, 'and a very excellent fellow he is in the latter department'. The innkeeper, come out of retirement, 'tosses up such a number of fine dishes that we are distracted in our choice when we set down to table, and obliged to hold a long consultation upon the subject before we can determine what to attack.' He added, 'Oysters & Lobsters make a very conspicuous figure upon the table, and never go off untouched. Tell Madam Washington this.' He hoped this report would 'have some effect (as she is remarkably fond of these fish)', and hasten her journey to New York: 'we are extremely desirous of seeing her here'.

Washington wrote to Adams on the 10th: 'Many things which appear of little importance in themselves and at the beginning, may have great and durable consequences from their having been established at the commencement of a new general Government.'[5] Heated debates in Congress about the title or titles by which Washington should be known had earlier ensued. Adams had considered a 'royal or princely title' necessary to uphold the President's authority. 'His Highness' and 'Excellency' were suggestions. The anti-federalist Senator, William Maclay, fulminated: 'a Court, our House seems determined on, and to run into all the fooleries, fopperies, fineries, and pomp of royal etiquette; and all this for Mr Adams'.[6] Ultimately the House of Representatives prevailed. It was decreed, on 14 May, that Washington should bear the title of 'the President', *tout simple*.

Washington canvassed numerous members of those who would form the Federal Cabinet for their opinions on 'the etiquette proper to be observed by the President'. Hamilton was firm on 5 May: 'The President to have a levée day once a week for receiving visits . . . The President to accept no invitations: and to give formal entertainments only twice or four times a year on the anniversaries of important events in the revolution . . . The President on the levée days either by himself or some Gentleman of his household to give informal invitations to family dinners on the days of invitation'. It was a proscribed existence that Hamilton advocated: 'The President to accept no invitations . . .'[7]

Washington, having digested Hamilton's answers, asked Adams if his appearance – '*rarely*' at tea parties – might be permissible.[8] Perhaps he contemplated Martha's reaction to come to the confined life sketched out. Ostensibly Adams's opinion, given on 17 May, allowed the President some latitude: 'There can be no impropriety, in the President's, making or receiving informal Visits, among his Friends or Acquaintances at his Pleasure. Undress [informal attire], and few Attendants will Sufficiently Shew, that Such Visits, are made as a Man and a Citizen, a Friend or Acquaintance.' Adams, who had no taste for frivolities himself, continued: 'The President's pleasure Should absolutely decide, concerning his Attendance at Tea Parties, in a private Character . . . The President's private Life, Should be at his own discretion, and the World Should respectfully acquiesce . . .' What followed undercut the above: 'as the President he Should have no intercourse with society, but upon public Business, or at his Levees.'[9]

The term 'levee' had, to say the least, unfortunate connotations. It derived from French court ritual and denoted a formal reception following the king's rising from his bed. When courtiers, government ministers and foreign dignitaries spoke or wrote of attending 'the levee' in England or in France, the king's levee was always meant, and his presence implied. In colonial America, George III's portrait hung on the wall of the different gubernatorial residences, the Governor's Palace in Williamsburg included. The King's representatives had confined their entertainments to assemblies and balls. Allusions to levees, whether in colonial days or in revolutionary America, had always been satirical. And now the levee had come to New York.

Referring to public dinners that he hosted from early in the Presidency every Thursday, Washington wrote to Stuart in July, 'it was thought best to confine *my* invitations, to official characters and strangers of distinction'. Some in Congress had bitter memories of what they considered profligate public dinners given by presidents of the Continental Congress. They called on the President to renounce the practice of giving dinners entirely. This 'line of conduct', however, Washington rejected, not least because, in England, King George III dined always in private. He told Stuart: 'first, the novelty of it would, I well knew, be considered as an ostentatious imitation, or mimicry of Royalty – and secondly . . . so great a seclusion wd stop the avenues to useful information from the many, & make me dependent on the few in whose vortex I moved'.[10]

At Mount Vernon Martha, in no sanguine mood, was preparing to follow her husband to New York. A colonel, who brought her letters and a package from Washington in early May, told the President that he was 'much affected at some of her observations on your both being oblig'd to leave Mount-Vernon once more'.[11] Washington's nephew, Bob Lewis, who was to serve as a third secretary to his uncle, went with his aunt on the journey north later that month. He recorded the leave-taking at Mount Vernon: 'The servants of the House, and a number of the field negroes made their appearance – to take leave of their mistress – numbers of these poor wretches seemed greatly agitated, much affected – My Aunt equally so.' Moll and Oney, dower slaves, went with Martha as her maids. Possibly some of the slaves lamented more their departure than that of Mrs Washington. When the party stopped at Abingdon, the commotion was still greater 'the family in tears, the children a-bawling, everything in the most lamentable situation'.[12] Martha was taking ten-year-old Nelly and Wash, aged six, with her to New York. The tears of their elder siblings, Bet and Pat, may have been born of frustration that they were not going instead.

After Martha dined with James McHenry at Baltimore, the former aide-de-camp addressed the President: 'I was sorry we were obliged to harass her with company (her stay being so very short) but our neighbours who visited her, would never have forgiven me if they had not been asked to supper.'[13] At Philadelphia Thomas Mifflin, now President of the Supreme Executive Council of Pennsylvania, and the First City Troop, escorted Martha into town. With Mrs Robert Morris and that lady's daughters she made the last leg of the journey north. The President and Morris, now a senator, met their wives on the Jersey shore, and the party was rowed over to New York – 'in the fine Barge you have seen so much said of in the papers', Martha informed Fanny on 8 June, 'with the same oarsmen that carried the P. to New York'. She added, 'dear little Washington seemed to be lost in a maze at the great parade that was made for us all the way we come'.

'I have not had one half hour to myself since the day of my arrival,' Martha told Fanny on the same date. Her hair was 'set and dressed' every day. She added, 'I have put on white muslins for the summer – you would, I fear, think me a good deal in the fashion if you could but see me.' Fanny was to send her a 'black lace apron and handker-chief [neckerchief]' – she thought they were 'in one of my drawers in the chest of drawers in my chamber'– and some thread lace or joining net to be found 'in one of the baskets on the shelf in my closet'. A postscript reads: 'Give my love to Harriot [Washington, a niece of the President's in residence at Mount Vernon] and send me the meas-ure of her foot.'[14] At Philadelphia, Martha had commissioned stays and shoes to be dispatched to Fanny, and to Nelly Stuart and the girls at Abingdon. Foreign ministers, government officials, New York residents and their ladies might require entertainment. The needs of family in Virginia must also be accommodated.

Washington's Tuesday levee remained strictly for gentlemen and occupied only an hour, from three to four in the afternoon. He told David Stuart in June 1790: 'These visits are optional – They are made without invitation. Gentlemen – often in great numbers – come and go – chat with each other – and act as they please. A Porter shews them into the room, and they retire from it when they please, and without ceremony. At their *first* entrance they salute me, and I them, and as many as I can talk to I do . . .' At 'the visits every Friday afternoon', though the President was always in attendance, Martha was now the hostess. These 'visits', he wrote, though similar in form to the Tuesday levee, were 'of a more familiar and sociable kind'.[15] Husbands and wives came, and brought their sons and daughters to be presented too.

This August Abigail Adams, wife of the Vice President, noted: 'The company are entertained with Lemonade & Ice Creams . . .'[16] Tobias Lear or David Humphreys was on hand to escort each visiting lady to Mrs Washington, to whom they curtseyed. The visitors then seated themselves, and the President came up and addressed them individually in conversation. Thereafter they were free to circulate until their departure, which they prefaced with another curtsey to Martha.

Just as the Tuesday assembly was known as the 'levee', so, that on the Friday became known as the 'drawing room'. The proceedings took the form of an evening reception and served as an opportunity for ladies to display elaborate coiffures and elegant gowns. Though there was some mockery of Martha's 'company days' as 'Queenly drawing rooms' – Queen Charlotte in England hosted such weekly entertainments in London – they never attracted such obloquy as would, in time, the Tuesday levee.

To confound those who would have liked to criticize the President's consort, there was no 'Tincture of hauteur about her'. So Abigail Adams discovered on coming to town in June and encountering Martha for the first time. Mrs Washington had received her at Cherry Street, she wrote, 'with great ease & politeness. She is plain in her dress, but that plainness is the best of every article . . . Her Hair is white, her Teeth beautiful, her person rather short than other ways . . . Her manners are modest and unassuming, dignified and feminine.' A further visit in July compounded Mrs Adams's respect. She described Martha as 'one of those unassuming characters which creates Love & Esteem. A most becoming pleasantness sits upon her countenance & an unaffected deportment which renders her the object of veneration and Respect. With all these feelings and Sensations I found myself much more deeply impressed than I ever did before their Majesties of Britain.'[17]

Martha was no doubt easier in her mind in July. A lesion on Washington's thigh the previous month had required surgery, and weeks of convalescence had followed. The *Massachusetts Centinel* was obsequious, on 27 June, in its report: 'His Excellency was attended by the principal physicians of New-York – and chains were extended across the streets, to prevent carriages passing before his door.'[18] Following his recovery, the levees and drawing rooms resumed. Abigail Adams wrote of one Friday evening in August that Washington conversed with ladies 'with a grace dignity ease, that leaves Royal George far behind him'.[19]

Vice President John Adams was unpopular with many, following the 'monarchical' line he had taken when debating titles for the President. David Stuart told Washington, in July, that stories were circulating that the Vice President never ventured out without six horses to his carriage. This Washington disputed: 'One of the Gentlemen whose name is mentioned in your letter [John Adams] though [high ton]ed, has never, I believe, appeared with more than *two* horses in his Carriage.'[20] The honours accorded the Adamses, however, when John had been Minister at the Court of St James's, had marked the couple, and made them believe more firmly in form than did others in government circles. Power, Adams had none, unless Washington should perish; with form he and Abigail must be content. Writing of the Friday drawing rooms, Abigail remarked to her sister: 'My station is always at the right hand of Mrs W; through want of knowing what is right, I find it sometimes occupied.' Martha's friend, Mrs Robert Morris, is noted in some contemporary accounts as having occupied this prized 'station'. Abigail wrote with satisfaction, 'the President never fails of seeing that it is relinquished . . . they have now learnt to rise and give it me . . .'[21]

Nathanael Greene had died in Georgia, shortly after settling near Savannah with his family at the war's end. The Washingtons afforded widowed Caty every courtesy when she visited New York this summer, to press for settlement of her husband's Revolutionary War accounts. The President himself handed her to her carriage on 'company days'. Only General Montgomery's widow received similar dues. Caty was not especially grateful. She wrote, on 7 August, to a friend, regarding Washington: 'on levée Days No person presumes to sit in his presence – and he is treated in most respects as if he had a crown. He, however did me the honour to give me a kiss for which I made my best courtesy and thanked him.'[22]

In August 1789, following the death of his mother in Fredericksburg, Washington ordered for the household at Cherry Street 'mourning Cockades & Ribbon'. He himself adopted a suit of imported black velvet for 'full dress' occasions. Many in New York adopted mourning in turn – 'black crape or ribbon on the arm or hat, for gentlemen, and a black ribbon and necklace for ladies'.[23] Such was the mourning prescribed at the Court of St James on the death of a member of the relevant royal family. Questions were inevitably raised about the legitimacy of recognizing Washington's private grief in this public fashion.

Washington made his own rules in certain respects. Though the period of mourning for his mother in due course ended, he continued conspicuous by his majestic, velvet-clad figure at levees and drawing rooms. When in 'undress' at home, he wore what Walter Buchanan, a visiting godson, described as 'pepper-and-salt coloured clothes'.[24] Homespun, which he had worn for his inauguration, no longer featured in his wardrobe.

On the education and upbringing of the Custis children in their care, both George and Martha continued to exercise thought. Martha's first care, she told Fanny in June, had been to search out 'a good school' for the children.[25] She wrote indulgently of Nelly this same summer: 'she is a little wild creature and spends her time at the window looking at carriages etc passing by which is new to her and very common for children to do'. However, she noted, the following week her granddaughter was to begin 'Musick'.[26] Patsy Parke Custis's spinet, exported from London thirty years before, was duly exchanged for a pianoforte, and 'Entrance money' paid to Alexander Reinagle, musician and composer, to teach Nelly.[27] Wash, years later, in his unreliable memoirs, recalled: 'The poor girl would play and cry, and cry and play, for long hours, under the immediate eye of her grandmother, a rigid disciplinarian in all things.'[28] She became a fine performer. At Mrs Graham's in Maiden Lane, the school for young ladies where she was inscribed in the late autumn, Nelly was a conscientious student. Artist William Dunlap, who had so revelled in life at headquarters at Rocky Hill, gave her lessons in 'drawing etc'.[29]

Like father, like son. Eight-year-old Wash was, from the beginning, inattentive to his lessons. After an experiment with a tutor, he was enrolled at Patrick Murdoch's school on Greenwich Street, behind Trinity Church.[30] Among other pupils were the sons of Alexander Hamilton and Henry Knox.[31] Martha declared herself, to Mercy Otis Warren in December, grateful for the 'advantages of education' that New York offered her grandchildren.[32] There were also metropolitan amusements, of which their siblings at Abingdon could only dream. Nelly and Wash went out daily in the carriage with Martha. The President attended them as often as he could. The children visited a waxworks museum and other curiosities of the town, and visited 'the play' with a chaperone or in a party with young friends.[33]

When George III in London showed himself at Drury Lane in London, he received ovations. The *Gazette of the United States* recorded Washington's attendance at the Ford Theatre in John Street on 24 November: 'The audience rose, and received him with the warmest acclamations.' The play he watched was *The Toy, or A Trip to Hampton Court*, and with him were Caty Greene, Abigail Adams, the Hamiltons, and Betsy Hamilton's parents, General Philip Schuyler – now a senator – and Mrs Schuyler.[34]

His patronage of the different theatres of New York afforded Washington a rare opportunity to relax. Henry Knox, Secretary of War, his wife Lucy, Baron von Steuben and Robert Morris were other regular guests. Martha, however, more sociable than her husband, felt very much the sacrifice of 'private life'. Rather than quibble over what that constituted, Washington abjured, as Adams had advised, almost all 'intercourse with society, but upon public Business'.[35]

'I lead a very dull life here,' Martha wrote to Fanny in October, 'and know nothing that passes in the town. I never go to any publick place, – indeed I think I am more like a state prisoner than anything else, there is certain bounds set for me which I must not depart from.' Martha ended defiantly: 'and as I cannot do as I like, I am obstinate and stay at home a great deal'.[36] At the time she wrote, Washington was away, on a lengthy journey eastward to survey those states with which he was least familiar. During his absence, despite her words to Fanny, she was not wholly unsociable. She asked 'Mrs Adams and family' to dinner and to accompany her thereafter to 'the concert'.[37] The Adamses inhabited the house on Richmond Hill which had briefly served the Washingtons as a home during the war. With them were living their daughter 'Nabby' – another Abigail – and her husband, a former aide to Washington, and their children. In early November Martha accepted an invitation to dine, in her turn, with the children at Richmond Hill. For company, she told Abigail, she would be 'very happy with General Knox and the ladies mentioned or any others you please'.[38]

Before he left for the east, the President had proclaimed that Thursday 26 November was to be a day of thanksgiving and prayer throughout the United States. Citizens might acknowledge divine favour and 'the opportunity peaceably to establish a form of govern-ment for their safety and happiness'.[39] Though critics disputed the right of Congress to proclaim such a day, Washington was not deterred, noting in his diary for November: 'Thursday 26th. Being the day appointed for a thanksgiving I went to St. Pauls Chapel though it was most inclement and stormy – but few people at Church.'[40] He could at least reflect that, in comparison with both their former enemy and their former ally, the United States were tranquil. England had suffered political turmoil in October 1788 when King George III became mentally and physically incapacitated and a Regency crisis developed. This spring the King had been restored to health, but divisions within the Royal family and political parties had been laid bare. Across the Channel, following the storm-ing of the Bastille in July, a National Assembly in Paris had been legitimized as a new French government. The King, Louis XVI, was now titular head of state only. The abolition of feudalism, among other measures, followed.

Following her husband's return to New York in the late autumn of 1789, Martha was more resigned to her lot, if we may trust her letter of 26 December to Mercy Otis Warren. Mrs Warren had been an outspoken critic of the new Constitution, and some amanuensis at Cherry Street framed the emollient sentences that flowed from Martha's pen: 'The difficulties which presented themselves to view upon his first entering upon the Presidency seem to be in some measure surmounted...' However, the letter may have accurately reflected Martha's state of mind. Had she been younger, she wrote, she would probably have enjoyed 'the innocent gaieties of life' that her residence in New York afforded. She was not dissatisfied with her elevated situation: 'no, God forbid, for everybody and everything conspire to make me as contented as possible in it'. She was, she wrote, determined to be cheerful and happy, having learnt from experience that 'the greater part of our happiness or misery depends upon our disposition'.[41]

There was no thought of leaving New York at Christmas. In late February 1790 the Presidential household took possession of a house on Broadway that the Comte de Moustier had lately vacated. As Minister Plenipotentiary to the United States, he had proved a dilatory negotiator of matters outstanding from the war and of new commercial treaties in concert with John Jay, Secretary of Foreign Affairs – from September 1789, Secretary of State. Moustier had, however, been a lavish host at his house, arguably the most elegant in New York. It enjoyed sweeping views, from the balcony on the garden front, of the Hudson and of the western waterfront of Manhattan. Now, leaving a chargé d'affaires to act with Jay, he returned home to France.

The owner of the house occupied, with his family, a portion of it. Congress took a year's lease on the remainder. Reception rooms on either side of the hall were lavish in size and in decoration. The furniture that Moustier had left and which was to be sold was 'well adapted to particular public rooms', Washington noted, when he inspected the house on 3 February.[42] Washington, easier in office now, had less compunction about displays of grandeur where he judged them fitting. Congress had prevailed on him in September to accept an annual 'Compensation' of $25,000. Adams received $5,000. Martha sent to Fanny in March at Mount Vernon to search out 'a silver seal' which bore her late father John Dandridge's arms, and take an impression of it. Her niece was to send this to New York as soon as possible, with a 'white necklace' and 'some small mother of pearl beads' that she would find in one of the drawers of her aunt's 'cabinet'.[43]

Before George and Martha left Cherry Street, however, they faced further criticism. In New York and elsewhere, Washington's birthday in February 1790 was made the occasion of celebration. In America before the Revolution, King George III's birthday – 4 June – had been the most important day of celebration in the secular calendar, the Queen's birthday – 19 May – the second. Was New York society now to glitter in February rather than on the glorious Fourth of July? Moreover, though all direct enquiries met a civil response from the President that he observed his birthday on 22 February, some celebrated on the 11th, as Rochambeau had before them. Levees, multiple birthdays, drawing rooms – Jefferson, who took up his duties as Secretary of State in March, was later to growl that Washington had intended all along to introduce these trappings of the English court, with the aim, ultimately, of establishing a constitutional monarchy.

The opulent house on Broadway was a backdrop for costly Presidential entertainment. Tobias Lear, who kept the household accounts, wrote to Washington in the early autumn: 'When we lived in Cherry Street, we could not have more than 12 or 15 persons to dine weekly, exclusive of our own family. Since we have been in Broadway there has seldom been less than 20.' Two additional servants had swelled the 'family', the house 'requiring more work in cleaning &ca than that in Cherry Street. We have had some extraordinary dinners, and the Company which has visited Mrs Washington on Friday evenings has been much more numerous than it could be in the other house.'[44]

The public dinners that the President gave each week were never a success. The Washingtons sat opposite to each other. The ladies were ranged alongside Martha, the gentlemen on either side of the President. 'Small images [porcelain figures], flowers (artificial) etc.', Senator Maclay noted, decorated the table. The food was good and nourishing. Soup, fish, 'meats, gammon and fowls, etc.' preceded desserts of some splendour – 'first apple pies, pudding, etc, then iced creams, jellies, etc, then water-melons, musk-melons, apples, peaches, nuts'.[45] But Martha was apparently unwilling to initiate conversation where the President was host. He had always been accustomed to following her lead, speaking only when a subject under discussion interested him. The dinners passed in near silence, till Washington toasted all those present, and the uncomfortable meal was at an end.

As Washington stamped authority on the office, as protocol and etiquette were, month by month, established, criticism of the executive branch dimmed in some quarters. Lund Washington, at Hayfield, Virginia, even heard that Washington's gouty neighbour George Mason's 'acrimony agnst the Constitution' was much abated. Mason condemned, however, 'the Pomp & parade that is going on at New York, and tells of a number of useless ceremonies that is now in fashion'. The master of Gunston Hall swore: 'by G–d [that] if the President was not an uncommon Man – we should soon have the Devil to pay – but hoped & indeed did not fear, so long as it pleased God to keep him at the head . . . it would be out of the power of those Damnd Monarchical fellows with the Vice president, & the Women to ruin the Nation'.[46]

This summer, Washington posed for artist John Trumbull in military uniform and with an arm laid across the saddle of his riding horse for a 'history painting', to be entitled *Washington and the Departure of the British Garrison from New York City*. It shows Washington as vigorous in health as he had ever been. The President, wearing his uniform, ushered a number of elders of the Creek tribe, in New York at this time to negotiate a treaty, into the 'painting room'. They were apparently rendered 'mute with astonishment' when they confronted a second 'Great Father'.[47] Washington was not, however, immune to the onset of age. He was increasingly deaf, and his teeth were a trouble to him. He told John Adams that this was the result of a youthful habit of employing them to crack walnuts.

For a few days in May 1790, it appeared as if the Vice President might soon succeed Washington. Abigail Adams was to write afterwards of this period: 'I never before realized what I might be called to, and the apprehension of it only for a few days greatly distressed me.'[48] Influenza was raging in New York. On the 10th the President was laid low with a severe inflammation on the lungs. Martha had charge of the sickroom, while her husband battled to breathe. Doctors from Philadelphia as well as medics in New York were called to the case. His condition, nevertheless, worsened. On the 15th a caller at the mansion on Broadway found the household in tears and 'his life despaired of'.[49] That same day, at four o'clock, Washington began to perspire copiously, his breathing eased. Within days he was declared safe. The opportunity for prolonged convalescence would only come when Congress rose, but tranquillity was restored. On 5 July – when the anniversary of independence was celebrated this year, the 4th falling on a Sunday – the President recorded, 'Members of Senate, House of Representatives, Public Officers, Foreign Characters &ca. The Members of the Cincinnati, Officers of the Militia, &ca., came with the compliments of the day to me.'[50]

George and Martha took advantage of the Congressional recess to visit Mount Vernon. But the President had little time to manage the plantation. He and Martha were soon to set off for Philadelphia where a new Presidential mansion awaited them. In July Washington had signed a Residence Act, creating a federal district, to be named the District of Columbia, centring around Georgetown in Maryland, on the Potomac. Distinct from the other states, it was to accommodate a new national capital. This Federal City was to occupy an area of ten square miles – much of it currently woodland and farmland and belonging to different landowners, from whom it must be acquired. Ten years was to be devoted to its building. In the interim, the federal government would have its home in Philadelphia, where Independence Hall and other buildings dating from the colonial period were to be adapted for its needs.

Philadelphia was replete with friends from the Washingtons' many sojourns there during the war. It had the added advantage of being relatively near to Mount Vernon. George Augustine, who had charge of the estate, was not in good health, and Fanny's domestic management caused her aunt anxiety. Martha told her niece to be firm with the house slaves when they pleaded sickness: 'Charlotte will lay herself up [take to her bed] for as little as anyone will,' she wrote.[51] Though she might exhibit signs of distress on her departure for Presidential residences, Martha had no mind to let anyone imperil the good management of Mount Vernon during her absence.

Market Street, Philadelphia, 1790–1793

. . . events which are governed by the public voice . . .

The Washingtons had often stayed at the house on Market Street in Philadelphia which served as the Presidential mansion from late November 1790. It belonged to the Robert Morrises, who had agreed, earlier in the year, to lease it and move to a smaller house they owned on the same street. In September, on his way from New York to Mount Vernon with Martha, the President formed a firm idea of which rooms should be appropriated for 'public rooms', which for official business, and which for the family's private use.[1] Alterations, including the installation of a double-height bow window or bay, to extend the dining room and drawing room above it to the south, were decided upon. Work on the house proceeded, if slowly. Mary Morris fell ill and she and her husband were still *in situ* in the third week of October. Relations between the Washington and Morris families, however, remained cordial.

Tobias Lear, the President's private secretary, acted as surveyor of works while Washington was in Virginia. In late October Lear began to make disposition in the Market Street house of some of the inventory from New York, and his employer advised him: 'Mrs Morris, who is a notable lady in family arrangements, can give you much information in all the conveniences about the

House & buildings, and I dare say would rather consider it as a compliment to be consulted in these matters (as she is so near) than a trouble to give her opinion of them or in putting up any of the fixtures as the House is theirs & will revert to them.'² The lady, Lear reported for days later, 'appeared much flattered by your opinion of her Housewifery and taste . . .'³ Places were found for looking glasses, lustres, sideboards, moreen curtains and carpets. Sèvres china purchased at the Comte de Moustier's sale and Angoulême biscuit groups and figurines, and mirrored silver plat-ters, acquired by Gouverneur Morris in Paris, were unpacked. The Morrises' mangle – for wringing sheets – was the subject of some discussion before Mrs Morris bore it off. Lear installed one that had served the Washingtons in New York.

Lear had taken a bride from his native New Hampshire, Polly Long Lear, in April. They had lodged elsewhere in New York, but it was Martha's wish that, at Philadelphia, they inhabit the Presidential mansion. Polly was termed by Washington 'an amiable, & inoffensive little woman' but she was timorous.⁴ 'Mrs Lear was in to see me yesterday,' wrote Abigail Adams to her sister, while Bush Hill, her own new residence in Philadelphia, was still in disarray, 'and assures me that I am much better off than Mrs Washington will be when she arrives, for that their house is not likely to be completed this year.'⁵

Despite these prognostications, the house on Market Street was habitable when the Washingtons took possession in late November. On the first floor a yellow drawing room in front served for more intimate occasions. The green drawing room measured thirty-five feet in length. On the ground floor the Washingtons breakfasted and usually dined in a blue room at the front. The weekly Thursday gath-ering, now commonly known as 'the Congress dinner', took place in the large dining room at the back. When not in use, the three Angoulême 'groups' were housed there under large glass covers. 'The Save [Sèvres] and Cincinnati China – the plate and other things which are not used common' were housed in a closet in the steward's room opposite.⁶ Elsewhere in the house was a study at the back for Washington and a parlour for Martha. In their bedchamber Martha had a new bed installed. The children, the Lears, secretaries and numerous servants were accommodated above.

The Washingtons had been at some pains to assemble a household in Philadelphia to suit them. In September the President had named, among servants who should transfer from New York to Philadelphia, 'the Wives of the footmen – namely James & Fidas. The Washer Women I believe are good . . .' He did not, however, wish for others: 'the dirty figures of Mrs Lewis [kitchen maid and temporary cook in New York] and her daughter will not be a pleasant sight in view (as the Kitchen always will be)'.[7] Hercules, one of two cooks at Mount Vernon, travelled to Philadelphia instead.

Hercules, according to the later recollection of Wash Custis, was something of a dandy, and liked to walk the streets, elegantly dressed, after serving the Thursday 'Congress dinner'.[8] Guests congregating in the new bay windows of the 'public rooms' which abutted the kitchen block presumably found him a 'pleasant sight in view'. Hercules's son Richmond accompanied his father, Washington bowing, in September, to the cook's 'desire to have him as an assistant'.[9] John Hyde, who had replaced Fraunces in New York, remained as steward, but the President was not enthusiastic: '. . . I strongly suspect that *nothing* is brought to my table of *liquors*, *fruits* or *other things* that is not used *as profusely* at his.'[10] Hyde must for the time being serve as housekeeper as well. In the northern city his wife had undertaken these duties: 'superintending the women of the family in washing the linen – cleaning the house &ca – taking care of the linen of the family – preparing the desert [*sic*] for dinners – making Cake, tea & Coffee – and assisting Mr Hyde in such parts of his duty as lay within the house'. Mrs Hyde told Lear in September she was no longer fit for work. Her health had given way, under the strain of serving 'in so large a family'.[11]

The Washingtons observed in Market Street the same weekly routine as they had in New York. On Tuesdays the President held his levee at the house, and gentlemen mounting the staircase found him, dressed in his customary black velvet, in the green drawing room, silhouetted effectively against the light and illumined further by 'lustres' or chandeliers above. At Martha's drawing rooms, as at

New York, he wore no sword, nor did he carry a hat. This signified that he appeared in a private character and was, like others, a guest at his wife's assembly. Once ladies had curtseyed to Mrs Washington, and were in circulation or seated on green damask sofas and chairs formally arranged around the room, they could hope that conversation with Washington would follow.

General Montgomery's widow, Janet, returning to New York after a period in Europe, expressed regret that the Washingtons no longer resided in that city. Replying in January 1791, Martha wrote, 'I have been so long accustomed to conform to events which are governed by the public voice that I hardly dare indulge any personal wishes that cannot yield to that.'[12] Philadelphia, however, suited both Washingtons very well. Grown in confidence, they no longer abjured 'private life'. They dined in town and in the country with friends – the Morrises, the Powels, the Willings, the Shippens and the Penns. In town the Washingtons and the children saw much of the Adams, Hamilton and Knox families. Invitations to the Presidential mansion were no longer confined to the public dinners. One gentleman, commanded to attend at an early hour, was disappointed by the simplicity of the Market Street breakfast. Nelly and Washington Custis were at table, and Mrs Washington herself made the tea and coffee. Only one waiter, not in livery, was in attendance, the visitor remarked, and 'a silver urn for hot water, was the only article of expense on the table'. There was not even fish offered, he complained, but only slices of tongue, 'dry toast, bread and butter, etc'.[13]

In late March 1791, prior to embarking on a tour of southern states, Washington met on the Potomac with commissioners – among them David Stuart – appointed in accordance with the Residence Act of the previous summer. He consulted with them and with Andrew Ellicott and Pierre L'Enfant, surveyor and architect, respectively, for the new Federal City. Following skilful negotiations with the owners of land that fell within the proposed federal district, he proclaimed, on the 30th at Georgetown, the quadrilateral area it would occupy. Washington was a happy man. Mount Vernon, lying along the western bank of the Potomac only fifteen miles below the site of the future city, was greatly enhanced in value. Congress was to decree, however, that all public buildings in the Federal City were to be built on the Maryland bank of the Potomac, between Georgetown and the eastern branch of the river.

Travelling further south, Washington wrote to Lear that Paris, one of the slaves with duties as groom or postilion, had become 'so lazy, self-willed & impudent, that John' – Fagan, coachman – 'had no sort of government of him; on the contrary, John say's it was a maxim with Paris to do nothing he was ordered, and every thing he was forbid'. Another slave, coachman Giles, was a permanent invalid. Washington wanted Lear to hire replacements in town – 'low & squat (well made) boys, would suit best'.[14]

During his absence in the south, Edmund Randolph visited Martha. The Attorney General, a fellow Virginian, informed her that 'three of his Negroes had given him notice that they should tomorrow take advantage of a law of this State, and claim their freedom'.[15] Pennsylvania's Gradual Abolition Act, passed eleven years earlier, was the law in question. With some exceptions, 'domestic slaves' belonging to citizens from out of state and who resided with their owners in Pennsylvania longer than six months by law became 'freemen and Freewomen'.

Among those excepted were 'the domestic Slaves attending upon Delegates in Congress from the other American States, foreign Ministers and Consuls, and persons passing through or sojourning in this State, and not becoming resident therein'.[16] Though the law had been amended in 1788 in a bid to prevent slave owners rotating slaves in and out of the state, still, no exception to the six-month rule existed for 'domestic' slaves belonging to members of the executive branch. While members of Congress could keep their slave servants with them as long as they liked, Washington and his Cabinet enjoyed no such impunity. The Attorney General's slaves appear to have been among the first to have been led to an understanding of this.

Randolph 'mentioned it to her', Lear wrote to the President on 5 April, following the Virginian's visit to Martha, 'from an idea that those who were of age in this family might follow the example, after a residence of six months should put it in their power'.[17] Washington from the south countered that he qualified as 'passing through or sojourning in this State, and not becoming resident therein'.[18] Randolph opined to Lear that this was a moot point: 'there were not wanting persons who would not only give them (the Slaves) advice; but would use all means to entice them from their masters'. The Attorney General gave this advice, ignoring the 1788 amendment, as Lear informed the president on 24 April: 'if, before the expiration of six months, they [the slaves in question] could, upon any pretence whatever, be carried or sent out of the State, but for a single day, a new era would commence on their return . . .'[19]

Martha and Lear acted. Scullion Richmond was dispatched by water the next day for Alexandria, and Lear told Washington that he would hold out a lure to Hercules himself: 'by being at home before your arrival he will have it in his power to see his friends – make every necessary preparation in his Kitchen &c'. If Hercules declined to travel to Virginia, the secretary noted, it would be 'a pretty strong proof of his intention to take the advantage of the law at the expiration of six months'. Lear was an efficient if unhappy agent: 'no consideration should induce me to take these steps to prolong the slavery of a human being, had I not the fullest confidence that they will at some future period be liberated'. In his native New Hampshire such measures were slowly under way. He soothed his conscience. The slaves' situation at Market Street, he believed, was 'far preferable to what they would probably obtain in a state of freedom'. Martha herself, adaptable to much, was fiercely possessive of the slaves that were hers by dower right. They would pass, following her death, to her grandchildren. She had her own plans, Lear told Washington, for Oney Judge, her maid, and Christopher Shiels, footman, 'which will carry them out of the State'.[20] When she and the children visited members of the Dickinson family at Trenton, maid and footman went too. On the return of the party to Philadelphia, a 'new era' of servitude began. Though it contravened state law, from now on the Washingtons observed a systematic rotation of their slaves in and out of Pennsylvania.

The white servants and stable staff in Market Street posed other problems. Black Sam Fraunces returned to displace Hyde as steward. Martha, while Washington was in the south, hired a housekeeper,

Mrs Emerson. Her greatest difficulty, Lear wrote Washington on 15 May, would be managing the other servants. Given the importance of their master's office, they were all 'impressed with an idea that they are the best Servants that can be obtained'. Yet insubordination was rife. With the aid of Mrs Washington, Lear was confident that order would be restored before the President came north.[21]

As the children grew older, their schooling and their holidays governed Martha's movements. Lear wrote to the President, while he was still in the south, that, after the Easter holidays, Wash, aged ten, would be 'put to Cyphering immediately'. Particular attention would be paid to 'his writing, reading & as well as to Latin'.[22] Both children – Nelly was now twelve – were taught to dance by English émigré James Robardet. In January 1791 Martha warmly invited 'Miss [Caroline Amelia] Smith', Abigail Adams's granddaughter, to join the class. A year later Washington praised Robardet's 'attention to my grandchildren, and the progress which they have made under his instruction'.[23] Dancing slippers as well as the necessary accoutrements for learning – slates and pencils, a 'silver pencil case', 'Elements of Geography' – were purchased for Nelly.[24] She now did her lessons, including French, drawing and watercolour, with masters at home, and was becoming an accomplished musician under the supervision of Alexander Reinagle, who had followed Congress to the city.[25]

Martha did not forget her elder grandchildren. She sent Bet and Pat – now fifteen and fourteen and known as Betsy and Patty – muffs, stays made by 'Mr Serres', and painting materials: '1 palette, 3/9 [that is, 3s 9d in New York money], a cake of black paint 5/. Ditto of white do 1/10, 4 brushes 2/1, 1 Indian rubber 1/10'.[26] Members of the extended clan, including Fanny and Harriot Washington and Nelly Stuart, too, received stays, ribbon, cambric, nankeen and shoes. But her attention was focused on Nelly and Wash. Martha made, with purchases for herself at fashionable emporia, others for Nelly – gloves, muffs, cloaks, bonnets, hats, handkerchiefs and fans, as well as costly fabric for habits, dresses and gowns. Suitable friends – the Robert Morrises' daughter, Maria; Attorney General Randolph's daughter, Susan; and a cousin of Miss Randolph, Elizabeth Bordley – provided companionship for Nelly.

Both Washingtons were uneasy on a number of scores about their home in Virginia. George Augustine was spitting blood and had a severe pain in his chest that no 'blister' – liniment – could relieve. At the end of August he went over the mountains to Berkeley Springs in search of a cure. Anthony Whitting, hired to manage the mansion farm alone, administered the estate. There were other causes for concern about George Augustine. He exercised little control over the overseers, and expressed dismay when a slave, whom he had authorized an overseer to punish, subsequently died. As aide-de-camp to Lafayette during the war, the young man had often heard the Marquis express his horror of the institution of slavery. His stewardship of Mount Vernon may have sat uncomfortably with ideas he had imbibed from the Marquis, ideas that indeed underlay recent legislation in other states as well as Pennsylvania. Only in Massachusetts, in 1783, had immediate abolition been enacted. But New Hampshire, Connecticut and Rhode Island, too, had passed Acts for the 'gradual abolition of slavery', following the Pennsylvanian model of March 1780, which deemed all children of slaves born in the state thereafter to be free.

The President had no high opinion of the overseers' humanity at Mount Vernon. He relied, however, on these man managers to extract the due portion of work from a 'people' disinclined to render it. Lear, writing home to New Hampshire, noted: 'The negroes are not treated as blacks in general are in this Country. They are clothed and fed as well as any labouring people whatever, and they are not subject to the lash of a dominating overseer – *but still they are slaves.*'[27] The President did his duty, as he saw it, by his 'people', including, in a memorandum this summer for his nephew, the instruction: 'Huts, or some kind of covering will be wanting at Dogue-run; some of the People at that place complain much of the Leakiness of their Houses.'[28]

Though the Washingtons, approaching sixty, were still energetic, many of the house slaves on whom they had relied at home were now 'past service'. Doll, whose housekeeping skills Martha had respected, was listed five years earlier by Washington as 'almost past service'.[29] George Augustine's wife, Fanny, was neither a good housekeeper nor did she exercise sufficient authority at the mansion house. Frank Lee, steward, was prone to drink, and Nathan, the cook, was slovenly. Martha wrote in August of Charlotte, sempstress, to Fanny, 'She is so indolent, that she will do nothing but what she is told. She knows what work is to be done.' Martha dismissed out of hand the slave servants' protests to her niece that they were fully occupied, making 'the people's clothes' – the clothing given out annually to the field slaves. 'If you suffer them to go on so idle, they will in a little time do nothing but work for themselves.'

Martha, adamant that Fanny must stir herself, wrote of an impending visit home in September: 'I shall leave all the housekeeping to you.' There would be 'company' staying, she informed her niece, the whole time she and the President were in residence. 'I shall not concern in the matter at all. Make Nathan clean his kitchen and everything about it very well.' Charlotte and her fellow sempstresses must endeavour to get all other business done 'as fast as they can'. Martha would be bringing up 'work' – or sewing – from Philadelphia for them to do.[30]

Those for whom the Washingtons felt responsibility were many. The President had reflected the previous autumn, 'The easy and quiet temper of Fanny is little fitted, I find, for the care of my Niece Harriot Washington, who is grown almost, if not quite a Woman.'[31] Ultimately the girl was dispatched to her aunt, Betty Lewis at Fredericksburg, with this injunction from her uncle: 'I wish you would examine her Cloaths, and direct her in the use and application of them – for without this they will be (I am told) dabbed about in every hole & corner – & her best things always in use.'[32]

Harriot continued to press for 'best things', asking her uncle in subsequent years to fund a dress, and a 'silk jacket and a pair of shoes', for her to wear on 'the Birth night' [Washington's birthday].[33] If Harriot was unsatisfactory, their uncle approved of her brothers, George Steptoe and Lawrence who were studying at the College in Philadelphia. The President had, in 1790, judged them 'well disposed Youths – neither of them wanting capacity; and both, especially the first, very desirous of improvement'.[34] One of Martha's nephews, Bartholomew Dandridge, served Washington as an assistant secretary, and he or the Washingtons' boys sometimes accompanied the children to the 'play' or concerts.

Martha and the President had plenty of curiosity themselves to see the sights of the city. In 1792 Washington paid to view a 'sea leopard [leopard seal]' on display. Martha visited at least once the famous 'flower garden' – or botanic garden – that John Bartram had established outside the city. Bowen's Waxworks – now transposed to Philadelphia and incorporating a scene from *The School for Scandal* – was another destination. The whole family inspected the natural history exhibits at Charles Willson Peale's museum that included in 1792 an 'Otaheitian [Tahitian] dress'.[35]

Martha had firm ideas about the upbringing of the children, including the need to control their diet. When her niece Fanny Washington was later to write that her young daughter Maria was ill, Martha was swift in her diagnosis: 'Children that eat everything as they like and feed as heartily as yours does must be full of worms. Indeed my dear Fanny I never saw children stuffed as yours was when I was down . . .'[36] Mr Spence, dentist, cleaned the children's teeth and supplied toothbrushes and tooth powder. In addition, Washington's own hairdresser, Durang, attended to her grandson's hair. A 'pair of skeats [skates]', noted in the household accounts, in December 1792, as well as innumerable handkerchiefs and items such as '10 pairs of stockings', hint at Wash's predilection for outdoor activities.[37]

At Georgetown this summer Washington had inspected, as he wrote to Lear from Mount Vernon, 'many well conceived & ingenious plans for the Public buildings in the New City'. It had been 'a pleasure indeed, to find – in an infant Country – such a display of Architectural abilities'.[38] Irish emigrant James Hoban had been chosen to design the President's House, and they were digging out its foundations. Washington had written to Jefferson in April 1791, 'The most superb edifice may be erected.' He wished their inhabitants much happiness. 'I shall never be of their number myself.'[39]

The Washingtons' sojourn at Mount Vernon in the summer and autumn of 1792 was tinged with sadness on more than one account. This year the Stuarts, with the Parke Custis girls and their many half-siblings, removed to a smaller and more isolated home, Hope Park, some way west of Alexandria. Abingdon, the estate Jacky had acquired with such enthusiasm, was sold. Moreover, Washington wrote to Lear on 21 September, George Augustine was 'but the shadow of what he was; he has not been out of his room & scarcely from his bed these six weeks'.

Washington was in a quandary. Should he yield to the pleas of his friends, as well as Cabinet colleagues of all political colours, and serve a second Presidential term? Doing so was not merely contrary to his inclination; George Augustine's wasted state added, as he wrote to Lear in September, 'not a little to my distress & perplexity on a subject you are already acquainted with'.⁴⁰ If he were to serve again, to whom should he look to manage the estate?

Whether he served a second term or not, he must renew the lease on the Morris house in Philadelphia. It would soon expire, even before the Presidential term was up in April 1793. When Lear called in July on Mr Morris to secure another year, the financier 'hoped to God' that love of country would persuade the President to serve another term. 'He thought', reported Lear, 'the reasons for your continuing were, if possible, more strong than those which first induced your acceptance of the Office.' Lear had taken other soundings, at Washington's request. He noted: 'The general idea seemed to be, to say nothing of the fatal effects expected from divisions & parties, that most of the important things hitherto done under this government, being, as it were, matters of experiment, had not yet been long enough in operation to give satisfactory proof whether they are beneficial or not.' A second term would accord an opportunity for a 'fair experiment'.⁴¹

'Divisions and parties' already played a lively part in governmental politics. Madison and others vehemently favoured the empowerment of the different states and opposed the establishment of a national bank. Hamilton in the Senate was prominent among those who wished further powers to accrue to federal government. Jefferson, inimical to Hamilton and all 'monarchical' tendencies, tired of the federalist press attacks, wrote to Washington in September of his own wish to retire. When the Secretary of State called in at Mount Vernon in early October on his way to Philadelphia, however, Washington was persuasive. It was important, he said, to preserve what he called 'the check' of his fellow Virginian's opinions in the administration. The President denied that Hamilton, Adams and others wished to transform the country into a constitutional monarchy on the British model.

Washington, at this exchange of views, was still undecided whether to serve another term. He told Jefferson, as the Secretary of State reported: 'nobody disliked more the ceremonies of his office, and he had not the least taste or gratification in the execution of its function'. Declaring himself 'happy at home alone' at Mount Vernon, the President observed that 'his presence there was now peculiarly called for by the situation of Major Washington whom he thought irrecoverable'. If his aid, however, was thought necessary to 'save the cause to which he had devoted his life principally', he would 'make the sacrifice of a longer continuance'.[42]

The question was unresolved when the Washingtons returned to Philadelphia. George Augustine, Fanny and their three children made a slow journey to Eltham, where attempts would be made to nurse the invalid back to health. Frank Lee, steward, and his wife, Lucy, were deputed to look after the mansion house. The plantation was left in the hands of Anthony Whitting. The President closed a long list of instructions for the manager: 'Although it is last mentioned, it is foremost in my thoughts, to desire you will be particularly attentive to my Negros in their sickness.' Every overseer, moreover, was to do likewise, and send for Dr Craik if the case demanded it. 'I am sorry to observe that the generality of them [the overseers], view these poor creatures in scarcely any other light than they do a draught horse or Ox; neglecting them as much when they are unable to work; instead of comforting & nursing them when they lie on a sick bed.' This ill-treatment had cost him dear, he wrote severely. He had, he wrote, 'lost more Negros last Winter, than I had done in 12 or 15 years before, put them altogether'.[43]

In conversation with Jefferson in February 1793, Washington was to declare that 'strong solicitations' the previous autumn led to his remaining in office. But he also told his fellow Virginian that he mentioned 'his purpose of going out', or intention not to serve a second term, to no one except to his Cabinet colleagues and Mr Madison.[44] In fact, among those with whom he had discussed his quandary was Mrs Powel, with whom he entered into the subject in a conversation in Philadelphia on Thursday 1 November 1792. She docketed a draft of a letter which she subsequently sent Washington: 'To the President of the United States on the Subject of his Resignation November the 4th 1792'. She began: 'After I had parted with you on Thursday, my Mind was thrown into a Train of Reflections in Consequence of the Sentiments that you had confided to me.' The arguments which she marshalled proved she knew well the man she addressed: 'Your Resignation wou'd elate the Enemies of good Government and cause lasting Regret to the Friends of humanity . . .'

The 'enemies of good government' – anti-federalists – would, she continued, 'urge that you, from Experience, had found the present System a bad one, and had, artfully, withdrawn from it that you might not be crushed under its Ruins'. They would use his resignation as an argument for dissolving the Union. The federalists were keen to hand him the Presidency, she wrote. They 'gave what a great and generous People might offer with Dignity and a noble Mind receive with Delicacy . . .' Would he withdraw his aid 'from a Structure that certainly wants your Assistance to support it? Can you, with Fortitude, see it crumble to decay?'

Mrs Powel went so far as to attack his wish to live in retirement at Mount Vernon as selfish and misguided: 'you have frequently demonstrated that you possess an Empire over yourself. For Gods sake do not yield that Empire to a Love of Ease, Retirement, rural Pursuits, or a false Diffidence of Abilities which those that best know you so justly appreciate.' One wonders if Washington showed this letter to Martha. Mrs Powel went on to ask: 'admitting that you could retire in a Manner exactly conformable to your own Wishes and possessed of the Benediction of Mankind, are you sure that such a Step would promote your Happiness? Have you not often experienced that your Judgement was fallible with Respect to the Means of Happiness? Have you not, on some Occasions, found the Consummation of your Wishes the Source of the keenest of your Sufferings?'[45]

Washington did not withdraw his name, but made 'the sacrifice of a longer continuance'. He was returned unanimously by the electoral college on 5 December 1792. The 132 electors supplied by the states, now numbering fifteen with new-minted Vermont and Kentucky, each had two votes. Adams received seventy-seven of the second votes and was elected Vice President once more. John Adams wrote on 28 December to his wife in Massachusetts: 'The Noise of Election is over . . . Four years more will be as long as I shall have a Taste for public Life or Journeys to Philadelphia. I am determined in the meantime to be no longer the Dupe, and run into Debt to Support a vain Post which has answered no other End than to make me unpopular.'[46] Washington too harped on his reluctance to serve. Early in the new year, in response to a letter of congratulation, he wrote to Henry Lee in Virginia: 'my particular, & confidential friends well know, that it was after a long and painful conflict in my own breast, that I was withheld . . . from requesting, *in time*, that no votes might be thrown away upon me.'[47]

Before Washington took the oath of office in Philadelphia, on 4 March 1793, any faint hopes that George Augustine might recover his strength and return to manage Mount Vernon were blasted. Washington's nephew died at Eltham in early February. Nevertheless, as Washington wrote to widowed Fanny, offering her and her children a home at Mount Vernon, matters there were 'now so arranged as to be under the care of responsible persons'.[48] Whitting was proving a conscientious estate manager, and Catherine Ehlers, wife of the German gardener, supervised the 'spinners', following instruction from Martha.

Had the President had the gift of second sight, he might have quailed at the four years of faction and personal attacks on him that lay ahead. The anti-federalists were calling for the government to support republican France. Washington and his fellow federalists, however, favoured strengthening ties with Britain, America's principal trading partner since the war. Mrs Powel had prophesied the previous autumn that, if he retired, 'a great Deal of the well earned Popularity that you are now in Possession of will be torn from you by the Envious and Malignant'.[49] As it turned out, he was to be stripped of it in office.

Second Term, 1793–1797

. . . the Turpitude of the Jacobins touches him
more nearly than he owns . . .

When Washington took his oath of office on 4 March 1793, news of Louis XVI's execution in Paris on 21 January had not yet reached Philadelphia. Reports the previous year, however, had thrilled anti-federalists. In August 1792 a coup in Paris had placed radicals in power in France, driving from office the constitutional government that Lafayette, among others, had done much to establish. The Marquis fled the country. Against all expectations, a French army then defeated Austrians and Prussians at Valmy on 20 September 1792. The French monarchy was abolished the day after, and a republic was established.

Edward Thornton, a secretary to the British legation in Philadelphia, wrote in early February 1793: 'the doctrines of liberty, and equality gain daily proselytes; public dinners, congratulations, civic feasts in honour of the French Victories are given throughout the United States, and the appellation of citizen is used on all these occasions'.[1] In this libertarian atmosphere, the style if not the substance of Washington's own government came under attack. The *General Advertiser*, an anti-federalist paper, purported, on 2 January, to seek a poet laureate: 'monarchical prettinesses must be highly extolled, such as levies, drawing rooms, stately nods instead of shaking hands, titles of office, seclusion from the people, &c. &c. . . .'.[2]

John Adams wrote of such jibes at the President to his wife Abigail: 'I have held the office, of Libellee General long enough: The Burthen of it ought to be participated and equalized according to modern republican Principles.'[3] For his part, in conversation with Jefferson in February, the President 'expressed the extreme wretchedness of his existence while in office, and went lengthily into the late attacks on him for levees &c.' He explained, noted the Secretary of State, 'how he had been led into them [the levees] by the persons he consulted at New York, and that if he could but know what the sense of the public was, he would most cheerfully conform to it.'[4]

Washington did not, however, alter by a jot the stately gatherings over which he and Martha presided, nor did he call a halt to the national celebrations of his birth night. He might not be a friend to monarchy, but, as Chief Magistrate of the United States, he must receive the envoys of foreign monarchs as well as those of foreign republics. He would do it in a style which he believed upheld the dignity of the country.

Washington was at Mount Vernon in April 1793, when Lear wrote from Philadelphia, enclosing newspapers of a February date from London: France had declared war on Britain and on Holland. The secretary, who was well placed to seek many opinions, wrote a digest of views: 'it becomes a question with every one – what will be the event to the United States? And the universal hope is that they may not be drawn into it.'[5]

At all costs, to Washington's mind, commerce with Britain must be put on a sure footing. Hamilton at the Treasury and Thomas Pinckney, Minister Plenipotentiary in London, must redouble their efforts to resolve issues including British withdrawal from frontier forts and bad American debts still outstanding ten years after the war. The American government cried off the war debt owed France on the ground that it had been owed to the French Crown. In retaliation French ships pillaged American merchant ships in the Atlantic.

Thornton, who studied the President closely, had detected in him a year earlier 'a certain degree of indecision . . . a want of vigour and energy . . . in some of his actions . . . the obvious result of too refined caution'.[6] At that time, in the spring of 1792, Washington himself, aged sixty, had told Jefferson that he 'really felt himself growing old, his bodily health less firm, his memory, always bad, becoming worse'.⁷ Now the President did not falter. He signed, on 22 April 1793, the Neutrality Proclamation: 'the duty and interest of the United States require that they should with sincerity and good faith adopt and pursue a conduct friendly and impartial toward the belligerent powers . . .'⁸ Legal proceedings were threatened against any American who aided any of the belligerents. In March the young French republic made declarations of war on the kingdoms of Spain and Portugal. Washington accepted Jefferson's resignation later in the year. It was inevitable, given the Secretary of State's passionate advocacy of republican France. To other protests Washington turned a deaf ear, as he was to be impervious when still greater dissension flared two years hence.

A pressing local issue diverted the attention of all in Philadelphia, including the President, from international politics. A drought had succeeded heavy spring rains. Pockets of standing water abounded where flies and mosquitoes thrived. An epidemic of yellow fever developed in the city in July and August. The role of the female mosquito and her bite in transmitting the virus was not then understood. Some said the disease had been brought by immigrant planters, who had hurriedly left the French West Indies, following the abolition of slavery there. Despite the best efforts of doctors, thousands were to die.

In mid-September Dr Benjamin Rush came down with the fever. The sweats he endured, he noted, were 'so offensive as to oblige me to draw the bedclothes close to my neck, to defend myself from their smell'.⁹ Bloodletting and purging cured him. Alexander and Betsy Hamilton, too, recovered. Countless others did not survive. Carts loaded with coffins crowded the streets. Henry Knox wrote mid-September: 'the great seat of it at present seems to be from 2d to 3d street, and thence to Walnut Street. Water Street however continues sickly. But the alarm is inexpressible. Every body who could, has removed into the Country.'¹⁰

Many decamped for Germantown, high across the river, which remained free of contagion. Others from out of state sought safety at home. The Washingtons themselves left the plague town on 9 September after some argument between them. Washington had wanted earlier to dispatch Martha and the children to Mount Vernon, 'The house in which we lived being, in a manner blockaded by the disorder which was becoming every day more & more fatal.'[11] When he spoke of remaining longer himself, Martha was adamant she would not leave without him. They offered to take Mrs Powel with them to Virginia, but she remained. Her husband, Speaker of the Pennsylvania Senate, she reported, was not 'impressed with the degree of Apprehension that generally pervades the Minds of our Friends'.[12]

Washington left Knox in charge of a skeleton government in Philadelphia. Samuel Fraunces, steward, and Mrs Emerson, house-keeper, remained in charge of the house on Market Street. The President consulted from Mount Vernon with Cabinet members by letter. The epidemic continued into October, in one week claiming over 100 victims. The Wigton family alone, which had supplied Nelly with a tutor, lost five members in as many weeks.[13] Samuel Powel, sanguine though he had been, died, after visiting a stricken employee. The French Consul died, and others in government perished: 'six Clerks of the Treasury Department, seven persons employed by the Collector of the Customs – a number of Clerks in the different Banks and three persons in the Post Office'.[14] Nor did the Washingtons' household in Market Street escape the scourge. Will Osborne, Washington's valet of recent years, died in hospital. In the course of the summer and autumn, more than 4,000 lost their lives.

At Mount Vernon the death in June of Anthony Whitting, farm manager, had been a serious blow. Cotton factory manager, William Pearce, was to take Whitting's place only in December. The Washingtons enjoyed no respite from duty. Both of them were exasperated by countless vices that they discovered obtained among servants, indoors and outdoors, overseers and field slaves. The President would ask Pearce to address the following when he arrived:

The Gardener has too great a propensity to drink, and behaves improperly when in liquor; admonish him against it as much as you can, as he behaves well when sober – understands his business – and I believe is not naturally idle – but only so when occasioned by drink . . . Do not suffer the Quarter Negro Children [house servants' children] to be in the Kitchen, or in the yards unless brought there on business – As besides the bad habit – they too frequently are breaking limbs, or twigs from, or doing other injury to my shrubs – some of which at a considerable expense, have been propagated.[15]

Washington left Mount Vernon for rented lodgings in Germantown at the end of October. Following Will's death, Christopher Shiels, one of the Mount Vernon house slaves, now acted as the President's valet. It was anticipated that the town would serve as emergency quarters for Congress, if Philadelphia was still contagious at the opening of the new session in December. Steward Fraunces, however, was optimistic on the 23rd: 'The House is clean and ready for your return and every thing in proper order – I long to see you home where I think you will be as safe as any where – as our Neibourhood is entirely clear of any infection.'[16]

The city was declared safe, the session of Congress took place in its accustomed meeting place, and Martha and the children joined the President in the city in mid-December. She was to write, however, the following January: 'almost every family has lost some of their friends – and black seems to be the general dress of the city'.[17] Neither theatre nor assemblies were permitted. She noted a month later, in February 1794: 'A great number of people in this town are very much at a loss how to spend their time agreeably . . .'[18]

Within the President's house, there were changes to accommodate. Polly Lear, who had been Martha's willing companion out shopping or visiting friends, had died unexpectedly in the summer of 1793, before the outbreak of yellow fever took hold of the city. For lack of other feminine company in the house, Martha's relationship with her granddaughter Nelly, now fifteen, became almost too close. Lear himself, intelligent, efficient and industrious, left the President's employ at the end of 1793. He meant to establish himself in Georgetown as a shipping agent. Washington could not depend, as he had on Lear, on Martha's nephew, Bartholomew Dandridge, who became principal secretary. His own nephew, Howell Lewis, became second secretary.

In February 1794 Martha's two eldest granddaughters, Betsy and Patty, paid a visit of some weeks to Philadelphia. Accompanying them was Mrs Robert Peter. Her husband, a merchant and mayor of Georgetown in 1790, had profitably sold land in that town to the Federal City Commissioners. Their son, Thomas Peter, who was courting Patty, was among those now investing in the new City. Though some, like David Stuart and Pierre L'Enfant, were no longer involved, the wharves on the Potomac were crowded with cargo ships laden with building materials. Washington himself, in the autumn of 1792, had laid the foundation stone of the President's House, on a site adjacent to Georgetown. William Thornton had won a competition the following spring to build, at the far end of the new city, a home for the legislature, to be called, by Jefferson's wish, the Capitol. Lodging houses and hotels were full, and speculators and contractors made daily applications to the Commissioners' Office in Georgetown for permission to build. Lots in the squares laid out on either side of a grand boulevard, Pennsylvania Avenue, that connected these two edifices and on sites close to them sold briskly.

The projected marriage of Patty Parke Custis, aged seventeen, and Mrs Peter's son Thomas met with Martha's approval. She wrote to Fanny on the 15th: 'I am the more anxious that she should marry well as I am sure it will be an advantage to her younger sister [Nelly].'[19] At the beginning of March she was content: 'from what I can hear Patty and Mr. Peter is to make a match.' Referring to a marriage settlement Patty's stepfather had proposed, she wrote: 'The old gentleman' – Thomas Peter's father, Robert – will comply with Dr. Stuart's bargain'. Mrs Washington characterized her second granddaughter as 'a deserving girl'.[20] Apparently Thomas thought so too. In late summer, with a wedding in the New Year and residence in the Federal City to come, Patty conceived herself 'near the *Pinnacle* of Happiness'.[21]

Washington sent the bride-to-be, at her request, a miniature of himself. This provoked Patty's elder sister Betsy to demand one for herself. 'I hope you will believe me sincere', she wrote on

7 September, 'when I assure you, it is my first wish to have it in my power to contemplate, at all times, the features of one, who, I so highly respect as the Father of his Country and look up to with grateful affection as a parent to myself and family.'[22] The Washingtons were at Germantown at this time, where they had taken a house to escape the summer heat of Philadelphia. The President apparently gratified Betsy's request and – unusually – offered matrimonial advice. Possibly tempestuous Betsy – irked by her younger sister's forthcoming marriage – had found an unsuitable candidate for herself: 'Do not . . . in your contemplation of the marriage state, look for perfect felicity before you consent to wed,' he advised her on 14 September. A partner for life should possess, in his view, 'good sense – good dispositions – and the means of supporting you in the way you have been brought up. Such qualifications cannot fail to attract (after marriage) your esteem & regard, into wch or into disgust, sooner or later, love naturally resolves itself; and who at the same time, has a claim to the respect, & esteem of the circle he moves in.'[23] The 'esteem and regard' which the President felt for Martha, as well as the 'respect and esteem' that others felt for her, cannot have been far from his mind.

Martha's love for her niece Fanny, widowed in early 1793, had recently been tested at times. Washington had pointed out the advantages of a home at Mount Vernon. 'You can go to no place where you will be more welcome – nor to any where you can live at less expense, or trouble,' he had written.[24] Fanny, though expressing herself eager for advice, resolved instead to occupy, with her three children, one of Washington's rental houses in Alexandria. Washington's gentle words of March 1793 went unheeded: 'with the best œconomy I conceive it must be expensive to purchase furniture & keep a house'.[25] Fanny became one more dependant, and one who requested, in November, that an additional storey to be added to the house she was to occupy. The President wrote in January 1794 to Pearce, the new manager at Mount Vernon: 'The house in Alexandria must be repaired & in order for Mrs [Fanny] Washington to go into in April, as I have promised this. When it is got in order, & made perfectly clean, I shall send paper from hence for the rooms.'[26]

Martha urged Fanny on 15 September 1794 to pay attention to her financial affairs: 'I wish you to be as independent as your circumstances will admit . . . a dependence is, I think, a wretched state and you have enough, if you will manage it right.'²⁷ Widowed Fanny's response to this call to arms was in its way eloquent. She sought her aunt's and uncle's advice about a proposal of marriage from widower Tobias Lear, who was now in business at Georgetown. Martha, while praising the former secretary's character, would not be drawn, in her reply of 29 September: 'You must be governed by your own judgment . . . it is a matter more interesting to yourself than to any other.' The President, wrote his wife, stood by his determination – 'as you have often heard him say' – that he never would 'intermeddle in matrimonial concerns'.²⁸ When Fanny accepted Tobias's hand, the Washingtons offered them as a home the River Farm, within easy reach of Georgetown. Here the couple were to settle, with Fanny's children and Lear's young son, Benjamin.

In Philadelphia Martha and her husband continued the precept that she had urged on her niece, and pored over reports from Pearce at Mount Vernon. No doctor, the President had written in January 1794, was to minister to a field slave, Sam. Claiming an asthmatic condition, he was off sick: 'he has had Doctors enough already, of all colours & sexes, and to no effect. Laziness is, I believe, his principal ailment.'²⁹ (No one could ever have accused George Washington of this vice.) Pearce followed the absent but assiduous President's instructions to the letter. While he remained at Mount Vernon, Washington's anxious care about the plantation was much abated. Fanny, however, who was deputed to oversee household affairs at Mount Vernon and act as hostess when visitors came during the proprietors' absence, was less reliable. Following a discovery the President had made on a visit home, Martha reproached her niece in November: 'it never was his intention to give wine or go to any expense to entertain people that came to Mount Vernon out of curiosity . . . rum may always be had'.³⁰ Though the Washingtons did not attend either wedding, the marriages of Fanny and of Patsy in the autumn of 1794 and winter of 1795 were at least occasions for pleasant sentiments to be expressed in correspondence with the bridal couples.

When Betsy Parke Custis came to stay again in the spring of 1795, her grandmother was disconcerted to find her, as she wrote to Fanny, 'very grave. I was in hope that being in the gay world would have a good effect on her, but she seems to wish to be at home.' While her younger sister Nelly and her grandmother went to the assembly, she stayed at home. Church every Sunday – a very social affair in Philadelphia – 'she thinks too fatiguing', Martha reported to Fanny Washington in Alexandria. She concluded: 'the girls have lived so long in solitude that they do not know how to get the better of it'.[31]

Nelly, more sociable than her elder sister, when on visits to her mother at Hope Park, pined for her 'beloved grandmamma' and for her life in Philadelphia.[32] Now that Nelly was sixteen, her education was mostly musical, and included lessons from masters on the guitar and pianoforte – she became a proficient performer on both instruments. She and her friend, Elizabeth Bordley, were, in addition, taught to sing in Italian by impresario Filippo Trisobio.[33] There was good reason for Nelly to dislike dark, secluded Hope Park, overrun with younger half-siblings, and for her elder sisters to wish to find early on husbands and a home elsewhere. Their mother only gave birth to the last of thirteen Stuart children a year after Patsy was married. Their stepfather had withdrawn from the world in recent years, resigning his post as Commissioner to the Federal City. His stepdaughter Betsy was later to dub him a 'gloomy mortal'.[34]

From afar Martha fussed. When Nelly wrote of having toothache, she sent 'brushes and tooth powder', and advised: 'you should be very careful how you go out in the cold to keep your feet dry and take care of your teeth to clean them every day'.[35] Two weeks later, she reminded Nelly, still resident at Hope Park: 'it is necessary for you to be careful of your clothes and have them kept together and often look over them'.[36]

Wash Custis's visits to his mother at Hope Park proved still less satisfactory. Dr Stuart complained, in the autumn of 1794, of his stepson's ignorance. The boy was then thirteen and attending a college on Fourth Street. 'He attends as constant as the day comes,' wrote Martha defensively to Fanny in September, 'but he does not learn as much as he might, if the master took proper care to make the children

attentive to their books.' She wrote of the college: 'it is a very indifferent one for big boys; little ones are not attended to at all'.[37]

Washington had little time to attend to these domestic matters.
The British government had aroused the ire of its former subjects
when the Royal Navy seized more than 200 American ships, on
the ground that they were trading with the French West Indies. At
Washington's instigation John Jay, special envoy, successfully nego-
tiated in London in the course of 1794 a treaty to settle these and
other disputes outstanding from the war. When Jay returned home
with the treaty, however, in the summer of 1795, and when its terms
became known, he was reviled by merchants, landowners, munici-
palities and anti-federalists alike. They believed that the Jay Treaty, as
it became known, grossly favoured British interests. Washington and
Hamilton, closely associated with the negotiations, were also abused
as the Senate vote on the treaty neared. A steady stream of addresses
to the President from protesting bodies required response. To them
all he gave an identical reply: 'the constitution is the guide, which
I never will abandon. It has assigned to the President the power of
making treaties, with the advice and consent of the senate.'[38]

Washington's authority and Hamilton's influence secured the
required two-thirds majority needed in the Senate for the treaty. The
President, however, did not forget the attacks he had endured. On
leaving office two years later, he was to meditate including in his
farewell address to the Senate a protest against newspaper paragraphs
teeming with 'all the Invective that disappointment, ignorance of
facts, and malicious falsehoods could invent, to misrepresent my
politics and affections; to wound my reputation and feelings; and to
weaken, if not entirely destroy the confidence you had been pleased
to repose in me'.[39] Jefferson's private encouragement of the anti-federalist press was known to both Washingtons. Years later, Martha
had not forgiven him, and named him, to a federalist Reverend, 'one
of the most detestable of mankind'.[40]

Slowly as the benefits of the commercial treaty accrued, some
of Washington's popularity returned. But in Philadelphia the anti-
federalist newspapers remained on the attack. In March 1796 Vice
President John Adams wrote: 'the Turpitude of the [American]

Jacobins touches him more nearly than he owns in Words. All the studied Efforts of the Feds, to counterbalance Abuses by Compliments don't answer the End.'⁴¹ Days earlier 1,000 people had gathered to celebrate Washington's birthday at a ball 'in a vast Room a Circle of 80 feet Diameter'.⁴² A few months later Jefferson, referring to 'the colossus of the President's merits with the people', predicted that his successor, 'if a monocrat', would be 'overborne by the republican sense of his constituents'.⁴³ The kingly trappings that had accreted to the office, while the 'colossus' occupied it, would prove hard to dislodge. But it would be for others to participate in that struggle. In the last year of office, the Washingtons were already preparing for retirement.

John Adams, dining with the Washingtons in February 1796, heard that Betsy Custis was to marry an 'English East India Nabob' and settle in the Federal City. The bride's grandmother, Martha, was 'as gay as a Girl', the Vice President wrote to his wife, 'and tells the story in a very humerous stile. Mr Law says he is only 35 Years of Age and altho the Climate of India has given him an older look Yet his Constitution is not impaired beyond his Years. He has asked Leave and a Blessing of The President and Mrs W. He is to finish a House in the Federal City and live there. He has two' – actually three – 'Children born in India: but of whom is not explained.' Adams added: 'Nelly is with her sister Patcy at Georgetown – married to Mr Peters [Peter], son of a Maryland Nabob. Thus you see that Fortune is the Object in our Country not Family. No, that would be Aristocratical.'⁴⁴

To Law, a bishop's son and an East India Company man for the last twenty years, an alliance with the President's granddaughter and purchase of land in the Federal City no doubt seemed promising investments. But Washington had originally discouraged the match, when Betsy – now, by Thomas's wish, called Eliza – and her husband-to-be wrote with news of their forthcoming nuptials. 'No intimation of this event', Washington responded to Law on 10 February, 'from any quarter, having been communicated to us before, it may well be supposed that it was a matter of Surprize . . .' He hoped, 'as the young lady is in her non-age [a minor], that preliminary measures' – a settlement on Eliza – 'has been, or will be arranged with her Mother and Guardian, before the Nuptials are Solemnized'.[45]

Outwardly the principal occupants of the house on Market Street appeared little changed in the last year of his office from when they had first appeared in public as the President and his lady – he tall, dignified and courtly, she small, robust and lively. Age had not diminished their spirit. Martha, however, suffered more than ever from stomach and bilious complaints, and her small white teeth were no longer her own. Gilbert Stuart, who painted the couple in Washington's last year of office, defended himself against criticism of the President's grim mien: 'he had just had a set of false teeth inserted, which accounts for the constrained expression so noticeable about the mouth and lower part of the face'. He had consented to be painted on this occasion only to oblige his wife, who had seen him painted for others so often, and now wanted a souvenir for herself. Martha was not to have her prize. Stuart never finished the portraits, and kept them in his studio, using that of the President as a model for many copies that he worked up and sold.

Though Washington's habitual reserve was both lauded and castigated, Stuart affected to observe 'a man of terrible passions'. He told his friend John Neal: 'the sockets of his eyes; the breadth of his nose and nostrils; the deep broad expression of strength and solemnity upon his forehead, were all a proof of this'.[46] Washington's anger did erupt at moments of frustration during the war and, according to Jefferson, at least once during Cabinet. His friendship for Mrs Powel, even during her widowhood, suggests that passion of another kind still stirred him. In a teasing and tantalizing letter of June 1796, she wrote: 'Feeling myself incapable of nourishing an implacable Resentment, and in conformity with your better and dispassionate Judgment I have, after maturely considering all that passed Yesterday, determined to dine with you Tomorrow, when I will endeavour to meet your Ideas with Fortitude.'[47] Washington's other correspondence sheds no light on 'all that passed yesterday', but it may have been a clash of political views.

While at Mount Vernon this summer, the Washingtons were busy preparing to make it their permanent residence the following year.

They were missing one member of the household whom Martha deemed crucial to her happiness. Just before they left Philadelphia, Oney Judge, the house slave who served as one of Martha's maids, had run away. Forty years later, Oney was to give this account of the day she sought her freedom: 'Whilst they were packing up to go to Virginia, I was packing to go, I didn't know where; for I knew that if I went back to Virginia, I should never get my liberty. I had friends among the colored people of Philadelphia, had my things carried there beforehand, and left Washington's house while they were eating dinner.' Oney seems to have feared, too, that she would be given as a 'wedding present' to Eliza Law. Her sister, Delphy, passed into Mrs Law's keeping.

There were sightings of Oney in New York before she was firmly located in the autumn in Portsmouth, New Hampshire. Conversations were held with her there, as she seemed wishful to return to her native Virginia.[48] Washington himself, on 28 November, gave this account: 'there is no doubt in this family, of her having been seduced and enticed off by a Frenchman, who was either really, or pretendedly deranged; and under that guize, used frequently to introduce himself into the family'. The President heard that the Frenchman had subsequently tired of her, and that she had 'betaken herself to the Needle – the use of which she well understood – for a livelihood'.

Just before yellow fever afflicted Philadelphia in 1793, Washington had signed into law the Fugitive Slave Act, which empowered a slave owner or his agent to arrest any slave who had fled into another state. It was the duty of a local judge or magistrate, upon production of satisfactory proof of ownership, to give a warrant for the slave's removal from the state. Children born of slave mothers were classed as slaves themselves. Accordingly, this Act and the fear of arrest extended unto succeeding generations. In this case Washington wished Joseph Whipple, the Collector of Customs in Portsmouth, to proceed cautiously. If possible, he should make no arrest. A Gradual Abolition Law had been passed in New Hampshire. The citizenry, as well as the free black community among whom the girl was living, would undoubtedly react badly if she were taken by force.

A curious stand-off developed between master and fugitive slave. The President struggled to gratify his wife's wishes and square his own conscience. Oney, bartering for her freedom, offered the Portsmouth officials a compromise. She would return to Martha's side, if her manumission, following Washington's death and that of her mistress, was guaranteed. This, Washington refused as a matter of principle. 'However well-disposed I might be to a gradual abolition, or even to an entire emancipation of that description of People (if the latter was in itself practicable at this Moment),' he wrote, 'it would neither be politic or just, to reward unfaithfulness with a premature preference.' It would breed discontent in her fellow servants' minds. If she returned voluntarily, he suggested, 'her late conduct will be forgiven by her Mistress'.

At first Oney said she would return. Then, no doubt advised by her friends, she changed her mind. Fear of obloquy deterred Whipple from dispatching her, unwilling, to Virginia. Still at large in January 1797, she married seaman Black Jack Staines and was soon with child. That child, of course, like Oney herself, was liable to arrest and dispatch to Mount Vernon, should Washington decide at any time to employ what he termed, in November 1796, 'violent measures'.[49] Martha must take another maid.

There were other losses threatening a peaceful retirement. Martha's niece, Fanny, had died this spring of the same tuberculosis that had afflicted her first husband, George Augustine. The mistress of Mount Vernon must look to Nelly to aid her in household management. Pearce, moreover, an effective farm manager, was too ill from a rheumatic complaint to continue long in his post. James Anderson, who would succeed him in January 1797, was to prove to have little experience of managing a slave workforce.

Martha's granddaughter Eliza was delighted with her new position in the Federal City as Mrs Thomas Law, and was soon expecting a child. With Nelly at home and the Laws and Peters in the Federal City, only Wash Custis would be far off when George and Martha retired to Mount Vernon in March 1797. In the autumn of 1796 he was installed in Nassau Hall, the university in Princeton. The President had been alarmed by some of the company his ward was keeping while at school in Philadelphia. Under no illusions about the young man's habits, he opined that Custis would least like having to rise an hour before daybreak to begin his studies.

In November John Adams, federalist, was elected President and Jefferson, anti-federalist, Vice President. On 22 February 1797, for the last time during the Washingtons' residence in Philadelphia, society thronged the rooms of the Market Street house, for 'birthday' celebrations. Martha received the ladies above. Washington, the order of the Cincinnati on his chest, welcomed those – Knox, Hamilton and others – similarly bedecked, and, among the members of his Cabinet, foreign ministers, senators, congressmen and businessmen, the friends with whom he and Martha had dined and visited these years he was in office.

Arrangements and preparations and farewells now filled the Washingtons' days. Lear was overseeing the packing up of the house as he had seen to the installation there of the Washingtons' belongings. Mrs Powel offered to buy from the President his carriage horses on her nephew's account: 'If my dear Sir it will be any accommodation to you to anticipate the payment for the Horses, intimate it to me, it will at any Moment be perfectly convenient to me to draw a Check on the Bank for the Amount.' As she did not speculate, she wrote, she was 'always in Cash'.[50] After his departure for Virginia, Washington instructed Lear to send Mrs Powel, as a gift, two mirrors, lamps and brackets. She was warm in her thanks: 'From you they are acceptable tho from no other Being out of my own Family would I receive a pecuniary Favor, nor did I want any inanimate Memento to bring you to my Recollection.' She begged only her 'best wishes to Mrs Washington and Miss Custis'.[51]

Days before he and Martha departed for Virginia, the President was to tell Mrs Liston, wife of the British Minister, he was 'like a Child within view of the Holydays, I have counted the months, then the weeks, & I now reckon the days previous to my release'.[52] On the eve of John Adams's inauguration, a large company, including the President-elect and his wife, dined at Market Street. Conversation stopped when Washington rose and filled his glass: 'Ladies and gentlemen, this is the last time I shall drink your health as a public man. I do it with sincerity, and wishing you all possible happiness.'[53]

Now it was for the Adamses to rent and inhabit the Market Street house. Mrs Adams wrote to a government wife in February in preparation: 'I will thank you if you can inform me what Number of domesticks the President's Household consisted of, how many female Servants? I can carry four from hence.' She added: 'To be the Successor of Mrs Washington and to make good her place will be an arduous task.'[54] On the 9th of the month she wrote to Martha herself, asking for guidance: 'the Tongue of Slander, the pen of Calumny, nor the bitterness of envy have never once to my knowledge assailed any part of your conduct . . . I will endeavour to follow your steps and by that means hope I shall not essentially fall short of my amiable exemplar . . .' Abigail was anxious to learn the 'Rules' which Mrs Washington had instituted and followed: 'as it respected receiving & returning visits, both to Strangers and citizens as it respected invitations of a publick or private nature'. She paid due tribute to her correspondent's 'experience and knowledge of persons and Characters'.[55]

Martha responded on the 20th: 'I never dined nor supped out, except once with the Vice President, once with each of the governors of the state where we have resided – and (very rarely) at the dancing assemblies.'[56] She was content to withdraw from public scrutiny. 'The curtain is falling,' wrote that most undramatic of women to Caty Greene – now Mrs Phineas Miller – in Georgia, and she looked forward to a 'more tranquil theater'.[57]

Retirement, 1797–1798

Rooms to Paint – Paper – Whitewash &ca &ca . . .

Washington celebrated the resumption of private life in Virginia to which he had so long looked forward with an economical diary entry for 16 March 1797: 'At home all day alone. Wind at East & very cloudy all day.'[1] On their way from Philadelphia to Mount Vernon he and Martha and Nelly had dined with the Laws in their house near the Capitol, and lodged with the Peters in Georgetown on their way home. Martha was not often again to visit the Federal City, now known also as the 'city of Washington'. Her husband was to lodge alternately with the Laws and Peters when inspecting lots at either end of the city that he had bought four years earlier. The progress of the public buildings, too, was to attract his attention.

At first, both Washingtons stayed close to home. A change in the weather a few days after their arrival at Mount Vernon caused Nelly to write to her friend Elizabeth Bordley in Philadelphia: 'this has been a charming morning – and everything appears to be revived. The grass begins to look green. Some trees are in blossom, others budding. The flowers are coming out – and the numerous different birds keep up a constant serenading.'[2] The inhabitants of the house included the Marquis de Lafayette's son, and his tutor. The arrival of this young namesake, George Washington Motier Lafayette, in America two years earlier had not been without embarrassment for the President. The boy's father had been denounced in France as a traitor to the revolution and by the allied powers as a traitor to the defunct King whom he had once served. After he fled France in 1792, Lafayette was captured by Austrian forces and imprisoned in a series of jails. Washington had won the approval of Congress, before he issued an invitation to George and his tutor to reside at the Presidential mansion. They continued the Washingtons' guests at Mount Vernon.

George and Martha had at first little opportunity to appreciate the natural beauty of their home, and the General, little time to attend to his farms. There were still matters arising from their leave-taking of the house on Market Street. Washington's ardent admirer, Mrs Powel, had bought the writing desk he had used as President. She wrote in mid-March: 'Suppose I should prove incontestably that you have without Design put into my Possession the love Letters of a Lady addressed to you under the most solemn Sanction; & a large Packet too.' After some raillery, she had pity on him: 'to keep you no longer in Suspense, tho' I know that your Nerves are not as irritable as a fine Ladies, yet I will with the Generosity of my Sex relieve you, by telling you – that upon opening one of the Drawers of your writing Desk I found a large Bundle of Letters from Mrs Washington bound up and labled with your usual Accuracy.'³ Washington denied in answer that he had any 'love letters' to lose. He was, however, discomfited by his error in not having emptied the drawers, and thanked Mrs Powel for her 'delicacy' in ensuring he received the letters safely and unread by others. Had they fallen into 'more inquisitive hands', he asserted, the correspondence would have been found to be 'more fraught with expressions of friendship, than of *enamoured* love'. So as to confer 'warmth, which was not *inherent*', on the correspondence, an illicit reader with ideas 'of the *Romantic order*', he wrote with ponderous humour, might have committed the letters to the flames.⁴

The Washingtons had left behind the 'furniture of the Green Drawing Room' – scene of so many successful receptions – as well as their splendid town coach, in hopes that Adams would decide to acquire them.⁵ Mrs Powel had written to Washington in February: 'if Mr Adams lays the same stress on the association of Ideas that I do, both with respect to our Pleasures, and our Consequence, I think he will gladly become the Purchaser of not only your Coach, but of every Article that the World have been accustomed to see you make use of; and that you are disposed to part with'.[6] John and Abigail Adams had other ideas. Furniture and vehicle were, in consequence, put up for sale, with the pictures that had adorned the public rooms – 'fancy pieces of my own chusing', Washington told Mary White Morris in May, and no longer required.[7] To the disappointment of auction-goers, Washington reserved for their home in Virginia what Lear termed in March 'the Paintings, Prints &c'. – images of the President.[8]

Washington listed to Mrs Powel, on 26 March, 'Rooms to Paint – Paper – Whitewash &ca &ca – But although these things are troublesome, & disagreeable as they will involve us in a good deal of litter & dirt, yet they will serve to give exercise both to the mind & body.'[9] Three months later Martha confessed to David Humphreys that they were still 'more beginners than old established residents'. They had, she wrote, found 'everything in a deranged [condition] and all the buildings in a decaying state'.[10] Among other defects in the mansion house, the Washingtons found the fireplace in the parlour all but out of its moorings and the house steps worn down. Problems continued to present themselves. A chance discovery that a girder underpinning the floor of the New Room was 'much decayed' averted disaster. Washington told Bartholomew Dandridge in December that, had action not been taken to make it good, 'a company only moderately large would have sunk altogether into the Cellar'.[11]

Rooms, once painted, were readied to receive furniture sent by water from Philadelphia. Lear supervised the loading aboard the sloop *Salem* in March of 'ninety seven boxes; fourteen trunks; forty three Casks; thirteen packages; three hampers', besides seven band-boxes, bedsteads, a bidet, 'one Tin shower bath', kitchen equipment and much else.[12] In due course this freight was unpacked and installed or stored at Mount Vernon. Places were found for the Sèvres, and the Cincinnati china was put away, as well as a new service known as the 'States china'. Each piece was inscribed with the names of the American states and featured Martha's initials. A Dutch merchant had commissioned the service in Canton, and recently presented the set to Martha.

The Washingtons entertained continually, despite the inconvenience of having workmen in the house. Unfortunately a man hired in Philadelphia to perform the duties of steward proved more hindrance than help. Martha wrote, in May, to Mrs Powel: 'he knows nothing of cooking, arranging a table, or servants, nor will he assume any authority over them'.[13] Efforts by Mrs Powel to secure a better candidate were not successful, nor were those of friends and relations nearer to hand. In August, Martha told her sister Betsy Aylett Henley, she was still being obliged to be her own housekeeper: 'which takes up the greatest part of my time'.[14]

Nelly Parke Custis wrote to Miss Bordley in Philadelphia, immediately after their arrival home in March, that she was 'deputy housekeeper, in which employment I expect to improve much, as I am very partial to it'. However, Nelly did not take her duties too seriously. Once her harpsichord arrived, she told her friend in Philadelphia, she meant to practise a great deal and make 'my Sister' – Eliza Law and Ann Stuart both had trained voices – 'sing your parts of our Duetts'.[15] Only in December did the advent of a satisfactory employee, Mrs Eleanor Forbes, release Martha from what her husband had earlier termed 'the drudgery of ordering & seeing the Table properly covered – & things œconomically used'.[16]

The Washingtons were as much at a loss for a cook as a housekeeper. 'Altogether', Martha, usually resilient, told her sister, 'I am sadly plagued.'[17] While they were still on their journey home from Philadelphia in March, Hercules, who had been left at Mount Vernon the previous December, had run away. Both George and Martha strongly suspected he was living among the free black community in Philadelphia, and over subsequent months made efforts to recover him, to no avail.[18] Washington feared that to supply a cook he would have to break his resolve 'never to become the master of another Slave by *purchase*'. He told his nephew George Lewis in November, 'I have endeavoured to hire, black or white, but am not yet supplied.'[19] In the meantime, Nathan and other house slaves performed cooking duties.

Now that she was returned home for good, Martha took stock of the neighbourhood. She told Humphreys in June: 'Our circle of *friends* is of course contracted without any disposition on our part to enter into *new friendships*, though we have an abundance of acquaintances and a variety of visitors.'[20] A year later she was to hunger after old friends, writing to Sally Fairfax in England: 'It is amongst my greatest regrets now that I am again fixed (I hope for life) at this place, at not having you for a neighbour and companion.' She had not felt this loss so acutely, she added, employing a homely metaphor, 'while I was a kind of perambulator [traveller]'. Now many of their friends from before the war were dead. Lund Washington had left his wife a widow at Hayfield the previous year. Martha added, 'our visitors on the Maryland side are gone, and going likewise'.[21]

Washington, in September 1797, refused an invitation to a family wedding party in another part of the state that, in former times, he and Martha might once have accepted. 'Wedding assemblies are better calculated for those who are *coming in* to than to those who are *going out* of life', he told his nephew, the bridegroom. 'You must accept the good wishes of your Aunt and myself in place of personal attendance, for I think it not likely that either of us will ever be more than 25 miles from Mount Vernon again, while we are inhabitants of this Terrestrial Globe.'[22]

The Washingtons were generous in their welcome to younger generations of neighbours. But George, in particular, found the demands of this hospitality great, and the rewards scanty. His widowed sister Betty Lewis had recently died and he put this proposition to her son Lawrence in August, that he should come to live at Mount Vernon: 'to ease me of the trouble of entertaining company; particularly of Nights'. Washington wanted to escape, either to his study or to bed, soon after tea had been drunk and the candles lit. If Lewis would remain host after the master and mistress had retired, his uncle wrote, 'it would render him a very acceptable Service'.[23]

Lawrence Lewis accepted the position as one, though without salary, with prospects. He had inherited a farm in Frederick County at his father Fielding's death in 1781, and could at least usefully learn from his uncle how best to manage it. The fortunes of his family had declined. Soon after his mother Betty's death, Millbrook, the fine hours in Fredericksburg where the Washingtons had often stayed, was sold to pay off debts. Lawrence proved a satisfactory secretary to his uncle George and a dutiful surrogate host. Nelly Parke Custis, deputing for her grandmother, brought a vivacity and charm to the task of entertaining visitors that Lewis lacked. She was now, at eighteen, much admired. Benjamin Latrobe, a visiting artist, wrote of her 'perfection of form, of expression, of colour, of softness'. He marked, too, her 'firmness of mind'.[24]

A year hence, a Polish nobleman, Julian Ursyn Niemcewicz, visiting Mount Vernon, was to encounter, besides Lewis, George de Lafayette, whom Nelly termed her *young adopted brother*'.[25] But the foreigner's eyes were all for Nelly: 'one of those celestial figures that nature produces only rarely, that the inspiration of painters has sometimes divined and that one cannot see without ecstasy'. He recorded: 'she plays the harpsichord, sings, [and] draws better than any woman in America or even in Europe'.[26] Her Philadelphia masters would have been pleased to hear it.

Nelly turned heads in Alexandria when she visited girlhood friends. While she stayed with her sister Patty Peter in Georgetown, she partnered a young man, Charles Carroll, for six dances at a ball held at the Union Tavern. But, she told Miss Bordley in Philadelphia, it was the custom at Virginia and Maryland assemblies to have one partner all evening. 'When I *have* anything to impart, I shall rely upon your secrecy.'[27] She wrote again, aggrieved by 'meddling *reporters*' who were 'perpetually *engaging her to those whom she never had a chance of marrying* and *never wished* to be united to'. She referred to George de Lafayette. Until she met a man she could love '*with all my heart* – that is, *not romantically,* but *esteem & prefer him before all others*', she would remain '*E P Custis*'. Should she never meet such a paragon, she was content to stay '*spinster for life*'.[28] Gossips would soon cease to link her name with Lafayette's son. Under the terms of the Treaty of Campo Formio, the Marquis was released from prison. The young man left America and joined his parents and sisters in Europe.

When the Listons from Philadelphia visited Mount Vernon in the late autumn of 1797, the Minister's wife pressed Nelly to spend a few weeks with them in Philadelphia, where her former friends – and beaux – abounded. But Miss Custis declined the opportunity. 'I have not spent a winter here for eight years,' she explained. She wrote of 'the winter weather, the trees, grass, houses, etc. all covered with ice. The appearance is beautiful and the river looks so wide and desolate – the Maryland shore so bleak and sublimely horrifying that I am quite delighted.' These romantic pleasures aside, she wrote, 'I could not leave my Beloved Grandmama so lonesome . . .'[29] She stayed on at Mount Vernon, apparently happy to read a nightly chapter and psalm to her grandmother rather than enjoy a greater world.

Washington Custis was, with Lawrence Lewis, newly of the household and supposedly studying at home. Faculty records show that, on 7 September 1797, the young man was suspended from Princeton 'for various acts of meanness and irregularity'.[30] In early October he reached Mount Vernon. There was apparently no question of his return to the college. Washington wrote to its President on 9 October, regretting his ward's 'conduct and behaviour' and requesting a tally of accounts to pay.[31] The shameful secret was kept from Martha and from Wash's mother, Nelly.

Thereafter the General was driven distracted by Washington Custis's unsystematic mode of life, as a series of injunctions he laid down on 7 January 1798 shows. Hours spent studying between breakfast and dinner, 'instead of running up & down stairs, & wasted in conversation with any one who will talk with you', would enable the young man to advance in his studies. Moreover, Wash was to be 'in place' at the usual breakfasting, dining and tea hours. 'It is not only disagreeable, but it is also very inconvenient, for servants to be running here, & there, and they know not where, to summon you to them.'[32] A bare two weeks later Washington wrote to inform the boy's stepfather that another solution must be found. It was, in his view, impossible to make him 'attend to his books' at home, 'without an able Preceptor, always with him'.

After much consultation between Hope Park and Mount Vernon, Dr Stuart inscribed his stepson in March in the college of St John in Annapolis. Washington would have liked to send Wash off to

Harvard, but considered in January that Martha would find the distance 'too heartrending'.³³ The boy was enjoined to write home once a fortnight. In mid-June Washington rebuked him for failing to do so, 'knowing (as you must do) how apt your Grandmamma is to suspect that you are sick, or some accident has happened to you, when you omit this'.³⁴ A previous letter Wash wrote in April, remarking on Charles Carroll's pursuit of his sister, earned this rebuke: 'Young Mr C came . . . to dinner, and left us next morning after breakfast. If his object was such as you say has been reported, it was not declared here . . . the less is said upon the subject, particularly by your sister's friends, the more prudent it will be . . .'³⁵

Nelly herself wrote in May to Miss Bordley to deny that Mr Carroll had ever told her of any attachment 'by *tongue* or *pen*'. If this was a disappointment, she had much to tell her friend. Of one 'charming dance' in Alexandria in February she wrote: 'I danced twenty-four dances, sets, cotillions, reels, etc, sung twelve songs, and at five [in the morning] went to *roost*; got up at seven.' Visits to 'Sister Law' and 'Sister Peter' in the city furnished other material for comment. The latter now had a second child, she informed her friend, named Columbia Washington – 'after the City, and District of Columbia. It is one of my sister's and my choosing,' she wrote, 'and I am to be her godmother.' Old friends in Philadelphia also occupied her. Robert Morris, who had financed the Revolutionary army, had over-invested in the Federal City, was bankrupt, and would soon enter a debtors' prison. The afflictions of his family perturbed Nelly, as they weighed on her grandmother and the General. '*Innate worth* is not diminished by loss of *wealth*,' she wrote.³⁶

New rebuke fell on Wash Custis. Washington wrote to the graceless scholar in June : 'we have, with much surprise, been informed of your devoting much time, to paying particular attentions to a certain young lady of that place!'³⁷ Custis allowed that he had informed a Miss Jennings – daughter of an Annapolis merchant – of his affections and of his prospects. He had begged her to wait till he was of age, in the hope that he could 'bring about a union at some future day'. Custis wrote stiffly: 'The conditions were not accepted.' He had the good sense, on 17 June, to allege his youth as 'an obstacle to the consummation of my wishes at the present time (which was farthest from my thoughts)'.[38]

The Washingtons were not entirely reassured. The General was displeased by Custis asking for more funds. He hoped that his ward had not indulged a taste for 'fanciful dresses, or misspent time in company – perhaps in taverns'. Custis also enquired whether his education was complete, following a course of Euclid. This question, wrote Washington on 24 July, 'really astonishes me! For it would seem as if *nothing* I could say to you made more than a *momentary* impression.'[39] The boy, in short, was to continue studies at the college.

Washington had other anxieties besides the conduct of his reprobate ward. Though he paid no visits to Philadelphia, James McHenry, now Secretary of War, was one of many who had written to him to outline the growing hostility between the American government and the French republic. The French Directory, now the revolutionary government in power, objected to the Jay Treaty between Britain and America, and had refused, in December 1796, to accept the credentials of the new American ambassador in Paris. Anti-French feeling among federalists in Philadelphia built further when French privateers seized American ships trading with Britain. Adams, in his annual address to Congress in the winter of 1797, spoke of French intransigence and aggression and of the need to place his country 'in a suitable posture of defence'.[40] War between the two former allies seemed possible.

Now, in June 1798, Adams wrote to Washington: 'In forming an Army, whenever I must come to that Extremity, I am at an immense Loss whether to call out all the old Generals or to appoint a young sett . . . I must tap you, Sometimes for Advice. We must have your Name, if you, in any case will permit Us to Use it. There will be more efficacy in it, than in many an Army.'[41] Washington had not served the country in a military capacity for fifteen years and was now sixty-six. He responded, on 4 July, 'it will not be an easy matter, I conceive, to find among the *old set* of Generals, men of sufficient activity, energy & health, and of sound politics, to train troops to the *quick step*, long Marches, & severe conflicts they may have to encounter'. He suggested, rather, looking to younger officers who had proved themselves in the revolutionary conflict.[42]

Experienced officers of the late war still in government – McHenry, Timothy Pickering, Secretary of State, and others – feared the worst. France and Spain had allied in 1796. With friendly Spanish bases in the southern territories of the American continent to supply its needs, the hostile French republic might successfully send an army north to combat the United States. In this heightened state of alarm numerous volunteer corps formed. Washington, Dr Craik and others in Alexandria established a home guard, composed of citizens over forty-five and so exempt from militia service. It went by the name of the 'Greyheads', or 'Silver Greys'. Martha later in the year was to present to the regiment its colours. A company of volunteer dragoons was similarly honoured by Nelly.[43] Meanwhile on the Fourth of July a 'large company of the civil and military of Fairfax company' dined at Spring Gardens outside Alexandria. The General, wearing 'full uniform', reviewed the different corps as they paraded and manoeuvred, before all attended a service in Christchurch, where the Reverend Davis officiated.[44]

Five days later, in Philadelphia, Congress, having previously rescinded treaties with France on 6 July, authorized attacks on French warships. At sea America was at war with its former ally. McHenry sent to Washington, with a few perfunctory lines, a newspaper announcement. By Act of Congress, the General was once more appointed Commander-in-Chief of the United States army. It stood, since a reorganization two years earlier, at 3,000 men. The very first intimation he had had, Washington later told Knox, 'that such a measure was in contemplation, was contained in a News-paper, as a *complete Act* of the President & Senate'. He was magnanimous: 'if affairs were in the alarming state they are represented to be . . . it was not a time to complain, or stand upon punctilios'.[45]

McHenry himself arrived, bearing the General's commission as Commander-in-Chief. He had with him also, for Washington's perusal, a '*pending* Bill for augmenting the Army of the U. States'. Washington's immediate response was to urge delay in passing this hasty Bill. Nevertheless, on 16 July Congress authorized the establishment of a provisional army, to be called up only in case of need. Twelve new infantry regiments and six troops of light dragoons were provided for. The 'American Cincinnatus', though he accepted the military post thrust upon him, exacted this condition. Except for such time as he should spend in Philadelphia making appointments in these regiments, he would remain at home until the opening of hostilities. Martha and he must hope that the French, for want of money, and believing the United States well armed, would not venture an attack.

Understanding that Congress wished Hamilton – no longer Secretary of the Treasury – to serve as Inspector General, the Commander-in-Chief offered the next senior command to Thomas Pinckney, lately minister in London. To his former right-hand man, Henry Knox, he offered the junior command of the three. Washington opined to Hamilton on 14 June, 'if the French should be so mad as to Invade this Country in expectation of making a serious impression . . . their operations will commence in the States South of Maryland'. In that event 'the services and influence' of southerner Pinckney would be crucial.[46]

Knox, offended and wounded, protested to his former commanding officer at the end of July. But Washington, as ever, was firm where he saw his duty to the country. Knox declined to serve, but the appointments of Pinckney and Hamilton were confirmed. While the summer tide of visitors and family ebbed and flowed at Mount Vernon, Washington compiled lists of those officers who had served in the late war and might serve again. He sifted the letters of those who recommended sons, relatives and young men of their acquaintance. He and Martha remained uneasy about her grandson.

Duly admonished, Custis had left his belongings behind at college when he came home for the summer holidays. But, the General wrote to Dr Stuart in August, the young man appeared 'to be moped & Stupid, says nothing – and is always in some hole or corner excluded from Company'.[47] The Stuarts and Washingtons came to suspect that Wash still hankered after Miss Hodgson. Nelly Stuart, who had personal experience of an impetuous Parke Custis pressing his suit, was particularly anxious that her son should not return to Annapolis.

With reluctance, in September, Washington addressed the President of St John's College in a letter that the young man delivered at Annapolis. The boy returned only to 'pack up for good', the General wrote.[48] By the late autumn, after Lear had attempted to tutor his former pupil at home, the General had 'a thorough conviction that it was a vain attempt to keep Washington Custis to any literary pursuits, either in a public Seminary, or at home under the direction of any one'.[49] He took Lear with him to Philadelphia to act as his secretary. Wash, at age seventeen, was free to chat away the day and roam all hours with his gun.

In Philadelphia, where he had formerly lived in splendour, Washington took lodgings in November in a boarding house on 8th Street. He wrote from there to Lawrence Lewis from Philadelphia two weeks after his arrival, on 2 December: 'Making a selection of Officers for the twelve new Regiments . . . is a work of infinite more difficulty than I had any conception of . . . When this will be accomplished I am not yet able to say.' They were not to rise from their work until 13 December, having been a full month at it. The Commander-in-Chief wrote of having little respite from his labours: 'In order to bring it to an end we sit from ten o'clock until after three – & from Seven in the evening until past nine.'[50] He dined abroad with friends in the interval between the daily and evening sessions, and took tea elsewhere afterwards. He dined too, on one occasion, with Robert Morris in the debtors' prison on Prune Street. Adams and others in government were also his hosts.[51]

Washington wrote to Mrs Powel on 17 November, a week after he had arrived in the city: 'I am to dine this day at Mr Willing's' – Thomas Willing, her brother – 'and if you are disengaged, will have the honor of drinking Tea with you in Third Street, afterwards.'[52] He proposed himself, on 1 December, as her breakfast guest the following day, a Sunday.[53] No record of either tea or breakfast appears in his diary, but the General and the lady were in constant communication in these early days of December, as his business wound to a close. She hoped, on the 3rd, that he was none the worse for his 'wet Sunday walk' of the day before.[54] On the 4th he acknowledged her 'kind, and obliging offer to choose some thing handsome, with which to present Miss Custis'. She had suggested a muff. He thought Nelly was already provided with one: 'of a tippet I am not so certain; but a handsome Muslin, or any thing else, that is not the whim of the day, cannot be amiss'. He asked her also: 'Is there any thing – not of much cost – I could carry Mrs Washington as a memento that she has not been forgotten, in this City?'⁵⁵

Mrs Powel duly supplied a piece of muslin for sixty-five dollars, a thread case at seven, and also dolls, for Martha's great-granddaughters. On 7 December, having named the total sum of her expenditure as seventy-four dollars, Mrs Powel wrote additionally: 'My Heart is so sincerely afflicted and my Ideas so confused that I can only express my predominant Wish – that God may take you into his holy keeping and preserve you safe both in Traveling and under all Circumstances, and that you may be happy here and hereafter is the ardent Prayer of Your affectionate afflicted Friend.'⁵⁶

What prompted this sophisticated woman to tell of a 'sincerely afflicted' heart and of 'confused' ideas? Had she or Washington or both declared or acted on a feeling for the other that was forbidden, given his marriage to Martha? Had she misunderstood the nature of the friendship that brought Washington to her door to breakfast and take tea? In response to this effusion Washington wrote unexceptionably: 'For your kind and affectionate wishes, I feel a grateful sensibility, and reciprocate them with all the cordiality you could wish, being My dear Madam Your most Obedt & obliged Hble Servant.'⁵⁷

Mrs Powel wrote, next day, to ask Washington to dine on the 9th. He declined courteously: 'I feel much obliged by your kind & polite invitation to dine with you to day, but am under the necessity of denying myself that pleasure.' He had 'requested Generals Hamilton & Pinckney to come prepared this morning, at their usual hour – ten O'clock – for the whole day; that a few moments for dinner *only* might interrupt our daily labour'.⁵⁸ Washington departed south for Mount Vernon, with the purchases Mrs Powel had made for him, without seeing her again, nor did they resume a correspondence.

While in Philadelphia, it had occurred to the Commander-in-Chief that a place might be found, subject to his mother's and grandmother's approval, for Washington Custis in a regiment. 'The only hesitation I had, to induce the caution before mentioned', he later wrote to Dr Stuart, 'arose from his being an only Son; indeed the only male of his Great great Grandfathers family.' It had been decided that Lawrence Lewis was to captain a regiment of light dragoons, and Custis's name was provisionally inscribed in this corps as a cornet of horse. Lear, who had not understood that the appointment was conditional on others' approval, wrote to seek the young man's own consent. Washington Custis was 'highly delighted'. Martha, who may have believed, with her husband, that a French invasion was unlikely, raised no objection, nor did Custis's mother. Washington wrote wryly to Stuart on 30 December: 'At least it might serve to divert his attention from a Matrimonial pursuit (for a while at least) to which his constitution seems to be too prone.'[59]

Washington Custis was zealous in his wish to assume the trappings of an officer, including a sword, 'silver mounted'. 'Daily, fruitless enquiries are made of me to know when they may be expected,' Washington told McHenry the following summer. 'If you were to jog Mr [Tench] Francis, the *Purveyor* [of Public Supplies], the sooner they might be *Purveyed*, and the young Gentleman gratified. I wish them to be handsome, and proper for an Officer, but not expensive.'[60]

One of the Mount Vernon household declined, however, an appointment for which he had previously been eager. Washington informed McHenry in February 1799, that during the previous autumn, while he was in Philadelphia, Lewis had been making 'overtures of marriage to Miss Custis'. These overtures had made no apparent impression, until Nelly learned that her beau was about to serve as a Captain in the Regiment of Light Dragoons, and 'try his fortune in the Camp of Mars'. This, Washington wrote, 'brought into activity those affections for him, which *before* she conceived were the result of friendship *only*'.[61] Their betrothal followed, while Washington was still in Philadelphia, Nelly imposing the condition that Lawrence was to 'relinquish the field of Mars for the Sports of Venus'. Washington had been so eager to divert Wash Custis from matrimonial adventures, he confessed to Martha's nephew, Bartholomew Dandridge, that he had had no suspicion that the boy's sister was romancing.[62] He and Martha, however, welcomed a match for Nelly that kept her for the moment at Mount Vernon, while Lewis remained in his uncle's employ.

29

The Death of a President, 1799

I die hard; but I am not afraid to go.

Aged nearly twenty, Nelly was in high spirits when she wrote on 3 February 1799 to her friend Miss Bordley. 'Cupid, a small mischievous Urchin', she declared, had taken her by surprise, just when she had resolved to pass through life a *'prim starched Spinster'*. She wrote of colourless Lawrence Lewis as 'universally esteemed'. Her happiness was only clouded when she thought of leaving her 'Beloved Grandparents . . . and this dear spot – which has been my constant *Home*, since my first remembrance . . .'[1] Those grandparents may have thought lovely Nelly thrown away on a man whose only asset was a farm he had inherited in distant Frederick County. Lewis's decision not to serve in the dragoons after all may not have endeared him to his uncle. But family feeling was strong in them both. Washington wrote to his nephew on 23 January: 'I presume, if your health is restored, there will be no impediment to your Union.' Two days before writing, the General had served as Nelly's guardian in Alexandria, so that she could obtain a licence for the nuptials.[2]

Lawrence's health held. At Nelly's wish, they were wed on the General's birthday. Washington marked in his diary: 'The Revd. Mr Davis & Mr Geo. Calvert came to dinner' – one of Nelly's uncles – '& Miss Custis was married abt. Candle light [at dusk] to Mr Lawe Lewis.'[3] A 'routine of ceremonious dinners, parties, visits; some agreeable, others tiresome', which Nelly described to

Miss Bordley, followed the wedding.⁴ Joshua Brookes, a young English visitor who dined at Mount Vernon during this time of festivity, found the Washingtons their usual, hospitable selves. Martha, who sat with him half an hour, was as imperturbable as ever. Brookes noted that she wore a 'Mazarin blue satin gown with three belts over her handkerchief across the body', and her grey hair was combed straight under a loose cap. She asked for news, 'said she was no politician but liked to read the newspapers'. Her 'affability, free manner and mild, placid countenance', wrote Brookes, brought to mind his mother.⁵

When Nelly in the guise of Mrs Lawrence Lewis next wrote to Miss Bordley, in November of this year, she and her husband were back at Mount Vernon. They intended to spend the winter there, and she was expecting a child. They had embarked, in May, on a series of visits to different seats belonging to relations of Lawrence's. They had also visited the White House, in New Kent County – now the property of her brother – which Nelly had never seen. Lawrence, however, had suffered from ill health for much of the year. At Marmion, his brother George Lewis's property near Fredericksburg, he had been confined, Nelly told Miss Bordley, 'for four weeks to a dark room with an inflammation in one of his eyes'. There had been no time to make their house in Frederick ready for the winter, as Lewis had never been well enough to visit that county. Nelly, a songbird even in winter, wrote that she had been busily engaged in 'providing little trappings' for the baby to come, as had her grand-mother. 'Think, My Dear Eliza, what a pleasure I shall have in seeing her fondle my child.' Martha, she told Miss Bordley on 4 November, had been severely unwell for several weeks before the Lewises' arrival at Mount Vernon, but was now better. 'Grandpapa is quite well.'⁶

George had recently given Lawrence congenial news, writing in September, 'From the moment Mrs Washington & myself adopted the two youngest children of the late Mr Custis, it became my intention (if they survived me, and conducted themselves to my satisfaction) to consider them in my will, when I was about to make a distribution of my property. This determination has undergone no diminution, but is strengthened by the connexion which one of them has formed with my family.' He understood, 'from expressions occasionally dropped from (Nelly Custis, now) your wife', that the Lewises wished to settle in the neighbourhood. His intention was to bequeath the young couple a part of his estate. Should they wish to do so, the Lewises might build a dwelling on the land now, and continue to live at the Mount Vernon mansion till it was ready.[7] It was an offer that Nelly and Lawrence gratefully accepted.

The Washingtons, when in good health, were enjoying a tranquil autumn. In the Federal City, two brick houses were rising on lots north of the Capitol that Washington had bought the previous September, and he made frequent visits to inspect progress. Difficulties with farm manager Anderson inclined him to realize a plan he had harboured for some years, to sell off a large part of the Mount Vernon plantations and manage the mansion house farm himself. But as yet he had made no move to do this.

Discontent among the slave workforce, both among the field 'people' and among those within the house, continued. Christopher Shiels, who had been Washington's 'body servant' (valet) during the Presidency, was discovered in a plot to abscond with a new wife, a 'mulatto girl', property of a neighbour.[8] Martha had no good opinion in general of slaves. To her niece Fanny she had written in May 1795, following the death of a child, her niece's property, 'I hope you will not find him too much loss. The blacks are so bad in their nature that they have not the least gratitude for the kindness that may be showed to them.'[9] Yet Martha was, by her standards, kind to the Mount Vernon slaves. While in Philadelphia she had regularly paid for Hercules and other members of the household enslaved to see 'the play', and made them presents. She called in doctors when they were sick. She never thought, however, of attending to their spiritual welfare. Though her maids were in the room when she read the Bible and devotional literature first thing in the morning and last thing at night, she never had them join her in prayer.

Though Martha had employed others at Mount Vernon as her maids, she still hankered after Oney, the domestic slave who had run away in the summer of 1797. This August Washington wrote to Burwell Bassett Jr, now the owner of Eltham following his father's death three years earlier, asking him to make efforts to recover the errant maid, who was believed to be still in Portsmouth, New Hampshire: 'it would be a pleasing circumstance to your Aunt'. He added, in a letter only partially legible, that, if the young woman put him to 'no unnecessary trouble and expence', and conducted herself well, she would 'be treated according to her merit[s]'. To promise more would be an impolitic '& *dangerous*' precedent.[10] Oney Judge Staines, now a married woman and a mother, was warned that Bassett was looking for her, and she temporarily left town, avoiding arrest.* Martha at last admitted defeat. No further attempts were made to recover Oney.

This summer Nelly's marriage and the death of his one remaining full brother, Charles, had prompted Washington to make a new will. It provided for the establishment of a number of educational institutions, namely, a free school in Alexandria, a university in the District of Columbia, and a national university in a central part of the United States. In this latter place, he envisaged, students from all parts of the country, forgoing both halls of learning in Europe and state colleges, would freely associate with one another.

He left the use and profit of his 'whole estate' for life, barring bequests to her grandchildren, to his 'beloved wife'. Thereafter Mount Vernon and the rest of his estate would pass to his nephew Bushrod Washington. There was one provision which was the product of much thought. Upon the decease of his wife, Washington stated, his slaves were to be manumitted. It was not in his power to free the dower slaves who would pass, on Martha's death, back to the Parke Custis estate and become property of her grandchildren. 'To emancipate them during [her] life', wrote Washington of the slaves he owned, 'would, tho' earnestly wish[ed by] me, be attended with such insu[pera]ble difficulties on account of thei[r inter-m]ixture by Marriages with the [dow]er Negroes.' He had no wish to 'excite the

---

* Following her husband's early death, Oney Judge Staines struggled to rear their three children, fell on hard times, and ended her days a ward of the New Hampshire county where she lived. She never repented her flight from the Presidential home. By it, she was to tell enquirers in the 1840s, she had gained freedom, learned to read and become a Christian. Technically, as she knew well, she remained a slave till her death in 1848.

most pa[in]ful sensations, if not disagreeabl[e c]onsequences', which would follow, if the Mount Vernon slaves went free, while their near relations among the dower slaves remained at the estate.[11] The separation of the Washington and dower slaves following Martha's death was the lesser evil.

Henrietta Liston, who visited with her husband Robert in the late autumn of 1798, noted of the General: 'His figure, always noble, appeared less, & an approaching deafness, had in some degree affected his spirits.'[12] This winter the managers of the Alexandria assemblies who hoped that the Washingtons would attend their revels received this reply from George: 'alas! our dancing days are no more; we wish, however, all those whose relish for so agreeable, & innocent an amusement, all the pleasure the Season will afford them'.[13] The daily routine at Mount Vernon offered both Washingtons occupation and interest, and gatherings of the younger generation, provided additional zest.

On 27 November 1799, Nelly Parke Custis Lewis gave birth at the mansion to her first child – a daughter, given the name Frances Parke Lewis, and known as Parke. Both Dr Craik and a midwife were in attendance. Nothing untoward occurred. On 9 December, Lawrence Lewis and Washington Custis, father and uncle of the newborn, set off on a journey to inspect the latter's New Kent County estate. The morning, Washington recorded in his diary, was 'clear and pleasant'. Visitors including 'Lord Fairfax, his Son Thos. and daughter and his lady' – Bryan Fairfax had lately inherited the title from his cousin Robert – came to dinner two nights later. That evening, the General noted, there was 'A large circle round the Moon . . . About 1 o'clock it began to snow – soon after, to Hail, and then turned to a settled cold Rain.'[14]

Disregarding the weather conditions, Washington made his usual round of the estate. When he came in, Lear, who was present, observed, 'the snow was hanging upon his hair'.[15] As he was late for dinner, the General did not change his dress. The following day, Friday the 13th, he made this entry in his diary: 'Morning Snowing & abt. 3 Inches deep. Wind at No[rth]. E[as]t. & Mer[cury]. at 30. Continuing Snowing till 1 O'clock and abt. 4 it became perfectly clear. Wind in the same place but not hard.'[16]

He had developed a sore throat. Nevertheless he went out on to the snowbound front lawn to mark some trees he had in mind to cut. In the parlour that evening, after dinner, and in the company of Martha and Lear, he read the newspapers, which had just arrived. About nine o'clock, the secretary recorded later, Martha 'went up into Mrs Lewis' room'. Nelly was still keeping to her room and nursing. Washington and Lear remained, reading the papers. 'He was very cheerful,' Lear recorded, 'and when he met with anything interesting or entertaini[n]g, he read it aloud as well as his hoarseness would permit him.'[17]

Washington rejected Lear's recommendation to take something for his cold. In the night – some time after two in the morning – he woke Martha and reported that he was very unwell. He had suffered an 'ague', or paroxysm of chills. Martha saw that her husband could scarcely speak and breathed with difficulty. He refused, nevertheless, to allow her to get up and send a servant for help. He did not want his wife to catch cold, Martha later told Lear. The couple lay there together until daybreak, when Caroline, the maid, customarily came in to make up the fire. In subsequent days Martha was to act with great immediacy and firmness. Possibly, in these early hours of 14 December, husband and wife contemplated together the possibility of his death and decided on certain protocols to follow, should it occur. Later in the day, he was to say to Lear: 'I believed from the first that the disorder would prove fatal.' He told Dr Craik, 'I believed from my first attack, that I should not survive it.'[18]

Caroline, at first light, alerted Lear, who sent for Dr Craik. After Martha dressed, she remained with her husband in the bedchamber. Numerous remedies were attempted in the early hours, while they waited for professional assistance. Washington almost suffocated when attempting to swallow a drink intended to ease his throat. An overseer came in, 'soon after sunrise', to try bleeding him. Martha, 'not knowing whether bleeding was proper or not in the General's situation, begged that much might not be taken from him, lest it should be injurious'. The General insisted the procedure continue. 'Mrs Washington', recorded Lear, 'being still very uneasy lest too much blood should be taken, it was stop'd after taking about half a pint.'[19]

No relief was to be had. Even when his throat was bathed externally, Washington said, ''Tis very sore.' Martha told Lear to send for Dr Brown of Port Tobacco, 'whom Dr. Craik had recommended to be called, if any case should ever occur that was seriously alarming'.[20] Even so, the General insisted on being dressed. He was helped to a chair by the fire, where he was sitting when Craik arrived at about eight o'clock in the morning.

After a couple of hours Washington could sit no longer and returned to lie down on the bed. Christopher, Washington's body servant, stood at its head. Martha took up a seat at the foot. She watched while Craik applied a blister to her husband's throat and tried to make him gargle. Again Washington nearly suffocated. Moll, Caroline and Charlotte, and housekeeper Mrs Forbes, came and went, tending to the fire, bringing hot water and other supplies. More doctors arrived mid-afternoon – Dr Dick from Alexandria and Dr Brown. They counselled more bleeding: 'the blood came very slow, was thick, and did not produce any symptoms of fainting'.

Washington, calling Martha to his bedside about half-past four, had her go down into his study below and bring him the two wills in his desk there. On his instructions, she then burnt the 'useless' one and preserved the other in her closet. It was an orderly passing, despite the agonizing pain. He told Lear: 'arrange & record all my late military letters and papers – arrange my accounts and settle my books'. Soon after six the General dismissed Dick and Brown from the room: 'I pray you to take no more trouble about me, let me go off quietly; I cannot last long.' To Craik, who remained, he had already said, 'I die hard; but I am not afraid to go.' He motioned Christopher, who had been standing all day, to be seated.

Craik stole some moments in the course of the long evening that succeeded to leave his patient and sit by the fire, 'absorbed in grief'. Martha remained seated 'near the foot of the bed'. Some time after ten, Lear called Craik to the bedside. Together doctor and secretary witnessed the General's demise. Martha asked, 'with a firm & collected Voice, "Is he gone?"' Lear responded with a gesture. ''Tis

well,' said she, in the same voice. 'All is now over, I shall soon follow
him! I have no more trials to pass through.'

Dry-eyed she had been all day, and apparently dry-eyed and
focused Martha, widowed, remained. She told Christopher to take
'the General's keys and things' out of his deceased master's coat
pockets and give them to Lear for safe keeping.[21] Near midnight, the
General's heavy corpse was taken down through the house and laid
out on the dining-room table in the New Room. Early the following morning, on Martha's instructions, Lear sent to Alexandria for a
mahogany coffin. It was to accommodate a body six feet three and a
half inches long, one foot nine inches 'Across the Shoulders' and two
feet 'Across the Elbows'.

It had been determined not to delay burial until Wash Custis,
Lawrence Lewis and other family members far off should arrive.
Instead, the funeral was held on the Wednesday, the fourth day after
Washington's death. The vault in the grounds, where Patsy Parke
Custis had been laid a quarter of a century earlier and which would
receive the new coffin, was unbricked. Martha gave orders, however,
that a wooden door should take the place of bricks, when it came
to close the vault once more.[22] It would not be long before she
joined her husband, she averred, displaying a 'pious fortitude' that
unnerved Lear and others. She had retreated to a small bedchamber
on the attic storey, and apparently did not again enter the room that
she and her husband had shared for forty years and where he had
died. 'The world now appears to be no longer desirable to her,' Lear
wrote to his mother on 16 December, 'and yet she yields not to that
grief which would be softened by tears'.[23] Throughout, Thomas Law
wrote to his brother in England, she 'displayed a solemn composure
that was more distressing than floods of tears'.[24]

Dissolution, 1799–1802

. . . we found this excellent Woman grieving incessantly.

Martha had done her best to meet the 'express desire' her husband had stated in his will, that his corpse be 'Interred in a private manner, without parade, or funeral Oration'.[1] On 18 December 1799 the General's riderless horse and Alexandria Freemasons formed part of the procession that accompanied the coffin from the New Room to the vault. Guns sounded on a schooner on the river. Dr Thomas Davis of Alexandria, who had so recently married Nelly and Lewis, officiated at a relatively simple funeral service at the tomb. Martha's former daughter-in-law Nelly Stuart and Hannah Bushrod Washington, widow of Washington's brother John Augustine, were chief mourners. Martha herself, with Nelly and baby Parke, remained within the mansion.

Other services held elsewhere on the day and a national parade in Philadelphia on 26 December – culminating in a funeral oration delivered by General Henry 'Light Horse Harry' Lee – were beyond her control. In that oration, which found widespread approval, her husband's former comrade paid full tribute to Washington's character as a husband: 'First in war, first in peace, and first in the hearts of his countrymen, he was second to none in humble and endearing scenes of private life . . . To his equals he was condescending, to his inferiors kind, and to the dear object of his affections exemplarily tender . . . The purity of his private character gave effulgence to his public virtues . . . Such was the man for whom our nation mourns.'[2]

Martha was not proof against the wishes of Congress, which President Adams made known to her in a letter, brought to her by his nephew and private secretary William S. Shaw at the end of December. Shaw brought, too, a letter of condolence from the President's wife, Abigail. Neither letter was lengthy, but Lear, who delivered the letters, told the waiting Shaw that the widow was 'two hours getting through them'. Abigail, on 7 January 1800, informed her sister that only then did Mrs Washington weep.[3] There was good reason in the contents of Adams's letter for Martha to cry.

President Adams had made known to her the resolution of both Houses: 'that a marble monument' – or sarcophagus – 'be erected by the United States in the Capitol, at the City of Washington; and that the family of General Washington be requested to permit his body to be deposited under it; and that the monument be so designed as to commemorate the great events of his military and political life'.[4] Martha did not wish her husband's body to be removed from the vault where it had been so recently placed, behind a door that, she had intended, would be opened hereafter to receive her own remains. It was repugnant to Martha that, though joined in life to her husband, she would be separated from him in death.

She strove, according to Abigail, while Shaw awaited her response, to 'get resolution sufficient' to see the President's secretary, but finally excused herself. 'She had the painful task to perform, to bring her mind to comply with the request of Congress,' Abigail told her sister.[5] Martha's response, which Shaw took to Adams at the end of two days, was dutiful: 'Taught by the great example which I have so long had before me, never to oppose my private wishes to the public will, I must consent to the request made by Congress, which you have had the goodness to transmit to me . . .' It was not, however, without bite: 'In doing this, I need not, I cannot, say what a sacrifice of individual feeling I make to a sense of public duty.'[6]

Dr William Thornton, architect of the Capitol, was moved by reports of Martha's distress. He wrote, early in January 1800, to

Secretary of State John Marshall to suggest that, upon Martha's own demise, her remains join those of her husband under the proposed monument. He argued:

> if an intimation could be given that she should partake merely of the same place of deposit, it would restore to her mind a calm and repose that this acquiescence in the national wish has in a high degree affected. You, who know her, are not unacquainted with her high virtues, and know that her love for the departed would be the only reason why such a wish could be entertained. She cannot be more honoured than she has been and, were it possible, the nation would give a still further proof of sensibility on this melancholy occasion, by a resolution in favour of her who possessed the heart of the late Friend of Man.

Thornton suggested a 'secret vote of the House', the result only to be made known after Martha's death.[7]

The matter hung fire. For the time being, as the city of Washington would not become the seat of government for a full year, and as the 'marble monument' was as yet uncommissioned, Washington's coffin remained in the vault behind the wooden door in the grounds of Mount Vernon. Should she be so minded, Martha might visit it daily.

Another resolution of Congress, passed on 28 March, was more welcome. It decreed that 'all letters and packets to Mrs Martha Washington, relict of the late General George Washington, shall be received and conveyed by post, free from postage, for and during her life'.[8] The residuary heir, Bushrod Washington, now a Supreme Court judge in Richmond, was acting as executor for his uncle's estate from afar. Lear and Lawrence Lewis took care of Washington's affairs in Alexandria. In the Federal City Messrs Peter and Law consulted with Thornton on the houses nearing completion there that Washington had commissioned him to build on lots he owned. At Mount Vernon Martha had been inundated with letters of condolence from those she knew and from those she did not. Tobias Lear wrote suitable replies, but the postal costs grew prohibitive. This resolution, in late

March 1800, that in future her letters be franked, relieved her of worry in this regard.

Few letters prompted Martha to return a personal answer. She did reply, on 5 April 1800, to the widow of General Montgomery: 'my own experience has taught me that griefs like these cannot be removed by the condolence of friends, however sincere.'⁹ Martha had been overwhelmed when her daughter, Patsy, and, later, her son, Jacky, died. The Listons, who visited Mount Vernon in July 1800 while on a Virginia excursion before sailing for Europe, were now bewildered by Martha's sorrow. 'Washington was more a respectful than a tender Husband . . .', was Mrs Liston's opinion, 'yet we found this excellent Woman grieving incessantly.' Martha repeatedly told them that 'all comfort had fled with her Husband, & that she waited anxiously her dissolution'. Indeed, Mrs Liston noted, 'it was evident that her health was fast declining & her heart breaking'.¹⁰

In December 1800 Mrs Adams noticed a degree of neglect about the mansion. The President's wife visited at a time of upheaval and distress. Martha had, that month, on advice – no doubt that of Bushrod Washington – signed a deed of manumission, freeing her late husband's slaves, 123 all told. Abigail wrote: 'In the state in which they were left by the General, to be free at her death, she did not feel as tho her Life was safe in their Hands, many of whom would be told that it was their interest to get rid of her.' When making his will Washington had failed to take into account this risk, that either household or field slaves, eager to hasten the promised day of freedom, might murder Martha. On the first day of the new century, 1801, Washington's slaves would begin a life of freedom. 'Many of those who are liberated have married with what are called the dower Negroes, so that they all quit their [family] connections, yet what could she do?' Abigail wrote to a sister. The Parke Custis slaves – 153, with husbands, wives and children among those who went free – remained enslaved on the estate.¹¹

Family, friends and pilgrims to Mount Vernon continued to receive a welcome. When the city of Washington became the seat of government, members of the outgoing and incoming administrations, senators and congressmen paid formal visit to the widow. Naval vessels sailed up the Potomac on their way to the new Navy Dockyard in the District of Columbia. On passing by the Washingtons' home, they formed the habit of honouring the President's tomb, visible in the grounds above, with a gun salute. Charles Morris, a young midshipman on board the thirty-six-gun frigate USS *Congress*, later remembered one such occasion in May 1801. 'Everyone was on deck to look upon the dwelling where Washington had made his home. Mrs Washington and others of the family could be distinguished in the portico which fronts the river.' A mourning salute of thirteen guns was fired, and Morris recalled 'the echo and re-echo of that sound from the near and distant hills, as it died away in the distance, the whole ship's company [with heads] uncovered and motionless.'[12]* Martha took pride in all honours done to the memory of her late husband as she had done in those paid George in his lifetime.

A visit that Thomas Jefferson, newly President, paid her on 1 June that year won him no favours. It had been, Martha was later to tell a group of visitors, including the Reverend Manasseh Cutler, an event only marginally less distressing than the demise of her husband. 'We were all federalists, which evidently gave her particular pleasure,' Cutler noted. 'Her remarks were frequently pointed and sometimes very sarcastic on the new order of things and the present administration. She spoke of the election of Mr Jefferson, whom she considered as one of the most detestable of mankind, as the greatest misfortune our country has ever experienced.'[13]

---

* President Theodore Roosevelt, cruising on the Potomac on the yacht *Mayflower* in 1906, was much impressed by the ceremony observed. Finding that the passing honours were not official, he issued General Order no. 22, 2 June 1906, to apply to all vessels of the US Navy passing Mount Vernon between sunrise and sunset: 'Marine guard and band paraded; bell tolled and colors halfmasted at the beginning of the tolling of the bell. When opposite Washington's Tomb, buglers sound taps, marine guard present arms, and officers and men on deck stand at attention and salute. The colors will be mastheaded at the last note of taps which will also be the signal for "carry on."' The playing of the national anthem was subsequently added.

Martha was still an outspoken hostess. She occupied herself with family business, as she had always done. Nelly and Lewis, as well as Wash Custis, were still resident and a comfort to their grandmother and aunt. But both within and without the mansion, there was now a degree of neglect. Philadelphia merchant Thomas Cope was to observe in May 1802: 'in general it may be said of the furniture, chairs, carpets, hangings, &c. that they have seen their best days'.[14]

John Pintard, of New York, who dined at Mount Vernon in late July 1801 found no fault with Martha as a hostess: 'She converses without reserve & [with] seeming pleasure on every subject that recalls the memory & virtues of her august consort.' Pintard saw a miniature that Martha had recently commissioned from British artist Robert Field, and called it a 'striking likeness'. Watercolour on ivory, the miniature shows Martha, in a loose cap with mourning ribbon and long lappets, with a decisive expression to her hazel eyes and set mouth. Martha, who had always understood the uses of imagery in the promotion of her husband's career, in this commission could indulge her 'private wishes'. She told Pintard she had had it drawn, 'to please her grandchildren, that they may see her . . . in her every day face . . .'[15]

The reverse of the miniature is ornamented with sixty-seven pearls, Washington's age at the time of his death, and an inscription, 'Join'd by Friendship, Crown'd by Love'. In a tiny scene Martha's chopped hair, mingled with that of her husband, forms the ground below a hymeneal altar. Above, a cupid offers a laurel wreath, and two birds fly from each other, bearing in their beaks ribbons which form a lover's knot.

Martha also commissioned from Field a miniature of her husband, with his hair woven on the reverse and surmounted by his initials in gold. Washington, in this companion piece, is depicted in his prime, in the buff and blue uniform that he wore as Commander-in-Chief during the Revolutionary War. As Colonel Washington, he came courting Martha Dandridge Custis, and as General Washington she remembered him. If Congress were to remove his remains, she had her memorial.[16] She had no wish for others to read her voluminous correspondence with her husband. 'Shortly after General Washington's death', according to the later testimony of her grand-daughter Patty Parke Custis Peter, Martha burnt their letters to each other.[17] The fires that Caroline and the other maids laid each morning provided a convenient means of destruction.[*]

Nelly and Lawrence were now ready to build a home on the acres Washington had willed them. In August 1801 the William Thorntons stayed at Mount Vernon, so that the doctor could inspect the ground and furnish the Lewises with a plan for building. Mrs Thornton thought Martha 'much broke since I saw her last'. She noted that the mistress of Mount Vernon seemed very anxious on account of her grandson Washington Custis, 'in whom she seems quite wrapt up', and who was ill.[18] Nelly was nursing a new daughter, named Martha, a sister for two-year-old Parke.

This autumn, during a severe illness, Martha Washington had a white dress laid aside for a time that was not to be long in coming.[19] During a bout of fever early the following summer, a 'chilly fit deprived her, during the paroxysm, of the power of speech'. She promised Dr Craik she would remove, if she recovered, to a more airy and 'commodious' part of the house – she was still living in the 'small, inconvenient, uncomfortable apartment' on the attic storey to which she had retreated when Washington died. No such recovery took place. Less than a week later, on 22 May, at noon, Martha passed away. It is said that the parrot, bought to amuse her daughter Patsy nearly thirty years before and an inhabitant of an aviary at the mansion ever since, flew away the same day.[20] The local newspaper, the *Alexandria Advertiser*, spoke for many when reporting Martha's death: 'She was the worthy partner of the worthiest of men, and those who witnessed their conduct could not determine which excelled in their different characters, both were so well sustained on every occasion.'[21] Congress had never yet made good on their

* Only a few items survive. Martha's addenda to Lund's and Jacky's letters to Washington of 1767 and 1777, respectively, were overlooked. The letters that the General had written in June 1775 before setting out for the war were later found, caught behind a drawer in Martha's writing desk. Thirdly, the letter of introduction to Martha that Washington wrote in 1782 for James Brown of Rhode Island remained, undelivered, in the latter's keeping.

resolution to remove her husband's remains to a marble home in the Capitol. Three days after her death Martha was laid to rest in the vault near the mansion at his side. On the day of the funeral, Nelly Parke Custis Lewis, six months pregnant with a third child, was a 'Picture of Woe', according to a cousin, but shed no tears: 'Never did I see silent Grief so strongly marked as in her countenance.'

Nelly's second child, Martha, aged ten months, had contracted measles the night of her great-grandmother's death, and did not survive. This August a son who might have brought happiness, died shortly after his birth.[22] Consolation for such misfortunes, guidance for Wash Custis and the other grandchildren, were now for others to afford. Martha, a woman of strong faith, never doubted that when she went to meet her Maker, there she would find her husband and, with him, renewed happiness.

Washington, provident to the end, had left instructions in his will: 'The family Vault at Mount Vernon requiring repairs, and being improperly situated besides, I desire that a new one of Brick, and upon a larger Scale, may be built at the foot of what is commonly called the Vineyard Inclosure . . .'[23] In the early 1830s there was no further thought of the removal of Washington's remains to the Capitol. John Augustine Washington II, then owner of Mount Vernon, acted. Besides the Washingtons themselves and Bushrod Washington, all others who lay in the old tomb at that time – Patsy Parke Custis, George Augustine Washington and Fanny Bassett Washington Lear included – were transferred to a new vault. There, in marble sarcophagi, side by side to this day, George and Martha Washington lie, 'Join'd by Friendship, Crown'd by Love'.

NOTES

Abbreviations

Family

AMB	Anna Maria 'Nancy' Dandridge Bassett: wife of BB, sister of MW
BB	Burwell Bassett: husband of AMB, father of FBW, brother-in-law to GW and MW
DPC	Daniel Parke Custis: first husband of MW; father of JPC and EPC
ECC	Eleanor 'Nelly' Calvert Custis (Stuart): wife of JPC, as widow of JPC, wife of David Stuart: mother of Eliza, earlier Bet and Betsy, Parke Custis, Martha, earlier Pat and Patty, Parke Custis, EPC and GWPC; later, mother of other Stuart children
EPC	Eleanor 'Nelly' Parke Custis (Lewis): daughter of JPC and ECC, granddaughter of MW, later wife of Lawrence Lewis
FBW	Frances 'Fanny' Bassett Washington (Lear): daughter of AMB and BB, niece to MW, wife of GAW and, as widow of GAW, wife of Tobias Lear
GAW	George Augustine Washington: son of JAW, nephew of GW, sometime Mount Vernon agent, husband of FBW
GW	George Washington
GWPC	George 'Wash' Washington Parke Custis, later known as Washington Custis: son of JPC and ECC, grandson of MW
JAW	John Augustine 'Jack' Washington: younger brother of GW
JPC	John 'Jacky' Parke Custis: son of MW and of DPC father of Eliza, earlier Bet and Betsy, Parke Custis, Martha, earlier Pat and Patty, Parke Custis, EPC and GWPC
LW	Lund Washington: cousin of GW, sometime Mount Vernon agent
MPC	Martha 'Patsy' Parke Custis: daughter of MW and of DPC
MW	Martha Dandridge Washington, wife of GW: earlier wife of DPC, mother of JPC and MPC
SW	Samuel Washington: younger brother of GW

Documentary Sources and Journals

AHR	*American Historical Review*
FUL	Fordham University Library, New York City, New York
GLC	Gilder Lehrman Collection, The Gilder Lehrman Institute of American History, located at N-YHS, New York City
HSP	Historical Society of Pennsylvania, Philadelphia, Pennsylvania
JHB	*Journals of the House of Burgesses*
LOC/AM	Library of Congress, Washington, DC, American Memory
LOC/AM/AATC	An American Time Capsule: Three Centuries of Broadsides and Other Printed Ephemera
LOC/AM/CL	Century of Lawmaking
LOC/AM/CL/JCC	Journal of Continental Congress
LOC/AM/CL/LDC	Letters of Delegates to Continental Congress
LOC/AM/GWP	Presidents: George Washington Papers, 1741–1799
LOC/AM/TJP	Presidents: Thomas Jefferson Papers, 1606–1827
LOC/WFP	Library of Congress Manuscripts Division, Washington DC, Washington Family Papers
MHS/AFPDE	Massachusetts Historical Society, Boston: Adams Family Papers Digital Edition
MVLA	Mount Vernon Ladies' Association, Mount Vernon, Virginia
N-YHS	New-York Historical Society, New York City, New York
N-YHSQ	*New-York Historical Society Quarterly*
PGWDE	The Papers of George Washington Digital Edition, ed. Theodore J. Crackel
PGWDE/EA	The Papers of George Washington Digital Edition: Founders Early Access [draft, unannotated material]
PJADE	The Papers of John Adams Digital Edition, ed. C. James Taylor
PJADE/EA	The Papers of John Adams Digital Edition, ed. C. James Taylor: Founders Early Access [draft, unannotated material]
PMHB	*Pennsylvania Magazine of History and Biography*
Proc. MHS	*Proceedings of Massachusetts Historical Society*
PTJDE	The Papers of Thomas Jefferson Digital Edition, ed. Barbara B. Oberg and J. Jefferson Looney
PTJDE/EA	The Papers of Thomas Jefferson Digital Edition, ed. Barbara B. Oberg and J. Jefferson Looney: Founders Early Access [draft, unannotated material]
RCHS	*Records of the Columbia Historical Society*
VHS	Virginia Historical Society, Richmond, Virginia
WGWEE	*The Writings of George Washington from the Original Manuscript Sources, 1745–1799*, ed. John C. Fitzpatrick: Electronic edition
WLU	Washington and Lee University, Lexington, Virginia
WMQ	*William and Mary Quarterly*
VMHB	*Virginia Magazine of History and Biography*
YUAG	Yale University Art Gallery, New Haven, Connecticut

Prologue: Casting Lots for his Garments, July 1802

1 LOC/WFP, Box 1, 'Private sales, which took place upstairs [sic] among the legatees . . . 22 July 1802'.
2 LOC/AM/TJP, William Thornton to Thomas Jefferson, 28 July 1802.
3 Prussing, *Estate of George Washington, Deceased*, p. 453.
4 Fields, "*Worthy Partner*", p. 412, 'Account of Sales . . .' 1802; Detweiler, *George Washington's Chinaware*, p. 185.
5 Lee, *Funeral Oration*, p. 10.
6 YUAG, Robert Field, *George Washington*; ibid., Robert Field, *Mrs George Washington*.
7 Adams, ed., *John Adams, Works*, Vol. 6, p. 462.
8 Fields, "*Worthy Partner*", pp. 414–15, 'Account of Sales . . .' 1802.
9 Custis, *Recollections*, p. 65.
10 Rasmussen and Tilton, *Washington: Man behind the Myths*, p. 266.
11 Horrell and Oram, 'George Washington's "Marble colour'd folio book"', p. 253.
12 VHS, Custis Family Papers, Sections 25, 27.
13 LOC/AM/GWP, Series 5, Ledger Book 2, f. 111 [1774].
14 Horrell and Oram, 'George Washington's "Marble colour'd folio book"'.
15 Thane, *Mount Vernon is Ours*, p. 16.
16 MVLA, Minutes (1874), p. 5, Ann Pamela Cunningham to MVLA Board, 1 June 1874.
17 PGWDE, GW to Elizabeth Powel, 26 March 1797.
18 Showman et al., eds, *Greene Papers*, Vol. 2, p. 54.
19 MVLA, Eleanor Roosevelt, Franklin Delano Roosevelt and Soong May-ling (Madame Chiang Kai-shek), 22 February 1943 [photograph: George R. Skadding].
20 Franklin D. Roosevelt Presidential Library and Museum, Eleanor Roosevelt Papers, Box 1401, carbon copy, radio broadcast text, 22 February 1935. Courtesy of Ms Nancy Roosevelt Ireland.
21 Johnson, *Story of a Shrine*, p. 75; Mount Vernon lore.

Chapter 1 – Colonial Colonel

1 PGWDE, GW to John Stanwix, 4 March 1758.
2 Ibid., GW to John Stanwix, 4 March 1758.
3 Weems, *Life of Washington*, pp. 21, 12.
4 Freeman, *Washington*, Vol. 3, p. 6, n. 10.
5 PGWDE, GW to Sarah Cary Fairfax, 15 November 1757.
6 Sparks, *Life of Washington*, Vol. 2, p. 10.
7 Freeman, *Washington*, Vol. 1, pp. 198–9.
8 PGWDE, GW to JAW, 31 May 1754.
9 Washington, *Rules of Civility*.
10 Henriques, 'Washington versus Green', p. 252.
11 Brown, *Virginia Baron*, p. 59.
12 Ibid.
13 PGWDE, GW to 'Robin' [1749–50].
14 Ibid., GW to George William Fairfax, 27 February 1785.
15 Ibid., Sarah Fairfax Carlyle to GW, 17 June 1754.
16 Ibid., GW to Sarah Cary Fairfax [7 June 1755].
17 Ibid., Sarah Cary Fairfax et al. to GW [26 July 1755].
18 Ibid., GW to Sarah Cary Fairfax [4 March 1758].
19 LOC/AM/GWP, Series 5, Ledger Book 1, f. 38, entries for 15, 25 March 1758; ibid., f. 39, entry for 5 June 1758.

Chapter 2 – Dandridge's Daughter

1   PGWDE, Robert Stewart to GW, 29 December 1758, n. 5.
2   Zuppan, *Letter Book of John Custis IV*, p. 15.
3   VHS, Custis Family Papers, *Custis v. Moody*, Section 11, Deposition of Anne Moody.
4   Fields, *"Worthy Partner"*, p. 432 and n.
5   VHS, Custis Family Papers, Custis-Lee family Bible, giving date of marriage.
6   Fields, *"Worthy Partner"*, p. 435, quoting HSP, Etting Collection, DPC to R. Cary, 5 May 1755.
7   Bryan, *First Lady of Liberty*, p. 29 n. 8, quoting Richard Pye Cook to Mrs John Stewart, 16 July 1887.
8   WLU, Lee Chapel & Museum, John Wollaston, *John and Martha Parke Custis*.
9   VHS Collection, Matthew Pratt, *Custis Children*.
10 VHS, Custis Family Papers, DPC, Invoice Book, 1749–57.
11 Ibid.
12 Lynch, *Custis Chronicles*, p. 114 and n. 384.
13 VHS, Custis Family Papers, DPC to John Mercer, 2 November 1754.
14 VHS, Custis Family Papers, DPC, Invoice Book, 1749–57.
15 Freeman, *Washington*, Vol. 2, p. 298.
16 VHS, Custis Family Papers, DPC, Invoice Book, 1749–57.
17 WLU, Lee Chapel and Museum, John Wollaston, *Daniel Parke Custis*; *Martha Dandridge Custis* [MW]; *John and Martha Parke Custis*.
18 Fields, *"Worthy Partner"*, pp. 15–16.
19 VHS, Custis Family Papers, DPC, Invoice Book, 1749–57.
20 Fields, *"Worthy Partner"*, pp. 5–6, Martha Dandridge Custis [MW] to Robert Cary & Co., 20 August 1757.
21 VHS, Custis Family Papers, DPC, Invoice Book, Martha Dandridge Custis [MW] to R. Cary, Invoice 20 August 1757.
22 Fields, *"Worthy Partner"*, p. 21, Martha Dandridge Custis [MW] to John Hanbury & Co., 20 December 1757.
23 Ibid., p. 56, John Mercer to Martha Dandridge Custis [MW], 2 November 1758.

Chapter 3 – North and South

1   LOC/AM/GWP, Series 5, Ledger Book 1, f. 38, entry for 15 March 1758; PGWDE, GW to Richard Washington, 18 March 1758.
2   Ibid., GW to John Forbes, 23 April 1758, n.
3   Ibid., GW to John Forbes, 23 April 1758.
4   LOC/AM/GWP, Series 5, Ledger Book 1, f. 38, entries for 16, 25 March 1758.
5   Custis, *Recollections*, pp. 499–502.
6   PGWDE, Robert Stewart to GW, 16 January 1759.
7   LOC/AM/GWP, Series 5, Ledger Book 1, f. 38, entry for 16 March 1758.
8   Fields, *"Worthy Partner"*, pp. 3–4.
9   PGWDE, Robert Carter Nicholas to GW, 5 January 1758.
10 Tinling, ed., *Correspondence of Byrds*, Vol. 2, p. 646 and n.
11 PGWDE, GW to Richard Washington, 7 May 1759.
12 Ibid., GW to Richard Washington, 20 September 1759.
13 Ibid., GW to Elizabeth Parke Custis, 14 September 1794.
14 Ibid., GW to Francis Dandridge, 20 September 1759.
15 Fields, *"Worthy Partner"*, p. 44, MW to John Hanbury and Co., 1 June 1758.
16 Ibid., pp. 25–8, MW to Robert Cary & Co. 1758.
17 LOC/AM/GWP, Series 5, Ledger Book 1, f. 39, entry for 5 June 1758.

18 PGWDE, GW to Francis Fauquier, 17 June 1758.
19 Fields, *"Worthy Partner"*, pp. 25–6, MW to Robert Cary & Co. 1758.
20 PGWDE, GW to Sarah Cary Fairfax, 12 September 1758.
21 Ibid., GW to Sarah Cary Fairfax, 25 September 1758.

Chapter 4 – Mount Vernon, Fairfax County

1 PGWDE, James Craik to GW, 20 December 1758.
2 Ibid., GW to the Officers of the Virginia Regiment, 10 January 1759.
3 Cadou, *George Washington Collection*, p. 244.
4 Harris, *Old New Kent County*, Vol. 1, pp. 118–19; Custis, *Recollections*, p. 11.
5 St Peter's Church, New Kent, Archives, Robert E. Lee to [parishioner] Virginia [surname illegible], 23 October 1869; Lee, *My Father, Lee*, p. 364.
6 PGWDE, GW to BB, 23 May 1785.
7 Ibid., GW to Robert Cary, 1 May 1759.
8 *JHB: 1758–1761*, Resolution [26 February 1759].
9 PGWDE, GW to John Alton, Thursday morning [5 April 1759].
10 Ibid., Invoice from GW to Richard Washington, 10 November 1757.
11 Ibid., GW to Richard Washington, 15 April 1757.
12 Ibid., Invoice from Richard Washington, 10 November 1757.
13 Ibid., Enclosure, Invoice to Robert Cary & Co., 1 May 1759.
14 Ibid., George William Fairfax to GW, 15 April 1761.
15 Ibid., GW to Robert Cary, 26 April 1763.
16 Ibid., GW to Richard Washington, 20 September 1759.
17 Fields, *"Worthy Partner"*, p. 129, MW to AMB, 1 June 1760.
18 PGWDE, GW to Robert Stewart [27 April 1763].
19 Ibid., Enclosure, Invoice to Robert Cary & Co., 1 May 1759; Ibid., GW to Robert Cary, 1 May 1759 and n.
20 Ibid., Guardian Accounts, 12 April 1762.
21 Fields, *"Worthy Partner"*, pp. 147–8, MW to AMB, 28 August 1762.
22 Ibid., pp. 131–2, MW to Margaret Green [29 September 1760].
23 PGWDE, Diaries, entry for 9 April 1760.
24 Ibid., GW to John Armstrong, 20 March 1770.
25 Fields, *"Worthy Partner"*, p. 146, MW to AMB, 6 April 1762.
26 PGWDE, Diaries, entries for January 1760.
27 Ibid., entry for 12 January 1769.
28 Ibid., entry for 15 February 1760.
29 Fields, *"Worthy Partner"*, p. 129, MW to AMB, 1 June 1760.
30 Ibid., p. 146, MW to AMB, 6 April 1762.
31 Ibid., pp. 147–8, MW to AMB, 28 August 1762.
32 PGWDE, GW to Robert Cary, 26 April 1763.
33 Ibid., GW to Robert Stewart, 27 April 1763.

Chapter 5 – Family Affairs

1 PGWDE, GW to BB, 5 July 1763.
2 *JHB: 1761–1765*, 171, Francis Fauquier to House of Burgesses, 19 May 1763.
3 PGWDE, GW to Lord Dunmore, 2 November 1773.
4 Ibid., Memorandum, 15 October 1763.
5 Ibid., GW to BB, 5 July 1763.
6 Ibid., Guardian Accounts, III, Accounts, 1762–73.
7 Ibid., GW to Jonathan Boucher, 30 May 1768.
8 Ibid., MW to Mrs Shelbury, 10 August 1764.
9 Ibid., Guardian Accounts, 6 May 1765.

10 Ibid., Diaries, entry for 13 March 1770; ibid., Guardian Accounts, 1 May 1771.
11 *WGWEE*, 'Invoice of Sundries, to be shipped by R. Cary . . .', 12 October 1761.
12 LOC/AM/GWP, Series 5, Ledger Book 1, f. 231, entry for 7 May 1766: 'Cash paid Mr Stedlar for teaching Mrs Washington and two children music, £38.14.0'.
13 PGWDE, GW to Jonathan Boucher, 30 May 1768.
14 Ibid., Guardian Accounts for JPC [5 May 1769], entry for 18 May 1767.
15 Ibid., GW to Francis Dandridge, 20 September 1765.
16 Ibid., Diaries, entries for 21 March 1763, 29 March 1764.
17 Sparks, *Life of Franklin*, p. 294.
18 PGWDE, GW to Francis Dandridge, 20 September 1765.

Chapter 6 – Acts and Associations

1 PGWDE, Robert Stewart to GW, 18 August 1765.
2 Ibid., GW to Francis Dandridge, 20 September 1765.
3 Ibid., Robert Stewart to GW, 18 August 1765.
4 Van Schreeven et al., eds, *Revolutionary Virginia*, Vol. 1, pp. 17–18.
5 Randolph, ed., *Memoir, Correspondence of Jefferson*, p. 6.
6 Wirt, *Sketches of Henry*, p. 65.
7 Carter, ed., *Gage Correspondence*, Vol. 1, p. 67.
8 *Virginia Gazette*, 26 September 1766, Account of John Mercer, 17 October 1765, reprinted.
9 *Virginia Gazette*, 26 September 1766, John Mercer to Printer, 12 September 1766.
10 *JHB: 1761–1765*, lxix, Francis Fauquier to Board of Trade, 3 November 1765.
11 Ibid., lxix–lxx.
12 Van Schreeven et al., eds, *Revolutionary Virginia*, Vol. 1, pp. 22–6.
13 McGaughy, *Richard Henry Lee*, p. 80 and n. 20.
14 PGWDE, George Washington to Francis Dandridge, 20 September 1765.
15 Ibid., GW to Robert Cary & Co., 22 August 1766.
16 Ibid., GW to George Mason, 5 April 1769.
17 *JHB:1766–1769*, 13, 6 Nov 1766.
18 Ibid., LW to GW, 30 March 1767, with Postscript [MW to GW].
19 Ibid., Diaries, 31 October 1768 n.
20 Ibid., 2 November 1768 n.
21 Ibid., GW to George Mason, 5 April 1769.
22 Ibid., George Mason to GW, 5 April 1769.
23 Ibid., George Mason to GW, 28 April 1769, n. 1.
24 Ibid., George Mason to GW, 28 April 1769.
25 *JHB: 1766–1769*, 215–18.
26 Van Schreeven et al., eds, *Revolutionary Virginia*, Vol. 1, pp. 74–7.
27 *Virginia Gazette*, 25 May 1769.
28 PGWDE, GW to BB, 18 June 1769.
29 Ibid., GW to Robert Cary, 25 July 1769.
30 VHS, Jennings Lee Papers, Francis Lightfoot Lee to William Lee, 17 December 1770.
31 PGWDE, GW to George William Fairfax, 27 June 1770.
32 Ibid., Fairfax County Associators to Peyton Randolph [c.1 July 1771].
33 Ibid., Fairfax County Associators to Peyton Randolph, [c. 1 July 1771], n.2.
34 Ibid., Enclosure, invoice to Robert Cary & Co., 18 July [1771].

Chapter 7 – Fevers and Physicians

1 PGWDE, LW to GW, 17 August 1767.
2 Ibid., Diaries, entries for 24, 25, 27 February 1768.
3 Ibid., entries for 14 June, 11 July 1768.

4 Ibid., entry for 31 July 1770 and n.
5 Ibid., entry for 17 December 1768.
6 Ibid., entry for 22 July 1768.
7 LOC/AM/GWP, GW to Robert Cary & Co., 20 June 1768.
8 PGWDE, GW to Jonathan Boucher, 4 Septermber 1768.
9 Ibid., Jonathan Boucher to GW, 5 September 1768.
10 Ibid., Diaries, entry for 20 September 1768.
11 Ibid., Diaries, 9 November 1768; ibid., 6 January 1769; VHS, Custis Family Papers, William Rumney, receipt, 18 February 1769.
12 PGWDE, GW to Jonathan Boucher, 26 January 1769.
13 Ibid., Diaries, entries for 30, 31 January 1769 and n.
14 Ibid., 16 February 1769 and n.
15 Ibid., Cash Accounts [February 1769].
16 Ibid., GW to BB, 18 June 1769.
17 LOC/AM/GWP, Ledger Book 1, f. 299, entry for 16 December 1769; PGWDE, Diaries, entries for November, December 1769.
18 Ibid., GW to Thomas Johnson, 20 July 1770.
19 Ibid., GW to Boucher, 26 March 1772, n.1.
20 Ibid., GW to Jonathan Boucher, 5 June 1771.
21 Ibid., Guardian Accounts [3 November 1773]: for MPC, entries for 7 May 1771, 21 November 1772.
22 Ibid., GW to Jonathan Boucher, 3 February 1771.
23 Miller et al., eds, *Peale Papers*, 2:2:695.
24 *WGWEE*, MW to Mrs S. Thorpe, 15 July 1772; ibid., GW to Robert Cary, 15 July 1772.
25 PGWDE, Cash Accounts, April 1770; ibid., Diaries, entry for 16 July 1772.
26 VHS, Custis Family Papers, Section 27, Guardian Accounts for MPC, 1761–1772.
27 Fields, *"Worthy Partner"*, p. 151. MW to Mrs S. Thorpe [15 July 1772].
28 Miller et al., eds, *Peale Papers*, 2:2:695.

Chapter 8 – The Schooling of Jacky Custis

1 PGWDE, Enclosure, invoice to Robert Cary & Co., 18 July [1771].
2 Ibid., Invoice to Robert Cary & Co., 15 July 1772.
3 MVLA, Charles Willson Peale, *Martha Washington* [miniature, 1772]; VHS, Custis Family Papers, Section 25, Guardian Accounts for JPC, entry for 30 May 1772.
4 PGWDE, Jonathan Boucher to GW, 9 May 1770.
5 Ibid., GW to Jonathan Boucher, 9 July 1771.
6 Ibid., GW to Jonathan Boucher, 3 February 1771.
7 Ibid., GW to Jonathan Boucher, 20 April 1771.
8 Ibid., Jonathan Boucher to GW, 11 April 1771.
9 Ibid., GW to Jonathan Boucher, 20 April 1771.
10 Ibid., Jonathan Boucher to GW, 19 April 1771.
11 Ibid., Jonathan Boucher to GW, 3 May 1771.
12 Ibid., GW to Jonathan Boucher, 5 June 1771.
13 Ibid., Jonathan Boucher to GW, 21 May 1770.
14 Ibid., GW to Jonathan Boucher, 9 July 1771.
15 Ibid., GW to Jonathan Boucher, 5 June 1771.
16 Ibid., GW to Jonathan Boucher, 9 July 1771.
17 PGWDE, GW to Jonathan Boucher, 21 May 1772.
18 WLU, Lee Chapel and Museum, Charles Willson Peale, *George Washington*, 1772.

19 PGWDE, GW to Jonathan Boucher, 21 May 1772.
20 MVLA, Charles Willson Peale, *Martha Washington*, *John Parke Custis*, *Martha Parke Custis* [miniatures, 1772].
21 Ibid., GW to Jonathan Boucher, 16 December 1770.
22 Ibid., Jonathan Boucher to GW, 18 December 1770.
23 Ibid., GW to Jonathan Boucher, 3 February 1771.
24 Ibid., GW to Jonathan Boucher, 5 June 1771.
25 Ibid., Jonathan Boucher to GW, 19 November 1771.
26 Ibid., GW to Jonathan Boucher, 9 July 1771.
27 Ibid., GW to Jonathan Boucher, 7 January 1773.
28 Ibid., Jonathan Boucher to GW, 19 January 1773.
29 Ibid., Jonathan Boucher to GW, 8 April 1773, n. 2, quoting Myles Cooper to Jonathan Boucher, 22 March 1773.
30 Ibid., GW to Benedict Calvert, 3 April 1773.
31 Ibid.
32 Ibid.
33 Ibid., Benedict Calvert to GW, 8 April 1773.
34 Ibid., Jonathan Boucher to GW, 8 April 1773.
35 Ibid.
36 Ibid., GW to BB, 20 April 1773.
37 Ibid., Diaries, entries for April, May 1773.
38 Ibid., GW to Myles Cooper, 31 May 1773.
39 Ibid., JPC to GW, 5 July 1773.

Chapter 9 – Death and Adjustment

1 PGWDE, Diaries, entries for June 1773; ibid., Account of the Weather in June [1773].
2 Ibid., GW to BB, 20 June 1773.
3 Sparks, *Life of Washington*, p. 522, quoting letter, EPC to Jared Sparks, 26 February 1833.
4 PGWDE, GW to BB, 20 June 1773.
5 Ibid., GW to BB, 20 April 1773.
6 Ibid., GW to BB, 20 June 1773.
7 Ibid., GW to Robert Cary & Co., 26 July 1773, n. 1.
8 Ibid., GW to Robert Cary & Co., Enclosure, Invoice, 10 July 1773.
9 Ibid., GW to Robert Cary & Co., 12 July 1773 and n.
10 Ibid., GW to BB, 20 June 1773.
11 Ibid., GW to Robert Cary & Co., 10 November 1773.
12 Ibid., JPC to GW, 5 July 1773.
13 Fields, *"Worthy Partner"*, pp. 152–3, JPC to MW, 5 July [1773].
14 PGWDE, John Vardill to GW, 20 September 1773.
15 Ibid., GW to Robert Cary & Co., 6 October 1773.
16 Ibid., Diaries, entries for November 1773.
17 Ibid., GW to Myles Cooper, 15 December 1773.
18 Ibid., Diaries, entries for 3, 30 [31] January 1774, and nn.
19 Ibid., entries for February 1774.
20 Ibid., GW to Myles Cooper, 15 April 1774.
21 Fields, *"Worthy Partner"*, pp. 152–3, JPC to MW, 5 July [1773].
22 PGWDE, Diaries, entry for 24 February 1774.
23 Ibid., entry for 7 May 1774.
24 Ibid., William Ramsay, Robert Adam and Carlyle & Dalton to GW and John West, 16 May 1774.
25 Ibid., Diaries, entry for 4 June 1774.

26 Ibid., GW to Robert Cary & Co., 10 November 1773.
27 Ibid., LW to GW, 12 November 1775.
28 Ibid., GW to George William Fairfax, 10[–15] June 1774, and nn. 3, 25.
29 Ibid., Hugh Mercer to GW, 21 March 1774 and n. 1.
30 Ibid., GW to Robert Cary & Co., 1 June 1774.
31 Ibid., GW to George William Fairfax, 10[–15] June 1774.

Chapter 10 – Continental Army

 1 Randolph, ed., *Memoir, Correspondence . . . of Jefferson* (1829), pp. 1, 5.
 2 PGWDE, GW to George William Fairfax, 10[–15] June 1774.
 3 Ibid., Fairfax County Resolves [18 July 1774].
 4 Mays, ed., *Pendleton*, Vol. 2, p. 98.
 5 PGWDE, GW to Bryan Fairfax, 24 August 1774.
 6 MHS/AFPDE, John Adams to Abigail Adams, 25 September 1774.
 7 Ibid., John Adams Diary 22a, Notes on debates . . . 6 September 1774.
 8 LOC/AM/CL/LDC, Silas Deane to Elizabeth Deane, 10[–19] September 1774.
 9 PGWDE, Diaries, entries for September 1774.
10 Ibid., GW to Robert McKenzie, 9 October 1774.
11 Ibid., Fairfax Independent Company to GW, 19 October 1774, n.; ibid., Diaries, entry for 16 January 1775.
12 Ibid., Resolutions of Fairfax County Committee [17 January 1775].
13 Van Schreeven et al., eds, *Revolutionary Virginia*, Vol. 2, pp. 366–9.
14 PGWDE, GW to JAW, 25 March 1775.
15 Ibid., Edmund Pendleton to GW, 21 April 1775, n. 2.
16 Ibid., Spotsylvania Independent Company to GW, 26 April 1775.
17 Ibid., GW to George William Fairfax, 31 May 1775.
18 VHS, Lee Papers, Richard Henry Lee to William Lee, 10 May 1775.
19 'a tyrannical ministry': LOC/AM/CL/JCC, 11 May 1775, recording Letter from the Provincial Congress of Mass., 3 May 1775.
20 MHS/AFPDE, John Adams to Abigail Adams, 29 May 1775.
21 LOC/AM/CL/JCC, 12 June 1775.
22 Alden, *General Gage*, p. 204, Gage to William, Earl of Dartmouth, 25 June 1775.
23 LOC/AM/CL/JCC, 2 June 1775, recording Letter from the Provincial Congress of Mass., 16 May 1775.
24 Ibid., 14 June 1775.
25 Ibid., 15 June 1775.
26 MHS/AFPDE, John Adams autobiography, pt. 1, sheet 20/53, June–August 1773.
27 PGWDE, GW to MW, 18 June 1775.
28 Ibid., Address to the Continental Congress [16 June 1775].
29 Ibid., GW to MW, 18 June 1775.
30 Ibid., GW to Officers of Five Virginia Independent Companies, 20 June 1775.
31 MHS/AFPDE, John Adams to Abigail Adams, 11–17 June 1775.
32 PGWDE, GW to MW, 18 June 1775.
33 Ibid., GW to BB, 19 June 1775; ibid., GW to JPC, 19 June 1775.
34 Ibid., GW to JAW, 20 June 1775.

Chapter 11 – Taking Command

 1 PGWDE, GW to MW, 18 June 1775.
 2 Ibid., GW to MW, 23 June 1775.
 3 Ibid., GW to Philip Schuyler, 25 June 1775.

4   Ibid., GW to John Hancock, [25] June 1775 and nn. 1–4.
5   Ibid., GW to JAW, 27 July 1775.
6   LOC/AM/GWP, Series 5, Revolutionary War Expense Account, f. 2, 15 July 1775.
7   Ibid., 19 July 1775.
8   Ibid., 24 July 1775.
9   PGWDE, GW to JAW, 27 July 1775.
10   Ibid., GW to LW, 20 August 1775.
11   Ibid., General Orders, 4 July 1775.
12   Ibid., General Orders, 23 July 1775.
13   Ibid., General Orders, 5 August 1775.
14   Ibid., GW to LW, 20 August 1775.
15   MacDonald, *Documentary Source Book*, pp. 189–90.
16   Ibid., GW to John Hancock, 4 August 1775.
17   Ibid., GW to LW, 20 August 1775.
18   Ibid., BB to GW, 30 August 1775.
19   Ibid., John Hancock to GW, 10 July 1775.
20   Ibid., Peyton Randolph to GW, 6 September 1775.
21   Ibid., GW to Samuel Washington, 30 September 1775.
22   Ibid., LW to GW, 5 October 1775.
23   Ibid., LW to GW, 15 October 1775.
24   Ibid., LW to GW, 29 October 1775.
25   Ibid.
26   Ibid., LW to GW, 5 October 1775.
27   Ibid., GW to JAW, 13 October 1775.
28   Ibid., LW to GW, 29 October 1775.
29   Ibid., LW to GW, 5 November 1775.
30   Ibid., Fielding Lewis to GW, 14 November 1775.
31   Ibid., LW to GW, 14 November 1775.
32   Ibid., LW to GW, 24 November 1775.
33   Ibid., Fairfax County Committee of Correspondence to GW, 14 November 1775.
34   Ibid., LW to GW, 14 November 1775.
35   Ibid., GW to Joseph Reed, 20 November 1775.
36   Fields, *"Worthy Partner"*, pp. 164–6, MW to Elizabeth Ramsay, 30 December 1775.
37   LOC/AM/CL/LDC, John Adams to Mercy Otis Warren, 25 November 1775.

Chapter 12 – Besieging Boston

1   LOC/AM/CL/JCC, 20 October 1774.
2   Duane, ed., *Remembrances of Marshall*, p. 53.
3   Ibid.
4   MHS/AFPDE, John Adams autobiography, pt. 1, sheet 32/53, 26 February–14 March 1776.
5   PGWDE, Benjamin Harrison to GW, 21[–24] July 1775 and n.
6   Fields, *"Worthy Partner"*, pp. 164–5, MW to Elizabeth Ramsay, 30 December 1775.
7   Ibid.
8   PGWDE, Charles Lee to GW, 19 February 1776.
9   PGWDE, GW to Joseph Reed, 20 November 1775.
10   Ibid., GW to Joseph Reed, 23 January 1776.
11   Ibid., William Bartlett to GW, 9 December 1775, n. 3.
12   LOC/AM/GWP, Series 5, Ebenezer Austin, Revolutionary War Household Expense Accounts, 1775–6, entries for 11, 12, 22 December 1775.
13   Fields, *"Worthy Partner"*, pp. 164–5, MW to Elizabeth Ramsay, 30 December 1775.

14 PGWDE, Pierre Penet and Emmanuel de Pliarne to GW [18 December 1775].
15 Cooper, *Diary of Samuel Cooper*, p. 328.
16 PGWDE, GW to Hancock, 4 December 1775.
17 Ibid., Diaries, entry for 4 January 1775 and n.
18 Fields, *"Worthy Partner"*, pp. 166–7, MW to AMB, 31 January 1776.
19 Hoyt, 'Self-Portrait: Eliza Custis', p. 93.
20 Fields, *"Worthy Partner"*, pp. 164–6, MW to Elizabeth Ramsay, 30 December 1775.
21 [Cambridge], *An Historic Guide to Cambridge*, p. 88.
22 PGWDE, GW to John Hancock, 25 December 1775.
23 Ibid., GW to John Hancock, 31 December 1775.
24 Ibid., GW to John Hancock, 4 January 1776.
25 Ibid., GW to Joseph Reed, 4 January 177[6].
26 Sparks, *Library of American Biography*, Vol. 17, pp. 405–6.
27 Book of Common Prayer, Prayer for the King's Majesty.
28 Sparks, *Library of American Biography*, Vol. 17, pp. 405–6.
29 PGWDE, General Orders, 1 January 1776.
30 *Parliamentary History*, Vol. 18, pp. 695–7.
31 Ibid., GW to John Hancock, 4 January 1776 and n. 6.
32 Ibid., GW to John Adams, 7 January 1776.
33 Fields, *"Worthy Partner"*, p. 166, MW to Mercy Otis Warren, 8 January 1776.
34 PGWDE, GW to Joseph Reed, 14 January 1776.
35 MHS/AFPDE, John Adams Diary, entry for 24 January 1776.
36 Fields, *"Worthy Partner"*, pp. 166–7, MW to AMB, 31 January 1776.
37 PGWDE, GW to John Hancock, 18[–21] February 1776.
38 Ibid., Invitation to Henry and Lucy Flucker Knox, 1 February [1776].
39 Ibid., GW to BB, 28 February 1776.
40 Ibid., GW to Joseph Reed, 26 February[–9 March] 1776.
41 GLC/N-YHS, Henry Knox Papers, Henry Knox to Lucy Flucker Knox, c. 5–17 March 1776.
42 PGWDE, GW to John Hancock, 19 March 1776.
43 LOC/AM/GWP, Series 5, Ebenezer Austin, Revolutionary War Household Expense Accounts, March 1775–6, entry for 1 April 1776.
44 Butterfield et al., eds, *Adams Family Correspondence*, Vol. 1, pp. 385–6.
45 PGWDE, GW to JAW, 31 March 1776.

Chapter 13 – New York and Philadelphia

1 PGWDE, GW to John Hancock, 23 April 1776.
2 Ibid., GW to John Hancock, 5 May 1776.
3 Ibid., GW to John Hancock, 25[–26] April 1776.
4 Ibid., JPC to GW, 10 June 1776.
5 Ibid., GW to JAW, 29 April 1776.
6 Ibid., JPC to GW, 10 June 1776.
7 Ibid., John Hancock to GW, 21 May 1776.
8 Ibid., GW to JAW, 31 May[–4 June] 1776.
9 Ibid., GW to BB, 4 June 1776.
10 Ibid., GW to JAW, 31 May[–4 June] 1776.
11 Metropolitan Museum, NY, Joseph Hiller, after Charles Willson Peale, *His Excellency George Washington, Esq.* [mezzotint, c. 1777]; Hiller, after Peale, *Lady Washington*, mezzotint [after 1776].
12 MHS/AFPDE, John Adams to Abigail Adams, 25 August 1776.
13 YUAG, Charles Willson Peale, *Martha Washington* [miniature, 1776]; MVLA, Peale, *Martha Washington*, [miniature, 1772].

14   MVLA, Charles Willson Peale, *George Washington* [miniature, 1776].
15   PGWDE, GW to JAW, 31 May[–4 June] 1776.
16   Van Schreeven et al., eds, *Revolutionary Virginia*, Vol. 7, p. 450.
17   PGWDE, GW to JAW, 31 May[–4 June] 1776.
18   Van Schreeven et al., eds, *Revolutionary Virginia*, Vol. 7, p. 650.
19   PGWDE, GW to JAW, 31 May[–4 June] 1776.
20   Ibid., John Hancock to GW, 10 June 1776.
21   LOC/AM/CL/JCC, 7 June 1776.
22   Ibid., John Hancock to GW [10] June 1776.
23   Ibid., GW to James Clinton, 28 June 1776 and n. 1.
24   PGWDE, GW to John Hancock, 10 July 1776.
25   Ibid., GW to JAW, 22 July 1776.
26   Fields, *"Worthy Partner"*, p. 171, JPC to MW, 21 August 1776.
27   PGWDE, GW to LW, 19 August 1776.
28   Fields, *"Worthy Partner"*, p. 172, MW to AMB, 28 August 1776.
29   Ibid., pp. 170–1.
30   PGWDE, GW to LW, 26 August 1776.
31   Ibid., GW to John Hancock, 31 August 1776.
32   Ibid., GW to John Hancock, 8 September 1776.
33   Ibid., GW to LW, 30 September 1776.

Chapter 14 – Retreat to the Delaware

1   PGWDE, GW to LW, 30 September 1776.
2   Ibid., GW to LW, 6 October 1776.
3   Ibid., GW to SW, 5 October 1776.
4   Ibid., GW to John Hancock, 2 September 1776.
5   Ibid., GW to LW, 30 September 1776.
6   Ibid., GW to LW, 19 August 1776.
7   Ibid., LW to GW, 31 January 1776.
8   Ibid., LW to GW, 8 February 1776.
9   Ibid., GW to LW, 30 September 1776.
10   Ibid., LW to GW, 15 February 1776.
11   Ibid., GW to JPC, 24 July 1776.
12   Ibid., JPC to GW, 10 June 1776.
13   Ibid., LW to GW, 10 December 1775.
14   Ibid., LW to GW, 24 December 1777.
15   Ibid., LW to GW, 17 January 1776.
16   Ibid., GW to LW, 30 September 1776.
17   Ibid., John Hancock to GW, 28 October 1776 and nn. 1, 2.
18   Ibid., William Howe to GW, 11 November 1776.
19   Ibid., GW to John Hancock, 14 November 1776.
20   Ibid., John Hancock to GW, 28 October 1776, n. 2.
21   Ibid., GW to John Hancock, 14 November 1776.
22   Ibid., GW to JAW, 6[–19] November 1776, n. 10.
23   Ibid., GW to Joseph Reed, 30 November 1776, n. 1.
24   Ibid., GW to John Hancock, 19[–21] November 1776.
25   Ibid., GW to Joseph Reed, 30 November 1776, n. 1.
26   Ibid., GW to John Hancock, 23 November 1776, n. 2.
27   Ibid., GW to John Hancock, 30 November 1776.
28   Ibid., GW to Joseph Reed, 30 November 1776, n. 1.
29   Ibid., GW to Joseph Reed, 30 November 1776.
30   LOC/AM/AATC [Paine], *The American crisis (No. 1)* [Boston, 1776], broadside.
31   PGWDE, GW to LW, 10[–17] December 1776.

32 Ibid., Bartholomew Dandridge to GW, 16 January 1777.
33 Ibid., GW to LW, 10[-17] December 1776.
34 Ibid., GW to SW, 18 December 1776; ibid., GW to JAW, 18 December 1776.
35 Happel, *Chatham*, p. 14.
36 PGWDE, GW to Joseph Reed, 23 December 1776.
37 Ibid., GW to John Hancock, 27 December 1776.
38 Butterfield, ed., *Rush Letters*, Vol. 1, pp. 125-7.
39 PGWDE, GW to John Hancock, 7 January 1777.
40 PGWDE, GW to John Hancock, 5 January 1777.
41 LOC/AM/AATC [Paine], *The American crisis (No. 1)* [Boston, 1776], broadside.
42 Sellers, 'Peale, Artist-Soldier', p. 283.
43 PGWDE, GW to Robert Morris, 5 January 1777.
44 Ibid., GW to Robert Morris, 13 January 1777.
45 Ibid., GW to JPC, 22 January 1777.
46 Ibid., Bartholomew Dandridge to GW, 16 January 1777.
47 Fitzpatrick, *George Washington's Accounts*, pp. 97-8.
48 PGWDE, GW to the Commanding Officer in Philadelphia, 6 March 1776.
49 Ibid., GW to SW, 15 March 1777.
50 Ibid., GW to John Hancock, 29 March 1777.
51 Ibid., GW to SW, 5 April 1777.

Chapter 15 – Morristown and Brandywine

1 Ibid., John Armstrong to GW, 30 December 1777.
2 Showman et al., eds, *Greene Papers*, Vol. 2, p. 54.
3 Moore, *Diary*, Vol. 1, p. 192.
4 PGWDE, GW to MW, 18 June 1775.
5 MVLA, Thompson, '"As if I had Been a Very Great Somebody"', pp. 42-3 and p. 43 n. 76, citing Proceedings of the New Jersey Historical Society (Newark, July 1933), p. 152, Martha Dangerfield Bland to Frances Bland Randolph, 12 May 1777.
6 Idzerda et al., eds, *Lafayette in the American Revolution*, Vol. 1, p. 225.
7 PGWDE, GW to Robert Morris, 2 March 1777.
8 PGWDE, GW to John Hancock, 5 February 1777.
9 Ibid., GW to John Hancock, 14 March 1777.
10 Ibid., GW to Patrick Henry, 13 April 1777.
11 Ibid., GW to Landon Carter, 15 April 1777.
12 Ibid., GW to John Hancock, 9 April 1777.
13 MVLA, Thompson, '"As if I had Been a Very Great Somebody"', pp. 42-3 and p. 43 n. 76, citing Proceedings of the New Jersey Historical Society (Newark, July 1933), p. 152, Martha Dangerfield Bland to Frances Bland Randolph, 12 May 1777.
14 LOC/AM/GWP, Caleb Gibbs and Mary Smith, 1776-80, Revolutionary War Household Expenses, entry for 11 April, March 1777.
15 Ibid., entry for 7 May 1777; PGWDE, GW to Caleb Gibbs, 1 May 1777 and nn. 3 and 5.
16 Ibid., Thomas Mifflin to GW, 11 June 1777, n. 2.
17 *Virginia Gazette*, 8 August 1777; Moore, *Diary*, Vol. 1, p. 477.
18 PGWDE, General Orders, 6 July 1777.
19 Ibid., GW to Philip Schuyler, 15 July 1777.
20 Ibid., GW to John Hancock, 25 July 1777.
21 Ibid., GW to Jonathan Trumbull Sr, 31 July 1777.
22 Du Motier, *Memoirs of Lafayette*, Vol. 1, p. 19.
23 PGWDE, GW to Jonathan Trumbull Sr, 4 August 1777.

24 Ibid., Bartholomew Dandridge to GW, 22 August 1777.
25 Ibid., JPC to GW, 8 August 1777.
26 Ibid., JPC to GW, 11 September 1777.
27 Ibid., JPC to GW, Postscript, MW to GW, 11 September 1777.
28 Ibid., GW to John Hancock, 11 September 1777.
29 Ibid., GW to Thomas Nelson, 27 September 1777.
30 Ibid., GW to SW, 27 October 1777.
31 Ibid., GW to Benjamin Harrison, 5 October 1777.
32 Ibid., GW to JAW, 18 October 1777.
33 Ibid., JPC to GW, 26 October 1777.
34 Ibid., GW to JPC, 14 November, 1777.
35 Ibid., JPC to GW, 26 October 1777.
36 Ibid., GW to SW, 27 October 1777.
37 Fields, *"Worthy Partner"*, pp. 174–5, MW to AMB, 18 November 1777.
38 Ibid., pp. 175–6, MW to BB, 22 December 1777.
39 PGWDE, LW to GW, 24 December 1777.
40 Ibid., JPC to GW, 14 January 1778.
41 Ibid., GW to JPC, 1 February 1778.

Chapter 16 – Valley Forge

 1 PGWDE, GW to Henry Laurens, 23 December 1777.
 2 Ibid., GW to John Banister, 21 April 1778.
 3 Ibid., GW to Henry Laurens, 23 December 1777.
 4 Ibid., General Orders, 18 December 1777.
 5 Ibid., GW to Continental Congress Camp Committee, 29 January 1778.
 6 Ibid., Nathanael Greene to GW [January 1778].
 7 Ibid., GW to Henry Laurens, 31 January 1778.
 8 Ibid., Henry Laurens to GW, 27 January 1778, n. 1.
 9 Henkles, ed., *Robert Morris Correspondence*, pp. 165–7.
10 PGWDE., Lafayette to GW, 30 December 1778.
11 Ibid, GW to Henry Laurens, 31 January 1778.
12 Sparks, ed., *Writings of Washington*, Vol. 5, p. 508.
13 Henkles, ed., *Robert Morris Correspondence*, pp. 17–19.
14 PGWDE, GW to Jonathan Trumbull Sr, 6 February 1778.
15 Ibid., GW to William Buchanan, 7 February 1777.
16 Ibid., GW to Thomas Wharton, 10 April 1778, n. 2.
17 LOC/AM/CL/LDC, Committee at Camp to Henry Laurens, 12 February 1778.
18 PGWDE, General Orders, 15 February 1778, source note.
19 Duponceau, 'Letters of Duponceau', p. 180.
20 Fields, *"Worthy Partner"*, pp. 177–8, MW to Mercy Otis Warren, 7 March 1778.
21 LOC/AM/GWP, Series 5, Caleb Gibbs and Mary Smith, 1776–80, Revolutionary War Household Expenses, entries for February, March 1778.
22 Duponceau, 'Letters of Duponceau', pp. 179, 181.
23 PGWDE, GW to Thomas Wharton, 6 April 1778, n. 1.
24 Boudinot, *Life of Boudinot*, Vol. 1, pp. 106, 115.
25 Fields, *"Worthy Partner"*, pp. 177–8, MW to Mercy Otis Warren, 7 March 1778
26 Ibid., pp. 178–9, JPC to MW, 3 April 1778.
27 Miller et al., eds, *Peale Papers*, Vol. 1, pp. 266, 271.
28 PGWDE, GW to JPC, 1 February 1778, n. 1.
29 Ibid., GW to LW, 28 February 1778.
30 Ibid., LW to GW, 22 April 1778.
31 Ibid., LW to GW, 8 April 1778.
32 Simms, ed., *Laurens Army Correspondence*, pp. 114–8, 124–5.

33 PGWDE, Nicholas Cooke to GW, 23 February 1778.
34 Ibid., GW to LW, 15 August 1778.
35 Ibid., LW to GW, 18 February 1778; ibid., LW to GW, 4 March 1778.
36 Baker, 'Exchange of Major-General Charles Lee', pp. 31–2.
37 PGWDE, GW to John Banister, 21 April 1778.
38 Ibid., GW to Henry Laurens, 20 April 1778.
39 Baker, *Itinerary*, p. 128.

Chapter 17 – Philadelphia and Middlebrook, New Jersey

1   PGWDE, GW to Henry Laurens, 18 June 1778.
2   Ibid., GW to Charles Lee, 26 June 1778.
3   Ibid., GW to JAW, 4 July 1778.
4   Ibid., Benedict Arnold to GW, 30 June 1778.
5   Ibid., JPC to GW, 11 May 1778.
6   Ibid., GW to JPC, 26 May 1778.
7   Ibid., GW to JPC, 3 August 1778.
8   Ibid., GW to JPC, 26 May 1778.
9   Ibid., JPC to GW, 15 July 1778.
10 Ibid., GW to JPC, 3 August 1778.
11 Ibid., John Sullivan to GW, 23 August 1778, n. 2.
12 Ibid., Thomas Nelson to GW, 11 August 1778.
13 Ibid., GW to Thomas Nelson, 20 August 1778.
14 Ibid., GW to JPC, 12 October 1778.
15 Ibid., GW to James Hill, 27 October 1778.
16 Ibid., GW to Burwell Bassett, 30 October 1778.
17 Ibid., GW to JAW, 26 October 1778.
18 Fields, *"Worthy Partner"*, pp. 180–1, MW to Bartholomew Dandridge, 2 November 1778.
19 PGWDE, John Mitchell to GW, 16 October 1778; ibid., John Mitchell to GW, 20 October 1778.
20 Ibid., GW to John Mitchell, 11 November 1778.
21 Ibid., GW to Nathanael Greene, 4 December 1778.
22 Showman et al., *Papers of Greene*, Vol. 3, p. 121.
23 PGWDE, GW to Alexander Stirling, 21 December 1778.
24 Ibid., GW to Continental Congress Committee of Conference, 8 January 1779.
25 Simms, ed., *Laurens Army Correspondence*, pp. 230–1.
26 Greene, *Life of Greene*, Vol. 2, p. 168.
27 PGWDE, GW to Philip Schuyler, 11 February 1779.
28 Fields, *"Worthy Partner"*, p. 181, MW to JPC and ECPC, 19 March 1779 [wrongly dated by MW 1778].
29 Papers of Benjamin Franklin, franklinpapers.org, 28:1778–9, Sarah Bache to Benjamin Franklin, 17 January 1779.
30 PGWDE, GW to Benjamin Harrison, 18–30 December 1778.
31 Ibid., GW to the Magistrates of Philadelphia, 25 December 1778, n., citing text of address made to him, 29 December 1778.
32 Ibid, GW to John Jay, 29 January 1779.
33 Morgan and Fielding, *Washington Life Portraits*, pp. 57–8.
34 PGWDE, GW to LW, 17 December 1778.
35 Ibid., GW to LW, 24 February 1779.
36 Ibid., GW to John Jay, 23 April 1779.
37 Ibid., GW to Gouverneur Morris, 8 May 1779.
38 Fields, *"Worthy Partner"*, p. 181, MW to JPC and ECPC, 19 March 1779 [wrongly dated by MW 1778].

39 Thacher, *Military Journal*, p. 157.
40 GLC/N-YHS, Henry Knox Papers, Henry Knox to William Knox, 28 February 1779.
41 PGWDE, GW to John Mitchell, 17 February 1779.
42 Showman et al., eds, *Greene Papers*, Vol. 3, p. 354.
43 Thacher, *Military Journal*, p. 159.
44 PGWDE, GW to LW, 29 May 1779, n. 7.

Chapter 18 – The Hard Winter: Morristown

1 *WGWEE*, GW to Nicholas Rogers, 28 May 1779 and n.
2 Ibid., GW to JAW, 20 June 1779.
3 Harbin, 'Letters from John Parke Custis', pp. 279–80.
4 WGWEE, GW to Philip Schuyler, 9 June 1779.
5 Ibid., GW to Anthony Wayne, 9 July 1779.
6 LOC/AM/GWP, Series 5, Caleb Gibbs and Mary Smith, 1776–80, Revolutionary War Household Expenses, entry for 25 December 1779.
7 LOC/AM/CL/LDC, John Jay to GW, 20 July 1779.
8 *WGWEE*, GW to Edmund Randolph, 1 August 1779.
9 Ibid., GW to John Cochran, 16 August 1779.
10 Fields, *"Worthy Partner"*, p. 181, MW to JPC and ECPC, 19 March 1779 [wrongly dated by MW 1778].
11 LOC/AM/CL/LDC, Henry Laurens to John Laurens, 27 September 1779.
12 Harbin, 'Letters from John Parke Custis', pp. 278–9.
13 LOC/AM/CL/LDC, Henry Laurens to GW, 7 October 1779.
14 LOC/AM/CL/JCC, 14 August 1779.
15 *WGWEE*, GW to Juan de Miralles, 16 October 1779.
16 LOC/AM/GWP, Series 4, GW to John Mitchell, 17 October 1779.
17 Ibid., Series 4, John Mitchell to GW, 30 October 1779.
18 Ibid., GW to Alexander Spotswood, 10 November 1779.
19 Ibid., John Mitchell to GW, 30 October 1779.
20 Harbin, 'Letters from John Parke Custis', p. 279.
21 LOC/AM/GWP, Series 4, GW to Nathanael Greene, 30 November 1779.
22 Parker, 'Journal of Lieutenant Robert Parker (concluded)', p. 23.
23 Thacher, *Military Journal*, p. 180.
24 Freeman, *Washington*, Vol. 5, p. 141 and n. 79.
25 *WGWEE*, Circular to Governors of the Middle States, 16 December 1779.
26 Ibid., GW to Philip Schuyler, 30 January 1780.
27 Ibid., General Orders, 29 December 1779.
28 LOC/AM/GWP, Series 5, Caleb Gibbs and Mary Smith, 1776–80, Revolutionary War Household Expenses, entry for 25 December 1779.
29 Thacher, *Military Journal*, p. 221.
30 Showman et al., eds, *Greene Papers*, Vol. 5, p. 252.
31 *WGWEE*, GW to Philip Schuyler, 30 January 1780.
32 Smith, ed., *Record of Service*, p. 135.
33 PGWDE/EA, GW to Lafayette, 18 March 1780.
34 *WGWEE*, GW to Nathanael Greene, 22 January 1780.
35 Ibid., GW to JPC, 20 January 1780.
36 Fields, *"Worthy Partner"*, p. 183, MPC to BB, 18 July 1780.
37 *WGWEE*, GW to Robert Morris, 4 February 1780.
38 LOC/AM/CL/LDC, John Fell to Robert Morris, 5 March 1780.
39 PGWDE/EA, GW to John Mitchell, 30 March 1780.
40 Ibid., GW to John Mitchell, 8 April 1780.
41 Fields, *"Worthy Partner"*, p. 182, MPC to Elizabeth Schuyler [Morristown, 1780].

42 Showman et al., eds, *Greene Papers*, Vol. 5, p. 426.
43 PGWDE/EA, Chevalier de La Luzerne to GW, 29 April 1780.
44 Freeman, *Washington*, Vol. 5, p. 158 and n. 113.
45 Thacher, *Military Journal*, p. 230.
46 PGWDE/EA, GW to John Laurens, 26 April 1780.
47 Idzerda et al., eds, *Lafayette in the American Revolution*, Vol. 3, pp. 3–6.
48 PGWDE/EA, GW to LW, 19 May 1780.
49 Reed, ed., *Life of Reed*, Vol. 2, p. 207.

Chapter 19 – Home and Headquarters

1 PGWDE/EA, GW to Henry Lee, 11 July 1780.
2 Ibid., GW to Comte de Rochambeau, 16 July 1780.
3 Ibid., GW to SW, 31 August 1780.
4 Ibid., GW to JPC, 6 August 1780.
5 Ibid., GW to John Cadwalader, 5 October 1780.
6 Fields, *"Worthy Partner"*, p. 183, MW to BB, 18 July 1780.
7 Hoyt, 'Self-Portrait: Eliza Custis', pp. 93–4.
8 Hoyt, 'Self-Portrait: Eliza Custis', p. 94.
9 Cadou, *George Washington Collection*, p. 90.
10 *Pennsylvania Gazette*, 21 June 1780.
11 PGWDE/EA, Esther Reed to GW, 4 July 1780.
12 Ibid., GW to Esther Reed, 10 August 1780.
13 PTJDE/EA, Martha Wayles Skelton Jefferson to Eleanor Conway Madison, 8 August 1780.
14 MVLA, Thompson, 'As if I had been a Very Great Somebody', pp. 9–10.
15 Fields, *"Worthy Partner"*, p. 184, MW to Arthur Lee, 15 September 1780.
16 Ibid., MW to Elizabeth Willing Powel, 20 September 1780.
17 PGWDE/EA, Nathanael Greene to GW, 13 November 1780.
18 Chinard, ed., *Washington as the French Knew Him*, p. 19.
19 Chastellux, *Travels in North America*, Vol. 1, p. 134.
20 PGWDE/EA, GW to Catharine Littlefield Greene, 15 December 1780.
21 Fields, *"Worthy Partner"*, p. 185, MW to Charles Willson Peale, 26 December 1780.
22 PGWDE/EA, GW to Henry Knox, 7 January 1781.
23 Ibid., GW to Philip Schuyler, 10 January 1781.
24 Ibid., GW to Nathanael Greene, 2 January 1781.
25 Ibid., GW to LW, 30 April 1781.
26 Fields, *"Worthy Partner"*, p. 186, MW to LW[?], 31 May 1781.
27 PGWDE/EA, GW to JPC, 31 May 1781.
28 Fields, *"Worthy Partner"*, pp. 186–7, Martha Mortier to MW, 15 June 1781 and nn. 1–2.
29 PGWDE, Diaries, entry for 5 September 1781.
30 Ibid., entry for 9 September 1781.

Chapter 20 – Victory on the York and Private Grief

1 Trumbull, 'Minutes of Occurrences', p. 333.
2 PGWDE/EA, GW to Benjamin Lincoln, 15 September 1781.
3 Ibid., GW to Thomas McKean, 23 September 1781.
4 PGWDE, Diaries, entry for 28 September 1781.
5 PGWDE, Diaries, entry for 9 October 1781.
6 Thacher, *Military Journal*, p. 340.
7 Harrison, ed., *Memoir of Tilghman*, p. 105.
8 Fields, *"Worthy Partner"*, pp. 187–8, JPC to MW, 12 October 1781.

9 GLC, Henry Knox Papers, Henry Knox to Clement Biddle, 11 November 1781.
10 Fields, *"Worthy Partner"*, pp. 187–8, JPC to MW, 12 October 1781.
11 GLC, Henry Knox Papers, Lucy Flucker Knox to Henry Knox, 8 October 1781.
12 Ibid., Henry Knox Papers, Lucy Flucker Knox to Henry Knox, 16 October 1781.
13 Ibid.
14 Ibid., Henry Knox Papers, Lucy Flucker Knox to Henry Knox, 23 October 1781.
15 Ibid., Henry Knox Papers, Henry Knox to Lucy Flucker Knox, 16 October 1781.
16 PGWDE, Diaries, entry for 17 October 1781.
17 PGWDE/EA, GW to Thomas McKean, 19 October 1781.
18 GLC, Henry Knox Papers, Henry Knox to Lucy Flucker Knox, 31 October 1781.
19 Wraxall, *Historical Memoirs*, 2:435.
20 GLC, Henry Knox Papers, Lucy Flucker Knox to Henry Knox, 23 October 1781.
21 PGWDE/EA, GW to George William Fairfax, 10 July 1783.
22 GLC, Henry Knox Papers, Henry Knox to Clement Biddle, 11 November 1781.
23 FUL, Charles Allen Munn Collection, Jonathan Trumbull Jr, 'Journal of Occurrences', entries for 5 and 6 November 1781.
24 PGWDE/EA, GW to Jonathan Trumbull Jr, 6 November 1781.
25 Ibid., GW to Marquis de Lafayette, 15 November 1781.
26 Ibid., GW to John Hanson, 6 November 1781.
27 GLC, Henry Knox Papers, Henry Knox to Clement Biddle, 11 November 1781.
28 PGWDE/EA, GW to Bartholomew Dandridge, 19 November 1781.
29 PGWDE, GW to Jonathan Trumbull Jr, 1 October 1785, quoting Laurence Sterne, *Tristram Shandy*, 9 vols (London, 1761), Vol. 3, p. 142.
30 PGWDE/EA, GW to William Ramsay, 19 November 1781.

Chapter 21 – Uncertainty and Disaffection

1 PGWDE/EA, GW to Nathanael Greene, 16 November 1781.
2 Ibid., Comte de Rochambeau to GW, 10 February 1782.
3 PGWDE/EA, GW to William Ramsay, 19 November 1781.
4 Chastellux, *Travels in North America*, Vol. 2, pp. 513–14.
5 Cadou, *George Washington Collection*, p. 78.
6 PGWDE/EA, GW to Robert Hanson Harrison, 18 November 1781.
7 Ibid., GW to John Hancock, 4 May 1782.
8 Ibid., Sir Guy Carleton to GW, 7 May 1782.
9 Thacher, *Military Journal*, pp. 371–2.
10 Balch, ed., *Blanchard Journal*, p. 32.
11 PGWDE/EA, GW to MW, 1 October 1782.
12 Ibid., GW to Nathanael Greene, 17 October 1782.
13 Ferguson et al., eds, *Robert Morris Papers*, 6–7:661.
14 PGWDE/EA, GW to William Heath, 5 February 1783.
15 Ibid., GW to Joseph Jones, 14 December 1782.
16 Ibid., GW to Daniel Parker, 22 January 1783.
17 Fields, *"Worthy Partner"*, p. 189, MW to Henry Knox [6 March 1783].
18 Freeman, *Washington*, Vol. 3, pp. 433–54 and nn. 33–9.
19 PGWDE/EA, GW to Marquis de Lafayette, 5 April 1783.
20 Ibid., GW to Alexander Hamilton, 31 March 1783.

Chapter 22 – Peace on the Hudson

1 PGWDE/EA, Proclamation for the Cessation of Hostilities, 18 April 1783.
2 Ibid., GW to Elias Boudimot, 22 April 1783.
3 Ibid., GW to Alexander Hamilton, 22 April 1783.
4 Ibid., GW to Tench Tilghman, 24 April 1783.

5 Ibid., GW to George William Fairfax, 10 July 1783.
6 Fitzpatrick, *George Washington's Accounts*, pp. 97–8.
7 PGWDE/EA, GW to JAW, 15 June 1783.
8 Ibid., GW to William Stephens Smith, 21 May 1783.
9 Ibid., GW to LW, 11 June 1783.
10 Ibid., GW to Daniel Parker, 18 June 1783.
11 Dunlap, 'Rise and Progress of Arts of Design', Vol. 1, pp. 253–4.
12 PGWDE/EA, GW to Bushrod Washington, 22 September 1783.
13 Ibid., GW to Tench Tilghman, 2 October 1783.
14 Ibid., GW to Clement Biddle, 2 October 1783.
15 *WGWEE*, GW to Wakelin Welch, 30 October 1783.
16 PGWDE/EA, GW to LW, 20 September 1783.
17 PGWDE/EA, Washington's Farewell Address to the Army, 2 November 1783
18 Freeman, *Washington*, Vol. 2, pp. 465–8.
19 Ibid., Vol. 2, p. 474 n. 33.
20 PGWDE/EA, GW to United States Congress, 23 December 1783.
21 PGWDE, GW to Charles Thomson, 22 January 1784.
22 Ibid., Charles Thomson to GW, 7 February 1784.
23 Fields, *"Worthy Partner"*, pp. 193–4, MW to Hannah Stockton Boudinot, 15 January 1784.

Chapter 23 – Mount Vernon

1 PGWDE, GW to Henry Knox, 20 February 1784.
2 Ibid., GW to Marquis de Lafayette, 1 February 1784.
3 Baker, *Washington after the Revolution*, p. 7.
4 PGWDE, GW to Marquis de Lafayette, 1 February 1784.
5 Ibid., GW to Marquise de Lafayette, 4 April 1784.
6 Ibid.
7 Fields, *"Worthy Partner"*, pp. 193–4, MW to Hannah Stockton Boudinot, 15 January 1784.
8 Baker, *Washington after the Revolution*, p. 7.
9 PGWDE, GW to Thomas Mifflin, 14 January 1784 and n. 2.
10 Fields, *"Worthy Partner"*, 194–5, MW to Hannah Bushrod Washington, 22 June 1784.
11 'Institution of the Society of the Cincinnati', 13 May 1783, societyofthecincinnati.org/pdf/SOTC_Institution.pdf.
12 Hünemörder, *Society of the Cincinnati*, p. 91.
13 Fields, *"Worthy Partner"*, pp. 205–7, MW to FBW, 25 February 1788.
14 Ibid., pp. 195–6, MW to FBW, 7 August 1784.
15 Ibid.
16 Idzerda et al., eds, *Lafayette in the American Revolution*, Vol. 5, pp. 237–8.
17 Ibid.
18 PGWDE, Diaries, entry for 4 October 1784.
19 Ibid., GW to Marquis de Lafayette, 8 December 1784.
20 PGWDE, GW to George William Fairfax, 27 February 1785.
21 PGWDE, Diaries, entry for 30 June 1785.
22 Watson, *Men and Times of the Revolution*, p. 244.
23 PGWDE, GW to Samuel Fraunces, 7 September 1785.
24 Ibid., GW to Richard Henry Lee, 22 June 1785.
25 Fields, *"Worthy Partner"*, pp. 196–7, MW to Mercy Otis Warren, 9 June 1785.
26 MVLA, Robert Pine, *Frances Bassett Washington* [half-length, 1785].
27 PGWDE, GW to BB, 23 May 1785.
28 *WGWEE*, GW to Thomas Montgomerie, 25 June 1785.

29 Fields, *"Worthy Partner"*, p. 197, MW to Thomas and Christian Scott Blackburn, 10 October 1785.
30 Cadou, *George Washington Collection*, p. 120.
31 PGWDE, Diaries, entry for 15 October 1785.
32 Ibid., GW to George William Fairfax, 10 November 1785.
33 Ibid., GW to Benjamin Lincoln, 6 February 1786.
34 Ibid., Benjamin Lincoln to GW, 9 May 1786, n. 1.
35 Ibid., Henry Lee to GW, 3 July 1786.
36 Ibid., GW to Mary Ball Washington, 15 February 1787.

Chapter 24 – Conventions and Elections

1   PGWDE, GW to Edmund Randolph, 28 March 1787.
2   Ibid., GW to Benjamin Harrison, 18 January 1784.
3   Ibid., GW to Edmund Randolph, 28 March 1787.
4   Ibid., Robert Morris to GW, 23 April 1787.
5   Ibid., GW to Robert Morris, 5 May 1787.
6   Fields, *"Worthy Partner"*, pp. 205–6, MW to FBW, 25 February 1788.
7   PGWDE, Diaries, entry for 3 May 1787.
8   Ibid., GW to Robert Morris, 5 May 1787.
9   Ibid., Address to the Continental Congress [16 June 1775].
10 Farrand, *Records of the Federal Convention, 1787*, Vol. 1, pp. 3–4.
11 PGWDE, GW to Elizabeth Willing Powel, 30 July 1787.
12 Ibid., Elizabeth Willing Powel to GW, 8 September 1787.
13 Ibid., GW to Elizabeth Willing Powel, 8 September 1787.
14 Ibid., GW to Marquis de Lafayette, 18 September 1787.
15 Ibid., Diaries, entry for 28 September 1787.
16 Ibid., Gouverneur Morris to GW, 30 October 1787.
17 Fields, *"Worthy Partner"*, pp. 200–2, MW to Elizabeth Willing Powel, 18 January 1788.
18 Ibid., pp. 205–6, MW to FBW, 25 February 1788.
19 PGWDE, Alexander Hamilton to GW, 13 August 1788.
20 Ibid., GW to Alexander Hamilton, 28 August 1788.
21 Ibid., GW to James Madison, 2 January 1789.
22 Ibid., Diaries, entry for 7 January 1789.
23 Ibid., GW to Henry Knox, 1 April 1789.
24 Fields, *"Worthy Partner"*, pp. 213–14, MW to John Dandridge, 20 April 1789.
25 Ibid.

Chapter 25 – New York Houses

1   PGWDE, First Inaugural Address, Final Version [30 April 1789].
2   Ibid., GW to John Adams [10 May 1789], source note.
3   Ibid., GW to David Stuart, 15 June 1790.
4   Ibid., GW to John Adams [10 May 1789], source note.
5   Ibid., GW to John Adams [10 May 1789].
6   Beard, ed., *Maclay Journal*, p. 29.
7   PGWDE, Alexander Hamilton to GW, 5 May 1789.
8   Ibid., GW to John Adams [10 May 1789].
9   Ibid., John Adams to GW, 17 May 1789.
10 Ibid., GW to David Stuart, 26 July 1789.
11 Ibid., William Heth to GW, 23 May 1789.
12 MVLA, Robert Lewis, 'A Journey from Fredericksburg Virginia to New-York', 13–20 May 1789, Ms.

13 PGWDE, James McHenry to GW, 24 May 1789.
14 Fields, *"Worthy Partner"*, pp. 215–6, MW to FBW, 8 June 1789.
15 PGWDE, GW to David Stuart, 15 June 1790.
16 Mitchell, ed., *New Letters of Abigail Adams*, p. 19.
17 Ibid., pp. 13–15.
18 PGWDE, James McHenry to GW, 28 June 1789, n .1.
19 Mitchell, ed., *New Letters of Abigail Adams*, p. 19.
20 PGWDE, GW to David Stuart, 26 July 1789.
21 Mitchell, ed., *New Letters of Abigail Adams*, p. 51.
22 PGWDE, Pierce Butler to GW, 6 August 1789, n. 1.
23 Ibid., Burgess Ball to GW, 25 August 1789, n. 3.
24 Cadou, *George Washington Collection*, p. 217.
25 Fields, *"Worthy Partner"*, pp. 215–16, MW to FBW, 8 June 1789.
26 Ibid., p. 217, MW to FBW [summer 1789].
27 Decatur, *Private Affairs of Washington*, pp. 33, 35.
28 Custis, *Recollections*, p. 408, n.
29 Decatur, *Private Affairs of Washington*, pp. 85–87.
30 Ibid., p. 102.
31 PGWDE, Tobias Lear to GW, 28 October 1790, n. 2.
32 Fields, *"Worthy Partner"*, pp. 223–4, MW to Mercy Otis Warren, 26 December 1789.
33 Decatur, *Private Affairs of Washington*, pp. 89–90, 62–3.
34 PGWDE, Diaries, entry for 24 November and n.
35 Ibid., John Adams to GW, 17 May 1789.
36 Fields, *"Worthy Partner"*, pp. 219–21, MW to FBW, 23 October 1789.
37 Ibid., p. 219, MW to Abigail Adams [October 1789].
38 Ibid., p. 221, MW to Abigail Adams [4 November 1789].
39 PGWDE, Thanksgiving Proclamation [3 October 1789].
40 Ibid., Diaries, entry for 26 November 1789.
41 Fields, *"Worthy Partner"*, pp. 223–4, MW to Mercy Otis Warren, 26 December 1789.
42 PGWDE, Diaries, entry for 3 February 1790.
43 Fields, *"Worthy Partner"*, p. 225, MW to FBW [22 March 1790].
44 PGWDE, Tobias Lear to GW, 12 September 1790.
45 Beard, ed., *Maclay Journal*, pp. 136–7.
46 PGWDE, LW to GW, 28 April 1790.
47 Trumbull, *Autobiography*, pp. 165–6.
48 Mitchell, ed., *New Letters of Abigail Adams*, p. 49.
49 Beard, ed., *Maclay Journal*, p. 269.
50 PGWDE, Diaries, entry for 5 July 1790.
51 Fields, *"Worthy Partner"*, p. 217, MW to FBW [July 1789].

Chapter 26 – Market Street, Philadelphia

1   PGWDE, GW to Tobias Lear, 5 September 1790.
2   Ibid., GW to Tobias Lear, 27 October 1790.
3   Ibid., Tobias Lear to GW, 31 October 1790.
4   Ibid., GW to Frances Bassett Washington, 28[–29] July 1793.
5   Adams, ed., *Letters of Mrs Adams*, Vol. 2, pp. 207–9.
6   PGWDE, Tobias Lear to GW, 31 October 1790.
7   Ibid., GW to Tobias Lear, 9 September 1790.
8   Custis, *Recollections*, p. 423.
9   PGWDE, GW to Tobias Lear, 22 November 1790.
10 Ibid., GW to Tobias Lear, 20 September 1790.

11 Ibid., Tobias Lear to GW 12 September 1790.
12 Fields, *"Worthy Partner"*, pp. 229–30, MW to Janet Livingston Montgomery, 29 January 1791.
13 Jeremy, ed., *Wansey Journal*, pp. 99–100.
14 PGWDE, GW to Tobias Lear, 19 June 1791.
15 Ibid., Tobias Lear to GW, 5 April 1791.
16 Laws of the Commonwealth of Pennsylvania, Vol. 1, pp. 492–93.
17 PGWDE, Tobias Lear to GW, 5 April 1791.
18 Ibid., GW to Tobias Lear, 12 April 1791.
19 Ibid., Tobias Lear to GW, 24 April 1791.
20 Ibid., Tobias Lear to GW, 24 April 1791 and nn. 2–7.
21 Ibid., Tobias Lear to GW, 15 May 1791.
22 Ibid., Tobias Lear to GW, 24 April 1791.
23 Founders Online, founders.archives.gov, Martha Washington to Abigail Smith Adams, 25 January 1791; PGWDE, GW to Betty Washington Lewis and Sarah Carlyle Herbert, 26 April 1792.
24 Decatur, *Private Affairs of Washington*, pp. 200, 207, 220, 240, 253, 292.
25 Britt, *Nothing More Agreeable*, pp. 30–2, 98, 105.
26 Decatur, *Private Affairs of Washington*, pp. 189, 226, 293.
27 Ibid., p. 315.
28 PGWDE, GW to Tobias Lear, 26 June 1791, n. 1.
29 Ibid., *Diaries*, entry for 18 February 1786.
30 Fields, *"Worthy Partner"*, p. 233, MW to FBW, 29 August 1791.
31 PGWDE, GW to Tobias Lear, 10 October 1790.
32 Ibid., GW to Betty Washington Lewis, 7 October 1792.
33 Ibid., Harriot Washington to GW, 5 January [1793]; ibid., Harriot Washington to GW, [7] January [1794].
34 Ibid., GW to Tobias Lear, 10 October 1790.
35 Decatur, *Private Affairs of Washington*, pp. 265, 226, 318–19, 322–3.
36 Fields, *"Worthy Partner"*, pp. 268–9, MW to FBW, 15 June 1794.
37 Decatur, *Private Affairs of Washington*, pp. 290, 313.
38 PGWDE, GW to Tobias Lear, 30 July 1792.
39 Ibid., GW to Thomas Jefferson, 1 April 1791.
40 Ibid., GW to Tobias Lear, 21 September 1792.
41 Ibid., Tobias Lear to GW, 21 July 1792.
42 Ibid., Thomas Jefferson's Conversation with GW, 1 October [1792].
43 Ibid., GW to Anthony Whitting, 14 October 1792.
44 Ibid., Thomas Jefferson's Notes on a Conversation with Washington, 7 February 1793.
45 Ibid., Elizabeth Willing Powel to GW, 17 November 1792.
46 MHS/AFPDE, John Adams to Abigail Smith Adams, 28 December 1792.
47 PGWDE, GW to Henry Lee, 20 January 1793.
48 Ibid., GW to FBW, 24 February 1794.
49 Ibid., Elizabeth Willing Powel to GW, 17 November 1792.

Chapter 27 – Second Term

1 Jackman, 'A Young Englishman Reports on the New Nation, p. 118.
2 *General Advertiser* (Philadelphia), 2 January 1793, 'To the Noblesse and Courtiers of the United States . . .'.
3 MHS/AFPDE, John Adams to Abigail Adams, 2 January 1793.
4 PGWDE, Thomas Jefferson's Notes on a Conversation with Washington, 7 February 1793.
5 Ibid., Tobias Lear to GW, 8 April 1793.

6   Jackman, 'A Young Englishman Reports on the New Nation', p. 104.
7   PGWDE, GW to Thomas Jefferson, 1 March 1792.
8   Ibid., Neutrality Proclamation [22 April 1793].
9   Flexner, *Doctors on Horseback*, p. 101.
10 PGWDE, Henry Knox to GW, 15 September 1793.
11 Ibid., GW to Tobias Lear, 25 September 1793.
12 Ibid., Elizabeth Willing Powel to GW, 9 September 1793.
13 State Society of the Cincinnati of Pennsylvania, pasocietyofthecincinnati.org/; ancestry.com, data for Lieut. John Wigton, d. 1793.
14 PGWDE, Oliver Wolcott to GW, 20 October 1793.
15 Ibid., GW to William Pearce, 23 December 1793.
16 Ibid., Samuel Fraunces to GW, 23 October 1793.
17 Fields, *"Worthy Partner"*, pp. 254–5, MW to FBW, 14 January 1794.
18 Ibid., pp. 256–7, MW to FBW, 10 February 1794.
19 Ibid., pp. 257–8, MW to FBW, 15 February 1794.
20 Ibid., pp. 259–60, MW to FBW, 2 March 1794.
21 PGWDE, GW to Elizabeth Parke Custis, 14 September 1794.
22 Ibid., Elizabeth Parke Custis to GW, 7 September 1794.
23 Ibid., GW to Elizabeth Parke Custis, 14 September 1794.
24 Ibid., GW to FBW, 24 February 1793.
25 Ibid., GW to FBW, 17 March 1793.
26 Ibid., GW to William Pearce, 12 January 1794.
27 Fields, *"Worthy Partner"*, pp. 274–5, MW to FBW, 15 September 1794.
28 Ibid., pp. 276–7, MW to FBW, 29 September 1794.
29 PGWDE, GW to William Pearce, 12 January 1794.
30 Fields, *"Worthy Partner"*, p. 281, MW to FBW, 30 November 1794.
31 Ibid., pp. 283–5, MW to FBW, 6 April 1795.
32 Brady, *Washington's Beautiful Nelly*, p. 21.
33 Ibid., p. 32; Britt, *Nothing More Agreeable*, p. 54.
34 Hoyt, 'Self-Portrait: Eliza Custis', 96.
35 Fields, *"Worthy Partner"*, pp. 288–90, MW to EPC, 3 January 1796.
36 Ibid., pp. 290–1, MW to EPC, 14 January 1796.
37 Ibid., pp. 276–7, MW to FBW, 29 September 1794.
38 PGWDE, Response to the Boston Selectmen [28 July 1795].
39 PGWDE/EA, GW to Alexander Hamilton, 15 May 1796 [First Draft] Farewell Address.
40 Cutler and Cutler, *Life of Manasseh Cutler*, Vol. 2, pp. 56–7.
41 MHS/AFPDE, John Adams to Abigail Smith Adams, 1 March 1796.
42 MHS/AFPDE, John Adams to Abigail Adams, 23 February 1796.
43 Simpson, *Lives of Washington and Jefferson*, p. 256.
44 MHS/AFPDE, John Adams to Abigail Adams, 23 February 1796.
45 *WGWEE*, GW to Thomas Law, 10 February 1796.
46 Barratt and Miles, *Gilbert Stuart*, pp. 152–3.
47 PGWDE/EA, Elizabeth Willing Powel to GW, 1 June 1796.
48 Frederick Lawler Jr, 'Oney Judge', ushistory.org/presidentshouse/slaves/oney. htm (with link to two 1840s articles on Oney Judge).
49 PGWDE/EA, GW to Joseph Whipple, 28 November 1796.
50 Ibid., Elizabeth Willing Powel, 8 February 1797.
51 Ibid., Elizabeth Willing Powel to GW, 11[–13] March 1797; ibid., Joseph Whipple to GW, 22 December 1796.
52 Nicholls, 'Henrietta Liston's Journal', pp. 511, 552.
53 Sparks, *Life of Washington*, p. 477.
54 PJADE/EA, Abigail Adams to MW, 9 February 1797.
55 Ibid., Abigail Adams to Mary Smith Gray Otis, [February] 1797.

56 Ibid., MW to Abigail Adams, 20 February 1797.
57 Fields, *"Worthy Partner"*, p. 297, MW to Catharine Littlefield Greene Miller, 3 March 1797.

Chapter 28 – Retirement

1 PGWDE, Diaries, entry for 16 March 1797.
2 Brady, *Washington's Beautiful Nelly*, p. 31.
3 PGWDE/EA, Elizabeth Willing Powel to GW, 11[-13] March 1797.
4 Ibid., GW to Elizabeth Willing Powel, 26 March 1797.
5 Ibid., GW to Bartholomew Dandridge [3 March 1797].
6 PGWDE/EA, Elizabeth Willing Powel to GW, 8 February 1797.
7 Ibid., Inventory of Goods in President's House, February 1797; PGWDE, GW to Mary White Morris, 1 May 1797.
8 PGWDE, Tobias Lear to GW, 15 March 1797.
9 Ibid., GW to Elizabeth Willing Powel, 26 March 1797.
10 Fields, *"Worthy Partner"*, pp. 304–5, MW to David Humphreys, 26 June 1797.
11 PGWDE, GW to Bartholomew Dandridge, 13 December 1797.
12 PGWDE, Tobias Lear to GW, 20 March 1797 and n. 1.
13 Fields, *"Worthy Partner"*, pp. 301–2, MW to Elizabeth Willing Powel, 1 May 1797.
14 Ibid., p. 307, MW to Betsy Aylett Henley, 20 August 1797.
15 Brady, *Washington's Beautiful Nelly*, p. 32.
16 PGWDE, GW to Samuel Fraunces, 7 September 1785.
17 Fields, *"Worthy Partner"*, p. 307, MW to Elizabeth Dandridge Henley, 20 August 1797.
18 PGWDE, GW to Frederick Kitt, 10 January 1798.
19 Ibid., GW to George Lewis, 13 November 1797.
20 Fields, *"Worthy Partner"*, p. 304, MW to David Humphreys, 26 June 1797.
21 Ibid., pp. 314–17, MW to Sarah Cary Fairfax, 17 May 1798.
22 PGWDE, GW to Lawrence Augustine Washington, 3 September 1797.
23 PGWDE, GW to Lawrence Lewis, 4 August 1797.
24 Latrobe, *Journal*, pp. 57–8.
25 Brady, *Washington's Beautiful Nelly*, p. 39.
26 Niemcewicz, *Under their Vine and Fig Tree*, p. 97.
27 Brady, *Washington's Beautiful Nelly*, p. 36.
28 Ibid., p. 39.
29 Ibid., p. 43.
30 Merritt, *The Best of PAW*, pp. 24–8: Virginia Kays Creesy, 'George Washington as a Princeton Parent'.
31 PGWDE, GW to Samuel Stanhope Smith, 9 October 1797.
32 Ibid., GW to GWPC, 7 January 1798.
33 Ibid., GW to David Stuart, 22 January 1798.
34 Ibid., GW to GWPC, 13 June 1798.
35 Ibid., GW to GWPC, 15 April 1798.
36 Brady, *Washington's Beautiful Nelly*, pp. 51–2, 48–9, 56, 55.
37 PGWDE, GW to GWPC, June 1798.
38 Ibid., GWPC to GW, 17 June 1798.
39 Ibid., GW to GWPC, 10 May and 24 July 1798.
40 LOC/AM/CL/SJ, 23 November 1797.
41 PGWDE, John Adams to GW, 22 June 1798.
42 Ibid., GW to John Adams, 4 July 1798.
43 Ibid., GW to James McHenry, 27 July 1798 and n. 1; ibid., James McHenry to GW, 13 August 1798, nn. 3 and 4.
44 Ibid., Diaries, entry for 4 July 1798 and n.

45 Ibid., GW to Henry Knox, 9 August 1798.
46 Ibid., GW to Alexander Hamilton, 14 July 1798.
47 Ibid., GW to David Stuart, 13 August 1798.
48 Ibid., GW to John McDowell, 2 September 1798, n. 2.
49 Ibid., GW to David Stuart, 30 December 1798.
50 Ibid., GW to Lawrence Lewis, 2 December 1798.
51 Ibid., Diaries, entries for 16 November–2 December 1798.
52 Ibid., GW to Elizabeth Willing Powel, 17 November 1798.
53 Ibid., GW to Elizabeth Willing Powel, 1 December 1798.
54 Ibid., Elizabeth Willing Powel to GW, 3 December 1798.
55 Ibid., GW to Elizabeth Willling Powel, 4 December 1798.
56 Ibid., Elizabeth Willing Powel to GW, 7 December 1798.
57 Ibid., GW to Elizabeth Willing Powel, 7 December 1798.
58 Ibid., GW to Elizabeth Willing Powel, 9 December 1798.
59 Ibid., GW to David Stuart, 30 December 1798.
60 Ibid., GW to James McHenry, 14 July 1799 and n. 2.
61 Ibid., GW to James McHenry, February 1799.
62 Ibid., GW to Bartholomew Dandridge, 25 January 1799.

Chapter 29 – The Death of a President

1 Brady, *Washington's Beautiful Nelly*, pp. 58–60.
2 PGWDE, GW to Lawrence Lewis, 23 January 1799.
3 PGWDE, Diaries, entry for 22 February 1799.
4 Brady, *Washington's Beautiful Nelly*, p. 62.
5 Vail, ed., 'A Dinner at Mount Vernon', pp. 76–7.
6 Brady, *Washington's Beautiful Nelly*, pp. 61–4.
7 PGWDE, GW to Lawrence Lewis, 20 September 1799.
8 Ibid., GW to Roger West, 19 September 1799 and n. 1.
9 Fields, *"Worthy Partner"*, pp. 287–8, MW to Frances Bassett Washington, 24 May 1795.
10 PGWDE, GW to Burwell Bassett Jr, 11 August 1799 and n. 1.
11 Ibid., George Washington's Last Will and Testament [9 July 1799].
12 Nicholls, 'Henrietta Liston's Journal', p. 517.
13 PGWDE, GW to Alexandria General Assemblies Managers, 12 November 1799.
14 Ibid., Diaries, entries for 20, 27 November, 9, 11–12 December 1799.
15 Ibid., I. The Journal Account [15 December 1799].
16 Ibid., Diaries, entry for 13 December 1799.
17 Ibid., II. The Diary Account, 14 December 1799.
18 Ibid., I. The Journal Account [15 December 1799]; ibid., II. The Diary Account, 14 December 1799.
19 Ibid., II. The Diary Account, 14 December 1799; MVLA, Thompson, '"The Lowest Ebb of Misery"', p. 15 and n. 20.
20 Ibid., I. The Journal Account [15 December 1799].
21 Ibid., II. The Diary Account 14 December 1799.
22 Washington, *Letters and Recollections*, p. 137.
23 MVLA, typescript, Tobias Lear to Mary Lincoln Lear, 16 December 1799.
24 McCallister, 'Law's Description of the Last Illness and Death of George Washington', p. 29.

Chapter 30 – Dissolution

1 PGWDE, George Washington's Last Will and Testament [9 July 1799].
2 Lee, *A Funeral Oration*, p. 10.

3   Mitchell, ed., *New Letters of Abigail Adams*, p. 227.
4   Fields, *"Worthy Partner"*, pp. 327–8, John Adams to MW, 27 December 1799; LOC/AM/CL/HJ, 23 December 1799.
5   Mitchell, ed., *New Letters of Abigail Adams*, pp. 226–8.
6   Fields, *"Worthy Partner"*, pp. 332–3, MW to John Adams, 31 December 1799; LOC/AM/CL/SJ, 8 January 1800.
7   Clark, 'Doctor and Mrs William Thornton', pp. 91–2.
8   LOC/AM/CL/HJ, 28 March 1800.
9   Fields, *"Worthy Partner"*, pp. 371–2, MW to Janet Montgomery, 5 April 1800.
10 Nicholls, 'Henrietta Liston's Journal', pp. 519–20.
11 MVLA, Thompson, '"To Follow her Departed Friend"', p. 15 n. 29; ibid., pp. 12–16.
12 Morris, *Autobiography*, p. 12.
13 MVLA, Thompson, '"To Follow her Departed Friend"', p. 7 n. 16.
14 Harrison, *Philadelphia Merchant*, p. 113.
15 N-YHS, John Pintard, ms. Diary, entry for 31 July 1801.
16 YUAG, Robert Field, *Martha Washington* [miniature, 1801]; Field, *George Washington* [miniature, 1801].
17 Adams, *Life and Writings of Sparks*, Vol. 2, pp. 46–7.
18 Ford, 'Diary of Mrs William Thornton', pp. 174–6.
19 McCallister, 'This Melancholy Scene', p. 15.
20 Harrison, *Philadelphia Merchant*, p. 112; MVLA, Thompson, '"To Follow her Departed Friend"', p. 18; McCallister, 'This Melancholy Scene', p. 15.
21 *Alexandria Advertiser*, 25 May 1802.
22 Torbert, *Eleanor Calvert*, pp. 99–100; Ribblett, *Nelly Custis*, p. 67.
23 PGWDE, GW, Last Will and Testament [9 July 1799].

BIBLIOGRAPHY

Archives

American Memory, memory.loc.gov/ammem/
>An American Time Capsule: Three Centuries of Broadsides and Other Printed Ephemera
>Century of Law-making
>>House Journal
>>Journal of Continental Congress
>>Letters of Delegates to Continental Congress
>>Senate Journal
>Presidents
>>George Washington Papers, 1741–1799
>>Thomas Jefferson Papers, 1606–1827

ancestry.com

Fordham University Library, New York, Charles Allen Munn Collection
>Box 6, item 37, Jonathan Trumbull, 1740–1809, 'Journal of Occurrences from 12 August to Siege of York, in Virginia – and return to Phila. Nov. 1781', Ms. Journal, 38pp

Founders Online, National Historical Publications and Records Commission/ University of Virginia, founders.archives.gov

Gilder Lehrman Collection, Gilder Lehrman Institute of American History, located at the New-York Historical Society, New York, gilderlehrman.org/collections

Henry Knox papers, 1750–1820

Library of Congress, Manuscript Division, Washington, DC, loc.gov
>Washington Family Papers

Massachusetts Historical Society, Boston
>Adams Family Papers: An Electronic Archive, masshist.org/digitaladams/

Mount Vernon Digital Collections, Mount Vernon, Virginia, mountvernon.org

Mount Vernon Ladies' Association, Mount Vernon, Virginia
>Lewis, Robert, 'A Journey from Fredericksburg Virginia to New-York', 13–20 May 1789, Ms., MVLA Library
>Thompson, Mary V., '"As if I had Been a Very Great Somebody": Martha Washington in the American Revolution: Becoming the New Nation's First Lady', Paper, 6 February 2002, typescript (amended 2012), MVLA Library
>Thompson, Mary V., '"The Lowest Ebb of Misery": Death and Mourning in the Family of George Washington', Symposium paper, Gadsby's Tavern Museum, Alexandria, 2 October 1999, typescript (amended 15 July 2003), MVLA Library
>Thompson, Mary V., ed., '"To Follow her Departed Friend": The Last Years and Death of Martha Washington', Report for MVLA Anniversaries Committee, 25 April 2000, typescript (amended 28 July 2006), MVLA Library

New-York Historical Society, New York City, New York, nyhistory.org
>John Pintard Papers, 1759–1844, Series I, Diaries

The Papers of Benjamin Franklin Digital Edition, Sponsored by the American Philosophical Society and Yale University, franklinpapers.org

The Papers of George Washington Digital Edition, ed. Theodore J. Crackel (Charlottesville: University of Virginia Press, Rotunda, 2008), rotunda.upress. virginia.edu/founders/GEWN.html

The Papers of George Washington Digital Edition, Founders Early Access (Charlottesville: University of Virginia Press, Rotunda)

The Papers of John Adams Digital Edition, ed. C. James Taylor (Charlottesville: University of Virginia Press, Rotunda, 2008), rotunda.upress.virginia.edu/founders/ADMS.html

The Papers of Thomas Jefferson Digital Edition, ed. Barbara B. Oberg and J. Jefferson Looney (Charlottesville: University of Virginia Press, Rotunda, 2009), rotunda.upress.virginia.edu/founders/TSJN.html

The President's House in Philadelphia, ushistory.org/presidentshouse/

Franklin D. Roosevelt Presidential Library and Museum, Hyde Park, New York, fdrlibrary.marist.edu/, Eleanor Roosevelt Papers

The Society of the Cincinnati, Washington, DC, societyofthecincinnati.org

State Society of the Cincinnati of Pennsylvania, pasocietyofthecincinnati.org/

Virginia Historical Society, Richmond, Virginia, vahistorical.org/collections-and-resources

Washington and Lee University, Lexington, Virginia, wlu.edu
Special Collections and Archives, James G. Leyburn Library

The Writings of George Washington from the Original Manuscript Sources, 1745–1799, ed. John C. Fitzpatrick (1931–44). Electronic Edition, ed. Frank E. Grizzard Jr, Washington Resources at the University of Virginia Library, Charlottesville, etext.virginia.edu/washington/fitzpatrick/

Yale University Art Gallery, New Haven, Connecticut, artgallery.yale.edu/

Books and Articles

Adams, Charles Francis, ed., *Letters of Mrs Adams, the Wife of John Adams*, 2 vols (Boston, 1840)

—, *The Works of John Adams*, 10 vols (Boston, 1856)

Adams, Herbert B., *The Life and Writing of Jared Sparks*, 2 vols (Boston, 1893)

Alden, John Richard, *General Gage in America: Being Principally a History of His Role in the American Revolution* (Baton Rouge, 1948)

Baker, W. S., 'Exchange of Major-General Charles Lee', *PMHB*, Vol. 15, No. 1 (1891), pp. 26–34

—, *Itinerary of General Washington from June 15, 1775, to December 23, 1783* (Philadelphia, 1892)

—, *Washington after the Revolution, MDCCLXXXIV–MDCCXCIX* (Philadelphia, 1898)

Balch, Thomas, ed., *The Journal of Claude Blanchard*, trans. William Duane (New York, 1969)

Barratt, Carrie Rebora, and Ellen G. Miles, *Gilbert Stuart* (New Haven, 2004)

Beard, Charles A., ed., *The Journal of William Maclay: United States Senator from Pennsylvania, 1789–1791* (New York, 1965)

Boudinot, Elias, *The Life, Public Services, Addresses and Letters of Elias Boudinot*, 2 vols (Boston, 1896)

Boyd, Julian P. et al., eds, *The Papers of Thomas Jefferson*, 37 vols (Princeton, 1950)

Brady, Patricia, *Martha Washington: An American Life* (New York, 2005)

—, ed., *George Washington's Beautiful Nelly: The Letters of Eleanor Parke Custis Lewis to Elizabeth Bordley Gibson, 1794–1851* (Columbia, SC, 1991)

Britt, Judith S., *Nothing More Agreeable: Music in George Washington's Family* (Mount Vernon, 1984)

Broadwater, Jeff, *George Mason: Forgotten Founder* (Chapel Hill, NC, 2006)

Brown, Stuart E., *Virginia Baron: The Story of Thomas, 6th Lord Fairfax* (Berryville, Va., 1965)

Bryan, Helen, *Martha Washington: First Lady of Liberty* (New York, 2002)

Butterfield, L. H., ed., *Letters of Benjamin Rush, 1746–1913*, 2 vols (Princeton, 1951)

Butterfield, L. H., Wendell D. Garrett et al., eds, *Adams Family Correspondence*, 11 vols (Cambridge, 1963–2013)

Cadou, Carol Borchert, *The George Washington Collection: Fine and Decorative Arts at Mount Vernon* (Manchester, VT, 2006)

[Cambridge], *An Historic Guide to Cambridge* (Cambridge, Mass., 1907)

Carp, E. Wayne, *To Starve the Army at Pleasure: Continental Army Administration and American Political Culture, 1775–1783* (Chapel Hill, NC, 1984)

Carter, Clarence Edwin, ed., *The Correspondence of General Thomas Gage* (New Haven, 1931)

Chadwick, Bruce, *George Washington's War: The Forging of a Revolutionary Leader and the American Presidency* (Naperville, Ill., 2004)

Chastellux, François Jean, Marquis de, *Travels in North America, in the Years 1780, 1781, and 1782*, ed. Howarth C. Rice, 2 vols (Chapel Hill, NC, 1963)

Chernow, Ron, *Washington: A Life* (New York, 2010)

Chesnutt, David R., ed., *The Papers of Henry Laurens*, 16 vols (Columbia, 1968–2002)

Chinard, Gilbert, ed. and trans., *George Washington as the French Knew Him* (Princeton, 1940)

Clark, Allen C., 'Doctor and Mrs William Thornton', *RCHS*, Vol. 18 (1915), pp. 144–208

Clark, Ellen McCallister, *Martha Washington: A Brief Biography* (Mount Vernon, 2002)

Conway, Moncure Daniel, ed., *The Writings of Thomas Paine*, 4 vols in 2 (New York, 1969)

Cooper, Helen A., David McCullough et al., *Life, Liberty, and the Pursuit of Happiness: American Art from the Yale University Art Gallery* (New Haven, 2008)

Cooper, Samuel, 'Diary of Samuel Cooper, 1775–1776', *AHR*, Vol. 6, No. 2 (January 1901), pp. 301–41

Cunliffe, Marcus, *George Washington: Man and Monument* (Mount Vernon, 1982)

Cunningham, John T., *The Uncertain Revolution: Washington and the Continental Army at Morristown* (West Creek, NJ, 2007)

Custis, George Washington Parke, *Recollections and Private Memoirs of Washington, with a Memoir of the Author by his Daughter*, ed. Benson J. Lossing (New York, 1860)

Cutler, William Parker, and Julia Perkins Cutler, eds, *Life, Journals and Correspondence of Rev. Manasseh Cutler, LL.D.*, 2 vols (Cincinnati, 1888)

deButts Jr, Robert E. L., 'Mary Custis Lee's "Reminiscences of the War"', *VMHB*, Vol. 109, No. 3 (2001), pp. 301–25

Decatur Jr, Stephen, *Private Affairs of George Washington, from the Records and Accounts of Tobias Lear* (Boston, 1933)

Detweiler, Susan Gray, *George Washington's Chinaware* (New York, 1982)

Duane Jr, William, ed., *Passages from the Remembrances of Christopher Marshall* (Philadelphia, 1839)

Du Motier, Georges, Marquis de la Fayette, ed., *Memoirs, Correspondence and Manuscripts of General Lafayette*, 3 vols (London, 1837)

Dunlap, William, *A History of the Rise and Progress of the Arts of Design in the United States*, 3 vols (Boston, 1918)

Duponceau, Peter S., 'Autobiographical Letters of Peter S. Duponceau', *PMHB*, Vol. 40, No. 2 (1916), pp. 172–86

Elliot, Jonathan, *The Debates in the Several State Conventions, on the Adoption of the Federal Constitution . . . in 1787*, 5 vols (Philadelphia, 1866)

Ellis, Joseph J., *His Excellency: George Washington* (New York, 2004)

Emory, John, ed., *The Works of the Reverend John Wesley*, 7 vols (New York, 1831)

Farrand, Max, ed., *The Records of the Federal Convention of 1787*, 3 vols (New Haven, 1911)

Felder, Paula S., *Fielding Lewis and the Washington Family: A Chronicle of 18th-Century Fredericksburg* (Fredericksburg, 1998)

Fenn, Elizabeth A., *Pox Americana: The Great Smallpox Epidemic of 1775–82* (New York, 2001)

Ferguson, James, et al., eds, *The Papers of Robert Morris, 1781–1784*, 9 vols (Pittsburgh, 1973–95)

Fields, Joseph E., ed., *"Worthy Partner": The Papers of Martha Washington* (Westport, CT, 1994)

Fitzpatrick, John C., ed., *The Diaries of George Washington, 1748–1799*, 4 vols (Boston, 1925)

—, *George Washington's Accounts of Expenses While Commander-in-Chief of the Continental Army, 1775–1783* (Boston, 1917)

Flexner, James Thomas, *Doctors on Horseback: Pioneers of American Medicine* (New York, 1939)

Floyd, N. J., *Biographical Genealogies of the Virginia–Kentucky Floyd Families* (Baltimore, 1912)

Ford, Worthington C., ed., 'Diary of Mrs William Thornton, 1800–1863', *RCHS*, Vol. 10 (1907), pp. 88–226

Frank, Robin Jaffee, *Love and Loss: American Portrait and Mourning Miniatures* (New Haven, 2000)

Freeman, Douglas Southall, *George Washington: A Biography*, 7 vols (New York, 1948–57)

Garrett, Wendell, ed., *George Washington's Mount Vernon* (New York, 1998)

Greene, George Washington, *The Life and Death of Nathanael Greene*, 3 vols (New York, 1867–71)

Happel, Ralph, *Chatham: The Life of a House* (Philadelphia, 1984)

Harbin, Billy J., 'Letters from John Parke Custis to George and Martha Washington, 1778–1781', *WMQ*, Third Series, Vol. 43, No. 2 (April 1986), pp. 267–93

Harris, Malcolm Hart, *Old New Kent County: Some Account of the Planters, Plantations, and Places in New Kent County*, 2 vols (West Point, NY, 1977)

Harrison, Eliza Cope, ed., *Philadelphia Merchant: The Diary of Thomas P. Cope, 1800–1851* (South Bend, Ind., 1978)

Harrison, Fairfax, *The Virginia Carys: An Essay in Genealogy* (New York, 1919)

Harrison, S. A., ed., *Memoir of Lieut. Col. Tench Tilghman* (Albany, NY, 1876)

Henkles, S. V., ed., *The Confidential Correspondence of Robert Morris* (Philadelphia, 1917)

Henriques, Peter R., 'Major Lawrence Washington versus the Reverend Charles Green: A Case Study of the Squire and the Parson', *VMHB*, Vol. 100, No. 2 (April 1992), pp. 233–64

Higginbotham, Don, ed., *George Washington Reconsidered* (Charlottesville, 2001)

Hildeburn, Charles R., 'Notes on the Stamp Act in New York and Virginia', *PMHB*, Vol. 2, No. 3 (1878), pp. 296–301

An Historic Guide to Cambridge, compiled by members of the Hannah Winthrop chapter, National Society, Daughters of the American Revolution (Cambridge, Mass., 1907)

Horrell, Joseph, and Richard W. Oram, 'George Washington's "Marble colour'd folio Book": A Newly Identified Ledger', *WMQ*, Third Series, Vol. 43, No. 2 (April 1986), pp. 252–66

Hoyt Jr, William D., 'Self-Portrait: Eliza Custis, 1808', *VMHB*, Vol. 53, No. 2 (April 1945), pp. 89–100

Hünemörder, Markus, *The Society of the Cincinnati: Conspiracy and Distrust in Early America* (New York, 2006)

Idzerda, Stanley J., Roger E. Smith et al., eds, *Lafayette in the Age of the American Revolution . . . 1776–1790*, 5 vols (Ithaca, NY, 1977–83)

Irvin, Benjamin H., *Clothed in Robes of Sovereignty: The Continental Congress and the People Out of Doors* (New York, 2011)

Ives, Mabel Lorenz, *Washington's Headquarters* (Upper Montclair, NJ, 1932)

Jackman, S. W., 'A Young Englishman Reports on the New Nation: Edward Thornton to James Bland Burges, 1791–1793', *WMQ*, Third Series, Vol. 18, No. 1 (January 1961), pp. 85–121

Jeremy, David John, ed., *Journal of an Excursion: Henry Wansey and his American Journal, 1794* (Philadelphia, 1970)

Johnson, Gerald W., *Mount Vernon: The Story of a Shrine: An Account of the Rescue and Rehabilitation of Washington's Home by the Mount Vernon Ladies' Association* (New York, 1953)

Journals of the House of Burgesses of Virginia: 1758–1761, ed. H. R. McIlwaine (Richmond, 1908); *1761–1765*, ed. John Pendleton Kennedy (1907); *1766–1769*, ed. Kennedy (1906); *1770–1772*, ed. Kennedy (1906); *1773–1776, including the records of the Committee of Correspondence*, ed. Kennedy (1905)

Latrobe, J. H. B., ed., *The Journal of [Benjamin] Latrobe . . . from 1796 to 1820* (New York, 1905)

Laws of the Commonwealth of Pennsylvania 1700–1810, 4 vols (Philadelphia, 1810)

Lee, Henry, *A Funeral Oration on the Death of General Washington . . . Delivered at the Request of Congress . . .* (Boston, 1800)

Lee, Robert E., *My Father, General Lee* (Garden City, NY, 1960)

Loane, Nancy K., *Following the Drum: Women at the Valley Forge Encampment* (Washington, DC, 2009)

Longmore, Paul K., *The Invention of George Washington* (Berkeley, 1999)

Lossing, Benson J., *The Pictorial Field-book of the Revolution*, 2 vols (New York, 1859)

Lynch Jr, James B., *The Custis Chronicles: The Virginia Generations* (Camden, Me., 1997)

MacDonald, William, *Documentary Source Book of American History: 1606–1898* (New York, 1914)

McCallister, Ellen, 'This Melancholy Scene', MVLA, *Annual Report 1981* (Mount Vernon, 1982), pp. 13–15

—, 'Thomas Law's Description of the Last Illness and Death of George Washington', MVLA, *Annual Report 1972* (Mount Vernon, 1973), pp. 28–31

McGaughy, Kent J., *Richard Henry Lee of Virginia: A Portrait of an American Revolutionary* (Lanham, MD, 2004)

Manca, Joseph, *George Washington's Eye: Landscape, Architecture, and Design at Mount Vernon* (Baltimore, 2012)

Marshall, Charles, *Autobiography of Commodore Charles Marshall* (USN, 2002)

Maxey, David W., *A Portrait of Elizabeth Willing Powel, 1743–1830* (Philadelphia, 2006)

Mays, David John, ed., *The Letters and Papers of Edmund Pendleton, 1734–1803*, 2 vols (Charlottesville, 1967)

Merritt, J.I., ed., *The Best of PAW: 100 Years of Princeton Alumni Weekly* (Princeton, 2000)

Miles, Ellen G., *George and Martha Washington: Portraits from the Presidential Years* (Washington, DC, 1999)

Miller, Lillian B., et al., eds, *The Selected Papers of Charles Willson Peale and his Family*, 4 vols (New Haven, 1983–96)

Mitchell, Stewart, ed., *New Letters of Abigail Adams, 1788–1801* (Worcester, MA, 1947)

Moore, Frank, *Diary of the American Revolution*, 2 vols (New York, 1859–60)

Morgan, John Hill, and Mantle Fielding, *The Life Portraits of Washington and their Replicas* (Philadelphia, 1931)

Morris, Charles, *The Autobiography of Commodore Charles Morris, US Navy* (Annapolis, 1880)

Neill, Edward D., *The Fairfaxes of England and America in the Seventeenth and Eighteenth Centuries* (Albany, NY, 1868)

Nicholls, James C., '[Lady] Henrietta Liston's Journal of Washington's "Resignation", Retirement, and Death', *PMHB*, Vol. 95, No. 4 (October 1971), pp. 511–20

Niemcewicz, Julian Ursyn, *Under their Vine and Fig Tree: Travels through America in 1797–1799, 1805*, ed. and trans. Metchie J. E. Budka (Elizabeth, NJ, 1965)

Parker, Robert, 'Journal of Lieutenant Robert Parker, of the Second Continental Artillery, 1779 (concluded)', *PMHB*, Vol. 28, No. 1 (1904), pp. 12–25

The Parliamentary History of England, from the Earliest Period to the Year 1803, 36 vols, London, 1806–20

Pickering, Octavius, and Charles W. Upham, *The Life of Timothy Pickering*, 4 vols (Boston, 1867–73)

Potter, Dorothy Bundy Turner, '*Food for Apollo': Cultivated Music in Antebellum Philadelphia* (Bethlehem, Pa., 2010)

Prussing, Eugene E., *The Estate of George Washington, Deceased* (Boston, 1927)

Randolph, Thomas Jefferson, ed., *Memoir, Correspondence, and Miscellanies, from the Papers of Thomas Jefferson*, 4 vols (Boston, 1830)

Rappley, Charles, *Robert Morris: Financier of the American Revolution* (New York, 2010)

Rasmussen, William M. S., and Robert S. Tilton, *George Washington: The Man behind the Myths* (Charlottesville, 1999)

Reed, William Bradford, ed., *Life and Correspondence of Joseph Reed*, 2 vols (Philadelphia, 1847)

Ribblett, David L., *Nelly Custis: Child of Mount Vernon* (Mount Vernon, 1993)

Russell, David Lee, *The American Revolution in the Southern Colonies* (Jefferson, NC, 2000)

Rutman, Darrett B., ed., *The Old Dominon: Essays for Thomas Perkins Abernethy* (Charlottesville, 1964)

Sellers, Charles Coleman, *Portraits and Miniatures by Charles Willson Peale* (Philadelphia, 1952)

Sellers, Horace Wells, 'Charles Willson Peale, Artist-Soldier', *PMHB*, Vol. 38, No. 3 (1914), pp. 257–86

Showman, Richard K., et al., eds, *The Papers of General Nathanael Greene*, 13 vols (Chapel Hill, NC, 1976–2005)

Simms, Wm Gilmore, ed., *The Army Correspondence of Colonel John Laurens in the Years 1777–8* (New York, 1867)

Simpson, Stephen, *The Lives of George Washington and Thomas Jefferson: With a Parallel* (Philadelphia, 1833)

Sizer, Theodore, ed., *The Works of Colonel John Trumbull: Artist of the American Revolution* (New Haven, 1967)

Smith, Stephen R., ed., *Record of Service of Connecticut Men in the I. War of the Revolution, II. War of 1812, III. Mexican War* (Hartford, CT, 1889)

Sparks, Jared, *The Library of American Biography*, 25 vols (New York, 1848–64)

—, ed., *The Life of Benjamin Franklin, Containing the Autobiography* (Boston, 1844)

—, *The Life of Washington* (Boston, 1853)

—, ed., *The Writings of George Washington*, 12 vols (Boston, 1833–7)

Sterne, Laurence, *The Sermons of Mr. Yorick*, 2 vols (12th edn, London, 1775)

Thacher, James, *Military Journal, during the American Revolutionary War, from 1775 to 1783* (Hartford, CT, 1854)

Thane, Elswyth, *Mount Vernon is Ours: The Story of its Preservation* (New York, 1966)

Thompson, Mary V., *'In the Hands of a Good Providence': Religion in the Life of George Washington* (Charlottesville, 2008)

Tinling, Marion, ed., *The Correspondence of the Three William Byrds of Westover, Virginia, 1684–1776* (Charlottesville, 1977)

Torbert, Alice Coyle, *Eleanor Calvert and her Circle* (New York, 1950)

Trumbull, John, *The Autobiography of Colonel John Trumbull, Patriot-Artist, 1756–1843*, ed. Theodore Sizer (New Haven, 1953)

Trumbull, John, 'Minutes of Occurrences Respecting the Siege and Capture of Yorktown, from the Journal of Col. Jonathan Trumbull', *Proc. MHS*, Vol. 14 (1875–6), pp. 331–8

Vail, R. W. G., ed., 'A Dinner at Mount Vernon: From the Unpublished Journal of Joshua Brookes', *N-YHSQ*, Vol. 31, No. 2 (April 1947), pp. 75–6.

Van Schreeven, William J., Robert L. Scribner and Brent Tarter, eds, *Revolutionary Virginia: The Road to Independence*, 7 vols (Charlottesville, 1973–83)

Washington, George, *Letters and Recollections of George Washington; Being Letters to Tobias Lear and Others* (New York, 1906)

—, *Rules of Civility & Decent Behaviour in Company and Conversation: A Book of Etiquette* (Williamsburg, 1971)

Watson, Elkanah, *Men and Times of the Revolution; or, Memoirs of Elkanah Watson, Including Journals . . . Correspondence . . . and Reminiscences* (New York, 1856)

Wayland, John W., *The Washingtons and their Homes* (1944; Berryville, Va., 1973)

Weems, Mason L., *The Life of Washington*, ed. Marcus Cunliffe (Cambridge, Mass., 1962)

Whiteley, Emily Stone, *Washington and his Aides-de-Camp* (New York, 1936)

Wirt, William, *Sketches of the Life of Patrick Henry* (Philadelphia, 1817)

Wraxall, Sir Nathaniel, *Historical Memoirs of His Own Times*, 4 vols (London, 1836)

Zuppan, Josephine Little, ed., *The Letter Book of John Custis IV of Williamsburg, 1717–1742* (Lanham, Md, 2005)

ACKNOWLEDGEMENTS

Throughout this project, I enjoyed the benign support of Michael Fishwick at Bloomsbury, who believed in the book from the beginning. Anna Simpson, too, was a fount of calm. I thank them, and all those, including Iris Weinstein and Ellen Feldman, who have made this book a pleasure to handle. In America, Robert Gottlieb guided and counselled me, and on the honing skills of my friend Peter James I additionally leant. In addition, I thank Leonora Clarke for her exemplary typing of the book from manuscript. Last but never least, Georgina Capel, my literary agent, encouraged me when I was faltering, and enthused at other times.

I thank Geraldine Bease for the meticulous index and David Lindroth for crafting the fine maps. I also thank Lesley Robertson Allen for energetic picture research.

I thank Cate Magennis Wyatt for first suggesting I visit Mount Vernon. Michele Lee, Special Collections Librarian, and Dawn Bonner, Photographic Resources and Rights Coordinator, gave me much welcome assistance there. I visited Morristown and other Revolutionary War headquarters and battlefields in New Jersey alone and in the dead of winter. On research trips to New York, Philadelphia, Brandywine and Valley Forge, I had the stimulating company of my daughter Stella Powell-Jones. With her brothers, Simon and Tommy Soros and their father Peter, I paid fruitful visits to Boston and Washington DC. I thank them all four, volunteers *extraordinaires*. I am also indebted to my mother, Antonia Fraser, for the excellent suggestions she made when the book was at draft stage.

The British Library and the London Library were rich resources, and the librarians at both institutions, as ever, helpful.

Mary V. Thompson, Research Historian at Mount Vernon shared with me – in person and in correspondence – some of her great fund of knowledge about the Washingtons. Frances S. Pollard, Vice President for Research Services at the Virginia Historical Society, Richmond, guided me through the Custis and Lee Papers. Jeffery M. Flannery, Head of Reference and Reader Services, steered me towards pertinent papers in the Manuscript Division at the Library of Congress, Washington DC. Professor Munro Price kindly commented on sections relating to French history and politics, and Stella Tillyard made valuable suggestions. I must also record my thanks to those at the University of Virginia who have led the publishing project. In particular I thank William M. Ferraro, Associate Editor, who read my manuscript and offered many helpful suggestions. All errors are my own, but I am grateful to all the above.

I thank Nancy Roosevelt Ireland for kind permission to quote from the papers of Eleanor Roosevelt. At Washington and Lee University, Lexington, Virginia, where Walter Robertson and Mary Frediani facilitated introductions, many souvenirs of the Washingtons' marriage are gathered. I profited greatly from conversation with Vaughan Stanley, Special Collections and Reference Librarian in Leyburn Library. At Washington and Lee, I thank Peter Grover, Linda Donald and Patricia Hobbs. Pie Friendly and Diana and Mallory Walker in Washington DC made helpful introductions for me in the museums and libraries world. At the Smithsonian Portrait Gallery, Washington DC, Ellen G. Miles was good enough to discuss with me, in front of the canvases, the Gilbert Stuart portraits of George and of Martha Washington. In addition, Leslie Buhler, Director of Tudor Place Historic House and Gardens, also in Washington DC, shared her knowledge of Washington artefacts. Thanks to the good offices of Carlos Picon and Carrie Rebora Barratt at the Metropolitan Museum in New York, I enjoyed an early viewing of Leutze's *Crossing the Delware*, restored and reframed, in the new American Wing. To Helen A. Cooper, among others at the Yale University Art Gallery, New Haven, I am indebted for information and assistance regarding images of the Washingtons in that rich collection. I thank, also, Robin Jaffee Frank, for showing me, when she was at Yale, Robert Field's miniatures of the couple, and Elizabeth Fairman, at the Yale Center for British Art, showed me valuable colonial maps.

David Michaelis paused often in his own work on Eleanor Roosevelt to pass me nuggets of information relevant to mine. Dr Quinn Peeper provided valuable insights into the epilepsy that affected Patsy Parke Custis. Stephen and Cathy Graham, Jeffrey and Elizabeth Leeds, Catharine Soros, Juliet Hughes-Hallett, Amelia Mendoza, Carla Powell, Annabel Fairfax, Hugh Fairfax, Katherine Bucknell, Marjorie Susman, Megan Gabriel, Amy Meyers, Joseph Gordon, William Richardson III, Richard Potter, Aileen Ribeiro, Philip Mansel, Lowell Libson, Dr and Mrs. Herbert A. Claiborne, Lea Carpenter Brokaw, Virginia Massie Valentine and the late Rick Mather all offered helpful suggestions, introductions or hospitality.

To the late Paul Soros I am indebted for raising numerous points that required answering. I shared early thoughts on the book with members – Val Paley, Susan Golden, Eileen West and Julia Ogilvy, among others – of my summer book club in Sconset, Massachusetts. And I bless my brother-in-law Edward Fitzgerald's Claiborne of Virginia roots.

INDEX

A NOTE ON THE AUTHOR

Flora Fraser is the author of acclaimed biographies of Emma Hamilton and of George IV's wife, Queen Caroline. More recently she has written Princesses: *The Daughters of George III* and *Venus of Empire: The Life of Pauline Bonaparte*. She lives in London with her children.

florafraser.com

A NOTE ON THE TYPE

The text of this book is set in Linotype Stempel Garamond, a version of Garamond adapted and first used by the Stempel foundry in 1924. It's one of several versions of Garamond based on the designs of Claude Garamond. It is thought that Garamond based his font on Bembo, cut in 1495 by Francesco Griffo in collaboration with the Italian printer Aldus Manutius. Garamond types were first used in books printed in Paris around 1532. Many of the present-day versions of this type are based on the *Typi Academiae* of Jean Jannon cut in Sedan in 1615.

Claude Garamond was born in Paris in 1480. He learned how to cut type from his father and by the age of fifteen he was able to fashion steel punches the size of a pica with great precision. At the age of sixty he was commissioned by King Francis I to design a Greek alphabet, for this he was given the honourable title of royal type founder. He died in 1561.